DEMOCRACY FOR SALE

DEMOCRACY FOR SALE

Elections, Clientelism, and
the State in Indonesia

**Edward Aspinall and
Ward Berenschot**

CORNELL UNIVERSITY PRESS   ITHACA AND LONDON

First published 2019 by Cornell University Press

Library of Congress Cataloging-in-Publication Data

Names: Aspinall, Edward, author. | Berenschot, Ward, author.
Title: Democracy for sale : elections, clientelism, and the state in Indonesia / Edward Aspinall and Ward Berenschot.
Description: Ithaca [New York] : Cornell University Press, 2019. | Includes bibliographical references and index.
Identifiers: LCCN 2018045944 (print) | LCCN 2018047964 (ebook) | ISBN 9781501732997 (pdf) | ISBN 9781501733000 (ret) | ISBN 9781501732973 | ISBN 9781501732973 (cloth) | ISBN 9781501732980 (pbk.)
Subjects: LCSH: Elections—Corrupt practices—Indonesia. | Patron and client—Indonesia. | Patronage, Political—Indonesia. | Indonesia— Politics and government—1998- | Democracy—Indonesia. | Political corruption—Indonesia.
Classification: LCC JQ779.A4 (ebook) | LCC JQ779.A4 A76 2019 (print) | DDC 364.1/32309598—dc23
LC record available at https://lccn.loc.gov/2018045944

Contents

List of Tables and Figures

Tables

Figures

Glossary

adat customary values and rules

aliran a "stream" or socioreligious current; in the 1950s and 1960s also a party and affiliated organizations based around such a current

bansos bantuan sosial; social assistance grants

BPS Badan Pusat Statistik (Central Statistics Agency)

bupati regent; executive head of a rural district or *kabupaten*

camat subdistrict head

DPR Dewan Perwakilan Rakyat (People's Representative Council), Indonesia's national legislature

DPRD Dewan Perwakilan Rakyat Daerah (Regional People's Representative Council), legislatures found at provincial and district levels

Forkabi Forum Komunikasi Anak Betawi (Communication Forum of the Children of the Betawi)

Gerindra Partai Gerakan Indonesia Raya (Greater Indonesia Movement Party)

Golkar Golongan Karya (Functional Group Party)

Hanura Partai Hati Nurani Rakyat (People's Conscience Party)

hibah grant money

kampung village or urban neighborhood

kyai traditionalist Islamic scholar

lurah appointed head of an urban precinct or *kelurahan*

majelis taklim grassroots Muslim prayer or study group

Masjumi Majelis Syuro Muslimin Indonesia (Council of Indonesian Muslim Associations), modernist-dominated Islamic party of the 1950s

Muhammadiyah mass-based modernist Muslim organization

musholla Islamic prayer hall

NasDem Partai Nasional Demokrat (National Democratic Party)

New Order Orde Baru, Suharto's authoritarian regime, 1966–1998

NGO nongovernmental organization

NTT Nusa Tenggara Timur (East Nusa Tenggara)

NU Nahdlatul Ulama, mass-based traditionalist Muslim organization

PAN Partai Amanat Nasional (National Mandate Party), party aligned with Muhammadiyah

Partai Demokrat Democrat Party

PDI-P Partai Demokrasi Indonesia Perjuangan (Indonesian Democracy Party—Struggle)

pilkada pemilihan kepala daerah secara langsung; direct elections of regional heads

PKB Partai Kebangkitan Bangsa (National Awakening Party)

PKI Partai Komunis Indonesia (Indonesian Communist Party)

PKK Pembinaan Kesejahteraan Keluarga (Guidance for Family Welfare movement), renamed in post-Suharto period the Family Empowerment and Welfare movement (community-level women's health groups)

PKS Partai Keadilan Sejahtera (Prosperous Justice Party)

PNI Partai Nasional Indonesia (Indonesian National Party)

PNPM Program Nasional Pemberdayaan Masyarakat Mandiri (National Program for Community Empowerment)

PPP Partai Persatuan Pembangunan (Unity Development Party)
PR Proportional Representation
proyek project
RT *rukun tetangga*; sub-neighborhood unit
RW *rukun warga*; neighborhood unit
tim sukses success team; election campaign organization or its individual members
tokoh masyarakat informal community leader
ulama Islamic scholar

TABLE 0.1 Indonesia's governmental structure

LEVEL OF GOVERNMENT	HEADS OF EXECUTIVE GOVERNMENT	LEGISLATIVE BODY
National	President and deputy—directly elected	Representative People's Council: DPR, Dewan Perwakilan Rakyat
Provinces	Governor (*gubernur*) and deputy—directly elected	Regional People's Representative Council I: DPRD I, Dewan Perwakilan Rakyat Daerah I
Districts Rural districts (*kabupaten*) Urban municipalities (*kota*)	District head (*bupati*) and deputy—directly elected Mayor (*walikota*) and deputy—directly elected	Regional People's Representative Council II: DPRD II, Dewan Perwakilan Rakyat Daerah II
Subdistrict (*kecamatan*)	Subdistrict head (*camat*)—appointed civil servant	—
Villages Rural *desa*	Village head (*kepala desa*)—directly elected	Village Consultative Body: BPD, Badan Permusyawaratan Desa
Urban precincts (*kelurahan*)	*Lurah*—appointed civil servant	—
Neighborhoods Urban neighborhood (*Rukun warga*, RW)	RW head (*ketua* RW)—varies, directly or indirectly elected, or appointed	—
Rural hamlet (*dusun*)	Hamlet head (*kepala dusun*)—varies, directly or indirectly elected, or appointed	—
Sub-neighborhoods *Rukun tetangga* (*Rukun tetangga*, RT)	RT head (*ketua* RT)—directly elected	—

Acknowledgments

The idea of coauthoring this book came at a point when each of us had begun separately researching grassroots politics in Indonesia and we were thinking about writing books of our own. Berenschot had come to the study of Indonesia after a long period of research on informal politics in India, and was struck by the similarities and differences he encountered in Indonesia. Aspinall had been researching Indonesian politics for around two decades but had recently begun working on a comparative project on "money politics" across Southeast Asia. When we met at workshops in Indonesia and elsewhere, the overlapping and complementary nature of our methods and findings was obvious. While both of us were immersing ourselves in fieldwork, Berenschot was also organizing a large expert survey, and Aspinall was helping to coordinate a multistranded project that involved a large team of fieldworkers as well as surveys. We decided to work together and found the process to be far smoother and more productive than we could have imagined, each learning a great deal from the other and working through our ideas together. We hope the benefits are obvious to our readers.

It is perhaps a cliché to say that academic research is a collective endeavor, but it is certainly true in the case of this book. Indeed, given our separate pathways, we incurred perhaps even more debts than are usual, and would not have been able to write this book without the support, encouragement, advice, and collaboration of a great many people. The book makes use, for example, of the expert survey that was designed by Berenschot and executed with the help of thirty-eight Indonesian researchers, who meticulously interviewed over five hundred experts in sometimes difficult circumstances. We are very grateful to these researchers: T. Muhammad Jafar, Aryos Nivada, Fauza Andriyadi, Siti Nur'aini, Tongam Panggabean, Sadri Chaniago, Irawati, Andri Rusta, Darmawan Purba, Muhammad Syarif Abadi, Ahmad Mafthuchan, Radjimo Sastro Wijono, Moh. Yasin, Akhriyadi Sofian, Dewi Herviani, Ahmad Zakiyuddin, Caroline Paskarina, Wachyu Ardiyanto, Aan Anshori, Muhtar Haboddin, Didik Hadiyatno, Alex Bhajo, Yanedi Yagau, Imam Trianto, Toto Widyanto, Irawan Amiruddin, Musaddaq, Eka Damayanti, Neni Kumayas, Yurnie Sendow, Steven Sumolang, Jusuf Madubun, Josef Emanuel Embu, Rudi Rohi, Siprianus Jemalur, Aprila Russiana Amelia, and Nasrul. Eddie Riyadi Terre-Laggut and Arni Riyani Putri were indispensable in overseeing the process. Likewise, the book draws on the insights contributed by the large team of researchers Aspinall worked with during the

2014 legislative election, in a project organized in collaboration with colleagues from the University of Gadjah Mada. Among the researchers who were most helpful, and from whom we learned the most, were Rubaidi, Ahmad Zainul Hamdi, Ahmad Taufik Dinamik, Rizkika Lhena Darwin, Aryos Nivada, Ibrahim, Alamsyah, Muhammad Mahsun, Gandung Ismanto, Idris Thaha, Ridho Taqwa, Tasman Sofyan, Sita Dewi, S. L. Harjanto, Olivia Purba, Aswad, Najib Husain, and Nono Sumampouw.

In organizing these large research efforts, we both benefited from working with inspiring colleagues at the Department of Politics and Government at the University of Gadjah Mada in Yogyakarta, especially Mada Sukmajati, as well as Wawan Mas'udi, Purwo Santoso, Amalinda Savirani, and Melathi Hingar.

For their highly capable and committed research assistance, Berenschot would like to thank Muhammad Syarif Abadi (North Lampung), Gita Nasution (Tangerang), and Yanedi Jagau (Gunung Mas). Likewise, outside of (and often in addition to) the 2014 election research mentioned above, many individuals collaborated with Aspinall, conducting field research and writing reports, coordinating visits and facilitating meetings, or running surveys and focus groups. Among those he learned most from were Noor Rohman, David Efendi, and Zusiana Elly Triantini (Central Java), Muhammad Uhaib As'ad (Banjarmasin), Sebastian Dettman (Palangkaraya), Marzuki Wahid (Cirebon), Rudi Rohi (Kupang), Parawansa Assoniwora (Samarinda), and Wijaya Kusuma and Thamrin Jaafar (Pontianak).

We discussed a first draft of this manuscript at a congenial session at KITLV, also known as the Royal Netherlands Institute of Southeast Asian and Caribbean Studies, where we benefited from helpful feedback from Nankyung Choi, David Henley, Gerry van Klinken, David Kloos, Henk Schulte Nordholt, Laurens Bakker, Wouter Veenendaal, Sarthak Bagchi, Wija Widyayanto, Adriaan Bedner, Jacqueline Vel, and James Scambary, as well as from the great PhD students and researchers there: Prio Sambodho, Retna Hanani, Zamzam Fauzanafi, Vita Febriany, Chris Chaplin, and Willem van der Muur. Anonymous reviewers for Cornell University Press also provided extremely useful feedback on the volume.

For Berenschot, KITLV has been an exceptionally pleasant and supportive home base for this project. As well as the above-mentioned colleagues, Berenschot also wishes to thank Ellen Sitinjak, Yayah Siegers, Jeannette Poestkoke, Gerd Oostindië, and Rosemarijn Höfte. Aspinall has equally benefited from working in a very supportive and stimulating environment for the study of contemporary Southeast Asia at the Department of Political and Social Change in the Coral Bell School of Asia Pacific Studies, Australian National University. His colleagues Marcus Mietzner and Greg Fealy, in particular, have long been wonderful sounding boards on contemporary Indonesian politics. Aspinall also benefited from working with a group of exceptionally knowledgeable and talented PhD students working on Indonesian politics and society. Two of them, Burhanuddin Muhtadi and Ahmad Muhajir, were themselves writing dissertations on vote buying in Indonesia, and helped Aspinall to organize aspects of the field and survey research, and to formulate his ideas. Eve Warburton was writing her PhD on a different topic but participated in the money politics research as well, and was always a source of great insight on contemporary Indonesia, as were other PhD students, including Liam Gammon, Thomas Power, Colum Graham, and Danang Widojoko. Aspinall also owes an enormous debt to his colleagues on the Southeast Asia money politics project, especially Meredith Weiss and Allen Hicken, who traveled with him for a time in Indonesia in 2014 and helped bring many comparative elements into focus, as well as Paul Hutchcroft, who especially helped to shape his early thinking on the politics of patronage.

Berenschot's fieldwork as well as the expert survey was funded by a VENI grant from the Netherlands Organization for Academic Research (NWO, grant number 451-12-013). Aspinall drew on several sources of funding, including a Future Fellowship (FT120100742) and two Discovery Grants (DP120103181 and DP140103114) from the Australian Research Council, without which he would not have had the time nor the resources to conduct the research. A grant from the Centre for Democratic Institutions at the ANU funded the 2014 legislative election research, and a fellowship for Aspinall at KITLV in 2016 allowed us to work intensively on the manuscript together.

At Cornell University Press we thank Roger Haydon and Sara Ferguson for their support and encouragement. Maxine McArthur and Glenn Novak provided expert copyediting. Kendra Millis prepared the index. Some passages in the book have appeared in other publications. Brief and scattered extracts are taken from articles by Aspinall: "A Nation in Fragments: Patronage and Neoliberalism in Contemporary Indonesia," *Critical Asian Studies* 45 (1) (2013): 27–54; "Indonesia's 2014 Elections: Parliament and Patronage," *Journal of Democracy* 25 (4) (2014): 96–110; "When Brokers Betray: Clientelism, Social Networks, and Electoral Politics in Indonesia," *Critical Asian Studies* 46 (4) (2014): 545–570; and "Vote Buying in Indonesia: Candidate Strategies, Market Logic and Effectiveness," *Journal of East Asian Studies* 17 (1) (2017): 1–27 (coauthored with N. Rohman, A. Z. Hamdi, and Z. E. Triantini). Parts of chapter 10 appear in Ward Berenschot, "The Political Economy of Clientelism: A Comparative Study of Indonesia's Patronage Democracy," in *Comparative Political Studies* (2018).

We also each owe personal debts, and here it is best to revert to the first person singular. From Aspinall: Thank you to my partner, Glenn Flanagan, who has always been my greatest source of support in my professional and other pursuits, and, once more, to my parents for introducing me to Indonesia long ago. From Berenschot: My greatest fieldwork supporters were Suzanne, Kas, Tamar, and Isa. It was such a blessing that you all agreed to move to Jakarta to make this research project possible. And I feel even more blessed knowing that this adventure was just one among many that we will have together.

DEMOCRACY FOR SALE

INDONESIA'S PATRONAGE DEMOCRACY

Abdullah (not his real name) is the head of an RW (*rukun warga*), or neighborhood, in one of the industrial zones in Tangerang district, just to the west of Jakarta. Most of the residents in his neighborhood, a working-class housing estate consisting of a few hundred households, work in a nearby textile factory. In the months leading up to the 2014 legislative election, Abdullah decided that if the residents of the RW united they would be able to leverage their voting power to gain benefits for their community. To this end, he contacted various candidates who were running for seats in the national, provincial, and district legislatures. At first, he negotiated with members of the Indonesia Democracy Party—Struggle (PDI-P) and found a national and a provincial candidate who were each willing to pay for regular insecticide spraying to kill the mosquitoes that spread dengue fever in the community, and to fund repairs to the community hall and sponsor parties organized by the local youth group. When a district PDI-P candidate failed to commit to a similar deal, Abdullah found a candidate running for the rival Golkar party, who contributed 50 million rupiah (about US$4,400) to pave 1.3 kilometers of road into the community.[1] In return for these benefits, Abdullah and his colleagues formed a team of brokers to deliver the votes these three candidates needed. Each sub-neighborhood (*rukun tetangga*, or RT) established a "victory team" composed of ten women and ten men whose job it was to talk to their neighbors and ensure they voted for the three candidates. They were also tasked with preventing teams working for rival candidates accessing the community and buying votes there.

This vignette, derived from field notes written in the lead-up to Indonesia's 2014 legislative election, describes a practice known as political clientelism. Political clientelism happens when voters, campaign workers, or other actors provide electoral support to politicians in exchange for personal favors or material benefits. Politicians who use clientelistic methods to win elections do so by distributing favors, goods, or cash to individuals or small groups of voters, whom they then expect to reciprocate with their votes. These goods and favors can come in multiple forms—from envelopes stuffed with cash to assistance in getting a child into a government scholarship program, from a job as a hospital janitor to a government construction contract.

The essence of clientelistic politics is the quid pro quo, or, as it is often described in the scholarly literature, "contingent exchange" (e.g., Stokes et al. 2013, 7; Hicken 2011, 291): politicians offer benefits in the hope and expectation that recipients will reward them with political support, or as a reward for such support offered in the past. This element of reciprocity distinguishes clientelism from programmatic politics, in which candidates or parties offer broad policies that confer benefits to large categories of persons—or even to an entire population—regardless of the political support those persons offer at election time.

Though it may sound like a technical, even abstract, term, the concept of clientelism allows us to unlock the inner workings and day-to-day politics of many countries around the world, including Indonesia. In much of the world, if we try to understand politics only by analyzing formal institutions, or even by observing only what is reported in the media, we can arrive at a picture in which electoral politics is primarily about battles among parties, political movements, and charismatic leaders offering competing visions for their country's future. Viewed up close, at the level of interactions between ordinary people, party workers, community leaders, and political representatives, what we often instead find is "the politics of the belly" (Bayart 1993), in which political actors of all sorts try to extract material benefits from the political system. At this level, politics is often conducted on a highly pragmatic basis, with the trading of favors, cash, material goods, and other benefits for political support being the daily stuff of politics. This netherworld of politics can become legible to outsiders briefly, such as when a newspaper reports on a high-profile corruption case linking a politician and a donor, or reveals a case of vote buying; but such publicly reported phenomena are typically mere instances in more widespread patterns of clientelistic politics.

Over the last decade or so, analysts and policy makers have recognized that across large swaths of the world, clientelism is both more common and more entrenched than was once thought. Not long ago, scholars expected that modernization, economic growth, and democratization would gradually force politicians to shed clientelistic practices and focus on the propagation of policy proposals as the principal means of wooing voters. Indeed, many theorists of democracy assumed that programmatic politics was the normal form of democratic competition.[2] Yet although programmatic politics can be observed in varying intensity throughout the world, there is little indication that it is on course to drive out clientelistic practices. The experiences of both relatively older, established democracies, such as India, as well new "third wave" democracies like Indonesia, suggest that democratization is making clientelistic politics less asymmetrical by strengthening the bargaining power of voters and grassroots brokers, but not making it less pervasive (Gay 1998; Kitschelt and Wilkinson 2007; Krishna 2007; Roniger 2004). On the contrary, a recurring theme in recent studies of politics from Eastern Europe to Africa, Asia, and South America is the centrality of clientelistic exchange in shaping interactions between citizens and the state (see for example Auyero 2001; Beck 2008; Collins 2006; Gay 1998; van Klinken 2009; Kopecký, Mair, and Spirova 2012; O'Dwyer 2006; van de Walle 2007). The term "patronage democracy" has gained currency to describe democracies where electoral mobilization primarily takes a clientelistic form (Chandra 2004), with the word "patronage," in our usage, referring to the goods and favors that politicians provide in exchange for electoral support (we discuss definitions at greater length in chapter 2). Given the centrality of clientelistic politics throughout the world, it could be argued that patronage democracies actually constitute the normal—in the sense of most common—form of democracy.

Growing awareness of the persistence and centrality of clientelism has led scholars to devote increasing intellectual effort to understanding how clientelistic systems work. This book extends that effort to the world's fourth-most-populous country, its third-largest democracy, and one of the great success stories of the so-called "third wave" of democratization: Indonesia. Throughout this book we argue that Indonesia's newly democratized political system is saturated with clientelism. At every level, formal political institutions are shadowed by informal, personalized networks through which material benefits and favors flow. Politicians win power, often, by distributing small-scale projects, cash, or other goods to voters or community groups; they gain the funds they need to campaign by trading contracts, licenses, and other favors with businesspeople; and they engage in constant battles with each other and with bureaucrats in order to wrest control over state resources and turn them to their personal political advantage.

The exchange of favors and material benefits at every stage of the electoral cycle is so pervasive that one is apt to think of democracy in Indonesia as being for sale. The sale of state power is a step-by-step affair that proceeds throughout the electoral cycle. It starts with the considerable amounts of money that many candidates pay to political parties to acquire the support they need to stand for election. During their negotiations with would-be candidates, party officials often extract stiff prices, as well as promises of future benefits, in exchange for their backing. Such auctioneering of support is also present when candidates build their campaign organizations. Candidates attract campaign workers by enticing them with monetary incentives and with promises of privileged access to projects, development schemes, and other state resources. These campaign organizers in turn acquire the support of community leaders by offering—as in the case of Abdullah—contributions for community infrastructure or activities, or simply by providing them with under-the-table payments. In the days preceding an election, campaigners take their auction to the streets and households of Indonesia, in the form of the so-called dawn attack, in which they distribute large amounts of money to voters. Not infrequently, voters have to weigh bids from several candidates before deciding on which they will support. After the election, it is payback time, and campaign donors and workers can expect to be rewarded by the winning candidates with jobs, contracts, credit, projects, and other benefits. The winners turn their thoughts to building up a war chest—typically by engaging in various forms of corruption—in anticipation of the next election. The huge amounts of money involved, and the pervasiveness of clientelistic exchange throughout the electoral process, mean that state power is, in effect, auctioned off.

Of course, in Indonesia, as in other countries, this is not how politicians present their election victories. Politicians and their supporters generally prefer to claim they win because voters prefer their persona or program over those of their competitors, rather than because they outbid them. And, of course, sometimes they are right. Candidate quality and programmatic offerings do count a great deal in at least some Indonesian elections (Aspinall 2013b; Fossati 2017; Mujani, Liddle, and Ambardi 2012), most obviously in presidential polls. In this book we confirm that there is scope for programmatic voting even in local elections in parts of Indonesia, especially urban regions of the most densely populated island, Java. By calling our book *Democracy for Sale* we do not mean that every political office is merely auctioned off, nor even that clientelistic politics boils down merely to a matter of monetary exchange. Even so, in many areas programmatic politics is mixed inextricably with clientelistic practices, and in some regions clientelism is so pervasive that the governing capacities or policy proposals of candidates have little impact on election results. The pervasiveness of clientelistic exchanges has turned elections into a contest of who dares to offer the most money and other resources. The pervasiveness of such clientelistic practices has given rise to the phrase *demokrasi wani piro* as a widely used descriptor for Indonesian democracy, where the Javanese phrase *wani piro* means "how much do you dare" (to pay)?

Treating Clientelism Comparatively

As well as describing how political clientelism works in Indonesia, our aim in this book is to place Indonesia's system in a comparative context and highlight what is distinctive about it. To allow us to begin this process, let us compare the story of Abdullah, with which we began this chapter, with two more vignettes, the first taken from Ahmedabad in Gujarat, India, the second from Buenos Aires in Argentina:

> Mahesh Varma [is] a party worker for the BJP [Bharatiya Janata Party]. Every morning [he] can be found at the side of one of the main roads . . . next to Pravin Dalal, the local municipal councillor, and four other party workers. At this roadside they receive a daily flow of local inhabitants, who come to ask for Pravin Dalal's help to deal with governmental institutions—for, for example, getting a loan, repairing broken paving, settling a police case, getting a proof of residence or reducing one's hospital fees. The party workers help Pravin Dalal in this process. . . . During elections [Mahesh Varma] helps to organise rallies, tours the neighbourhood—"I go from home to home and I tell people to vote for the BJP, because of the work it has done." (Berenschot 2014, 202–203)

> Cholo still distributes milk, food, and medicine and opens his UB [*unidades básicas*, a Peronist neighborhood committee] almost every day of the year. Many residents identify this UB with the municipality. Asking people whether they knew Cholo, I would often receive the same answer: "Yes, there in the corner, at the municipality." . . . In the end, it is the Peronist Party that has the most direct access at all levels—local, provincial, and national—to the resources of the state. In poverty-stricken neighborhoods, squatter settlements, and shanty-towns, the UBs constitute one of the most important places in which basic needs can be satisfied, through [which] basic problems can be solved. The UBs lend incredible organizational strength to the Peronist Party and ensure the party high (and unmatched) levels of territorial penetration. (Auyero 2001, 92 and 89)

Both of these quotations describe interactions that are clientelistic, as in the scene that opens this chapter. The first paints a typical picture of local politics in India, where party workers often act as fixers and problem solvers for their communities. Through such acts of support, these Indian party workers aim to generate a sense of obligation among their clients to vote for their party (e.g., Auerbach 2016; Witsoe 2013). The second describes politics in a poor neighborhood in Argentina's capital, where the Peronist party has historically possessed a deeply entrenched party machine and uses its control over municipal welfare programs to cultivate political support. Here, such deals sometimes remain implicit, as party activists assume that "in the act of getting help, problem holders become increasingly ensnared within the Peronist web" (Auyero 2001, 117). As with Abdullah in Tangerang, in both these cases we see how political actors provide various favors with the aim of generating support: all three cases are examples of political clientelism at work.

However, the careful reader will have already noted a similarity between the Indian and Argentinian examples that contrasts with Abdullah's story. Both feature political parties or, more precisely, grassroots party operatives, playing the role of intermediaries or brokers in clientelistic exchange. In contrast, what is striking about the story of Abdullah is how marginal political parties are to it. Yes, the candidates seeking office were party candidates. But the person initiating the deal, acting as these candidates' chief broker, and organizing their combined campaign in this neighborhood was not a party worker. He was instead a nonpartisan community leader *cum* low-ranking state functionary. RW heads are not civil servants, but in most places they draw a small stipend from the state, and much of their work concerns managing community-level official business: we explain their functions and authority at length in later chapters. Abdullah established a team of brokers who were themselves not connected directly to the candidates they were supporting, let alone to their parties. The fact that they were simultaneously working for candidates from rival parties was somewhat unusual, but not unique in the Indonesian context. And while it is more typical for the candidate to be the one to make the initial approach, we shall see in later chapters it is by no means rare for community leaders to seek out candidates at election time and offer them support in exchange for small-scale projects of the type Abdullah sought. Bargaining between politicians and community brokers over such deals is so common that there is even an Indonesian term that encompasses such deals, along with those made for cash or other material rewards: *politik transaksional*, or "transactional politics." While transactional politics can occur within political parties, it often takes place outside parties through deals that are ad hoc, temporary, even freewheeling.

Here we arrive at the nub of what makes Indonesia's system of clientelism distinctive. In many countries, political parties are the principal intermediaries in clientelistic politics. Classic studies of clientelism have focused on party machines. In the United States, scholars paid attention to the party machines that operated in working-class and migrant cities like Chicago and Philadelphia (Banfield and Wilson 1963; Scott 1969). More recent studies on clientelistic politics in countries like India, Argentina, Mexico, or Brazil highlight the central role of political parties in clientelistic vote mobilization (see Auerbach 2016; Auyero 2001; Berenschot 2011b; De Wit 2016; Levitsky 2003; Magaloni, Diaz-Cayeros, and Estévez 2007; Nichter 2014; Witsoe 2013). Indeed, as Hilgers (2012, 569) notes, the terms "machine politics" and "clientelism" are often used interchangeably. One recent influential cross-national comparative study of distributive politics considers clientelistic brokers solely as "agents of the party" (Stokes et al. 2013, 19) and assumes the distribution of clientelistic benefits to be the domain of political parties. This assumption is shared by much recent literature on the topic (see for example Calvo and Murillo 2004; Gans-Morse, Mazzuca, and Nichter 2014; Kitschelt and Kselman 2013; Kitschelt and Wilkinson 2007; Nichter 2008).

Indonesia is different. Political parties in Indonesia, as in most democratic systems, play an important role in politics. Indeed, as Mietzner (2013b) has persuasively demonstrated, Indonesia's parties are relatively strongly institutionalized, at least when compared to those of similar third-wave democracies. Yet parties are often strikingly marginal to the clientelistic exchanges that are so important to Indonesia's political life. At election times, most candidates build nonparty vote-brokerage structures known as "success teams," *tim sukses*, that sometimes draw on party cadres but are more likely to rely on community leaders and other citizens not affiliated to parties. Politicians themselves often have only tenuous links to the parties, or coalitions of parties, that nominate them for elective office. Many of the patronage goods and services that are the medium of exchange in clientelistic politics in other settings—social welfare programs, for example—remain largely outside the control of parties but are instead distributed at the discretion of bureaucrats, community-level elected officials, or by politicians whose party links are weak. Parties themselves are often reduced to the role of toll keeper, selling nominations to candidates but doing little to help them campaign or to discipline or direct their behavior once they hold office. Indonesia is not in this regard unique: in a range of countries, including neighbors such as the Philippines and Thailand, parties are relatively marginal in the organization of election campaigns and the organization of clientelistic exchange (see for example Callahan and McCargo 1996; Chattharakul 2010). But the Indonesian pattern of party marginality is striking, and, as we shall show in later chapters, it has also developed relatively quickly, in the space of less than two decades since the introduction of the country's new democratic system at the end of the last millennium.

In sum, Indonesia has a system that we characterize as *freewheeling clientelism*. Our book is devoted to outlining the features of this form of clientelism, explaining its internal logic, describing its origins, and explaining how it varies across different regions of Indonesia.

Framework and Arguments

We are now in a position to highlight our book's three main goals and arguments. Our first goal, and the one to which we devote most space through this book, is to describe and analyze the core features of Indonesia's patronage democracy and to highlight what makes it distinctive.

In order to do this, we need to come up with a framework that allows us to place the Indonesian system in comparative perspective. Although political scientists and other scholars have in recent years paid much attention to clientelism, there have been few efforts to systematically compare patronage democracies. We introduce a framework that allows us to do so in chapter 2. This framework focuses on four aspects: the *networks* through which politicians distribute patronage, the *patterns of discretionary control* they exercise over state resources, the varieties of *benefits* they provide to voters, and the *intensity* of clientelistic exchange. We maintain that such a framework highlights critical dimensions of clientelistic politics that differ across countries and could be used to systematically compare a large number of patronage democracies, though we lack space to do so in this volume. However, in order to bring the distinctive features of Indonesia's system into focus, we keep a comparative eye fixed on India and Argentina through the volume, returning from time to time to contrast Indonesia's experiences with those of these two important countries. We choose India and Argentina as our main comparators because they provide us with two well-studied examples of clientelistic political systems that are both, like Indonesia, large democracies that exercise great influence within their respective regions, and marked by significant social inequality.[3] Furthermore, one of us (Berenschot) has previously studied local politics in India. We hope that our efforts at formulating an analytical framework will help to stimulate more comprehensive efforts to compare patronage democracies in the future.

We elaborate in chapter 2 on the features that characterize Indonesia's system of freewheeling clientelism, but let us summarize them briefly here. First, and as already suggested, Indonesia's system is noteworthy for the fact that much of the clientelistic exchange takes place outside of political parties, and is instead organized through ad hoc campaign teams and informal social networks. This situation has historical roots, which we examine, but it also flows from a critical second feature of Indonesia's system of clientelism: parties largely lack the control over key state patronage resources enjoyed in places like Argentina and India. Instead, discretionary control over state resources is dominated by state actors, notably bureaucrats, and by elected local officials, many of whom are former bureaucrats who lack strong party ties. Parties are engaged in a long-term struggle to gain greater control over such resources, so this situation may change in the future, but for much of the post-Suharto period, parties have been only one player, and far from a dominant one, in Indonesia's patronage system. Third, in part owing to the difficulties that parties and other nonincumbent politicians have in controlling the spigot of state resources, Indonesia's patronage democracy is marked by the relative prominence of privately distributed patronage, such as vote buying, private gifts, and personal donations to community groups through ad hoc and short-term exchanges, rather than systematic and long-term cultivation of social constituencies through preferential access to state programs, as seen in countries like Argentina.

Our second major goal, after describing Indonesia's freewheeling clientelism, is to explain how and why this system has come into being. Our argument here stresses historical and institutional factors. Drawing on work that focuses on the sequencing of state and party formation, we emphasize the critical importance of the prehistory of Indonesia's patronage democracy in the long period of authoritarian rule that preceded it. Between 1966 and 1998, Indonesia was governed by the authoritarian "New Order" regime of President Suharto. The New Order was also a patronage polity, but it was one that was highly centralized and relatively closed, with the chief beneficiaries of patronage distribution being bureaucratic actors and other elites who formed the social base of the regime. For our purposes, two features of the New Order's patronage system are important: first, the government institutionalized patronage distribution through nonparty channels, including religious and other social networks, and through village-level quasi-state organizations; second, it put control over key state patronage resources in the hands of bureaucrats and community-level state officials. As a result, when democratization began in 1998, the parties were at a disadvantage because alternative mechanisms of patronage distribution were available to politicians. Parties were also locked out of many of the state patronage resources that sustain machine parties in other countries. Even so, party leaders began to construct organizations and scrambled to access state patronage to sustain them. It is possible that a party-centered system of machine politics would have developed over time. This trend was checked, however, by Indonesia's adoption of a series of reforms that shifted its electoral system away from being party focused to one that was instead candidate focused. This shift meant that political candidates had little to gain from coordinating their patronage distribution efforts through parties but had incentives to build personal teams, cultivate personal clienteles, and foster personal relationships with social networks. In sum: Indonesia's system of freewheeling clientelism can be explained by the legacies of Indonesia's authoritarian bureaucratic polity and the unintended consequence of electoral system design.

Our third goal is to analyze and account for variation in the patterns and intensity of clientelism *within* Indonesia. We use an expert survey to show that the intensity of clientelistic politics varies considerably across the country. Our explanation for that variation concerns concentrated economic control: where the major economic resources in an area are concentrated in the hands of a relatively small elite, clientelism is more intense. In contrast, economic diversification disperses material resources through a wider range of actors, which strengthens scrutiny and disciplining of politicians, thereby reducing clientelism. By using data generated by the expert survey, we demonstrate that this explanation best accounts for variations in the degree of clientelism across Indonesia.

This analysis of regional variation highlights a fundamental fact about clientelism: it both reflects and reproduces deep structures of social and economic inequality. While much of our analysis focuses on the micropolitics of clientelistic exchange and the institutional structures that shape such practices, we also interpret the pervasiveness of clientelism in the light of class and power inequalities. Scholars first developed the concept of clientelism in part to account for how wealthy landlords and poor tenants could maintain relatively harmonious relations in agrarian societies, even when landlords ruthlessly exploited the peasants. Paying attention to landlords' occasional provision of monetary or other assistance to their clients, and the cultural modes of deference and gratitude associated with such exchanges, helped scholars to understand how class inequalities were mediated, legitimated, and sustained in such societies. In Indonesia's mass democracy, clientelistic politics similarly entrench and reflect the dominance of economic elites. In a political arena in which the clientelistic distribution of cash and goods is a key to political success, wealthy politicians and their business allies have a natural political advantage. They use this advantage to win elections, access state resources, and so attain ever greater opportunities for economic accumulation. The regional comparative analysis we provide in chapters 9 and 10 illustrates the connection between clientelistic politics and economic inequality by showing that clientelistic practices are most pervasive in regions where economies are less diversified and where control over them is most concentrated in the hands of a narrow elite.

Researching Informal Politics

At this point it is important to explain a fundamental mission and underlying philosophy of this book. We intend our book to make the case that scholars of Indonesia, and of comparative politics more broadly, need to take informal politics more seriously. In most countries, formal political rules and institutions are shadowed by a netherworld of personalized political relationships and networks, secretive deal making, trading of favors, corruption, and a host of other informal and shadowy practices. As Alina Mungiu-Pippidi has recently argued, in most countries favoritism is "the main social allocation mode, with widespread use of connections of any kind, exchange of favors, and, in their absence, monetary inducements" (Mungui-Pippidi 2015, 22). In practice, scholars often recognize such features but treat them as aberrations from the formal rules and sanctioned patterns of behavior that we assume constitute the political system in the country concerned, or which we believe normatively *should*, or perhaps *will*, constitute it. Taking such informal politics seriously requires us to place them at the center of our analysis and not view them as deviations, failings, or epiphenomena (see also Berenschot and van Klinken 2018). It also requires us to develop conceptual tools to think systematically and comparatively about variations in patterns of informal and clientelistic politics, a challenge we take up in the next chapter.

The case of Indonesia certainly provides salutary lessons in this regard. In the early period of Indonesia's democratic transition, shortly after the collapse of the Suharto regime in 1998, there was considerable optimism among scholars and practitioners alike regarding the prospects of a new democratic order. Much attention was paid to the design of Indonesia's formal rules and institutions, including constitutional design, judicial reform, security sector reform, and the like (Horowitz 2013). To be sure, almost from the start, many scholars began to remark upon the persistence of corruption, patronage, and patrimonialism. In general, however, observers depicted such phenomena as being remnants of the Suharto period, vestiges of the pre-democratic order that would either be gradually eliminated as formal institutions consolidated and grew stronger, or which would undermine and cripple such institutions from within. The standard way to conceptualize informal politics was in a continuity-and-change mode, which located informality as a remnant of past practices, in contradiction, even at war, with the new democratic order that was being constructed. Of course, no serious scholar assumed that Indonesia was predestined to succeed in establishing a rational bureaucratic order or a fully consolidated democracy. But evidence of informal politics such as vote buying, political corruption, and money politics initially tended to be treated as signs of *dysfunction* within the system, rather than being seen as evidence of how the system was actually functioning.

It soon became obvious, however, that informal politics were not merely a lingering vestige of the past but were evolving, adapting, and even expanding as democracy settled into place. This adaptation was most apparent in studies of corruption, with one observer pithily remarking that Suharto had practiced a "better class" of corruption, because it was centralized and predictable, in contrast to the more fragmented and seemingly arbitrary corruption that arose after the New

Order (McLeod 2000). Likewise, Indonesia's "big bang" decentralization—in which significant political authority and fiscal powers were devolved to hundreds of district governments around the country—was in part initially conceived as a means of improving governance by bringing government close to the people and thus allowing better monitoring of the governmental "agents" by the popular "principals." It soon became obvious, however, that one primary effect of decentralization was to shift the locus of predatory behavior downward, allowing for the multiplication of sites for corruption and informal deal making, rather than their elimination (Hadiz 2010; Robison and Hadiz 2004).

Meanwhile, observers of electoral politics also began to observe oddities, such as the tendency of political parties not to seek to dominate elected executive office in Indonesia's regions, but simply to auction off such positions to the highest bidders (Hadiz 2004). In the new wave of local government-head elections from 2005, scholars noted that candidates relied more on informal personal networks than they did on parties and other formal structures (Buehler and Tan 2007). In virtually every sphere of state life, from the police (Baker 2013) to natural resources management (McCarthy 2004; Warren and Visser 2016), from the judiciary (Butt and Lindsey 2011; Pompe 2005) to the management of Indonesia's ubiquitous land conflicts (Lucas and Warren 2013), it became increasingly obvious that a "shadow state" (S. Hidayat 2007) of informal connections, payments, and networks determined how state officials functioned. Furthermore, the selection and promotion of civil servants turned out to be heavily influenced by personal connections and political expediency rather than professional capacity (Blunt, Turner, and Lindroth 2012a; Kristiansen and Ramli 2006). By about a decade after the fall of Suharto, such observations had accumulated to an extent that scholars were beginning to make informality central to their assessments of Indonesia's political system. Thus, it was argued that "illegality by state officials is as central to the way that the state operates in Indonesia as are the formal rules and bureaucratic structures that constitute the state on its surface" (Aspinall and van Klinken 2011, 22–23). Scholars characterized Indonesia as a "patronage democracy" (van Klinken 2009; Schulte Nordholt and van Klinken 2007; Simandjuntak 2010, 2012) and as a system of "fragmented clientelism" (Aspinall 2013a) where "what matters is who you know, what and who you pay, and to whom you pledge loyalty, [while] initiative, excellence and results matter little" (Blunt, Turner, and Lindroth 2012a, 215).

There is thus a rapidly developing scholarly literature on informal politics in Indonesia that we draw upon and to which we seek to contribute in this volume. However, even in much of this literature there is a tendency to view phenomena such as clientelism and corruption as signs of pathology, and as being secondary to the main game of formal politics. Take, for example, the important "oligarchy" literature on Indonesian politics produced by Richard Robison, Vedi R. Hadiz, and Jeffrey Winters (Hadiz 2010; Robison and Hadiz 2004; Winters 2011). In an influential series of works, these scholars have argued that political and economic life in Indonesia remains dominated by powerful and wealthy oligarchs who first rose to prominence under Suharto. These scholars propose that the informal fusion of political and economic power is critical to the continuing hold of this oligarchy. Yet if we carefully study these works, it becomes apparent that their major focus is predation by elites. Informal politics are presented to illustrate the basic message that elites exploit their power for material gain. These scholars provide little in the way of systematic analysis of the mechanics and modes of such behavior: their interest is in the brute facts of class power rather than in the methods by which it is maintained. Proponents of the oligarchy thesis have contributed much to our understanding of contemporary Indonesia, but their work illustrates a more general point: clientelism frequently attracts attention for its venality and its destructive impact, without paying attention to its forms, functionality, productive effects, and wider consequences.

In this book, we endeavor to place informal politics at the heart of our analysis, rather than viewing it as deviant. To be sure, formal institutions such as laws, policies, and official procedures do affect the functioning of state institutions. But the actual impact of regulations depends on the capacity of individuals and groups to use informal, personal exchange relationships to manipulate their implementation. Analysis of Indonesian politics should thus endeavor to understand the interplay between formal and informal dimensions of politics, and view informal politics as a constituent element of state power. In this sense, our book responds to recent calls for an "upside down view of governance" (Centre for the Future State 2010; Hickey 2012; see also Booth and Cammack 2013) that takes informal institutions more seriously (Helmke and Levitsky 2004; Lauth 2000). Developing a detailed and nuanced picture of the variants of informal clientelistic politics is critical for developing an accurate understanding of how government actually works in a country like Indonesia—and for whom.

Finally, we should stress that taking informal politics seriously does not mean turning our backs on its deleterious effects. On the contrary, we maintain that the comparative study of informal, clientelistic politics is important because clientelistic election campaigns shape not just electoral outcomes, but also the functioning of state institutions and the nature of governance. As will become apparent in this book, clientelistic politics is at the root of many of the challenges that Indonesia faces—ranging from environmental degradation, persistent social inequality, and weak spatial planning to inadequate public services and corruption. Addressing these challenges is not simply a matter of adopting better policies or improving the skills of government officials. Instead, it will involve dealing with a political system that thrives on the use of informal, personal relationships to capture and distribute state resources. We make the case that understanding informal politics is essential for finding ways to better deal with the governance problems experienced by a country like Indonesia. Rather than working against this system of informal politics—or pretending that it does not exist—strengthening governance often involves working along the grain of the incentive structure that a clientelistic political arena generates. We take up this challenge in the conclusion.

Methodology

Taking informal politics seriously also has implications for our research methods, requiring a combination of qualitative fieldwork and quantitative approaches. Fieldwork is necessary precisely because informal practices often take place behind closed doors, in the shadows cast by formal institutions. We can rarely learn about such practices by relying on media reports or other public sources. Instead, we need to observe them directly and to learn from practitioners. Accordingly, the study of clientelism was for a long time dominated by ethnographic studies (examples that inspired us include Auyero 2001, Chubb 1981, and Weiner 1967). These studies have provided a rich mosaic of descriptions of clientelistic practices in different country contexts.

The limitation of ethnographic accounts is that they allow us to develop an accumulation of snapshots of informal practices, without bringing into sharp focus how common these practices are, or whether and under what conditions clientelism varies. Without such a picture, we are limited in our ability to make inferences about causation. To do that, it is helpful to accumulate whatever statistical evidence we can about clientelistic practices. Accordingly, in recent times, researchers have started to apply various quantitative methods, including using surveys (Stokes 2005; Young 2009; Wantchekon 2003), statistical proxies (Keefer 2007; Keefer and Vlaicu 2008; Magaloni, Diaz-Cayeros, and Estévez 2007) and, more recently, a cross-national expert survey (Kitschelt et al. 2009) to identify conditions favoring or discouraging clientelism. These quantitative methods provide their own challenges precisely because of the invisibility of clientelistic practices in most formal records. Survey respondents, moreover, are often reluctant to discuss informal practices such as vote buying or influence peddling. To ensure reliability and analytical depth, integration of ethnographic and quantitative approaches is needed (see Hicken 2011; Kitschelt et al. 2009, 747; Kitschelt and Wilkinson 2007; Muno 2010).

The research we draw upon for this volume is based on just such a combination. It is founded on lengthy periods of fieldwork on election campaigns. Berenschot concentrated his field research on three districts: North Lampung in the south of Sumatra, Tangerang city on the outskirts of Jakarta, and Gunung Mas in Central Kalimantan. These sites were chosen as being representative of distinctive political economies as they have, respectively, an agricultural, an urban, and a natural-resource-based economy. In these areas, Berenschot conducted fieldwork during a period of fifteen months in 2013 and 2014, during which he observed campaigns in district-head, legislative, and presidential elections. During this fieldwork, Berenschot followed several campaigns and individuals—candidates, campaigners, bureaucrats, voters—throughout these electoral cycles. Aspinall, by contrast, ranged widely across Indonesia, visiting about sixty districts in eighteen of the country's thirty-four provinces, sometimes on repeat occasions, but with the goal of developing a sweeping picture of nationwide patterns and regional variations. Part of Aspinall's own research was conducted in conjunction with a project that involved extensive ethnographic research by fifty researchers located in twenty locations across the archipelago in the lead-up to legislative elections in April 2014. He was able to access the research summaries and interview notes produced by these researchers, adding to the breadth of our coverage. Both of us were fortunate to work with Indonesian colleagues and partners who could connect us to local networks. Overall, we were able to directly observe both the planning and execution of clientelistic campaigns, including practices such as vote buying.

Throughout the book, we draw on examples from our fieldwork to illustrate our arguments and explain how clientelistic politics works on the ground, where possible quoting directly from our informants to explain the logic of clientelism in the words used by its practitioners. We use examples from across the archipelago, both to point to variations in clientelistic practices and to underline their ubiquity. In addition, one connecting thread that runs through the chapters is a mayoral election in Tangerang, an urban district on the periphery of Jakarta. We use this contest to introduce chapters 3 through 8 and so take the reader through the different phases typical of an electoral campaign in Indonesia. We do not claim that Tangerang, a relatively wealthy and industrialized suburb of Jakarta, is representative of Indonesia as a whole, but by weaving the story of the campaign of mayoral candidate Arief Wismansyah through the analysis, we aim to provide readers with a sense of how core features of Indonesia's patronage democracy cohere.

In addition to using our fieldwork observations, we draw on quantitative methods, primarily on the findings of an expert survey that was designed by Berenschot. Throughout the book we supplement analysis based on direct observations of and interviews with politicians and brokers by drawing on data produced by the expert survey in order to show that we are not describing anomalous behaviors but phenomena that are widespread across Indonesia. Expert surveys, which seek informed opinion from qualified specialists on a topic, rather than from a cross-section of the general population, are an established and increasingly influential method in social science research. We chose this method because we believe it provides a more comprehensive and reliable source of data than the alternatives.

In recent times, some researchers have measured clientelism by using statistical proxies—such as corruption and rule-of-law measures (Keefer 2007; Keefer and Vlaicu 2008), the rate of government spending on personnel (Magaloni, Diaz-Cayeros, and Estévez 2007), or mayoral discretion in spending of welfare budgets (Weitz-Shapiro 2014). This body of research has produced numerous important findings, but the obvious drawback of using such proxies is that their link to clientelism is often questionable. It cannot always be assumed that more spending on government personnel, for example, will indicate higher intensity of clientelistic politics. The use of general population surveys has also become more common, such as those that measure citizens' involvement in, or knowledge of, vote buying (Brusco, Nazareno, and Stokes 2004; Stokes 2005). One problem with this method is that, because of the illegality or social illegitimacy of such practices, there can often be social desirability problems with such surveys, though innovative methods have been introduced to get around this problem, such as the use of survey experiments. Yet another problem with using either proxies or general surveys is that these methods generally focus on just one dimension of clientelistic politics. Voter surveys, for example, tend to study clientelism by looking at vote buying, and cannot uncover clientelism found in relations between politicians and other actors, such as donors or civil servants.

An expert survey has the advantage of allowing a more comprehensive assessment. Our survey paid attention to a range of objects of clientelistic exchange—from government jobs and contracts to public services and welfare support—across the country, and enabled us then to merge these measures into a single Clientelism Perception Index. Of course, expert surveys have their own challenges. The partisanship of experts might distort assessments. To be reliable, such surveys need careful implementation and clearly worded questions. We adopted various measures—such as a careful, balanced selection of experts with the help of locally based researchers, extensive training of these researchers, and the use of standardized questionnaires that were repeatedly piloted in the field—to minimize possible sources of distortion (see appendixes A and C for an overview of the survey method and the reliability of the results).

A particular potential drawback of using an expert survey is that its findings can still be considered proxies, since they gather *perceptions*—in this case, of how common clientelistic practices are. However, the relationship between perceptions and reality is complex when it comes to clientelism. On the one hand, one could advance various reasons—partisan bias and lack of information being chief among them—that could lead to over- or underestimation of clientelistic practices, though we made strong efforts to avoid such problems. On the other hand, it can be argued that the perceived reality of clientelistic practices is itself important. Perceptions are an important element of clientelistic exchange. The willingness of voters, campaigners, or campaign donors to enter into clientelistic relationships with political actors is informed by their *perception* that their access to state resources might be curtailed if they avoid such relationships. Arguably, from the viewpoint of a politician wanting to influence votes, that perception is as important as his or her actual ability to control the spigot of state funds. Perceptions that the distribution of state benefits is contingent on electoral support are thus more than a proxy for clientelistic practices. Such perceptions are part of that reality.

The expert survey used in this book was inspired by, and built upon, an earlier initiative that used an expert survey to compare clientelism between countries (Kitschelt et al. 2009). Between April and July 2014, Berenschot, together with a team of thirty-eight persons, most of whom were Indonesian university lecturers, executed a survey of 509 local political observers—journalists, academics, NGO activists, and campaigners—in thirty-eight districts in sixteen provinces. These four categories were chosen because their work enables these informants to follow local politics on a professional basis. With the help of our local researchers, we selected informants who were known for their knowledge of local politics. The researchers then conducted recorded interviews with these local experts, using a questionnaire that asked mostly multiple-choice questions on the character of election campaigns, vote buying, and the ways in which various politicians allocated different kinds of state resources.

Through this volume we use the assessments of these 509 local political observers to ascertain how common clientelistic practices are perceived to be across regions with different social and economic characteristics. We asked our survey respondents, for example, what percentage of government contracts were awarded to individuals who made donations to the election campaigns of local politicians, and what percentage of government servants received their postings as a reward for supporting a winning candidate. Such questions provide an assessment of how common such clientelistic exchanges are perceived to be. We find, for example, that more than half of all surveyed experts assess that at least 40 percent of all district-level government contracts are awarded to campaign supporters. A similar number of experts estimate that over 60 percent of all higher-level civil servants within district governments received their current position as a reward for campaign support.

We also use this material to trace variation across Indonesia. Clientelistic allocation of government contracts, for example, is perceived to be almost twice as common in Kupang as in Surabaya. Most experts in Jakarta assess that only between 20 and 40 percent of all government jobs are provided as clientelistic rewards, while in areas like Gunung Mas (Kalimantan) and Jayapura (Papua) almost all such government jobs are considered to be dependent on loyalty during election campaigns.

The survey questions covered a large range of benefits used for clientelistic exchange—not only contracts and jobs but also money, public services, social assistance funds, licenses, and access to welfare programs (for more on this survey instrument see appendix B). In chapter 10 we use this material to construct a Clientelism Perception Index to analyze the extent to which clientelistic practices are common across Indonesia, and to develop an explanation for the variation we find. The full results of the expert survey are available at this book's website, http://www.kitlv.nl/democracy-for-sale.

The Structure of This Book

In the next chapter we elaborate on the core concepts we use in the book and make the case for a comparative study of clientelist politics. After that, the book is divided into four sections, largely following the comparative framework we outlined above. In the first section, we discuss the institutional context that has shaped the evolution of Indonesia's contemporary patronage democracy. In chapter 3 we describe the historical background, noting how President Suharto developed a state-centered patronage system in which political parties played a relatively peripheral role. Chapter 4 discusses interaction between politicians and political parties. We argue that Indonesia's current electoral system has further weakened the role of political parties and prompted many politicians to adopt a very pragmatic relationship with them.

In the next section, on "networks and resources," we discuss how candidates mobilize electoral support, and the forms of resources they distribute when doing so. Chapter 5 discusses the functioning of success teams, the ad hoc campaign organizations that politicians rely on as an alternative to political parties. This chapter focuses on how these success teams organize vote-buying efforts, and how this campaign strategy is marred by problems of broker discipline. Chapter 6 discusses how politicians, in the absence of institutionalized networks such as those provided by deeply rooted parties, incorporate a wide range of social networks into their campaigns by drawing in community notables and providing collective forms of patronage.

The third section of the book, on discretionary control, relates the character of election campaigns to the nature of governance in Indonesia. These chapters discuss the ongoing struggle of politicians to gain more control over state resources. Chapter 7 discusses the ways in which three types of state resources—welfare programs, infrastructure funds, and social assistance funds—are being transformed into patronage that incumbent politicians can use for electoral purposes. We highlight, however, the considerable control that bureaucrats still exercise over these resources, and their tendency to use this control to shore up their own influence. Chapter 8 discusses the politicization of Indonesia's bureaucracy and the tendency of incumbent executive government politicians to use their control over postings and promotions to reward personal loyalty and electoral support. The chapter argues that local politicians use bureaucratic appointments to acquire control over distribution of state resources. We show how and why incumbent politicians enjoy electoral advantages.

The last section compares the intensity of clientelistic politics across Indonesia. Chapter 9 discusses why and how clientelistic elections foster a close embrace between politics and business in Indonesia. We highlight, however, that different local economic conditions generate considerable variation across Indonesia. In chapter 10 we employ the expert survey to study this variation in the intensity of clientelistic practices. Chapter 11 concludes with a plea for taking informal politics seriously in policy making and the design of electoral institutions.

2

CAPTURING VARIETIES OF CLIENTELISM

In this chapter we present a new framework for comparing patronage democracies and sketch out how we use it to analyze Indonesia's version of clientelism in the remainder of this book. We have been required to devise our own framework—though of course we do so by building on the works of others—because the existing political science literature has relatively little to say about variations between patronage democracies and types of clientelism.[1]

This dearth stands in sharp contrast to the richness of comparative study of formal dimensions of politics. Comparative analyses of such topics as political parties or electoral systems are major subfields within political science. In contrast, the comparative study of clientelistic politics has hardly begun (Helmke and Levitsky 2004; Lauth 2000). Handbooks of comparative political science, for example, rarely mention clientelism or other forms of informal politics; when they do, they usually subsume clientelism in sections on "political development" and mention it merely as an indicator of political underdevelopment or of weakness of political parties and other formal institutions.[2] As an example, Arendt Lijphart's oft-cited book, *Patterns of Democracy*, compares thirty-six democracies only in terms of formal dimensions: party coalitions, electoral systems, constitutional provisions related to executive-legislative relations, and so on (Lijphart 2012). This and similar volumes lack sections comparing informal, clientelistic dimensions of politics, giving the impression that these matters are irrelevant for understanding democracies. When comparative analyses include clientelistic practices, they usually do so only in terms of their relative presence or absence, contrasting clientelistic with programmatic political parties, for example, or clientelistic electoral behavior with ideological or policy-oriented patterns. This tendency to position clientelistic practices as deviations from a norm has discouraged systematic analysis of the different forms that clientelistic politics may take.

As a result, and despite the prevalence of clientelism, it is surprising how much we remain in the dark about this political practice, its determinants, and its variability. Overviews of the available literature conclude that we know relatively little about why some states are able to transition away from clientelism, while in others the practice adapts and endures (Hicken 2011, 206). Other accounts conclude that the study of conditions favoring political clientelism "is, perhaps surprisingly, still in its beginnings" (Roniger 2004, 369; see also Keefer and Khemani 2005, 23).

This blank spot extends to Indonesia, of which it has been remarked that "the literature on Indonesia says astoundingly little on the exact forms of clientelism" (Ufen 2012, 51). To be sure, terms like "clientelism," "patronage," and "patrimonialism" recur frequently in descriptions of Indonesian politics, and clientelistic exchange relations are regularly blamed for various problems, ranging from the weaknesses of the country's political parties (Buehler and Tan 2007; Mietzner 2013b) to ethnic conflict (Bertrand 2004; van Klinken 2007; Sidel 2006), weak provision of public services (Blunt, Turner, and Lindroth 2012a), and the political dominance of economic elites (Hadiz 2010; Hadiz and Robison 2013; Winters 2011, 2013). Yet these studies feature clientelistic politics mainly as an explanation for other phenomena; they offer relatively little insight into how clientelistic exchanges are actually organized, or why Indonesia's clientelistic politics take the forms they do. Likewise, we remain largely ignorant of differences in the nature and intensity of clientelistic practices across Indonesia's large and diverse archipelago.

In this chapter we sketch out a framework of potentially broad applicability for the study of patronage democracies. In a first section, we briefly review the large literature on clientelism and identify some of the conceptual and methodological challenges that have inhibited comparative analysis. Part of the problem is the gap between anthropological and political science approaches, with the former relying on single-sited ethnographies and the latter increasingly drawing on quantitative analysis. At the same time, three different traditions—culturalist, marketist, and institutionalist—approach the study of clientelistic politics in strikingly and, in our view, unnecessarily exclusionary ways. In the remainder of the chapter, we introduce our fourfold framework for analyzing patronage politics and explain how we apply it in our analysis of Indonesia.

Approaching the Study of Clientelism

Scholarship on political clientelism has occurred in two main waves. In a first wave during the 1960s and 1970s, pioneering scholars, most of them anthropologists working in predominantly agrarian countries in Southeast Asia, Latin America, and Southern Europe, observed how the patron-client relationships that had characterized interactions between landlords and tenants in these societies were being extended into the political domain. During times of hardship or major life events, peasants had often been able to turn for assistance to the landlords who normally exploited them. Now they were transferring their loyalties to these same landlords or their proxies as they moved into formal politics, or to the new breed of bureaucrats, professionals, and other party leaders who were displacing them. James Scott (1972a, 1972b), for example, famously argued that relations between landowners and tenants in many parts of Southeast Asia provided a template on which subsequent voter-politician interactions were modeled. Throughout the region, tenants provided services and labor to their landlords in exchange for protection and support in the face of adversity. By embedding themselves in such exchange relationships, clients managed to obtain some security in otherwise hostile and volatile environments. When elections made their entry into village life, "the client gained a new political resource, since the mere giving or withholding of his vote affected the fortunes of aspirants for office" (Scott 1972b, 109). Politicians and parties thus adapted to these centuries-old patterns, even if expansion of the colonial and postcolonial states often undermined the obligations that landowners and tenants felt toward each other.

It is thus important to note that the political relations we study in this book have deep roots in Indonesian history and are in many ways modern adaptations of long-standing modes of social interaction. A common theme in studies of Indonesia's precolonial kingdoms is that these polities relied on personalistic styles of rule. Both the large Majapahit and Mataram empires, as well as smaller sultanates, were built on largely uncodified, patron-client relationships between rulers and vassals infused with a strong sense of reciprocal obligation (Day 2002; Pelras 2000; Schulte Nordholt 2015). There was nothing unusual about this: as Mungiu-Pippidi (2015) and Fukuyama (2011) have pointed out, personalized exchange of favors has been a dominant form of social organization throughout human history.

This background in the study of agrarian societies helps explain why, during the first wave of research, scholars largely saw clientelism as a particular form of *relationship*. Lemarchand and Legg, for example, wrote that political clientelism could "be viewed as a more or less personalized relationship between actors, or sets of actors, commanding unequal wealth, status or influence, based on conditional loyalties and involving mutually beneficial transactions" (Lemarchand and Legg 1972, 151). Scholars frequently saw clientelism as involving "dyadic" relations between two persons of unequal status and power and, drawing on the prototype of relations between landlords and tenants, often saw these relations as multifaceted and extending over long periods of time (Scott 1972b, 8). There was debate about whether such relationships were exploitative or voluntary, and whether they ameliorated or merely masked class dominance, but the general consensus was that norms of solidarity were critical to clientelism, and that these exchanges involved trust and regular interaction between patrons and clients (see Eisenstadt and Roniger 1980; Lemarchand 1972; Schmidt et al. 1977; Weingrod 1968). These understandings largely drew on deep ethnographic research involving extended fieldwork. Indeed, given the often hidden nature of patron-client relations, such a method was a necessary condition for the emergence of theorizing about clientelism.

This early wave of scholarship gave rise to what might be thought of as a "culturalist" understanding of clientelism, which focuses on how social norms and ideas structure relationships between patrons and clients. Scholars drawing on this approach frequently observe that clientelistic relationships are animated and facilitated by a distinct morality in which "mutual expectations of partners are backed by community values and rituals" (Scott 1972b, 94). In this approach, clientelistic practices are attributed, above all, to the moral force that norms of reciprocity exert. Such practices are therefore more likely to be found in societies where moral conventions and "various conceptions of honor" as well as "otherworldly orientations" generate a strong sense of interpersonal obligations (Eisenstadt and Roniger 1980, 68). Emphasis on the cultural moorings of clientelism, and the social expectations that surround it, remains a powerful tradition in the literature (for recent works, see for example Finan and Schechter 2012; Lawson and Greene 2014; Piliavsky 2014).

Such culturalist approaches have their drawbacks. An emphasis on deep-seated cultural norms, especially when combined with an insistence that these "moral conventions persist across space and time" (Piliavsky 2014, 18), can involve essentializing particular cultures as sources of clientelistic practices and does little to help us identify whether and how clientelistic practices are changing. Nor do single ethnographies themselves allow for comparative analysis, though they of course provide a resource for comparativists seeking to mine them to identify variety in clientelistic forms.

From the beginning, however, the seeds of an alternative approach were visible. Especially in the United States, the first wave of research on clientelism was conceptualized primarily in terms of "machine politics." In the urban United States in the late nineteenth and early twentieth centuries, political parties used well-entrenched networks of local operatives and precinct captains who provided personal favors and cash when mobilizing electoral support. Studies of these political machines highlighted the pragmatic and instrumental nature of these exchanges, arguing that these machines were possible because voters "place a lower value on their votes than they do on the things which the machine can provide in exchange for them" (Banfield and Wilson 1963, 117; see also Scott 1969).

Such more instrumentalist interpretations of clientelistic politics became more prominent in the second wave of scholarship, which began around the year 2000. This second wave was spurred by the increasing realization on the part of many political scientists that clientelistic exchange, despite some early predictions, was not disappearing as a result of democratization and modernization. Partly displacing the earlier emphasis on ethnography, many scholars now used the techniques of quantitative analysis, especially surveys, in the process devising new techniques to measure key phenomena such as vote buying. Mirroring wider trends in the discipline of political science, scholars now placed greater emphasis on causal inference and the systematic identification of patterns, studying both the micro-foundations of clientelism (who gets targeted for clientelistic exchange and why?) and identifying key causal variables (how is clientelism linked to factors like poverty and multi-ethnicity?).

The political and social context for these new studies had changed considerably since the 1960s, contributing to new understandings of clientelism. Scholars were making their new findings in the context of mass democracies and in societies in which population growth, urbanization, social mobility, and commercialization were inhibiting the ability of politicians to build long-term, personalized relationships with clients. Observers of clientelistic politics now remarked that relations between politicians and their supporters "do not often amount to multifaceted, dyadic, relationships of patron-clientage" (Arghiros 2001, 8). The new scholarship saw brokers as key facilitators of clientelistic exchanges, and perceived brokers' relationships with both voters and politicians as more fleeting, pragmatic exchanges in which the role of social hierarchies was less marked than in the patron-client relationships that had characterized stable agrarian societies (e.g., Beck 2008; Brusco, Nazareno, and Stokes 2004; Gans-Morse, Mazzuca, and Nichter 2014; Stokes 2005, 2013; Szwarcberg 2012; Weitz-Shapiro 2014). Scholars began to downplay the durability, personal character, and unequal nature of clientelistic relationships. Instead, they increasingly recognized that clientelistic exchanges could be pragmatic, market-like deals in which the politician does not always have the upper hand (e.g., Chandra 2004; Gay 1998; Kitschelt and Wilkinson 2007; Larreguy, Marshall, and Queribín 2016; Nichter 2014; Schneider 2014).

All this contributed to a shift toward viewing clientelism as a particular type of political *exchange* rather than a form of relationship. To mention one widely cited definition, clientelism was now seen as involving "the proffering of material goods in return for electoral support, where the criterion of distribution that the patron uses is simply: did you (will you) support me?" (Stokes 2007, 605). Kitschelt and Wilkinson (2007, 2) offer a similar definition, describing clientelism as "the direct exchange of a citizen's vote in return for direct payments or continuing access to employment, goods, and services." In this study, we follow this emerging consensus to define political clientelism as the practice of exchanging material resources or benefits (cash, goods, jobs, public services, government contracts, etc.) for political support (votes, campaign donations, campaign support, etc.).[3]

Sometimes the term clientelism is used interchangeably with a related term: patronage. Following Shefter (1994, 283n3) and Hutchcroft (2014, 176–77), we prefer, however, to use "patronage" to refer specifically to the goods and benefits that are distributed through clientelistic exchange.[4] In other words, while clientelism refers to a particular *type* of exchange, patronage refers to what is exchanged. As such, we use the term patronage to describe the material goods and other benefits distributed by politicians in a manner contingent on electoral support. Patronage might thus range from a government job to access to a subsidized health care program, from a cash handout to a new water tap installed in a village, from a government contract given to a campaign worker to a new dome installed on a mosque. Patronage can be conferred on individuals or on groups— we use the term "club goods" to refer to gifts given to groups (see chapter 6). A patronage democracy is a democracy where politicians use the distribution of patronage as the primary means to cultivate electoral support.[5]

It is important to point out that clientelistic politics can involve benefits that are conferred privately (a gift of cash from a politician to a voter, for example) *or* state resources that are distributed as a result of a government policy. The defining characteristic of clientelistic politics is not the type of benefit that is offered, or even the electoral intent that motivates it, but the *terms* on which the benefit is offered. Politicians in all democracies promise to provide state resources in order to gain electoral support: for example, they offer pensions, scholarships, development projects, and similar schemes at election times. But such schemes are examples of programmatic politics if they are distributed according to criteria that are not explicitly tied to political support. Thus, a program of subsidized health care that is intended to win the support of poor voters is not clientelistic when each citizen who fits the criteria (e.g., an income test), irrespective of his or her vote or political loyalty, can access it. Such a program *can* be called clientelistic, however, if those distributing the program identify beneficiaries on the basis of their political allegiance or perceived voting behavior, and manipulate the rules to ensure that such persons get preferential access. As a result, clientelistic politics often involve substitution of formal criteria and procedures of selecting beneficiaries for the political criterion noted above: have you supported me, or will you support me? (Stokes 2007, 605; see also Hicken 2011; Kitschelt 2000). Club goods and pork-barrel spending are a particularly fuzzy category of exchange because, as we shall see in chapter 6, individuals may benefit from a gift—such as a new road in their village or a new sound system in their church—without voting for the candidate who provided the benefit. Yet candidates often approach such collective gifts with the same logic of contingent exchange as they use with individual patronage, targeting communities on the basis of deals struck with brokers who promise a bloc vote in exchange—like Abdullah in the story that began this book—and withholding or withdrawing the benefit if the broker fails to deliver the promised votes. For this reason, we treat candidates' practice of offering club goods in their election campaigns as a form of clientelistic exchange.

If early scholarship gave rise to a culturalist approach, emphasizing norms and relationships, the second wave of scholarship has been dominated by an approach that might be described as "marketist," insofar that it has emphasized calculations made by actors of the costs and benefits to be attained from clientelistic exchange. This understanding is informed by rational-choice models of political behavior, whereby citizens are seen as using their votes instrumentally to maximize their access to resources, and politicians target their resources to maximize electoral returns. Scholars working in this tradition often describe their focus as "machine politics" (e.g., De Wit 2016; Kramon 2016) because they pay explicit attention to the dependence of politicians on networks of brokers in facilitating and enforcing clientelistic exchanges and the element of calculation that underpins them. Adopting this approach has enabled scholars to focus on many critical aspects of clientelism. For example, researchers have examined whether politicians target swing voters or party loyalists with their vote-buying efforts (Stokes et al. 2013; Brusco, Nazareno, and Stokes 2004; Cox 2009; Dixit and Londregan 1996), and whether politicians purchase votes or just turnout (Nichter 2008; Gans-Morse, Mazzuca, and Nichter 2014), and they have identified possible gaps in incentives separating politicians and their brokers (Stokes et al. 2013; Larreguy, Marshall, and Queribín 2016; Szwarcberg 2012). Scholars using this approach have gone furthest in identifying the social conditions favoring or hampering clientelistic politics. Rational-choice models inform arguments about factors that might make clientelistic strategies more effective, such as poverty or inequality (Stokes 2007; Robinson and Verdier 2013), as well as factors that might make clientelistic strategies unrewarding, such as a large middle class and urbanization (Weitz-Shapiro 2014; Larreguy, Marshall, and Queribín 2016; Stokes et al. 2013).

This new wave of scholarship has thus opened many fruitful lines of inquiry and cast new light on many aspects of clientelism. Even so, critics—many of whom are anthropologists—are skeptical of what they say is the crude instrumentalism of these studies and the image they offer of "a billion profiteering voters wielding the abacus of rational choice" (Piliavsky 2014, 16; see also Björkman 2014). Scholars who have produced ethnographic studies sometimes point out a disjuncture between the expectations of marketist theory and findings in the field—for example, emphasizing that "neither patrons nor clients are willing or even able to describe the clientelistic relationship as a quid-pro-quo exchange" (Kitschelt and Wilkinson 2007, 19). Auyero, for example, emphatically states in his study of Peronist problem-solving networks in Argentina that it would be a "distortion bordering on disfigurement" to see political support offered by voters as a straightforward repayment for favors performed on their behalf. Rather, Auyero argues, such exchanges are ingrained at a much deeper level in social relationships: "people who receive things *know* that receiving favors implies a return. Such a return is one of the rules of the game . . . verbalized only when an explanation is explicitly requested" (Auyero 2001, 160; emphasis in original). Such critics also draw attention to the fact that politicians are often incapable or unwilling to effectively monitor the voting behavior of recipients of their money (Kramon 2016)—something which, as we will highlight, also holds true for most Indonesian politicians. The marketist approach struggles to explain why politicians would be willing to hand out large amounts of money without monitoring whether these gifts are actually repaid at the ballot box. Here and elsewhere, critics rightly point out that it is critical to maintain attention to the cultural scaffolding that supports clientelistic exchange.

A third approach to the study of clientelism, which can be labeled institutionalist, has also emerged over the last two decades. Scholars working in this tradition interpret clientelistic practices in the light of histories of state formation. Historical patterns in the development of state institutions, they argue, can generate opportunities or obstacles for politicians seeking to engage in clientelistic practices, and can be highly consequential for whether countries are able to emerge out of clientelism, or become trapped in a self-reinforcing clientelistic cycle (Golden 2003; Keefer 2007; Kenny 2015). This historical approach is somewhat less prominent in clientelism studies, partly because the relevant works often do not take clientelistic politics as their explicit focus, instead analyzing the impact of colonial rule (Chabal and Daloz 1999; Lange 2009; Mamdani 1996) or the *longue durée* of political development (Fukuyama 2014; North, Wallis, and Weingast 2009; Shefter 1994). Yet these studies hold important lessons, as they show how clientelistic practices in the contemporary world are typically products of prior historical development of state institutions. Particularly influential in this regard has been Shefter's work on the evolution of Germany, England, Italy, and the United States (Shefter 1977, 1994). He argued that clientelistic politics were less likely to develop if universal suffrage and mass electoral participation occurred *after* state bureaucracies had time to become strong and autonomous, developing the capacity to resist political interference in their internal workings. In such circumstances, habits and official procedures—Shefter called them a "charter for bureaucratic autonomy"—could prevent politicians from interfering in how bureaucrats implemented state policies, limiting the supply of clientelistic favors and pushing parties and politicians to instead develop programmatic strategies. When, in contrast, democratic politics were initiated *prior to* the development of autonomous state institutions, elected officials were typically able to capture the bureaucracy and direct state resources to particularistic ends. In such circumstances, such as in Italy, clientelism became pervasive and constituted an obstacle to strengthening of bureaucratic autonomy. In such societies, a "clientelist trap" can emerge: voters turn to politicians for the assistance that the state will provide only with their intercession, stimulating politicians to develop greater personal control over state resources, and further undermining bureaucratic autonomy. It is this self-reinforcing relationship between state institutions and political incentive structures that makes clientelistic politics so entrenched in many parts of the world, including, we argue, Indonesia.

One benefit of the institutionalist perspective is that it helps us interpret *both* the normative dimensions and the elements of calculation that underpin clientelistic politics. To interpret clientelism satisfactorily, we need not only to understand why personal obligations and norms of reciprocity carry a particular force (a focus of the culturalists), but also to understand why impersonal obligations—obedience to law, institutions, and interpretations of the public good—do not carry similar weight. The norms of reciprocity that culturalists highlight are themselves fostered by people's historical experiences of aloof, oppressive, and venal state institutions. When a state provides little to citizens in terms of social security, legal certainty, or welfare, they turn to networks of family, friends, and, often, patrons. And when citizens experience state institutions as tools used by elites to cement their dominance, it is also understandable that they will be more likely to heed personal obligations than impersonal obligations to the laws and procedures of the state. Indeed, in such circumstances these personal obligations can be so strongly engrained in a person's emotional makeup that one can speak of a "clientelist habitus" (Auyero and Benzecry 2017).

In this book, we derive inspiration from each of these three traditions and do not view our study as being confined to any one of them. From the culturalist approach, we derive our ethnographic method and sensitivity to the cultural logics and norms that shape how individuals engage in clientelistic exchanges. From the marketist approach, we take an emphasis on the strategic considerations that motivate many of the political choices that actors make within a clientelistic political context. Indeed, we frequently find it necessary to combine insights from both approaches: for example, when understanding the strategizing employed by politicians who buy votes, it is obvious that an instrumental, marketist logic is at play; when we turn to understanding how these cash payments achieve their desired goals, it is necessary to pay attention to cultural norms of reciprocity and proper behavior through which at least some recipients understand such gifts. Finally, in presenting our causal argument to explain how and why Indonesia's clientelistic system has evolved to assume its current form, we adopt a historical institutionalist account, emphasizing both the legacies of Indonesia's long period of bureaucratic-authoritarian rule under the Suharto regime, and the choices the country made when designing its electoral system in the post-Suharto period.

A Comparative Framework for Analyzing Patronage Democracies

It should already be obvious that a large and sophisticated comparative literature has been produced that throws light on key aspects of clientelism across many countries. It is our contention, however, that we still lack the analytical tools to properly understand the great variation in *forms* taken by patronage democracies. The widespread assumption that parties everywhere provide the brokers for clientelistic exchange is just one reflection of this collective failure to properly address the great variation in clientelistic systems across the globe. This failure, in turn, partly flows from the divide between anthropological and political science approaches to clientelism. The ethnographic, case study–based methodology of anthropologists has yielded much insight into the inner workings of clientelistic politics, but anthropologists have rarely used their insights for comparative analysis. Conversely, political scientists have developed a strongly comparativist outlook, but their frequent preference for quantitative methods has often precluded attention to the less visible, shadowy dimensions of clientelistic politics that can be observed only through fieldwork. One result, as we have already indicated, is that democracies are too rarely compared in terms of the character of their informal politics.

To help us describe Indonesia's distinctive variant of clientelism, and to facilitate comparative analysis of clientelistic systems more generally, we devise an explanatory framework that focuses on four key dimensions of clientelistic politics. These four dimensions are (1) the networks through which clientelistic exchange is organized; (2) the patterns of control through which discretion is exercised over state patronage resources; (3) the nature of the resources that are exchanged; and (4) the degree, or intensity, of clientelism. Using such a framework, we contend, helps us to locate Indonesia among the many patronage democracies, and goes some way toward providing a framework for wider comparative study of differences among patronage democracies.

The first dimension concerns the *nature of the networks* that are used to distribute patronage. As already noted, it is often assumed that parties provide the organizational apparatus for clientelist politics. The fact that this view is so widespread itself indicates that we need to think more comparatively about clientelist politics. Party networks are just one form of patronage networks. Detailed, ethnographic studies of local politics in, for example, Thailand (Arghiros 2001), Senegal (Beck 2008), or Central Asia (Collins 2006) illustrate that a wide variety of nonparty networks and organizations can facilitate clientelist exchanges, from bureaucratic networks and kinship groups and clans to religious organizations and ethnic communities. A range of brokers—party workers, state representatives, notables, and community leaders—can be identified across countries, and the relative prevalence of such brokers varies considerably.

This wide range of networks used by politicians to facilitate clientelist exchange can, in our view, be most fruitfully compared in two ways. First, patronage networks can be compared in terms of their degree of institutionalization. Networks can be considered highly institutionalized when most brokers are connected to political actors through shared membership of an organization or party. At the opposite extreme are networks where most brokers lack such ties and where their connection to, and support for, a politician is established only during an election campaign. The degree of network institutionalization shapes, in other words, the character of politician-broker relationships, and affects the nature of election campaigns. We posit that less-institutionalized patronage networks are more likely to see the defection of brokers, as politicians using them have fewer carrots and sticks at their disposal to ensure the loyalty of their brokers, lacking long-term organizational relationships with them.

A second important way to compare patronage networks concerns the character of voter-broker ties. Brokers may be distinguished between those whose authority and capacity to deliver votes is based on a proven capacity to represent voter interests, and those whose authority stems primarily from various forms of cultural capital, such as family status, religious learning, age, occupational status, and so on. On the one side of this spectrum are brokers whose capacity to deliver votes is based on their everyday capacity to help their neighbors. These brokers develop their status and their capacity to deliver votes by acting as problem solvers, which often takes the form of using political connections to facilitate access to state institutions. Descriptions of party activists and social workers in India (Berenschot 2014; De Wit 2016; Witsoe 2012) and Argentina (Auyero 2001; Szwarcberg 2015) most closely fit this ideal type. On the other side of the spectrum are brokers such as religious or customary leaders whose capacity to deliver votes is based not so much on their capacity to solve problems as on the forms of cultural capital that they possess. Accordingly, in chapter 6, we distinguish between networks of affect and networks of benefit. The distinction matters, because the prevalence of the two types of brokers shapes the pressure that voters can exert on state institutions, and thus their capacity to obtain access to state benefits. When the status of brokers is based on their capacity to represent voter interests, they face stronger incentives to busy themselves getting practical things done. We thus posit that where brokers of the cultural capital variety are more prevalent, citizens will lack effective avenues to pressure power holders.

Through this book we show that in Indonesia much patronage distribution occurs outside party structures. Instead, patronage flows to voters mostly through two forms of networks, which often overlap: the ad hoc "success teams" established by political candidates, and the formal and informal social networks that penetrate society and structure people's everyday lives—networks based on religion, ethnicity, friendship, and the like. Parties do play a role in clientelist exchange at election times, and patron-client relations are certainly rife inside parties, but they are far from being the dominant channel of patronage distribution. In sum: Indonesian clientelism occurs mostly through informal networks rather than through parties.

A second, related, comparative dimension concerns the *pattern of control* over the distribution of state resources and benefits, including grants, projects, welfare programs, and government budgets. Discretionary control over resources is critical to clientelist politics. In order for clientelism to work, a politician must be able to choose to reward a village that voted for her with a new water pump, bypassing a neighboring community that supported a rival, or to reward an especially hardworking campaign worker with a patronage job in the civil service, while withholding such a reward from a broker who absconded with money intended for voters. But who actually controls the distribution of such state resources? To what extent is this control shared or contested between different actors? Political parties certainly compete with one another to establish this control, but they can also compete with bureaucrats, with individual politicians, and sometimes with nonparty informal networks such as clans to ensure control of the state resources they need to generate support. The outcome of this competition will differ from country to country. Particular trajectories of state and party formation enable different kinds of actors to gain the upper hand in this competition. In some patronage democracies, including Argentina and India, parties have considerable control over who gets what resources; in others, parties are much weaker, and bureaucrats or individual politicians exercise much greater control.

The discretionary control over the distribution of state resources may also be compared in terms of the degree to which this control is concentrated. In some systems, authority to dispense patronage is highly centralized, resting in the hands of a single political party, clique, or leader. This will especially be the case in authoritarian, electoral authoritarian, or semi-democratic regimes. In such cases, clientelist networks form a "single pyramid" (Hale 2011, 585). Conversely, competing parties or factions can sometimes establish footholds in different levels or agencies of the state and develop the capacity to manipulate the distribution of state resources in ways that lack coordination and can even be at cross-purposes. Institutional dispersal of budgetary authority, such as can arise under federal or decentralized systems, or as a result of division of authority between the executive and legislature, can also fragment control over state resources. In such contexts, there may be multiple, competing clientelist pyramids. When control over state resources is dispersed among multiple actors, the relative power of voters vis-à-vis politicians will be greater, potentially allowing for greater democratic accountability than is typically expected in clientelist systems.[6]

In Indonesia, as a result of historical legacies and institutional features we explain through the book, parties lack leverage over many key patronage resources, which are instead allocated and distributed largely by state bureaucrats and community-level state representatives like village heads. There are exceptions to the general pattern, and parties have been trying to expand their discretionary control over state resources ever since the collapse of the Suharto regime. Even so, the relative weakness of party control of state patronage helps explain much about the ad hoc, nonparty, and transient nature of clientelist politics in the country. Another critical factor is the highly fragmented pattern of budgetary control that has emerged since Indonesia implemented sweeping decentralization reforms in the early 2000s. Control over much discretionary spending was dispersed to what are now more than five hundred districts around the country, each of which holds its own legislative and executive elections to select its political leaders, greatly reducing the potential for coordination in the distribution of patronage resources across the political system. In Indonesia, key state patronage resources lie beyond the control of party politicians, but are instead controlled by widely dispersed state actors.

Our third comparative dimension concerns the *nature of the resources* that are exchanged for political support. Clientelist politicians can entice their supporters with an almost endless range of benefits, from such staples of clientelist exchange as money, jobs, and road building or other community infrastructure, to more culturally specific examples such as sponsorship of mass circumcisions, bird-whistling competitions, pilgrimages to the tombs of saints, or the purchase of pigs for feast days (all examples we encountered in our research). There are various ways to categorize such benefits.

One distinction we repeatedly turn to throughout this book is between gifts that are directed at the individual voter (such as a gift of cooking oil or an envelope stuffed with cash) and those that confer a benefit on a group, whether members of an association (e.g., a new sports field for a village soccer club, a loudspeaker for a prayer group, or a cow for a farmers' cooperative) or a geographically defined community (a road for a village, street lighting for an urban alleyway, or a new neighborhood hall). Such collective gifts are generally known as "club goods" in the comparative literature on clientelism, and, as we shall see, they are all but ubiquitous in Indonesia. But so, too, are the more individualized forms of gifting, as witnessed by the widespread incidence of the "dawn attack" that occurs in the lead-up to elections. The provision of both types of gift can be termed clientelistic because in both cases the gift is provided in a manner conditional on electoral support.

However, individual and collective patronage raise distinctive organizational challenges and require different sorts of brokers. In the case of private gifts, the clientelist exchange taking place is between a voter and a politician through the mediation of a broker. In the case of collective gifts, the exchange is between a politician and a broker or community representative promising to deliver a certain number of votes. As we shall see in chapters 5 and 6, if political candidates seek to deliver gifts of cash or other goods effectively to individual voters in sufficient numbers to sway elections, they need to create mass brokerage networks consisting of large numbers of grassroots intermediaries, each of whom is tasked with persuading a small number of voters to take the gift and vote for the candidate. For politicians to make club-goods strategies effective, by contrast, they generally need to win the support of influential social notables—the leader of the prayer group that benefits from the loudspeaker, the head of the village that gets the new road, or the chief of the cooperative that gets the cow—who will broker the gift, endorse it, and persuade community members to reciprocate with their votes. The relative utility of each strategy will thus greatly depend not only on the candidate's resources, but also on local social structures. For example, in communities in which "traditional" informal institutions remain influential, such as those based on custom or village organization, the opinions of community leaders can carry great social weight, making club-goods strategies viable; in relatively atomized communities lacking strong ties of community solidarity, as is the case in many urban areas, candidates may need to rely on more individualized patronage.

An equally critical distinction concerns whether the patronage resources politicians distribute are privately provided, as when a candidate raises money personally to fund his vote-buying efforts and his donations to religious schools and houses of worship, or whether they are provided by the state, as when a victorious candidate manipulates a government program to make sure a village that voted for her is rewarded with a new bridge, or to ensure that her campaign workers are first in line for a new government micro-credit scheme. Of course, the boundary between these two categories can be blurred, especially when a candidate raises the money to fund his or her "private" gifts by engaging in corruption. Moreover, electoral campaigns in most countries are likely to see both types of resources employed. Even so, their mix can vary considerably between countries, and the distinction between private and public resources matters greatly for the nature of politics and governance.

When clientelist strategies revolve around the use of private resources, they are more likely to involve one-off transactions at election times. In a country like Indonesia, candidates often limit their interactions with voters to onetime distributions of cash or consumer goods, leading to regular complaints from citizens that they see their politicians only during elections. We label such clientelistic exchanges "retail clientelism" to denote the brevity of the interaction. In some other contexts, clientelist exchanges occur on a more sustained basis, such as when a party captures state power and uses its influence over budgetary planning and implementation to establish ongoing relations marked by repeated exchanges. Such ongoing relations of mutual support beyond an election period might be termed "relational clientelism" (Nichter 2011).

While distribution of private resources often takes place before elections, exchange of public resources often occurs afterward (Hanusch and Keefer 2013). In the slums of Buenos Aires, for example, Argentina's Peronist party set up local branches that act as problem solvers throughout the year. Through their contacts within the municipality, the Peronist party workers provide residents with subsidized milk, negotiate with the police, arrange government jobs, organize health care or school admission, and perform other day-to-day tasks. In this context, citizens' voting behavior is influenced by feelings of obligation and gratitude incurred through multiple interactions. Because Peronist voters know that they can turn to party workers after the election should they need to, cash payments during elections are less likely to be effective (Auyero 2001; Levitsky 2003; Szwarcberg 2015). For our purposes it is important to highlight that the development of such forms of relational clientelism requires parties and politicians to acquire a certain level of control over the bureaucracy and, consequently, capacity to manipulate the allocation of state resources. If, as is often the case in Indonesia, a party or politician lacks such

TABLE 2.1 Varieties of patronage

	PUBLIC	PRIVATE
Individual	Welfare benefits, patronage jobs, government contracts	Vote buying
Collective	Pork-barrel projects of community infrastructure. Government subsidies to associations	Private community donations to religious, sporting, and other associations

capacity, it is difficult to sustain longer-term clientelistic relationships beyond elections.

For analytical purposes, the wide range of patronage goods distributed by politicians can thus be classified according to two overlapping pairs of characteristics, given that both individual and collective patronage goods can be provided privately or publicly—see table 2.1. What sort of mixture is found in a particular country will depend on both social and political factors. For example, societies with relatively dense associational life or traditional informal institutions are likely to be more prone to club-goods strategies, but whether these are provided through public funds in the form of pork-barrel projects, or privately by politicians, will largely depend on the success that parties and politicians have achieved in gaining discretionary control over budgetary resources (for example, in the form of constituency development funds). Legal and normative prohibitions on vote buying can also play a role in impeding some forms of patronage while allowing others: even in established democracies such as the United States, pork-barrel projects in which elected representatives bring home projects and patronage jobs to their own constituencies can be an established part of political behavior, even though such practices are, at least ambiguously, a form of patronage politics (Bickers and Stein 1996). A comparative study of patronage democracies needs to pay attention to the relative prevalence in different countries of these different types of resources.

To summarize the nub of our argument on this third dimension: in Indonesia, clientelist strategies revolve relatively often around private vote-buying and community donations. Both club goods and private patronage are prominent, though there is some variation depending on the nature of local social institutions, with greater reliance on club goods in regions where customary and community-level leaders remain strong. We also argue that private rather than public forms of patronage are prominent largely because parties have difficulties securing control over potential sources of patronage, partly as a result of the continuing power of bureaucrats and the legacy of the Suharto period. Our explanation for the pervasiveness (in comparative terms) of vote buying and other forms of retail clientelism in Indonesia is that politicians lack the discretionary control over state resources needed to develop longer-term relational clientelism. Even so, we recognize that the situation is in flux. Over the two decades since the end of the Suharto regime, parties and elected officials have been devising methods to hijack government programs and use them for electoral purposes (chapter 7), meaning that the share of public versus private patronage is increasing.

At this point, it is worth pausing and pointing out that we have already progressed quite far in devising a framework for comparing patronage democracies. Indeed, it is now possible to schematize various ways to compare countries. One example, which focuses on the degree of centralized, party control over patronage resources, and the relative balance of private versus public patronage, is presented in figure 2.1. In this figure, we try to capture Indonesia's experience over the last two decades, starting by locating the country in the late Suharto period at the right, reflecting the fact that Indonesia at this time both had a highly centralized system of patronage, centered on the presidential palace, in which the regime's party, Golkar, and the regime itself were all but indistinguishable and possessed a system in which patronage resources were overwhelmingly public (see chapter 3 for elaboration). After democratization, both party control and centralization of

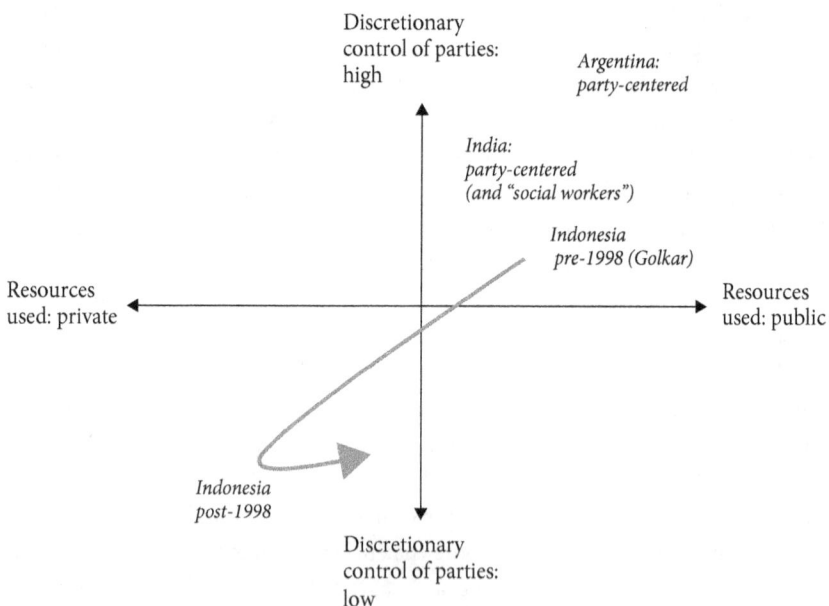

FIGURE 2.1   Varieties of patronage democracy: India, Indonesia, and Argentina

patronage resources declined steeply, while politicians increasingly used private funds to win elections (remembering the caveat that these funds were often corruptly obtained). The rightward movement of Indonesia on the chart indicates the ongoing efforts of parties and politicians to acquire greater control over state patronage resources in recent times (chapter 7). In contrast, we have placed India and Argentina in the top-right quadrant. In both India and Argentina, political parties and their grassroots representatives play a much more prominent role in the distribution of state benefits. However, accounts of local politics in India suggest that politicians also actively incorporate a more independent, nonparty type of broker (referred to as "social workers," "neighborhood leaders," or *naya neta*) into their election campaigns (Auerbach 2016; Berenschot 2011a; Krishna 2007). Because of this more fragmented nature of patronage networks, we place India closer to the center of the quadrant.

Finally, our fourth dimension refers to the *degree* of clientelism. This dimension is easiest to identify but hardest to measure. Political scientists have long observed that political systems may vary in the degree to which political relationships and resource distribution occur on a clientelistic basis. Political systems are never entirely based on clientelism nor entirely free of it. Instead, clientelist exchange typically exists alongside, and may be intertwined with, programmatic distribution.

In Indonesia, despite the saturating presence of clientelist exchange we have noted, the democratic period has also seen the rise of new forms of programmatic politics. Candidates for political office, especially in executive races, regularly promise improved development outcomes, better-quality bureaucratic performance, improved health care and other social services, and there has been dramatic expansion of public welfare programs of various sorts (Aspinall 2013b, 2014a). Many policies have been designed to allocate state resources and public spending according to standardized bureaucratic procedures in ways that insulate them from discretionary decision-making by public officials (though of course the mere presence of rules does not mean that they are always implemented rigorously or uniformly). Likewise, even in some countries where norms of "ethical universalism" (Mungiu-Pippidi 2015) generally apply, such as the United States, Japan, or the Netherlands, the politics of the quid pro quo can often be observed in matters such as pork-barrel spending, patronage jobs, or deals between campaign donors and politicians, even if practices such as vote buying are, by now, relatively rare.

The insight that clientelism may vary in intensity has certainly been recognized in the literature, but relatively few efforts have been made to assess it empirically. One challenge is that while it may be possible to ascertain levels of particular clientelist practices, such as vote buying, with some accuracy, it is harder to arrive at a rounded assessment encompassing clientelism in multiple dimensions, incorporating the prevalence of patronage jobs in the bureaucracy, pork-barrel spending, and so on. As we mentioned in chapter 1, a number of initiatives—largely based on general surveys or statistical proxies—have recently been undertaken to address this challenge. One effort from which we derive particular inspiration was launched by the political scientist Herbert Kitschelt. He used an expert survey to compare the intensity of clientelist efforts in eighty-one countries, using assessments made by political observers to characterize electoral strategies pursued by political parties in these countries (Kitschelt et al. 2009, Kitschelt and Kselman 2013). As we explained in the preceding chapter, we adapted and extended this expert survey to Indonesian conditions in order to measure how clientelism varies in shape and intensity across Indonesia. In chapter 10, we explain the findings, showing considerable variation in perceived intensity of clientelist practices. The assessments made by 509 local political observers suggest that vote buying is common throughout the country, while politicians' use of various kinds of state benefits to reward supporters is most pronounced in Kalimantan and eastern Indonesia, and less so in Java. We use this pattern to identify conditions fostering clientelist politics in chapters 9 and 10, noting how diversity in patterns of economic activity fosters more programmatic politics. Our conclusion: there is significant variation in the degree of clientelism across Indonesian provinces in a manner that largely corresponds with variation in the character of local economies.

In this chapter, we sketched a framework to analyze and compare the particular forms that clientelist politics may take, focusing on networks, discretionary control, resources, and intensity of clientelist exchange. We do not claim that these dimensions encompass all that might be said about variation in clientelist politics. There might be other elements that could also serve as fruitful bases for comparative analysis. We feel, however, that these four dimensions are particularly relevant for our purpose of analyzing the core features of Indonesia's patronage democracy, and for pointing out the ways in which this democracy is distinctive. As the titles of the different sections of this book indicate, our argument revolves around these comparative dimensions. We use these dimensions not only to describe the inner workings of Indonesian politics, but also how and why Indonesia stands out. In the next section we develop our explanations for why clientelism in Indonesia takes its particular freewheeling form, focusing on historical legacies as well as Indonesia's electoral system.

Part 1
INSTITUTIONS

3

HISTORICAL ORIGINS OF
FREEWHEELING CLIENTELISM

In his office, Tangerang's deputy mayor, Arief Wismansyah, seemed the embodiment of a new brand of Indonesian politician. Only thirty-six years old, Arief exuded an open, energetic youthfulness very different from the aloof attitudes of some of his older colleagues. Pictures of him in newspapers, inspecting public works and visiting neighborhoods affected by the region's frequent floods, standing ankle deep in water, must have helped him in the polls. This "*turun ke lapangan*" or "coming down to the field" style is favored by many new-generation politicians as a way to demonstrate they are different from the remote, desk-sitting leaders of old. Arief was also conversant with a new kind of political self-presentation that emphasized openness and inclusivity. We had barely been seated on one of the comfortable sofas in his office when he launched into a discussion of the lessons he had learned about running in an election during his four years in office. "We have to know what people feel. The candidate has to pass the test that he is really going to work for the people. A leader is needed who is close to people, who takes part in the life of people and who works for the people."

Arief was the deputy mayor of one of the fastest-developing districts of Indonesia. On the outskirts of Jakarta and helped by its proximity to Indonesia's main international airport, Tangerang had acquired the nickname of the "town of a thousand industries" because of the many factories that were built there, especially during the industrial boom of the 1980s and 1990s. Since that time, not only had working-class migrants flocked to Tangerang; but since around 2005, fancy, well-serviced residential areas had also mushroomed, attracting members of the burgeoning middle class who work in the offices of Jakarta. The appetite for new housing, offices, and malls seemed endless. It was this dizzying pace of development that made Tangerang a suitable site to study the upcoming elections for a new mayor. The popular outgoing mayor, Wahidin Halim, had finished the maximum two terms allowed him, and a new leader needed to be chosen. Tangerang, at the cutting edge of the country's urban and industrial development, seemed like a good place to observe the changing nature of Indonesian politics.

Yet, as the interview lengthened and the conversation turned to the upcoming elections, it became clear that in this bustling city, too, politics reflected a mixture of new and old. Arief was about to declare his candidacy for Tangerang's mayorship. He couched his decision to run in modest terms that are clichéd among Indonesian politicians. He said he had not wanted to run. His wife wanted him to step down after one term. It was, he emphasized, the polls that made him decide to stand. Showing the result of an opinion poll he had commissioned, he said, "There is a crisis of leadership in this city. My electability is at 90 percent, while that of the other candidates is low. So I have to be a candidate. I have nothing to lose. I just want what is best for the city."

But the list of candidates he pointed to showed that these politicians were not so new, after all. They all came from a very narrow political elite. Of Arief's four competitors, two were bureaucrats. The municipality's *sekretaris daerah*, or regional secretary—the highest-ranked civil servant in the district—was running. His office was just a few meters away, right down the corridor. Arief's closest competitor, Abdul Syukur, was the younger brother of outgoing mayor Wahidin Halim. As leader of the city branch of Golkar, the electoral vehicle of the former New Order regime, and former chair of once Golkar-allied organizations like the Pancasila Youth and the Indonesian National Youth Committee (KNPI), Syukur seemed very much a representative of old-style Suharto-era politics. Arief himself also represented an important continuity with the New Order. His rise in politics was made possible by the economic prowess of his family. The Wismansyah family owned several hospitals in the city. Rumor had it that four years earlier Halim had chosen Arief as his running mate because Arief's family had offered to shoulder the cost of the election campaign.

The continuities with New Order politics also became apparent when it came to Arief's campaign strategy. Political parties turned out to be absent in his campaign organization. Instead, Arief emphasized the broadness of his personal campaign network. "I build my network through contact with the people, and then I ask people to join. We now have a success team that consists of [various] organizations." He pointed to a list of groups with creative names. As Arief detailed how his network had representatives in neighborhoods throughout the city, he was dismissive about the capacity of political parties to provide a similar network. "People are tired of political parties. They choose the figure, not the party. I do not brand myself as a candidate of a party." Instead, Arief seemed confident that Tangerang's bureaucratic apparatus would help him. "The RT/RW [sub-neighborhood and neighborhood heads] and the *camat* [subdistrict heads], those are the people who can influence who gets the votes. If such a person tells people not to vote for you, your vote will go down. That is why [the elections] will be different for the other candidates." As a deputy mayor with control over the government apparatus, Arief felt he could use it to sway votes. Suddenly, Arief did not sound like a new politician anymore. He sounded like a Golkar strategist during the New Order, confident in his control of the bureaucratic machinery of power.

Arief's strategizing hints at three striking features of Indonesia's electoral politics in the post–New Order era: the relatively minor role played by political parties, the reliance on personal networks, and the importance of the government apparatus. We discuss these features in the coming chapters, when we dive into election campaigns in Tangerang and elsewhere. In this chapter we discuss the historical origins of Indonesia's contemporary system of freewheeling clientelism. We do so by making a historical institutionalist argument that stresses the ways the authoritarian New Order regime (1966–1998) left a legacy that shaped and constrained the range of clientelist strategies available to politicians during the post–New Order so-called *reformasi* period.

At first sight, our emphasis on this historical legacy may seem puzzling. Indonesia's contemporary patronage democracy differs in obvious ways from its authoritarian predecessor. A dizzyingly wide range of actors are patronage wielders in Indonesia's contemporary messy, multiparty democracy. Parties, bureaucrats, local state officials, candidates, brokers, social notables, and others form ever-shifting webs to distribute patronage, much of which, as we explore through this book, ends up in the hands of ordinary voters. Under the New Order, patronage was centralized in the state bureaucracy, and distributed to a much narrower range of beneficiaries. To be sure, at election times, Golkar, the bureaucracy's electoral vehicle, did distribute patronage goods. But most patronage politics occurred entirely outside the electoral sphere, which is not surprising, given that electoral legitimacy was never the basis of the New Order's authority. The key beneficiaries were the senior military officers, civil servants, businesspeople, and other notables whose support was needed to maintain stability.

Nevertheless, we argue that the New Order period laid the groundwork for Indonesia's current system. Most obviously, it did so by institutionalizing and even universalizing patronage distribution as a key feature of the political order. To be sure, patronage already played a part in political life in the 1950s, but that early phase of Indonesian democracy was also marked by ideological schism and identity-based mobilization. Contending political parties advanced dramatically opposed visions for Indonesia's future. Under the New Order, the military purged the body politic of ideological or programmatic contestation. Merely offering an alternative program to that promoted by the government was designated subversive. Instead, the regime legitimated itself by pursuing economic growth, promoting a developmentalist ideology and buying the acquiescence of key political and social elites with patronage, allowing military officers and bureaucrats to use public office for their private benefit.

By the time Indonesia began its transition to democracy in 1998, such elites were enmeshed in clientelist networks. Equally importantly, ordinary people, party activists, members of social organizations, and other actors knew that civil servants, and their political bosses and allies, had been milking the state for private benefit for decades. The entire citizenry had been witness to, and were habituated to, a style of politics based on informal relationships and connections, even if many ordinary Indonesians had been unable to benefit much from this system. Once the democratic transition occurred, ordinary people and, especially, middle-ranking actors in New Order structures now wanted to take their share, generating a strong demand for patronage that rapidly overwhelmed the developing party system. Viewed in this way, the key political shift that occurred with democratization after 1998 was a transition from a restricted, elite-focused form of patronage distribution to one that was massified.

In this chapter, we make two further points about the nature of the New Order that are critical for the analysis we present later in this book. First, we emphasize the *state-centered* nature of patronage distribution that became established during the New Order. In countries like India and Argentina, which we have presented as a contrast to Indonesian clientelism from the start of this book, parties were integral to clientelist politics—through the twentieth century in Argentina, and from independence in the case of India. A similar pattern of party-based clientelism began to develop in Indonesia in the 1950s but was ended by the New Order's proscription of competitive multipartyism and its centralization of control over patronage resources. To the extent that electoral politics mattered, under the New Order, low-level bureaucrats and community-level state officials such as village heads were the chief intermediaries through which patronage was dispensed to citizens as voters. Second, during the New Order years, the regime also used associational channels of patronage distribution, co-opting leaders of religious organizations, security groups, and other formal and informal bodies. Such leaders developed a patronage-seeking mentality, with formal and informal leaders learning how to leverage their social influence in order to access resources. Again, this authoritarian mode of patronage distribution through social associations had little to do with party politics; on the contrary, the two surviving nongovernment parties were deliberately cut off both from the state funds and the mass organizations that had sustained parties during the 1950s.

As a result of these factors, when Indonesia became democratic after 1998, shifting from elite to massified clientelism, not only did parties lack control over the levers of patronage, which remained embedded in the state bureaucracy, but there were also well-established nonparty mechanisms and channels for the distribution of patronage, which politicians could use when reaching out to voters. This legacy set the scene for the fragmented, largely nonparty forms of patronage distribution that came to dominate electoral politics in the post-Suharto period, as we explain through the remainder of this book.

The Rise and Fall of Party-Based Clientelism

If we focus on the earliest phase of post-independence politics, the parliamentary democracy period of 1950–1957, it is obvious that Indonesia was developing in the direction of being a party-based system of clientelism. During this period, the country was a lively democracy. Numerous parties, organizations, and individual candidates contested the country's first general elections in 1955, with four parties emerging as the dominant players: the Indonesian National Party (PNI); Nahdlatul Ulama (NU), representing traditionalist Muslims; Masjumi, representing modernist Muslims; and the Indonesian Communist Party (PKI).

Given that much (though not all) of political life was clustered around the four largest political parties, we might think of this as being a system of *pillared clientelism* (Aspinall 2013a). Every major party was surrounded by a range of affiliated organizations, or *underbouw*. These clusters of core parties and their mass affiliates were described by the renowned anthropologist Clifford Geertz as representing distinct *aliran* (or streams) in Indonesian political life. (Somewhat confusingly, Geertz also used the same term, *aliran*, to refer to the major variants of Javanese religion, each of which was also loosely affiliated to one or two of these parties—traditionalist Muslims to NU, modernist Muslims to Masjumi, and *abangan* or syncretist lower-class Muslims to PNI and PKI.) In a 1959 article, "The Javanese Village," Geertz (1959, 37) described *aliran* in the following way:

> An aliran consists of a political party surrounded by a set of voluntary social organizations formally or informally linked to it. In Java there are only four such alirans of importance: the PNI or Nationalists; the PKI or Communists; the Masjumi, or Modernist Moslem; and the NU, or Orthodox Moslem. With one or another of these parties as the nucleus, an aliran is a cluster of nationally based organizations—women's clubs,

youth groups, religious societies, and so on—sharing a similar ideological direction or standpoint. . . . An aliran is more than a mere political party, certainly more than a mere ideology; it is a comprehensive pattern of social integration.

Critically, Geertz argued that the flourishing of *aliran* politics stemmed from a failure of the state. In Geertz's view, the colonial and postcolonial state had failed to effectively penetrate village society. Largely as a result, the *aliran* acted as the basic skeleton of social organization there, performing a broad range of religious, educational, economic, and other integrative functions and organizing the "reconstruction of vigorous village life" (Geertz 1959, 37). These networks of mass organizations, each centered on a political party, substituted for effective state institutions. Through the *aliran*-linked organizations, villagers could arrange loans, secure assistance to harvest their crops or repair their houses, learn about national and international affairs, participate in or watch cultural performances, and engage in many other useful activities. Party membership was a path toward social prestige and material reward, and through it "an individual could often obtain protection, the redressing of grievances, and the informal adjudication of disputes by party leaders" (Feith 1962, 124).

In part, the *aliran* could play these roles because they were infused with traditional forms of agrarian clientelism. Leading figures in the PNI and NU, in particular, were often landowners with clienteles of tenants, sharecroppers, and agricultural laborers. The PNI was also closely associated with the *pamong praja*, or civil servants. NU and Masjumi leaders were also wielders of religious authority: NU was led by rural *kyai*, or religious scholars, while Masjumi leaders often had urban, educational, or commercial-sector backgrounds. The PKI was the major exception to this pattern, attempting to organize on the basis of horizontal class-based solidarity rather than vertical patron-client ties, especially from 1962, when it began to mobilize in favor of land redistribution. Even so, scholars have noted that it, too, grew in part by securing support from landowners and local notables in some regions (Mortimer 1974).

The *aliran* played integrative roles in Indonesia's largely rural society in part by organizing themselves on the basis of preexisting social ties and hierarchies, in part because they were the key means through which political actors could access state resources. In both the center and the regions, the parties competed for access to the patronage resources offered by the state—notably those that could be attained if they gained control of ministries or local governments—and they rewarded supporters clientelistically if they gained such access. In his classic account of politics in the 1950s, Herbert Feith sums up the situation as follows: "In effect the parties obliged the government to distribute its store of material and status rewards largely through them. . . . Coveted government posts, business opportunities, overseas trips, houses, and cars tended to go chiefly to those with party connections. At a lower level party membership was usually an advantage for ex-guerillas looking for white-collar employment or educational opportunities. Parties were a principal channel of access to the bureaucracy" (Feith 1962, 123).

At the national level, parties that gained control of ministries tended to treat these as patronage resources, rewarding their supporters with positions, access to government funds, business deals, and other perquisites. Moreover, party intervention in the bureaucracy increased through the 1950s, producing "an over-all increase in the dependence of civil servants on party leaders" (Feith 1962, 366). Had parliamentary democracy continued uninterrupted, a strongly party-focused system of patronage politics might have developed in contemporary Indonesia.

However, even at the height of parliamentary democracy, Indonesia's system of party-based clientelism was marked by two significant weaknesses. A first problem was that interparty competition was fragmented and unstable. Competition for ministries and other positions produced a constant churn of alignments and realignments in Jakarta, with seven cabinets in seven years. Contributing to the instability, the pattern of interparty competition was centrifugal (Mietzner 2008), with the parties not simply pursuing access to patronage but also having very different ideological visions for a future Indonesia. These tensions were demonstrated by a fissure in the Constituent Assembly that was elected in 1955 to draft a new constitution, but which deadlocked on the issue of whether Indonesia should become an Islamic state. Another destabilizing factor was the steady growth of the PKI, which elites of other parties viewed as an existential threat.

A second weakness was that the parties faced strong competitors for power. During the late colonial period, the Dutch had repressed the nationalist movement, including the first major unifying party, the PNI, established by Sukarno in 1927. The colonial government allowed representative councils that included moderate nationalists, but these were swept aside by the Japanese occupation (1942–1945), and their leaders never gained leadership of nationalist opinion. No single hegemonic party led Indonesia's independence struggle between 1945 and 1949. Instead, independence was won by the army, various militias, revolutionary bands, social organizations, a multiplicity of parties, and charismatic political leaders. In independent Indonesia, political parties thus had to compete with the army and a relatively independent bureaucracy over how to use state resources. The army, in particular, viewed itself as having saved the Indonesian republic during Dutch military advances, and began to press its claims to play a leading role in government. Once a state of martial law was declared to deal with regional rebellions in Sumatra and Sulawesi in 1957, the army began to shoulder past its civilian rivals and assert an increasingly dominant political role in the regions. It also began to build up its control over economic resources by taking over Dutch plantations, oil fields, and other assets after they were occupied by workers in the same year and later nationalized.

Contrast this situation to India, where the origins of party-mediated access to state resources can be traced back to the prominent role of the Congress Party in India's decolonization. At independence, the Congress Party was arguably the most strongly institutionalized party in the developing world (Rudolph and Rudolph 1987, 127). From the late nineteenth century, British colonial rulers enabled the early institutionalization of Congress by granting Indian representatives in municipal and district boards a growing degree of influence over the use of government funds. Furthermore, the heroism of Congress's independence struggle provided the party with the necessary symbolic capital to gain the upper hand in its dealings with bureaucrats. Its reputational strength enabled the party after independence to develop into a well-oiled political machine with extensive control over the distribution of state resources (Jalal 1995; Kothari 1964; Weiner 1967). In Argentina the Peronist movement gradually achieved similar dominance. Bolstered by strong labor unions and Peron's charismatic leadership, the Peronist party—the Justicialist Party—developed a strong organizational capacity, which it maintained during periods of authoritarian rule. In the 1950s, the Peronist movement established thousands of local party branches, which distributed material benefits and provided a space for political engagement of working-class Argentines (Levitsky 2003, 40).

In Indonesia, the closest equivalent was the PNI, but it was far from having the dominance of India's Congress or Argentina's Peronists, gaining only 22 percent of the popular vote in Indonesia's first post-independence election, compared to 45 percent for Congress in India's 1951–1952 election (Tudor and Slater 2016). Even President Sukarno, seeing himself as embodying the greater national will, did not directly lend his authority to the party, for example by becoming its president.

In the end, Indonesia's party system was unable to withstand the combination of internal and external pressures it faced. In 1959, President Sukarno dissolved the Constituent Assembly and returned to the authoritarian 1945 constitution, formalizing Indonesia's second system of government, which he labeled Guided Democracy. Under this system, the president accumulated great authority (in 1963 he was proclaimed president for life), but he also tried to maintain a precarious balance between the contending political forces, handing out ministries to most major parties and also trying to accommodate the rising power of the military. However, this system proved to be merely a transitional arrangement, and was unable to survive the mounting tension between the PKI and its allies on the left, and an anticommunist coalition coalescing around the army on the right. The army, led by General Suharto, emerged triumphant from this contest when it took advantage of an attempted leftist putsch on the night of September 30, 1965, to push Sukarno out of power and organize a brutal massacre of the PKI and its allies on the left, in one of the great mass killings of the twentieth century. Out of this bloody destruction, Suharto and his allies created one of the most resilient and effective authoritarian regimes of the late twentieth century, ruling Indonesia between 1966 and 1998.

The New Order and the Centralization of Patronage

According to Martin Shefter's (1977, 1994) influential analysis of the evolution of clientelist politics in Western Europe and the US, countries that develop a well-institutionalized, autonomous bureaucracy *before* the advent of mass democracy are more likely to avoid clientelist politics. An autonomous bureaucracy can resist political interference in the distribution of public goods, thus preventing politicians from rewarding supporters with personal favors. Parties that are locked out of state patronage resources, Shefter argues, are instead forced to appeal to voters through policy platforms rather than personal benefit. Such "externally mobilized" parties, he argues, can also resist the blandishments of patronage politics because they rely on mass organizations—labor unions, peasant associations, churches, and the like—that do "not need to be fueled by patronage" (Shefter 1994, 29). By contrast, parties that are established by actors who are entrenched in a ruling regime, especially in conditions in which rules and procedures for bureaucratic autonomy have not been well established, are likely to become patronage machines.

Indonesia in the 1950s presents a picture between these two extremes. A party system was emerging simultaneously with the rebuilding of the state bureaucracy from the ashes of the old colonial state. Some parties, notably the PNI, were embedded in the bureaucracy and built themselves by using public office for political gain. Others, such as the NU and the PKI, were externally mobilized parties, based on mass organizations that had historically not been part of the colonial apparatus, but which were doing what they could to penetrate the new Indonesian state, carve out patrimonial fiefdoms for themselves, and distribute their resources to their mass followings. Overall, the absence of a powerfully autonomous bureaucracy explains why the sudden onset of mass democracy in the 1950s set the country on the path toward party-led clientelism.

In Indonesia's next phase of political development, however, this path hit an abrupt dead end. Under the New Order, the state struck back and pushed the parties to the margins of political life. After destroying the left, Suharto and the military quickly brushed aside their erstwhile civilian allies in the Islamic parties and other groups. They built the New Order regime on a system of state corporatism, constraining the parties and independent associations by repression, or by pushing them into state-controlled corporatist bodies, or both. The military was now involved directly in both the legislative and executive branches, and it used coercion to suppress the regime's opponents. Alongside the army, an equally important pillar of the New Order was the civilian bureaucracy, which produced many of the leaders who filled key posts as ministers, governors, *bupati*, and mayors, and which ensured the implementation of regime programs. However, rather than being based on the sort of bureaucratic rationality and rule-based proceduralism that Shefter imagines as being the precursor of programmatic politics, both the military and civilian wings of the New Order bureaucracy were deeply infused by personalized networks and patronage politics.

To be sure, the form taken by Indonesian clientelism had now changed significantly. In contrast to the party-focused, pillared clientelism that was developing in the 1950s, the New Order represented a system of *centralized clientelism*. Electoral politics and parties were no longer important to this system, though they retained a role. Instead, patronage was distributed downward through a steeply pyramidal structure that centered at its apex on the presidential palace and which operated primarily through the bureaucracy and security apparatus, as well as through the state-controlled corporatist organizations and private business. Observers such as Crouch (1979) used the term "neo-patrimonial" to describe the fusion of public office and private interest that was involved, and to discuss the ways in which senior officials used their discretionary power over the distribution of state resources to gain supporters and wealth and to cement their own positions.

The New Order's centralized clientelism was a relatively closed system, in which the primary beneficiaries were state officials or business elites, and where patronage typically took the form not of the petty cash payments or club goods that oil electoral clientelism, but of lucrative bureaucratic positions and economic opportunities. Ross McLeod has argued that Suharto effectively turned the public sector into a "franchise system" in which "the fundamental purpose . . . was to use the coercive power of government privately to tax the general public and redistribute the revenue to a small elite" (McLeod 2011, 49–50). In McLeod's analysis, all officials were effectively licensed to turn their posts into profit-making enterprises. They could do so either by engaging directly in corruption (skimming resources from their budgets or levying fees on citizens) or indirectly, by distributing economic opportunities (business licenses, timber concessions, mining permits, and the like) to family members or cronies. Accordingly, deeply collusive relationships between private business and state functionaries were critical to the way the system operated, with Suharto and his family's close relationships with leading *cukong* (ethnic Chinese entrepreneurs) (Robison 1986) mirrored at the local level by minor functionaries' informal alliances with local rice traders, timber barons, retailers, and other economic actors. As salaries were low and departmental budgets inadequate, these arrangements formed part of the everyday operations of the state (Baker 2015). This "Suharto franchise" tied Indonesia's capitalists closely to the state as they realized that access to many business opportunities depended on cultivating contacts with Suharto and his circle. Politics acquired an oligarchic character, with elites using their control over state institutions to build their economic dominance (Robison and Hadiz 2004).

Given the structure of this system, it is not surprising that a scholarly consensus developed among observers that the New Order state was extremely dominant vis-à-vis society. Scholars such as Benedict Anderson (1983) and Heather Sutherland (1979) began to see the Indonesian state as acting as a "state-for-itself" that largely focused on serving its own interests—not unlike its extractive, aloof predecessor, the colonial state. Ruth McVey (1982, 88), too, described the New Order as representing the revival of the colonial *beambtenstaat*, arguing that "real politics takes place not in parliament or whatever organs may exist outside the bureaucracy, but in the government apparatus itself." In a somewhat different vein, Karl Jackson (1978) described the New Order as a "bureaucratic polity," based merely on "a small ruling circle whose members respond primarily, albeit not exclusively to the values and interests of less than one thousand persons comprising the bureaucratic, technocratic and military elite of the country." Jim Schiller (1996) wrote of the "powerhouse" state that dominated societal interests at the local level. Even neo-Marxist scholars like Richard Robison (1986), while stressing how the state was embedded in wider patterns of class relations, nevertheless saw the state not as an instrument of a capitalist class, but as the cauldron out of which such a class emerged through personalized relationships between state officials and rent-seeking entrepreneurs.

Such descriptions of the Indonesian state under the New Order contrast dramatically with analyses of the Indian and the Argentinian states in the same period. Scholars described the Indian state as "soft" (Myrdal 1968) or "weak-strong" (Rudolph and Rudolph 1987) because of the strong capacity of non-state actors to manipulate the implementation of state directives. While the Indian state did have an ambition to regulate many spheres of life, in practice "the state system in India is profoundly penetrated or influenced by social forces" (Fuller and Harriss 2001, 10). Indeed, its sovereignty was so fragmented (Hansen 2005) that the Indian state was best thought to be "not a discrete, unitary actor, because it does not consist of an 'actual' organization separated from society" (Fuller and Harriss 2001, 22).

Similarly the Argentinian state, despite experiencing—like Indonesia—periods of military, authoritarian rule (1966–1973 and 1976–1983), was considered to possess very limited autonomy: "public policies were constantly changing and never implemented, as the State danced to the tune of the dynamics of civil society. [The] State apparatus [was] extensively colonized by civil society [and] extraordinarily fragmented. . . . Such a State could not 'keep at a distance' from the governing alliance's immediate demands and interests" (O'Donnell 1978, 50). The contrast with Indonesia is illuminating. Argentina's authoritarian regimes depended, like Indonesia's, on its bureaucratic apparatus to maintain control—indeed the term "bureaucratic authoritarianism" was coined to describe Argentina (O'Donnell 1973). Yet two factors prevented the state from developing the kind of autonomy it acquired in Indonesia. First, in contrast to Indonesia, Argentina had a dominant class of landowning elites, a "pampas bourgeoisie." This class maintained such extensive control over the bureaucracy that it was argued that the Argentinean "state was the creation of the pampas bourgeoisie" (O'Donnell 1978, 25). Second, Argentina's more industrialized economy laid the basis for the development of a relatively strong labor movement, which gave the Peronist party great mobilizational strength and resilience (Levitsky 2003). Indonesia lacked both these countervailing powers. Large landownership was relatively rare, while its capitalist class was largely made up of ethnic Chinese whose political status was precarious. A more limited industrialization, combined with the anticommunist onslaught of 1965, meant that Indonesia's labor movement never became the kind of political force it was in Argentina. The Indonesian bureaucracy lacked competitors, particularly after 1965.

Indonesia's system of centralized, state-controlled clientelism had important implications for the subsequent development of political life in the post–New Order state. As we shall see in subsequent chapters, Indonesia embarked on its democratization process with a bureaucracy that enjoyed high levels of discretionary power over the distribution of state resources. In contrast to the situation in India and Argentina, where political parties and other pressure groups had long made the bureaucracy subservient to their interests, Indonesia's bureaucracy had remained largely independent of outside control. At the same time, if we return to Shefter's analysis of the historical origins of clientelism, the state was not particularly well-institutionalized. Civil servants had grown accustomed to seeing impersonal implementation of laws and policies being undermined by political and personal considerations. Moreover, the political manipulation of laws and regulations did not stem from *outside* actors such as political parties, but rather began *inside* the bureaucracy, at the instigation of senior bureaucratic officials themselves.

New Order Patronage at the Grass Roots

Despite the centralized, extractive, and relatively closed nature of the New Order patronage system, it is important to note that patronage distribution still played a role in the regime's efforts to bolster its legitimacy among wider social groups and the population at large. If the tip of Suharto's patronage pyramid was located at the presidential palace, its lowest reaches extended all the way down to local communities in even remote parts of the country. State officials drew support from—and rewarded with patronage—even small-time elites in rural villages and urban neighborhoods. They also had the ability to reward compliant populations with development goods. In this context, electoral politics retained an important function—not as a means of vertical accountability or of selecting government leaders as in a democratic polity, but as way of identifying and rewarding local notables and communities who demonstrated loyalty to the regime by voting for its electoral vehicle, Golkar. For that purpose, and to provide the regime with a fig leaf of democratic legitimacy in its international dealings, regular national elections continued to be held throughout the New Order period.

An important part of the context here was that the New Order oversaw sustained state building at the local level. When Geertz conducted his research in the 1950s, he concluded that the state was all but absent from Javanese villages. In stark contrast, when the Swedish political scientist Hans Antlöv conducted research in a West Javanese village of sixty-eight hundred inhabitants during the 1980s and early 1990s, he found a "complex village bureaucracy [that] abounds with associations and institutions" (Antlöv 1995, 50). Antlöv identified a total of 178 official positions in eighteen associations in this village, alongside a core leadership of fifty people (Antlöv 1995, 51). This number of political offices, in a village with only sixteen hundred households, he argued, was a "measure of how well higher authorities have penetrated the countryside" (Antlöv 1995, 144). He concluded that the state now played an omnipresent role in the lives of citizens, performing functions that in the 1950s had often been carried out by parties: "Through these officials, institutions and programmes, the Indonesian state is present in most spheres of people's lives. It tells them what to think about foreign policy, which variety of rice they should grow, and when it is ideal to get the first child—in short how to live as Indonesian citizens" (Antlöv 1995, 57). By the same token, the state absorbed community-level notables—village government officials, such as elected village heads, local economic elites such as landowners or traders, and traditional elites such as clan heads or religious leaders—into its own formal and informal structures of power. For example, when Gillian Hart conducted research in rural Central Java in the 1970s, she found that the government was increasingly relying on the cooperation and support of a narrow class of relatively large landowners at the village level (Hart 1986). In a study of community-level politics and state building in the petty kingdom of Bayan, on the island of Lombok, Sven Cederroth (2004) found a similar dynamic, with members of all three of the major noble families eventually lining up to support Golkar at election times. He concluded that "much of the politics of Indonesia can be explained in terms of its political culture: patron-client relationships, traditional authority, indigenous political forms" (Cederroth 2004, 79). Because landlords, traditional chiefs, low-level businesspeople, and similar community notables typically had their own clienteles of tenants, sharecroppers, employees, suppliers, and other hangers on, varied forms of traditional clientelism were thus grafted onto the state-based centralized system of clientelism that defined the New Order.

The relationship between local notables and officialdom was mutually advantageous. As with people closer to the center of power, community-level notables derived material benefits from supporting Golkar and the government. By building ties with bureaucrats, and security officials at the subdistrict or district level, they could access all sorts of opportunities: roles as contractors in local development projects, positions in state-controlled distribution chains, preferential access to land, contracts to supply government offices, help with dealing with unruly tenants or business rivals, and the like. Through such methods the Golkar-military state permeated local power relations and social structures. The formal structures of the bureaucratic state were uniform, even homogenizing. But its informal structures of control were remarkably flexible, adapting to the circumstances of local societies. Overall, the support of community-level notables was enormously beneficial for the New Order state, greatly expanding its social reach and control, and propagating its hegemony even through people's intimate interpersonal relationships.

These relationships also had an electoral dimension. During the New Order, elections were still held regularly, even if they were more of a "useful fiction" (Liddle 1996) rather than being essential to the regime's maintenance of power or a genuine test of its popular support. The political parties that survived into the early New Order were forced, in 1973, to merge into constrained, state-controlled parties: PNI, along with several minor nationalist and Christian parties, joined to form the Indonesia Democracy Party (PDI); NU and various other Islamic parties were fused into the Unity Development Party (PPP), which, tellingly, was not even able to refer to Islam in its name. These parties had little autonomy in, for example, candidate selection or campaign messaging. In a policy that the regime called "floating mass" (*massa mengambang*), the parties were obstructed in establishing branches below the district level. As Jackson (1978, 4) observed, parties were now marginal to political life: "The bureaucracy [is] not accountable to other political forces such as political parties. . . . Parties, to the extent that they exist at all, neither control the central bureaucracy nor effectively organize the masses at the local level." Harassed at the grass roots, cut off from sources of patronage, required to parrot regime ideology, and rent with internal divisions, PPP and PDI were unable to mount a sustained challenge to the regime. They occasionally channeled symbolic protest, but they no longer operated as effective clientelist machine parties because they had no significant patronage to dispense.

The regime's electoral vehicle, Golkar, by contrast, enjoyed huge advantages—the backing of the bureaucracy and coercive apparatus, blanket media support, unlimited funds—and won solid victories in every election, elections that in any case involved considerable electoral manipulation. Strictly speaking, Golkar was not a party at all—and regime leaders did not describe it as one. Instead, it was the electoral manifestation of the military and civilian bureaucracy—the yellow clothing that civil servants and soldiers donned at election time. It makes little sense to think of Golkar as having much independent existence outside the civilian and military bureaucracy, and its dependence on these branches of the state meant that Golkar never established capacity to discipline or control civil servants. Not only were most Golkar candidates drawn from the bureaucracy, but government officials also staffed its local branches (Liddle 1985, 72). During elections, local bureaucrats and soldiers were set vote targets by their superiors that they were expected to attain for the organization. Civil servants were expected to display "mono-loyalty," which meant in practice that they had to campaign for Golkar. As Liddle wrote, "Golkar's primary strategy in New Order elections has been to mobilize government officials, who are used in turn to mobilize the electorate. Regional officials at provincial, district, and subdistrict levels apply pressure on village heads to get out the vote for Golkar" (Liddle 1988, 181).

The critical role played by village heads deserves emphasis, because these actors play a crucial role in our account of post-Suharto clientelist politics. In their modern form, village heads are a creation of the New Order. In 1979, the government adopted a new village law, which aimed to standardize Indonesia's diverse forms of local customary leadership through the adoption of the Javanese *kepala desa* (village head) as the key village leader. The law stipulated that village heads would be elected by villagers every eight years, and they were not—unlike their functional equivalents in cities, the *lurah*—civil servants, receiving only a stipend for their services. This downward accountability did not, however, make village heads under the New Order much more independent than civil servants proper. Village heads were subjected to the same "screening" processes that kept persons with suspect political views or loyalties out of the civil service and parliaments. More important, their loyalty and obedience were achieved through the flow of state funding for special projects to build roads, schools, health centers, or markets, as well as by the informal opportunities to profit from such activities. Government projects were generally awarded to villages where the village head had shown loyalty and Golkar attained a strong vote. As village heads could generally take a few percent of project costs, the selective allocation of such benefits helped secure their loyalty. As Antlöv observed, "Village officials are more interested in maintaining smooth relations with supra-village officials than with the subordinate villagers. . . . The compulsory doctrine of 'mono-loyalty' makes it clear to all civil servants and village leaders that their first loyalty is towards the New Order and Golkar" (Antlöv 1994, 83).

To do their work, meanwhile, the village heads and their urban equivalents, the *lurah*, could lean on a range of local officials, heads of government-recognized associations, and, especially, neighborhood heads (*ketua RW, rukun warga*) or hamlet heads (*kepala dusun*), and, below that, sub-neighborhood heads (*ketua RT, rukun tetangga*). Each RT typically contained about twenty or thirty households, with several RT making up one RW. This system of RT/RW heads was introduced by the Japanese during World War II as a means of population surveillance. Elected by their neighbors, the RT/RW heads became in effect the most local representatives of the Indonesian state, even if they did not have civil servant status and were not salaried. Nevertheless, they performed a wide range of functions for the state, monitoring population movements and facilitating implementation of (and access to) a wide range of government programs. As one study put it, they "are presumed to be conduits to government help and also to serve as redistribution points for other *kampung* [community] social goods" (Newberry 2006, 36). At the same time, RT and RW heads played representational roles, negotiating on behalf of their communities, or individual residents, when they needed to deal with higher state authorities, managing community-level services such as garbage collection, and resolving community disputes (Guinness 2009, 41).

Local state representatives like village heads and RT/RW heads played an important role in maintaining support for the New Order, even if their relationship with the state was sometimes ambiguous. Their capacity to withhold access to important resources, in combination with the status associated with their position, meant that village heads (and, to a lesser extent, RT/RW heads) were generally considered capable of delivering a sizable portion of the votes during the New Order's controlled elections. Under Suharto it was quite common for village heads to manipulate the implementation of government programs to maintain support for themselves and to quell resistance to the New Order. Villagers needed, for example, to obtain letters attesting to good behavior signed by the village heads (as well as police and army officials) in order to get married, get a government job, or be admitted in school. "Even to get a sick-leave permission, without which a worker might eventually be fired, one must thus be on good terms with the *pamong desa* [village officials]" (Antlöv 1994, 82). Local state representatives were prone to present their provision of such benefits as entailing an obligation to reciprocate—either by supporting Golkar or themselves. At the same time, village heads had little formal power to extract more resources beyond demonstrating loyalty and cultivating the goodwill of higher state authorities. This combination of considerable discretionary power within their communities with high dependence on state authorities ensured that village heads played an important role in safeguarding the stability of the New Order.

This role was most obvious at election time, when the integration of the New Order's development machinery, the bureaucracy, Golkar, and the village heads and other community leaders into a single system meant that the regime's much-vaunted development programs could be used for distributing collective rewards and punishments. Grassroots studies of legislative elections during the New Order period show that a pork-barrel logic was central to the way the Golkar machine operated at the grass roots (Antlöv 1994; Cederroth 2004). In the lead-up to national elections, local bureaucrats, village-level officials, and allied notables made it clear to residents that neighborhoods, hamlets, and villages that supported Golkar would be rewarded with development projects. They often ascertained what a community most wanted—a water channel here, a new road or school building there—and explained that the desired project would be forthcoming if the community delivered a Golkar victory. Antlöv observed this process at firsthand in his field site in West Java, noting that "in many cases a hamlet or village leader would directly approach the sub-district branch of Golkar and suggest a project to be initiated if Golkar won by a certain percentage" (Antlöv 2004, 114). Occasionally, too, local state officials distributed cash or other goods directly to voters, but this was not the primary modus operandi: instead, the New Order acted largely to a punitive logic, withholding infrastructure, development projects, or other benefits from communities that failed to support Golkar by a sufficient margin. All of this, of course, was nested within a broader political context in which ordinary citizens were constantly bombarded with messages both in the formal media and from their community leaders stressing the regime's developmental goals and achievements, and contrasting these with the failures of predecessor regimes.

The system of highly coordinated, state-controlled electoral authoritarianism collapsed with the New Order. But we will see in later chapters that the heritage of Golkar's grassroots electoral apparatus still shapes the organization of clientelist exchange during elections and, consequently, the distribution of power. In particular, village heads and RT/RW heads have become highly sought-after brokers, delinked from Golkar, in Indonesia's post-Suharto patronage democracy. Their role in controlling access to government programs has increased and, combined with the legitimacy they enjoy as locally elected and respected community problem solvers, provides them with a power to influence local electoral outcomes that is enjoyed by few other actors. However, in sharp contrast to the New Order period, when they were shepherded and bullied to support Golkar, in post-Suharto Indonesia these grassroots officials are free to shop among parties and candidates to look for whatever deals might best advantage them and their communities.

The New Order and Social Organizations

A second way in which patronage politics remained broadly based even during the New Order years was through social organizations. Although the government weakened the political parties in the ways described above, many of the social and cultural organizations that had been connected to those parties survived; numerous other associations had never had strong party links. The government frequently courted the support of leaders of influential organizations in order to reach out to their constituencies and so promote government policies, bolster regime legitimacy, and ensure social stability.

This dynamic was most obvious among religious organizations. In the 1950s, religion and politics had become closely linked, with members of most of the country's major religious traditions establishing their own political parties. Under the New Order, even as the government constrained these groups' ability to operate freely as part of political society, the basic organizational infrastructure of religious life remained intact. For example, Nahdlatul Ulama (NU), the sprawling organization representing traditionalist Muslims, remained a powerful network through the New Order years, linking religious scholars (*kyai* or *ulama*) and their networks of religious boarding schools (*pesantren*) throughout the country (Fealy and Barton 1996). Vast numbers of people found their spiritual succor and were integrated into community life through organizations affiliated with NU, such as the women's associations Muslimat and Fatayat. Likewise, during the 1950s, leaders and members of the major modernist Islamic organization, Muhammadiyah, had mostly been aligned with the Masjumi party. Even though the government refused to unban Masjumi (it had been banned by Sukarno), and shepherded its remnants into the PPP in 1973, Muhammadiyah retained a formidable organizational presence through the New Order years. It ran a massive network of schools, colleges, universities, hospitals, and health centers. Likewise, the Protestant and Catholic parties were forced to merge into the PDI, but the church organizations survived, as did a large array of church-affiliated educational institutions, youth groups, women's organizations, prayer unions, and the like.

Such religious organizations developed a relationship with the New Order state that has elsewhere been described as semi-oppositional (Aspinall 2005). From time to time, their leaders criticized particular government policies or decisions—especially policies they saw as impinging on their corporate interests—and they often chafed at government restrictions. But they generally acceded to regime ideology and participated in government development programs. Importantly for our purposes, they also became conduits of patronage. At the local level, religious leaders were often treated in much the same way as other notables, being drawn into formal and informal government arrangements in their communities, and gaining access to patronage resources as a result. Religious leaders were often especially interested in attaining government assistance for the physical construction of houses of worship, schools, or other community facilities. It became something of a cliché of New Order election campaigning that Golkar leaders would appear at a campaign rally alongside an *ulama* or other local religious leader, and soon afterward trucks carrying sacks of cement to help expand the buildings of that leader's *pesantren*, school, or other institution would appear.

A similar logic applied outside the religious sphere. For example, although most formerly PNI-aligned Sukarnoists were affiliated with the PDI and were thus marginal to regime politics, a considerable number made peace with the government from its early years. In fact, given that the PNI had been the natural party of the bureaucracy in the 1950s and early 1960s, many village heads and civil servants—especially in regional Java—had PNI family backgrounds. By the time of the late New Order, government ministers who were alumni of the formerly PNI-aligned student organization, the Indonesian National Student Movement (GMNI), were openly sponsoring the organization and coordinating networks of alumni within government (Aspinall 2005, 80). And, of course, there was a much larger universe of organizations that had never been aligned to any pre-1965 political party but were instead affiliated directly to the government and Golkar through the latter's array of corporatist bodies: sports associations, youth groups, groups of *preman* or petty gangsters, labor unions, and so on. Such organizations also provided avenues down to the masses that could be used for patronage distribution and brokerage purposes.

In the villages, such groups included youth groups, farmers' cooperatives, and the ubiquitous Guidance for Family Welfare (PKK) organizations that notionally incorporated all women and ran everything from maternal and infant health programs to savings and credit schemes. Such organizations became avenues through which ordinary citizens could access government programs, whether by providing them with subsidized fertilizer and new seed varieties, as with many farmers' cooperatives, or merely enlisting women as "unpaid social welfare workers" (Newberry 2006, 16), as often ended up being the case with the PKK. Whatever their specific purpose, a rich web of associations connected the New Order state to ordinary citizens. This web survived largely intact into the post–New Order period and was to become thoroughly penetrated by political candidates and their operatives who turned it to election campaigning purposes.

The critical point with regard to the legacy for post-Suharto patronage politics is that although Indonesia had an authoritarian regime during the New Order years, it also retained a relatively rich associational landscape, but one that was de-linked from political party life. Particularly striking was the dense array of state or quasi-state organizations at the village and urban community level, as well as the larger national networks, most (but not all) of which were organized around religious identities. During the New Order period itself, scholars devoted much effort to explaining how the government co-opted such organizations through corporatist arrangements and patronage politics (e.g., Reeve 1990). However, as we shall see, such organizations proved readily adaptable to the more decentered and fragmented patterns of patronage distribution that were developed by politicians once political competition was liberalized after 1998. A multiplicity of ready-made vehicles for political mobilization and patronage delivery outside of party structures became available to politicians.

Again, it is useful to compare the Indonesian situation to our comparators, Argentina and India. In both places, linkages between parties and associational life remained relatively robust. In Argentina, which was governed for briefer periods by authoritarian military-based regimes, the Peronist party was able to maintain its connections with the trade union movement. The labor unions provided the party with an organizational backbone, as well as a channel to connect with voters, and enabled it to maintain its presence and popularity during periods of authoritarian rule (Levitsky 2003). In India, by contrast, there was never sustained authoritarianism, only a brief period of emergency rule in the 1970s. As a result, many important social organizations retained party links. For example, the Hindu Nationalist Party, BJP, is connected to a host of cultural and religious organizations that are at least nominally committed to promoting Hinduism (Jaffrelot 1996). Similarly, the Congress Party built its dominance in the first three decades after independence on close connections with numerous organizations, ranging from labor unions and cooperatives to landowners and caste leaders (Weiner 1967). In contrast, Indonesia experienced a three-decade period when the regime tried hard to break the ties between civil and political society. In the post-Suharto period, though leaders of Nahdlatul Ulama, Muhammadiyah, and some other religious organizations did successfully establish new parties that claimed to represent the interests of their respective communities, in reality these parties were never able to establish anything like a monopoly claim to the loyalty of these organizations or their mass constituencies. At the same time, Indonesia entered the new era of democratic competition with a multiplicity of religious and other social organizations, including many that were strongly rooted at the community level but which lacked party linkages. This environment provided a rich array of formal and informal networks that could be used by politicians to build links to voters, bypassing formal party institutions.

The Revival of Patronage Democracy

A few days before Indonesia's first post-Suharto election on June 7, 1999, Jakarta turned red. An estimated three million people clogged the streets of the city: on foot, on motorcycles, in cars and buses, and on the open backs of trucks. Almost everyone was wearing outfits in red, the trademark color of the PDI-P, the party led by Megawati Sukarnoputri, daughter of the first president. Many people were wearing hats, helmets, or face masks adorned with horns, representing the party symbol of the *banteng*, or bull; others were dressed as clowns, zombies, spacemen, or anything else that took their fancy. The city's *waria*, or transsexuals, were out in force, also dressed in red. Members of many poor *kampung* communities had pooled their resources to make giant papier-mâché bulls or other models, which they paraded around through the city on trucks. Many vehicles carried giant sound systems pumping out ear-splitting electronic dance music or *dangdut*, a form of Indonesian pop. The atmosphere was exhilaratingly festive. Though this was the largest election rally of that campaign season, it was far from being unrepresentative of the general mood. The 1999 election witnessed a vigorous renaissance of political party life. A total of forty-eight parties registered to contest the election, and mass rallies, party symbols, and party colors were the order of the day. A new age of parties had arrived, or so it seemed.

More than that, for a while it seemed as if a new version of the party-centered, pillared clientelism that had briefly held sway in the 1950s would now revive. Certainly, many of the conditions seemed favorable. Golkar lost its monopoly access to the channels of patronage delivery it had enjoyed under the New Order. In the lead-up to the 1999 election, under intense pressure to show that the polls would be free and fair, the government introduced new rules prohibiting bureaucrats from being members of political parties, or using the powers of their office to campaign for any group, as had been the norm under the New Order. The military and police, too, were for the first time required to be politically neutral. These were fateful decisions for Indonesia's subsequent political development: even after the initial tumult of the transition ended, Golkar was never able to reestablish its dominance over state resources and bureaucratic machinery, even as these factors once more became important in electoral politics.

In the aftermath of the collapse of the Suharto regime, a large number of new parties were formed, and old ones were revived. These parties tried to reconnect with local communities, building up their branches and recruiting members. Ambitious politicians and community notables around the country flooded into the parties. Many of the new parties bore more than a passing resemblance to the old *aliran*-linked parties of the 1950s, and could thus be expected to try to solidify their support by delivering patronage to the socioreligious communities on which they were based. The PDI-P was the direct descendant of the old PNI and Christian parties and had a strong traditional following in the *abangan* or religiously syncretic communities of rural Java and among secular urbanites and minority groups such as Hindus and Christians. Among the Islamic parties, the National Awakening Party (PKB) drew on the traditionalist Islamic community affiliated with NU and was thus particularly strong in East Java and other NU heartland areas, such as parts of Central Java and South Kalimantan. The National Mandate Party (PAN) was rooted in the modernist and more urban Muhammadiyah. PPP, along with several other Islamic parties, also competed for the support of the pious, as did a new party, the Justice Party, later renamed the Prosperous Justice Party (PKS), which was founded on a core of campus-based activists inspired by the Muslim Brotherhood in the Middle East. However, none of these parties—with the exception of the Justice Party, which appealed only to a narrow group—was able to claim a monopoly on the loyalties of its target group, each facing competition from numerous splinter identity-based parties and catchall parties (such as Golkar) that tried to reach across socioreligious divides. For example, PKB was never able to command the loyalty of an overwhelming majority of the influential traditionalist Islamic scholars, many of whom were affiliated to PPP, other Islamic parties, or even parties like Golkar, and it was certainly never able to command the vote of the entire NU community (national surveys routinely show that more than a third of the Indonesian population identify with NU; PKB won only 13 percent of the national vote in the 1999 election and has not since matched that result).

As the new democratic order settled into place, these parties began to engage in rent-seeking behavior that was also reminiscent of that practiced in the

1950s. The post-Suharto pattern of government formation has been memorably described by Dan Slater as constituting "collusive democracy" or "promiscuous power sharing" (Slater 2004; Slater and Simmons 2013). Beginning in 1999, post-Suharto cabinets have mostly been oversize "rainbow coalitions" that pay little heed to ideological distinctions but are instead based on a model of patronage sharing. The negotiations preceding the formation of such coalitions focus on the distribution of offices rather than policy, wherein cabinet posts represent "a gilded bridge between parliament and the presidency, providing a fortunate few with access to the bounteous patronage resources of the state executive" (Slater 2004, 66). From the early days of the new democracy, it became obvious that government ministers were accessing the resources they had in their departments to raise funds for their parties. In Indonesia's national parliament, the People's Representative Assembly (DPR), too, MPs became notorious for using the opportunities afforded them by their legislative and budgeting functions to extort cash payments or other benefits from government ministries, companies, and other parties interested in gaining a particular legislative outcome. Competition for the so-called "wet" commissions that dealt with lucrative areas of government spending such as public works or mining became intense (Sherlock 2010). As we discuss in the next chapter, these corrupt practices were one motivation for the adoption of electoral reforms that gradually restricted the prominence of political parties, ensuring that the age of parties never really arrived.

In the meantime, much of this kind of corruption served to strengthen party organization. National-level politicians started to use patronage goods to strengthen and build party networks. Indubitably, many politicians used the opportunity afforded by access to state power to engage in personal enrichment. But many also directed the resources they gained downward through their party structures, using them to build party machines, reward party supporters, and strengthen their own personal clienteles within their parties. Members of parliament from most parties, for example, had their pay docked to help fund the party machinery. Corruption could also be used for the same purpose: one of the more spectacular examples comes from somewhat later in the post–New Order period when Anas Urbaningrum, the chairperson of President Susilo Bambang Yudhoyono's Partai Demokrat, was sentenced to fourteen years' jail for his role in a large corruption scandal involving a massive markup in the construction of a sports center; Anas had used part of the proceeds to reward supporters at the party's 2010 congress, which elected him as its leader. Likewise, party politicians who controlled ministries could systematically use them to benefit fellow party members and appointees. Thus, PKS used its control of the Agriculture Ministry under Yudhoyono not only to extract funds (exposed by a massive beef import scandal late in the Yudhoyono presidency) but also to

direct programs, projects, and positions toward party members and supporters. In many parts of the country, PKS cadres were appointed as agricultural
extension officers, and the party used their networks to reach down to rural
areas and provide projects to farmers' groups who supported the party. The
Ministry of Manpower and Transmigration, when it was under the control of
PKB, did much the same, directing projects toward NU communities that were
viewed as being the party's main support base. Indeed, one of us interviewed a
former PKB parliamentarian who was given an advisory role in the ministry;
she described her real function as being to "manage Department of Manpower
and Transmigration programs for the purposes of [our] political interests"
(confidential interview, August 29, 2012). Such party-based clientelism could
have become even more prevalent, and parties could have become the coordinating centers for virtually all electoral clientelism. However, as we discuss in
the next chapter, subsequent electoral reforms discouraged politicians, especially regional politicians, from using their access to patronage goods to build
their parties. These reforms instead encouraged them to focus on their own
personal, nonparty networks.

Indonesia began its history of democratic government in the 1950s with a parliamentary style of government that pushed parties to the forefront of political life, even as the parties' competitors, notably in the army and other parts
of the state apparatus, were also consolidating their authority. Had the political
polarization and crises of the 1950s and 1960s been avoided, it seems likely that
Indonesia would have developed in the direction of a party-focused system of
mass clientelism, with party leaders gradually wresting control over sources of
government patronage and building the authority to direct civil servants to channel state resources in accordance with partisan interests. After the long authoritarian interlude of the New Order, at first it seemed that the evolution of such a
system would resume. A vigorous multiparty democracy was developing, parties
were rapidly recruiting members and building branches, and they also occupied a
large place in the public political imagination, inspiring both enthusiasm among
ordinary voters and suspicion among reformers. Party leaders began to gain
access to lucrative sources of state patronage in ways that might be expected to
assist party building. Certainly, when practices of "money politics" were exposed
by the media, members of Indonesia's vigorous civil society tended to criticize
the parties and accuse them of creating a political system in which the public
interest was subordinated to narrow and self-serving partisanship. In the early
2000s, it became common to hear media talk of Indonesia as being a "dictator-
ship" or an "oligarchy" of parties. It seemed reasonable to expect that party-led
clientelism was once more in the offing.

Much of the remainder of this book is devoted to explaining how and why Indonesia departed once more from this pathway, instead taking a direction that was virtually the opposite of those taken in the 1950s and 1960s. Rather than returning to a system of authoritarian, centralized clientelism, Indonesia became not only a vibrant democracy, but one in which clientelist networks were increasingly fragmented and freewheeling. As we explore in subsequent chapters, parties never became entirely marginal to political life, but a growing proportion of politicians at all levels bypassed them as their key networking and patronage instruments, instead turning to personalized networks to meet their alliance-building and campaigning needs. The party system itself began to change, with a growing proportion of parties being based on personalist appeals and resembling convenient vehicles for influential individuals and their networks. More and more politicians and voters lost interest in their parties' distinctive ideologies, programs, and identities.

Some of the reasons for this evolution have to do with the choices Indonesians made when designing the post-Suharto electoral system and Indonesia's institutional structure more broadly, reasons we explore in the next chapter. But many of the reasons can also be found in the historical account that we have provided in the preceding pages. The New Order was a political system in which not only was patronage distribution universalized as a mode of building political relationships, but in which patronage was distributed largely through nonparty channels—at the lower levels through community-level state functionaries and social organizations; at the higher levels through informal networks linking political, bureaucratic, and business actors. The legacy of this system meant that not only did politicians have available to them a variety of nonparty channels for distributing patronage to voters once the authoritarian system crumbled, but many of these politicians were themselves not particularly beholden to parties for their political authority or material resources. Instead, they were empowered by their connections to bureaucratic, business, and informal networks. Indonesia transitioned to democracy with a system where key patronage resources remained outside the control of party politicians, being instead deeply buried in the state apparatus. In the next chapter we examine what these legacies meant for the fate of the parties.

4

ELECTORAL INSTITUTIONS, POLITICAL PARTIES, AND CANDIDATES

The run-up to the 2013 election for Tangerang's new mayor was messy. On paper, it should have been easy for Arief Wismansyah to persuade parties to support his candidacy. He was the deputy mayor under the outgoing incumbent, Wahidin Halim, and in Indonesia such deputies often launch tilts at the top job after a period or two in office. Moreover, Arief's prosperous family ran a well-known chain of hospitals, and during his period as deputy mayor he had already built up much support. But his campaign team decided to put off engaging in negotiations with parties until the very last moment. Instead, they worked on building Arief's popularity and visibility by creating a local network of supporters. Six months before the election, they commissioned a survey that gave Arief a 20 percent lead over his main competitor, Abdul Syukur. They took this survey to political parties. Indonesia's electoral system required candidates running for mayor to have the support of political parties that together commanded at least 20 percent of the seats in the local parliament. To reach this threshold, Arief decided to negotiate not just with the Partai Demokrat—the party that had previously supported him—but also with leaders of PDI-P, PKB, PAN, the Greater Indonesia Movement Party (Gerindra), and the People's Conscience Party (Hanura). With such polling numbers, Arief was convinced he would be able to attract their support at a relatively low price.

Yet no party dared to declare its support. Wahidin Halim, the outgoing mayor and head of the local chapter of the Partai Demokrat, stood in the way. Wahidin was also the elder brother of Abdul Syukur, the leader of the local chapter of

Golkar, and Arief's strongest potential competitor. This family connection greatly complicated matters. Arief was the natural choice of Partai Demokrat—it had supported him to become deputy mayor previously, and he was a party member. But Wahidin wanted to support his brother. These clashing ambitions caused considerable tension and confusion within Partai Demokrat. Wahidin wanted Arief and Abdul Syukur to run as a pair, but Abdul resented playing second fiddle and wanted to run as mayor himself. This meant that the support of Partai Demokrat was not guaranteed. Of all the candidates, only Abdul Syukur had a background within a political party—but as Golkar's seat share was insufficiently large to nominate a candidate in its own right, Syukur also needed to build a coalition of various parties to support his candidacy. All the other candidates lacked strong ties with a political party.

As a result, the run-up to the Tangerang election was accompanied by frantic negotiations between party leaders and the five candidates. The candidates tried to woo the parties to support their candidacies with a mixture of promising poll results and promises of money and influence. Such promises were important to party bosses. Backing a winner in a local government race would be more beneficial than supporting a losing loyal party cadre. Supporting a winner would mean the party would be able to call in favors and access the government budget more readily. Yet this depended on concluding a good deal with a promising candidate. As negotiations stretched out, tensions rose: a week before the registration deadline, both Abdul Syukur and Arief Wismansyah had still not secured the necessary party support. Journalists held their breath: would the outgoing mayor Halim succeed in denying his deputy the backing he needed to run?

This chapter discusses the negotiated and pragmatic relationships between political parties and politicians that predominate in post-Suharto Indonesia. Describing the processes through which individuals become candidates for office, we relate the often surprisingly marginal role played by political parties in electoral competition. As in Tangerang, many political candidates elsewhere in Indonesia have only weak connections with the parties that nominate them for office. Indeed, candidates often talk about how they need to "*mencari perahu*" (look for a boat) as the first stage of electoral competition, viewing the political party (or coalition of parties) that will nominate them merely as a convenient vehicle that will get them through the nomination process. Candidates often forge connections with parties through cash transactions, purchasing the "boat" they need. After these initial transactions are complete, candidates often rely on nonparty networks to organize their election campaigns and to deliver patronage to voters and supporters. Parties are, in sum, just one of a number of networks that candidates can use for patronage purposes, rather than being *primus inter pares* of Indonesian clientelism.

This weak relationship between candidates and parties is to a large extent the product of Indonesia's electoral system. In the preceding chapter we already pointed to historical and structural factors that have helped generate Indonesia's freewheeling clientelism, but we also explained that there were early signs that Indonesia would revive its old system of party-based clientelism after Suharto fell. After this beginning, however, Indonesia made two fateful choices when redesigning its electoral system. First, the country moved from a system of indirect to direct elections of heads of executive governments. The first direct presidential elections were held in 2004, but the consequential shift for our purposes occurred in 2005, when direct elections of regional heads (*pilkada*) were introduced. A second change was the shift from closed-list to open-list proportional representation in Indonesia's parliaments, a shift that began in partial form in 2004 but was fully implemented in the 2009 election as a result of a decision by Indonesia's Constitutional Court. In an open-list system, citizens can vote not only for parties (as they do in closed-list systems) but also for individual candidates, giving rise to intense competition for personal votes, including between candidates running for the same party.

These shifts had profound effects on the nature of patronage politics. They did not generate patronage politics, but they changed its locus. Early in Indonesia's democratic transition, patronage politics occurred largely *inside* political parties and legislative institutions, in the form, for instance, of vote buying at party congresses or within regional legislatures, or the purchase of positions on party lists. It is one of the better established propositions of the comparative literature on electoral systems and clientelism that candidate-centered electoral systems frequently prompt "party leaders to allow or encourage candidates to cultivate a personal support network by directing (or promising to direct) pork and other particularistic forms of government largesse to a candidate's constituents" (Hicken 2007, 50). Accordingly, after the introduction of such systems in Indonesia, the major locus of patronage politics was between *candidates and voters and not between parties and voters*. There was a spike in retail vote buying, gift giving, and distribution of club goods to voters. The role of personal rather than party-based campaign teams and community-level vote brokers expanded dramatically. Overall, we might say that these electoral changes helped to democratize Indonesian patronage politics: during the New Order, patronage primarily circulated between members of the political elite; now, ordinary voters were a prime target of patronage. At the same time, the shifts made the individual candidate or officeholder, and the informal networks he or she created, rather than the party, the main hub in patronage distribution networks. Although candidates often still used party networks when organizing supporters and mobilizing voters, they more often turned to other sorts of networks to carry out these tasks.

Compared to many third-wave democracies, Indonesia's party system has remained relatively robust (Mietzner 2013b). But this continuing robustness of the formal party system *coexists* with the primacy of informal networks in electoral politics that is our focus in this book. This apparent paradox is due to the important *gatekeeping* role that political parties continue to play in Indonesia's system of patronage democracy. The power to nominate gives parties a linchpin role in Indonesia's system of freewheeling clientelism. In most cases ambitious politicians need to either join or strike deals with parties, even only temporarily, in order to run for office. In this sense, Indonesia's institutional architecture does favor parties. Yet this is a mixed blessing: by forcing executive candidates to build coalitions of different political parties—rather than requiring candidates to be supported by one party only—the electoral system generated a highly pragmatic, monetized deal-making political culture, which has weakened the loyalty of politicians to their parties.

Indonesia's Party System

Before we proceed, it is helpful for us to consider Indonesia's party system and the changes it has undergone since democratization began. As noted in the previous chapter, early in the post-Suharto period it was possible to imagine that Indonesia would develop in the direction of party-centered clientelism. Parties were accessing patronage resources and becoming conduits for their distribution. Many of the most important parties were rooted in distinctive social constituencies and therefore appeared to be potentially resilient.

In the decade and a half that followed, several important changes occurred. First, and most strikingly, there was a steep decline in the proportion of the population who identified with any party. Surveys have shown a dramatic plunge, with 86 percent saying that they felt "close" to a party in 1999, and that number sinking to only 15 percent in 2014 (Muhtadi 2018, 18). This decline of public support has many causes, but one driving it is elite capture of the parties, and their use as vehicles to extract rents from the state. As we pointed out in the preceding chapter, and has been argued repeatedly in the wider literature, under the New Order a new wealthy class had grown up that had enriched itself through privileged access to state office and the many opportunities for informal fees, budget skimming, licenses, contracts, subsidies, and other benefits such access provided. In order to protect their access, and to take advantage of the new opportunities afforded by democratization and, especially, by decentralization of political and economic power to the regions, many such individuals moved into the parties that were becoming so prominent in political life after the downfall of Suharto.

Many party officials and parliamentarians who lacked elite pedigrees also tried to benefit from the rent-seeking patterns that had been modeled under Suharto. The resulting steady stream of corruption scandals embroiling all the major parties at both national and local levels has meant that political parties and parliaments are routinely noted in surveys as among Indonesia's least trusted and respected institutions. At the same time, as Mietzner has pointed out, the fact that the state provides only minimal subsidies to parties undermines their financial sustainability and makes them even more vulnerable to capture by wealthy local elites in the regions and by national oligarchs at the center (Mietzner 2007, 2013a, 2013b).

A second, and related, feature of post-Suharto political life is the notable fluidity of party alignments and, for a time at least, their fragmentation. Because many of the individuals who join parties are primarily attracted by the patronage-hunting opportunities they offer, party loyalty can count for little. Accordingly, party leaders who lose out in internal faction fights often leave to join other parties, taking their retinues of followers with them. Rules governing the legislatures make it impossible for parliamentarians to swap parties midterm (parties can replace representatives who violate party discipline), but there is a great deal of party hopping between elections (Allen 2012). Indeed, many of the important new entrants to the political party scene, notably Partai Demokrat, Gerindra, Hanura, and the National Democratic Party (NasDem) (see table 4.1) were not really "new," in the sense that many of their leaders and cadres were individuals who had previously served in other parties.

Early in Indonesia's democratic transition, the same dynamic generated considerable fragmentation of the parties. Especially in rural and remote districts,

TABLE 4.1 National legislative election results for 1999, 2004, 2009, and 2014 (by percent of valid votes)

PARTY	1999 % OF VOTE	2004 % OF VOTE	2009 % OF VOTE	2014 % OF VOTE
PDI-P	33.7	18.5	14.0	18.9
Golkar	22.4	21.6	14.5	14.8
Gerindra			4.5	11.8
PD		7.5	20.9	10.2
PKB	12.6	10.6	4.9	9.0
PAN	7.1	6.4	6.0	7.6
PKS	1.4	7.3	7.9	6.8
NasDem				6.7
PPP	10.7	8.2	5.3	6.5
Hanura			3.8	5.3
Other	12.1	19.9	18.2	2.4
Total	**100.0**	**100.0**	**100.0**	**100.0**

many political candidates engaged in "party shopping" prior to legislative elections. This occurred when a local bureaucrat, businessperson, or other notable with a strong presence in a particular locale or some other mobilizational advantage—such as a powerful clan affiliation, a strong bureaucratic network, or simply enough money to buy his or her way to office—rather than subjecting himself or herself to a number-two position on a party candidate list dominated by a competitor, would simply switch parties. The result was a proliferation of micro-parties, such that in more remote regions, the ratio of parties represented in local legislatures to the number of seats was often 1:2 or even lower. In such areas, political fragmentation was almost complete, with local representative bodies merely representing individual leaders and their networks rather than collective interests or programs that could be connected to national-level politics. Institutional change eventually limited the extent of this fragmentation: more demanding registration requirements limited the number of parties that could compete. Parties had to show they had broad national representation: to register in 2014, a national party had to demonstrate, among other things, that it had functioning branches in all provinces, 75 percent of districts, and, within those districts, 50 percent of subdistricts; it also had to show it had a membership of at least one thousand people or 1/1000th of the population of the relevant districts (this was according to article 8 of Law Number 8 of 2012). Though forty-six national parties tried to register for the 2014 election, only twelve were allowed to run (down from thirty-eight in 2009, twenty-four in 2004, and forty-eight in 1999). Meanwhile, a "parliamentary threshold" set a minimum national result (3.5 percent in 2014) that parties needed to attain to win representation in the national legislature. Despite these restrictions, by 2014 Indonesia had a large number of medium-size and small parties, but no truly large ones, with no party winning more than 20 percent of the national vote in the legislative election that year.

A third shift occurred in the overall composition of the party system, with a decline of the vote share of parties based on resilient social identities, and the growth of catchall parties that function as patronage machines and are built around prominent individuals and networks. Unlike in many countries, since the 1960s, socioeconomic and class-based cleavages have played little role in structuring the Indonesian party system. Instead, at the outset of the democratic transition, most Indonesians voted for parties that tried to appeal to distinctive identity groups. These were, most obviously, the various Islamic parties, but also the PDI-P, which appealed strongly to non-Muslim minorities and to nominal, or non-devout, Muslims and could be relied on to promote consistently "pluralist" positions (Mietzner 2013b). In Indonesia's first post-Suharto legislative election in 1999, parties that mobilized socioreligious, ethnic, or similar identity-based appeals won about 75 percent of the total vote. By 2014, their total vote share had declined to 50 percent.

Another group of parties were "catchall" parties that tried to cut across socio-religious divides and relied more on patronage and personalized appeals, rather than identity loyalties. The lead example here is Golkar, which had been the electoral manifestation of the bureaucracy under the New Order regime. In the post-Suharto period, Golkar was able to reinvent itself as Indonesia's quintessential patronage machine, and it continued to draw primarily on bureaucratic and business networks, mobilizing voters through village chiefs and other community-level power brokers, though also drawing on religious and other networks whenever it could (Tomsa 2008). However, Golkar was not able to stave off challengers, despite the fact that the bureaucratic elite, as we will see in later chapters, continued to be a critically important source of politicians. The formal ban on involvement by bureaucrats in election campaigns was often ignored in practice, but it did mean that Golkar now lost its ability to monopolize access to the civil service and its resources, or to constrain the choices of local elites who wanted to compete for elected office. As Tomsa (2014, 265) explains, "As competitive elections became the norm in post-Suharto Indonesia, more and more locally powerful officeholders who had acted as important vote getters for Golkar in the past abandoned the former regime party and joined smaller parties." When local elites found themselves unable to secure a place on a Golkar ticket, they simply turned to the alternatives. The limited electoral success of Golkar in post-Suharto elections thus did not point to declining political influence of former bureaucrats and similar local elites; it simply indicated that the party, as capacious as it was, was no longer able to fully accommodate the political ambitions of these groups.

As a consequence of this dynamic, Golkar was joined by a series of new parties that tried to mimic its catchall approach, and which were led by similar mixes of former bureaucrats, military men, businesspeople, and other elites. In particular, from 2004, a growing share of the vote was taken by "presidentialist" parties—parties that were built to further the presidential ambitions of a single man. Beginning this trend was Partai Demokrat, the vehicle of President Susilo Bambang Yudhoyono, followed by Hanura (led by the retired general Wiranto), Gerindra (Prabowo Subianto, another former general), and NasDem (Surya Paloh, a business tycoon). These parties also tried to design cross-cutting appeals, symbolized by the Demokrat Party's designation of itself as "nationalist-religious" (Honna 2012). The combined vote share of the presidentialist parties increased from 9 percent in the 2004 legislative election to 34 percent in 2014. All four of these parties were led by men who were either former Golkar members or who hailed from social groups (such as the military) associated with Golkar. Viewed another way, therefore, almost half the vote in 2014 was won by Golkar and its successor parties. Given that these four parties were strongly reliant on patronage delivery and personalist appeals, their growing prominence was itself a sign of the changing shape of Indonesia's party system, and of the growing importance of patronage distribution in electoral politics.

Such trends have prompted debate among observers of Indonesia's politics. The political scientist Andreas Ufen identified a process of "Philippinization," arguing that Indonesian parties were coming to resemble the notoriously weak parties of the country's Southeast Asian neighbor, which are "characterised by a lack of meaningful platforms, by the high frequency of party-switching, short-term coalition-building, factionalism as well as numerous dissolutions and re-emergences" (Ufen 2006, 16). Mietzner (2013b) has countered by pointing out that, compared to the party systems of many third-wave democracies, including the Philippines, Indonesia's is relatively robust. He points out that the party system is not especially fragmented, nor is the level of electoral volatility unusually high. He also argues that many parties remain socially rooted, being "closely intertwined with mass organizations and movements" (Mietzner 2013b, 112) and that parties "remain the single most important entry point for citizens to engage in formal politics" (Mietzner 2013b, 198).

We accept Mietzner's judgments, though we would emphasize that the parties have been propped up largely by certain features of Indonesia's institutional design. Most obviously, only party nominees can stand for legislative office. As already noted, increasingly onerous national registration requirements for parties seeking to contest legislative elections constitute a significant barrier to entry, making it impossible for cliques of local politicians to establish their own micro-parties, as often happens in the Philippines. In Indonesia, elected legislators are also prohibited from switching parties while still holding their parliamentary seats, meaning legislators cannot desert their parties in favor of that of a newly elected president, another common pattern in the Philippines (instead, in Indonesia the pattern is that parties will move en masse to support a new president, hoping to join the government and access patronage resources that way). Parliamentary threshold rules have further checked the proliferation of small parties. In local government-head elections (*pilkada*), meanwhile, though the rules were changed from 2008 to allow independent candidates, the registration requirements for these candidates are onerous, such that a majority—such as Arief at the start of this chapter—prefer to seek party endorsement. In other words, even if personalization and patronage have been pushing Indonesian parties in the direction of a Philippinized system, aspects of Indonesia's institutional design have slowed—but not halted—this movement. And, as we shall see in a moment, in the electoral arena where institutions are least protective of parties—executive-government-head elections—their influence has declined most rapidly.

A more important point is that the relative robustness in terms of formal party system institutionalization *coexists* with the freewheeling clientelist politics and largely nonparty organization of election campaigns that are our focus in this book. Above all, parties play an important role as gatekeepers in electoral competition, largely determining who can compete for elective office. They thus remain an important entry point for politicians seeking to participate in representative institutions. There is great variation, however, in the extent to which the parties use their gatekeeper role to select candidates who will promote the party's ideology, adhere to its socioreligious identity, and promote party goals if elected. The Islamic parties tend to select more pious candidates; PDI-P will rarely nominate a person who would not defend socioreligious pluralism. But for many of the parties, even such goals are secondary, and what really counts is a potential candidate's financial resources, mobilizational power, and electability. Moreover, once this gatekeeping role is discharged, much electoral politics takes place informally, through personal and ad hoc networks rather than through formal party structures. In other words, the formal edifice of a reasonably robust party system survives, but it is to a large degree a façade, behind which much of the day-to-day business of politics is carried out informally.

Executive-Government Elections

In the years following the collapse of the Suharto regime, the nature of patronage politics in Indonesia changed dramatically. This change can be characterized as a shift from a closed system of patronage, in which patronage circulated primarily among unelected officials and allied economic actors, to a semi-open one in which elected politicians began to participate as central players, and finally to a fully open system of patronage in which ordinary voters became a primary target of patronage politics. Driving this shift was, first, democratization and decentralization and, later, the replacement of indirect with direct elections of government leaders. This rise of direct democracy occurred in two arenas: elections of executive government heads, discussed in this section, and legislative elections, which we discuss later. The resulting opening of Indonesia's political system, and the growing role of voters, did not destroy the influence of local oligarchs and other individuals who were already integrated into local circuits of bureaucratic and economic power, even if this was what some of the supporters of direct democracy had hoped for. But the opening of the system did mean that political leaders now needed to build clientelist networks that reached down into the community, drawing in grassroots brokers and ordinary voters.

Let us begin our analysis of these shifts by looking at how Indonesian presidents are appointed. The New Order regime used an indirect system to appoint the president. The People's Consultative Assembly (MPR, a body in which the majority of members were appointed, but which also included a substantial cohort of elected members of the DPR) "elected" the president every five years. These elections were tightly scripted, leaving no doubt that the outcome would always be Suharto's reappointment. After the transition to democracy, the system of indirect elections was retained but democratized: in 1999, the MPR elected Abdurrahman Wahid through a process marked by extensive "cow trading" (*dagang sapi*) of votes for promises of cabinet positions and other posts.

The introduction of a new system of direct presidential elections by popular vote in 2004 changed the role of parties in selecting Indonesia's presidents. To be sure, candidates still had to be nominated by parties or coalitions of parties that had won a certain percentage of the national vote in the preceding legislative election (5 percent in 2004, rising to 25 percent by 2014) or held a minimum proportion of seats in the DPR (3 percent in 2004, 20 percent in 2014), meaning that the cow trading largely shifted to the period when nominating coalitions were being formed. But the election of both Susilo Bambang Yudhoyono in 2004 and Joko Widodo in 2014 showed that politicians who lacked significant party bases could appeal over the heads of the parties directly to the people. Opinion polls showed that both men enjoyed great popularity, prompting parties to support them in the hope of later being rewarded with cabinet posts. Though the parties that nominated them played a role in campaigning, these candidates also relied on personal campaign teams that went by various names—success teams (*tim sukses*), volunteers (*relawan*), and so on. Television advertising and candidate appeal, rather than party machines, were also critical to both their campaigns.

Presidential elections have not been a major factor driving the massification of patronage politics, though they have helped to reduce the centrality of parties in Indonesia's electoral landscape. The massive scale of Indonesian presidential elections—plus the fact that they take place after, rather than coinciding with, parliamentary elections—has limited the reach of personalized patronage politics in them. Thus, by 2014, though individualized vote buying—payments of cash to individual voters—was widespread in legislative contests, it was rare in the presidential election. The vast size of Indonesia's population, which forms a single constituency in presidential elections, makes it prohibitively expensive and logistically difficult to organize vote buying on this scale. Instead, the organizers of presidential campaigns make great efforts to draw local government heads, politicians, and other notables into their ad hoc campaign teams, and can provide them with material benefits and promises of future advantage when doing so (see Aspinall 2015, 21–24, on the efforts of Prabowo Subianto in 2014 in this regard). Informal networking is thus important, but local power brokers generally lack strong incentives to deliver patronage to voters during presidential elections.

More important than the shift to direct presidential elections for our purposes was the parallel change at the subnational level. Indonesia's provinces and districts (rural *kabupaten* and urban *kota*) are headed by local officials—governors and deputy governors in the provinces, *bupati* and their deputies in the *kabupaten*, and mayors (*walikota*) and deputies in the urban municipalities. Indonesia's decentralization process gave local governments more budgets and responsibilities and so made these posts much more politically powerful and materially endowed than previously (Aspinall and Fealy 2003; Schulte Nordholt and van Klinken 2007). Consequently, contests to fill them became a major new focus of political contestation.

The first wave of post-Suharto reform gave local legislatures (DPRDs) full authority to choose these local government heads by way of a simple majority vote of members. The ensuing period of indirect elections of local government heads (1999–2004) provided the first sign to many reformers that something was going seriously wrong with Indonesia's electoral democracy, given the obvious role played by vote buying in these elections. Because of Indonesia's Proportional Representation (PR) system, single parties rarely held a majority of the seats in a legislature, so that candidates had to win support from DPRD members from various parties in order to be elected. The rallying of such support typically involved various forms of cow trading. What shocked many Indonesians, however, was that many of these DPRD elections involved trading not merely of political favors, but also of a sort that might be found in a real cattle market, with the currency being cash payments. Regional government heads had no cabinet posts to distribute (government departments, or bureaus, are headed by career bureaucrats, not politicians, at the provincial and district levels). As a result, party bosses and legislators who at the national level looked for cabinet seats in exchange for their support, at the regional level often wanted cash. The Indonesian media detailed dozens of cases of open vote buying in the legislatures. In fact, so blatant was the practice that in some cases candidates who had not received the number of votes they expected tried to sue the recipients of their bribes for failing to make good on their promises. These elections frequently split apart parliamentary party blocs (*fraksi*, is the Indonesian term), with members of one party deserting the candidate nominated by that party to support a rival nominee. Because the elections were by secret ballot, it was usually impossible to be sure who had voted for the winning candidate, and *fraksi* often splintered amid bitter accusations and counteraccusations of betrayal and treachery. Court cases, physical clashes, and demonstrations proliferated. All in all, rather than strengthening the parties, this form of parliamentary democracy at the regional level undermined party cohesion.

In response to such problems, and to further the democratization process, in 2005 Indonesia introduced the new system of *pilkada* or direct elections. In this system, local government heads were elected by popular votes by the populations of the regions concerned. As with presidential elections, parties still played the gatekeeping role: at first, all candidates were nominated by parties or coalitions of parties that held a certain percentage of the seats in the relevant local parliament (15 percent in 2005, rising to 20 percent in 2015) or had won a certain percentage of the popular vote in the preceding legislative election (15 percent rising to 25 percent). In 2007, the Constitutional Court ruled that independent candidates should also be allowed to run. While registration requirements to do so are demanding, by 2015 about one-sixth of candidates were independents. Importantly, the rules required candidates to run in pairs (a governor plus a deputy governor, and so on), a requirement that encouraged cross-party and cross-identity coalition building.

The introduction of direct local elections had dramatic effects. First, it meant that parties now needed to choose candidates who were popular with the electorate. Candidates could not simply buy their way to power by making payments to a few dozen legislators. Instead, they had to win the support of at least a plurality of the electorate (the rules stated that candidate pairs would avoid a runoff if one of them won at least 25 percent of the vote, a figure that was later raised to 30 percent). This shift had numerous effects. For example, it drove a dramatic growth of the public opinion polling industry (Mietzner 2009; Qodari 2010). Though money remained important, popularity with voters now became critical. As a result, as Mietzner (2006, 2010) has argued, the early round of *pilkada* delivered defeats for incumbents who were cashed up but who had reputations for excessive corruption or poor performance (he found that about 40 percent of incumbents were defeated: Mietzner 2010, 183). A new populist style emerged among regional leaders, with candidates striving to develop a popular touch—expressed through ubiquitous terms such as *merakyat* (being close to the people) and practices such as *blusukan* (meet-the-people-style visits to residential areas, marketplaces, and similar locations—a term first popularized by Jokowi).

A second effect was to accelerate the marginalization of parties. Local party leaders who held elected positions in the legislature were often poorly prepared to bid for executive power. The local legislatures were usually divided between several evenly matched *fraksi*, so that it was rare that a party politician would develop a sufficiently strong public record to compete convincingly in a local executive race. At the same time, though the DPRDs helped draw up local government budgets, and exercised oversight functions, their leaders lacked the control over the government apparatus and budget that senior bureaucrats possessed. As a result, the people who stood and won in these elections were not party politicians. In one first-cut analysis of fifty early polls, Mietzner (2006) found that 36 percent of candidates were career bureaucrats, 28 percent entrepreneurs, and 8 percent retired police and military officers; only 22 percent were party officials. As we discuss more extensively in chapter 9, in 2015 these numbers were largely comparable, with 27 percent of the candidates being bureaucrats and 25 percent businesspeople. In 2015, a negligible percentage—4 out of 696 candidates—presented themselves to the election committee only as party officials.

The adoption of direct elections did not end the auctioning of office by parties. Under the preceding system, party *legislators* had sold their votes to candidates; the new rules empowered party *boards* to sell nominations. Many party boards simply auctioned their nominations to the highest bidders, as we shall discuss in a moment. This process often generated conflicts between district, provincial, and national branches as these bodies endorsed, and took payments from, rival candidates. Aspiring candidates who tried to gain a party's support in a district race, if they were unsuccessful at that level, could lobby to have the decision overturned, and gain endorsement by a higher body. To be sure, there was some variation between the parties, with, for example, the PDI-P tending to favor party cadres as nominees more than some other parties. Overall, however, though parties played a gatekeeper role, this role was often simply akin to taking a fee at a tollgate, rather than exercising scrutiny over candidates for their ideological affinity or loyalty to the party.

A third major effect was to encourage candidates to rely on personal networks when it came to electioneering. Most contestants for local executive office had long-established links with the bureaucracy and other networks in their locales, rather than deep relationships with parties. For their part, parties often viewed these candidates as sources of funds, rather than wanting to invest time or effort into their elections. As a result, party structures often played an increasingly marginal role in organizing *pilkada* campaigns (Buehler 2009a; Mietzner 2010, 177–178; Tomsa 2009). Personal networks—the very networks that had been central to the New Order's informal power relations—came to the fore. In one early study from South Sulawesi, for example, Buehler and Tan (2007, 58) pointed to "efforts of power brokers—such as religious figures, large landholders, and bureaucrats—who could lobby in the subdistricts and who often distributed goods to the people." We discuss the use of such networks for electoral purposes in the next chapters.

Fourth, and closely related, the introduction of *pilkada* strengthened the role of vote buying and other forms of patronage politics in electoral politics or, more precisely, shifted its locus from inside formal institutions, notably parliaments, to relations between candidates and voters. Vote buying was, in other words, democratized. To be sure, *pilkada* also produced something of a shift toward programmatic delivery. Voters were now able to scrutinize and cast judgment on incumbents on the basis of policy, and there is evidence that local leaders began to introduce certain welfare policies—notably in the field of health—in response (Aspinall 2014a). But incumbents were even more likely to win reelection on the basis of pork-barrel spending in the form of local infrastructure and other development projects (Aspinall and As'ad 2015), and the new format also encouraged club goods, gift giving, and straight-out vote buying. There was a learning process involved here, however, and during our research in the lead-up to legislative elections of 2014, many local brokers and candidates recalled the most recent *pilkada* in their province or district—in other words, the second such election after the introduction of direct polls in 2005—as marking the beginning of mass-scale retail vote buying in their locale.

Not surprisingly, these shifts also dramatically increased the cost of campaigning. Paying for nomination fees, polling and political consultants, brokers, and advertising—to say nothing of vote buying—was costly (Mietzner 2007). It was generally only a few of the richest people in any district or province who were able to fund such campaigns personally, or raise enough cash through business networks and connections. These individuals tended to be bureaucrats or businesspeople who thrived in sectors dependent on state licenses and largesse, such as contracting or mining. As we discuss in chapter 9, a black economy of campaign financing thus grew in concert with *pilkada*, drawing on the corruption, kickbacks, and networking that had always been part of the system of the more elite-oriented patronage established during the New Order.

Negotiating Candidacy in the City of Tangerang

To illustrate these dynamics in action, let us shift gears and return to the nomination process for the mayoral elections in Tangerang. The process was chaotic—involving a scheming outgoing mayor, double-crossing political parties, and uncompromising candidates—but in ways that typify the complex negotiations between parties and candidates that occur in local direct elections.

One reason why the nomination process in Tangerang dragged on until the last week before the nomination deadline was that most aspiring candidates had close personal relations with the outgoing mayor, Wahidin Halim. Not only Wahidin's younger brother (Abdul Syukur) and vice-mayor (Arief) but also his regional secretary and his former success team head were in the running to replace him. None of them wanted be seen as going against Wahidin's wishes. For example, Arief wanted to free himself from Wahidin's influence but could not openly show this: both etiquette and strategy dictated that he should remain on a good footing with the popular and powerful outgoing mayor. So when Wahidin demanded that Arief team up with Abdul Syukur, Arief knew he could not openly reject this demand. Instead, he tried to stall the negotiations. As a result, nobody dared to make a move until the last week. Meanwhile, Wahidin did not want to endorse anybody until Arief and Abdul had agreed to join forces; Arief stalled the negotiations with Abdul; and the leaders of both Golkar and Demokrat did not declare support for either candidate out of calculated respect for Wahidin. Both Arief and Abdul, meanwhile, regularly traveled to Jakarta to meet national leaders of parties to lobby them for their support.

One critical factor here was finances. Parties regularly get paid *mahar politik*, or "political dowry," in exchange for nominating a candidate pair. In the Tangerang election, smaller parties like PKB, Gerindra, and Hanura were especially keen to keep negotiating with alternative candidates in order to see who was willing to pay the most. As one candidate lamented, "I talked to [the party leaders] for two hours, I exhausted myself talking about my vision and my mission. But in the end, they only asked me about how much money I was willing to pay." In Tangerang, political parties generally demanded 1 billion rupiah (about $88,000) per seat that the party controlled in the local parliament. Candidates in regional Indonesia commonly complain about such extortion from parties; indeed, negotiations over candidacy often founder when parties ask for too much, or when local and national boards cannot decide on how to divide the dowry.

However, money is not the only factor that drives such negotiations. In Tangerang, as elsewhere, a second critical element was calculations about which candidate had the best chance of winning. Parties face strong incentives to pick a winner: an electoral victory can mean privileged access to state resources and control over the local state bureaucracy, which yields increased income for the party and its local leaders, and can also provide access to local projects, too, for national party officials or their cronies. In Tangerang, with both parliamentary and presidential elections due in the coming year, support from the mayor could also strengthen parties' electoral prospects. As a result, candidates can use promises of future support to lower the price they have to pay for a party nomination. This helps explain the intense focus of parties and candidates on survey results: such promises are meaningful only if an electoral victory is likely. Positive survey data not only reassure parties; they can help candidates bargain down the price they pay for nomination.

At the same time, party leaders pay close attention to the choices being made by other parties, because those choices affect the benefits they can gain from a nomination deal. The prospective benefits that a party may gain from supporting a victorious candidate are partly dependent on whether the party is a major or a minor member of the coalition supporting that candidate. Each party—or, rather, its local leaders—will benefit less from supporting a likely winner in a broad coalition with many supporting parties. It is not only that parties will not be able to demand much money from a candidate who would easily gain enough party support elsewhere. Being a junior member in a big coalition is also unlikely to help the party and its members much in gaining access to state resources: elected politicians will have many other requests to entertain.

The calculations are often complex. On the one hand, party leaders thinking about the long term will be averse to supporting a candidate with poor prospects of victory. Yet, given the fact that local government heads cannot reward supporting parties with cabinet seats (as the president can at the national level), the incentives for political parties to support the winner are limited. A candidate with poor prospects might offer enough of an immediate monetary payoff such that being the leading party in a losing coalition might outweigh the benefits of joining an outsize winning coalition. Overall, such considerations stimulate the proliferation of candidates in elections for district head and governor. In the end the Tangerang elections had five candidate pairs contending, with at least two of them having poor prospects.

Table 4.2 illustrates that, comparatively speaking, this large number of contenders was somewhat unusual. In the 260 district-head elections held in 2015, on average just over three candidate pairs contested, with a sizable share of independent candidates. The table also shows that the party coalitions supporting candidates were generally quite big, as candidates had, on average, more than three parties supporting them. The number of contestants was kept low by the high threshold, because in 2015 candidates needed to have the support of parties holding 20 percent of the seats in local parliaments, up from 15 percent previously. The need to meet this threshold constituted another reason why local party leaders pay close attention to the strategies of other parties: they need to avoid committing to supporting a candidate who fails to put such a coalition together. That was a major challenge facing Arief: while Gerindra and PKB were willing

TABLE 4.2 Party coalitions in 2015 district-head elections

NO. OF DISTRICTS	AVERAGE CANDIDATE PAIRS PER DISTRICT	NO. INDEPENDENT PAIRS	AV. COALITION SIZE (NO. PARTIES)*	AV. SIZE SUPPORTING PARTY COALITIONS (SHARE OF DPRD SEATS)
260	3.2	147 (17.7%)	3.05	31%**

*Excluding independents

**n = 277 candidates

to support him, they did not want to sign up before any other party had done so. After weeks of stalemate, "Rahmat," a senior member of Arief's team, used a trick to prevent a stalemate: "In politics you sometimes have to lie a little, but it is for the glory of God. When I was meeting with Gerindra, I showed them the picture of me and Arief together with Muhaimin Iskandar and Ma'ruf Amin [the general head and the head of the advisory council of PKB]. I told them, 'These are the big leaders. What more do you need?' So they thought PKB supported us [and issued a letter to that effect]. Then I took the letter from Gerindra to PKB to get their support. . . . Later we laughed about it" (interview, March 13, 2014).

A third element in these negotiations was complex interactions between local and central leaders of the parties. Both Gerindra and Hanura leaders basically double-crossed the candidates: after local chapters received money from a candidate in exchange for promises of support, the central leadership boards of both parties decided to support a different candidate. Arief had almost completed the deal with the local chapter of PDI-P when Jakarta decided otherwise. The interests of local and national party leaders often differ: local leaders and cadres generally prefer someone they know and have access to; national party leaders think about wider considerations. In most parties the central leadership claims the privilege of deciding on supporting a candidate, and electoral rules eventually required this—hence the frequent trips of candidates to Jakarta. But local party leaders can do much to control the decision making. Going against the wishes of the local cadres—as in the case of PDI-P—risks weakening the subsequent election campaign and can cause local leaders to defect to another party. On the other hand, Jakarta's influence over appointments can sometimes lead to the selection of candidates from outside the party's local establishment, and national boards sometimes veto unpopular local party grandees in favor of outsider candidates whose popularity has been proven by opinion polls.

With the support of Gerindra and PKB now secured, Arief still needed the support of Tangerang's biggest party, Partai Demokrat. The obstacle was that the head of the party, Wahidin Halim, had realized that Arief did not want to partner with his younger brother Abdul Syukur. He now tried to prevent his party endorsing Arief. When Arief traveled to Jakarta to try to persuade the party's central leadership board to support him, Wahidin went the next day to advise against it. Yet the board looked at the poll results and, to break the deadlock, formed a selection committee that excluded Wahidin. This decision emboldened Arief's team, but it took until the final morning of nomination, after seemingly endless negotiations, to reach an agreement. As Rahmat explained, "After the fax came in [from Jakarta] at eight in the morning, I met with the DPC [district party board] at a coffee stall on a street corner. There they finally signed." The negotiations were lengthy not only because of Wahidin's obstruction, but also because of the amount of money involved: the party had initially asked a price of 500 million rupiah per seat it held in the local legislature, totaling 6.5 billion rupiah (about $575,000) for thirteen seats. Arief's campaign team managed to negotiate this down to 2 billion. The negotiators used two bargaining chips. They promised that Arief would build the party a new office in the town if he was elected, and appealed to their sense of party loyalty. As one of the negotiators later related, "I asked them to think realistically: 'You are not just selling your seats, you have to think of your party cadres. If you ask for so much money from your own cadres, people will not be willing expend any effort for the party.'"

The dramatic nomination process in Tangerang illustrates the calculated and negotiated nature of relationships between political parties and candidates. In this case the relationship was actually quite close: Arief was aligned with the Partai Demokrat from the start, even though his nomination created an eruption of conflict within the party. Very often, candidates are not formally aligned with any party, and they are thus quite free to shop around for support. Yet even for a candidate with relatively close bonds, party support depends on complex negotiations and extensive exchanges of favors, in which money plays an important part. An important effect of these monetary transactions is that elected district heads and governors often do not feel beholden to the parties that nominate them, believing they have already paid for their support. Ultimately, this weakens the access of political parties to patronage goods and, as a result, further undermines their mobilizational capacity.

Legislative Elections

Let us now turn to a sphere where, in theory, the bond between party and candidate is much stronger. Indonesia's legislative elections (always run concurrently at national, provincial, and district levels) in some ways entrench the role of the parties, by mandating that only members of registered parties can run. Moreover, party registration requirements have become increasingly onerous in the years since the fall of Suharto. And yet, personalized rather than party-centered campaigning has become more important in legislative elections, too, as a result of changes in electoral rules that have moved Indonesia toward a candidate-centered system. To illustrate the candidate-centered nature of legislative elections, let us take an example from Kupang, the capital of East Nusa Tenggara Province.

Partly in order to further his business interests, Vincent (not his real name) decided in 2013 he wanted to become a member of the local city council, the DPRD. He was a local contractor, which gave him plenty of incentives to involve himself in politics. The DPRD determines the city budget, in consultation with the mayor and the government agencies working under him. As a result, legislators are often able to collude with government officials in order to direct contracts toward relatives or cronies.

Vincent was not fussy about which party he would run for. For help, he turned to a patron from a local association of police families. This man was big in the contracting world and was connected to the Gerindra party. He put Vincent in touch with the party's provincial chairperson and gubernatorial candidate, Esthon Foenay. Vincent prepared all the necessary documents, and as a sign of goodwill he supplied three of his trucks to take supporters to an election rally attended by the party's national leader, Prabowo Subianto. But then, at the ceremony where Gerindra announced its party list—a day before the list was to be submitted to the election commission—party leaders told Vincent that there was no spot for him. He was not sure why he had lost the place he had been promised; he guessed it was because all the places were given to "people who were close by blood or marriage to the party bosses" (confidential interview, September 10, 2013).

Vincent did not give up. Though other parties had already prepared their party lists, and only twenty-four hours remained to change them, he began to call on other contacts. He needed to find, as he put it, "someone who already had a door" but did not "have masses." And he was willing to pay up to 30 million rupiah ($2,700) for such a position. Someone on the Partai Demokrat list fit the bill: this man had been the head of a church development committee and had not been able to account for all the funds that had passed through his hands. So he was unpopular in his local community, and party leaders now saw him as a liability. Vincent struck a deal with the party branch chair to take this man's place, and paid 20 million rupiah on the spot. Some of the money would go to the candidate whose place Vincent was taking; Vincent assumed most of the rest would go to the party chair, but he did not know for sure.

In any case, Vincent now had his "door" and was ready to roll out his strategy. For this, he did not need the party at all: he had assessed that his extended kin group was big enough in his electoral constituency to elect two DPRD members, if they voted solidly for a relative. Leading family members had already decided they needed someone to represent their interests in the council. So his strategy was based on recruiting influential kinsmen into his campaign team, or "family team," as he called it, holding regular family gatherings to let more distant relatives know that he was standing and, of course, distributing cash and other benefits to team members.

In some ways, Vincent's strategizing echoes Arief's experiences: like Arief, Vincent was very pragmatic about choosing a political party, and his relationship to the party that eventually nominated him was even more ad hoc and negotiated.

Yet Vincent's story represents an even more dramatic example of electoral system change. As indicated in the last chapter, Indonesia's first post-Suharto election was strongly party centered. Party cadres festooned the streets with party colors, symbols, and flags. Parties organized large rallies and street parades. This enthusiasm was partly a result of the democratic transition itself, but it was also a product of the closed-list electoral system inherited from the New Order. Under this system, voters in multi-member districts marked their ballots by punching a hole through the symbol of the party of their choice. Parties won a number of seats that matched the proportion of the popular vote they attained in that district. Individual candidates were allocated seats according to their place on the party list of candidates that had been prepared for that constituency prior to the election. If the party won one seat, the person at the top of the list won the seat; if the party won two seats, the first two got the seats, and so on. Under this system, the interests of candidates and party members were aligned: the higher the party vote, the greater the chances candidates lower down the list had of being elected. The system encouraged campaigners to promote parties, and voters to identify with them. Patronage was important, but it tended to be focused inside the parties: for example, it became critical for ambitious politicians to seize party branch leadership positions, because from these positions they could determine candidate lists. To do this, party officials had to build links with clients among the party membership and lower-level leaders, but it also helped to curry favor with more senior officials. It also became a common practice for party officials to take bribes in exchange for awarding top positions on party lists.

This electoral system changed piecemeal over following years, largely in response to public criticisms of the parties and their corruption. The second post-Suharto election in 2004 used a semi-open list: voters could now vote *either* for the party of their choice or for one of the individual candidates nominated by that party in their electoral district. There was a catch, however: to be elected on the strength of their individual vote, candidates had to win a proportion of the vote equivalent to or greater than the entire quota necessary to elect one representative in that electoral district (for example, 10 percent of the votes in a district with ten members). Where this figure was not reached, the party list determined who was elected. In the end, only two candidates passed this very high bar and were elected to the DPR in this way. In the lead-up to the 2009 election, parliament changed the rules again: now a candidate only needed to win individual votes amounting to 30 percent, rather than 100 percent, of a seat quota in order to trump the list order. This was itself a significant change, but a decision by the Constitutional Court before the 2009 election changed the system again, eliminating altogether the requirement for candidates to win part of a quota. Now, if a party achieved a large enough overall vote—consisting of the votes of people who voted for either the party symbol or the party's individual candidates—to meet the quota and have one or more of its candidates elected in a district, then it would be the candidate(s) with the largest individual vote who would take the seat(s).

As could be readily predicted from the experiences of other countries (Hicken 2009), the open-list system dramatically changed the nature of electioneering. It created a strong incentive for individual candidates to devote their resources to campaigning for themselves rather than for their party. Indeed, because candidates could use past results to predict in advance the number of seats their party was likely to win in a particular constituency (this was often just one, and rarely more than two or three seats), candidates typically viewed their chief rivals as being their own party colleagues. This changed incentive structure was reflected almost immediately on the streets of Indonesia during the 2009 election campaign: suddenly, in the place of party placards and flags, campaign workers began to erect posters and billboards bearing the images of individual candidates and extolling their virtues. By the time of the 2014 legislative election, candidates had had time to prepare their strategies. Now, candidates invested their efforts and funds in success teams outside party structures, and "ground war" campaigns focused on building community-level connections. We explore this pattern of organization in the next chapter, noting that this style of campaigning encouraged vote buying and other forms of patronage distribution as candidates tried to differentiate themselves from competitors and lock in voters' support. Indeed, by the time of the 2014 legislative election, candidates, voters, and observers alike frequently bemoaned that "money politics" was out of control.

Once again, all of this does not mean that parties no longer mattered. Parties retained an important gatekeeping role: recall that only candidates nominated by registered political parties could stand for legislative seats. At the minimum, this meant that individuals who wanted to run for office had to approach and persuade a party to nominate them, even if this took place through a straight-out economic transaction, as with Vincent. In fact, on a typical party list in most locations, a significant number (often around a third) of candidates would be party officials such as chairs or secretaries of local branches. Indeed, getting control of a local party branch was still a typical pathway for an ambitious politician who wanted to move into a local legislature. How deep such individuals' associations were with the party varied greatly, however. Some parties, such as PKS and PDI-P, had relatively resilient party structures; gaining a leadership position in such a party required demonstrating ideological affinity with it and serving some sort of apprenticeship. Most parties were less demanding; the presidentialist parties in particular grew simply by recruiting local notables (often disgruntled members of other parties) to take over their local party organs and bring their own clienteles with them. Party structures had little real meaning independent of the individuals who led them.

Most parties also gave a proportion of the positions on their candidate lists to nonparty community leaders or *tokoh masyarakat*—influential local business-people, former bureaucrats, religious leaders, and the like. Sometimes, as with Vincent, party officials simply sold off places on their lists for cash. But party officials who were themselves standing as candidates also had an incentive to recruit community leaders as "vote getters"—a popular individual might boost the total party vote in the constituency and thus increase its chances of winning seats. This was a risky calculus, however: include too few locally influential candidates on your list and the party might not win enough votes to win a seat; include one or two who enjoyed great personal popularity, or who had the riches to organize a formidable personal campaign, and they could gain a higher number of personal votes and take the party's quota of seats in the district, denying that prize to the party officials who invited them to stand.

As well as playing this gatekeeping role, parties still played a role in campaigning. To be sure, most candidates knew that they could no longer rely on the party to run their campaigns, simply because in every electoral district each party fielded several candidates (between three and ten in national seats and three and twelve in districts and provinces), who were effectively competing against each other. As a result, most candidates relied first and foremost on their personal success teams. But what happened with local party cadres, branch and subbranch structures in such circumstances? Two patterns predominated. First, and most commonly, one or two candidates who occupied important positions in the local party structure (typically, as chairs of local party branches) would dominate the party apparatus and use it for their own campaigning purposes. This pattern was facilitated by the fact that, very often, subbranch or village-level party functionaries owed debts and loyalties to such candidates. In such cases, competing candidates realized that they were outgunned inside the party and concentrated instead on building personal campaign teams outside it. Second, however, in some places the party machinery could become a site of intense competition between candidates, each of whom felt he or she had a claim on the loyalty and support of party members. This was particularly the case in locales where a party had a history of electoral strength. Thus, for example, one national PDI-P candidate in the city of Surabaya, traditionally a stronghold of that party, explained that "most of the competition is within the party," such that "you have to carefully read the dynamics at the local level, especially within the party. If you know that the subbranches or [leaders of the party] structure in a particular place are not happy with a particular candidate, then you can get access to that area" (Erma Susanti, interview, March 7, 2014). In these cases, personal success teams might predominate, but many of their members would be drawn from the party.

Though competition between candidates running for the same party was the common pattern, cooperation also occurred. For example, it was a consistent pattern that PKS—which prides itself as being a "cadre" party and is inspired by the Muslim Brotherhood—tended to run much more centralized and party-focused campaigns. Not only did their candidates rely more on party cadres for their grassroots campaigning; they also tended to be more disciplined about sharing resources and avoiding competition. For instance, PKS candidates frequently divided up an electoral district into different zones, which were then assigned to different candidates for their campaigning work (*zonafikasi* was the standard term for this practice).

Here and there during the 2014 election we encountered branches of other parties that successfully did the same, but in many cases party leaders who tried to introduce such policies failed. As a general rule, inter-candidate cooperation tended to be somewhat greater among parties based on long-standing *aliran* identities, such as PAN or PDI-P, than in Golkar and the presidentialist parties. But even in identity-based parties, cooperation between competing candidates was often difficult to achieve. For example, one provincial PDI-P candidate interviewed in Yogyakarta explained: "The zone system has totally broken down, and candidates are fighting against each other everywhere. Usually you go into a village where you have good connections with the branch or subbranch. But if you are blocked there, you can go in through different patrons, for example a businessman who got lots of benefits from the government and has been generous to the people. He's the patron. He can decide which candidate to facilitate" (confidential interview, March 27, 2014).

In the presidentialist and catchall parties like Golkar, Hanura, Gerindra, Nas-Dem, and Partai Demokrat, virtually everyone viewed them merely as vehicles for the expression and organization of their individual leaders' and candidates' interests. In such parties, cooperation between competing candidates in the same electoral district occurred only if a dominant local party leader believed his or her own prospects of reelection were so secure that party resources could be spared to boost other candidates and thus increase the party's representation in the legislature.

Though intra-party competition rather than cooperation was the order of the day, an exception was candidates running for seats in legislatures at different levels (district, province, and national). Because they were not directly competing against each other, candidates running at different levels commonly formed "tandem" arrangements, which involved establishment of joint teams, or at least coordination of teams and cost sharing for campaign events and vote buying. For higher-level candidates, this was a convenient way to access voters: rather than establishing separate teams in areas where lower-level candidates were already strong, they could simply piggyback on those teams. For lower-level candidates, joining a tandem typically meant gaining an injection of funds, campaign paraphernalia, and other resources from the richer, higher-level candidate. The lower candidates offered local knowledge and connections; the higher candidates had money, prestige, media access, and name recognition. Typically, such tandem deals were struck between candidates running for the same party, though they did occasionally cross party lines. Despite the strong incentive candidates had to cooperate in this way, tandems were often fraught, because they were vulnerable to free-riding. Candidates often accused their tandem partners of sharing expenses but then directing their own grassroots brokers to promote their own individual candidacies, without promoting their partners. They also feared that voters might receive a single payment or gift to encourage them to vote for three candidates, but choose to vote for only one, delivering the other two votes to rival parties whose candidates had also engaged in vote buying. Accordingly, many candidates were suspicious of tandems and preferred to organize campaigns they could control in their entirety.

Overall, the adoption of the open-party list system significantly eroded the coherence of the parties and their connections with voters. In our research during the election campaign of 2014, it was very common to encounter candidates, even from long-established parties such as PPP and PDI-P, bemoaning that parties had "lost their meaning" and explaining that what counted now were personal relations with campaign workers and voters, as well as "concrete" assistance in the form of cash, goods, and other gifts. Candidates often complained that they had to pay party workers for their support, and they speculated that the parties were becoming increasingly indistinguishable at the grass roots. Let us close with an observation made by a sitting member of the DPR representing PPP in Banten Province:

> Claims that some area is a base for party A or party B don't really make much sense now. The community is much more pragmatic. Moreover, parties A, B, C, and so on are not so different now at the level of ideas or programs. Including PPP. What Golkar, PPP, PDI-P, and the others sell . . . it's only the packaging that is different. . . . So I don't differentiate between base and non-base areas when I hand out assistance. It all depends on personal connections. For example, last night I helped [one community group by paying for] iron bars for their office. They asked me: "Sir, you are only on the yellow ballot, right?" [i.e., running for the national legislature]. I said yes. I didn't even try locking them

into supporting the others [i.e., the PPP candidates running at district and provincial levels]. They would have resisted. They told me [that at those levels] they would vote for candidates from other parties [who had given them different forms of assistance]. I had to compromise. It's all about the person now, not the party. (Interview, March 30, 2014)

Despite the gloom expressed by many party leaders, parties have not become irrelevant to Indonesian democracy. They are an enduring part of the electoral landscape, playing the key nominating role in electoral competition and still providing one of the organizations that candidates can use to run their election campaigns and reach down to voters. They also play an important role in organizing the alliances that constitute government at the center, something we have hardly touched on in this account. Moreover, at least some of the parties retain a social meaning and weight that extends beyond the influence of their individual leaders, retaining distinct social constituencies and targeting particular slices of the electorate. The attention that Indonesian parties have attracted in the scholarly literature is thus warranted.

However, changes in Indonesia's electoral system have tended to reduce the role of political parties to that of a gatekeeper, particularly in local executive government elections. While the legacy of Indonesia's authoritarian past had already weakened political parties—as discussed in the previous chapter—Indonesia's electoral reforms dealt political parties further blows. We have discussed three changes in Indonesia's post-Suharto electoral system—the open-list electoral system for legislative elections, direct elections for executive governments, and the requirement for candidates in such elections to build coalitions—which gave rise to more candidate-centered elections and weakened relations between candidates and their nominating political parties. These changes have undermined the party loyalty of candidates and elected politicians, in many cases limiting their interactions to pragmatic deal making at the start of a campaign. There are many exceptions to this overall pattern, but the general trend is unmistakable.

Furthermore, the electoral changes discussed in this chapter democratized clientelist practices. In 1999 and 2004, candidates were highly dependent on party bosses. Cash transactions between candidates and party leaders were critical to victory, in that key party functionaries received payments in order to secure candidates winnable positions. By 2014 the major locus of patronage was in relations between candidates and voters. This change was arguably a boost for democratic accountability, but it also led to a sharp increase in vote buying and the cost of election campaigns.

As we turn to discuss election campaigns and governance in the coming chapters, we highlight some of the effects of the candidate-party relationship we have sketched out here. In chapters 7 and 8 we discuss how the limited party loyalty of elected politicians affects patterns of governance, in particular the provision of public services. In contrast to our two comparator cases of India and Argentina, in Indonesia politicians face few incentives to involve political parties in the distribution of state benefits. Before coming to that, in the next two chapters we turn to election campaigns and describe the nonparty structures candidates use when organizing their campaigns and reaching down to voters. The weak mobilizational capacity of parties has generated an alternative form of campaign organization called *tim sukses*, as well as an intense politicization of social life, as politicians endeavor to incorporate a wide range of organizations and social networks into their election campaigns.

Part 2

NETWORKS AND RESOURCES

5

SUCCESS TEAMS AND VOTE BUYING

One week before the election, a crowd of about two hundred people assembled on the lawn in front of Arief Wismansyah's house. They were all dressed in the same blue-and-white shirts, which carried the names of Arief and Sachruddin (Arief's running mate) underneath the campaign slogan *Lanjutkan!* (Continue!). This group of people formed the core of Arief's grassroots campaign organization, or *tim sukses*. From all over Tangerang, the campaign's *korkel (koordinator kelurahan,* or precinct coordinators) and *korwe (koordinator* RW, or neighborhood coordinators) had come to receive their final instructions on how to prepare for election day. They had been working hard over the preceding weeks, organizing Arief's neighborhood visits, going from door to door to talk about Arief's achievements, and ferrying their neighbors to Arief's rallies and motorcades. Now, much of the focus was on the challenge of recruiting *saksi* or witnesses: on election day each of the thousand polling booths in the city needed to be staffed with poll observers to ensure a fair voting process.

When asked about their reasons for joining Arief's campaign team, none of those present mentioned a political party connection. Instead, it turned out that most coordinators had some personal or business connection with Arief: one had been the supplier of office stationery to Tangerang's government; another said that he was an old friend from school; a third was a contractor engaged in building roads in the municipality. Unusually, quite a few said they had been involved in setting up Tangerang's "garbage bank." This was a waste management program established by Arief that, as it turned out, was also a highly effective campaign tool. By allowing selected residents to collect and sell recycled waste, the garbage bank had become a source of livelihood for people throughout the city. Many of them decided to repay this favor by joining Arief's campaign team.

The first person to grab the microphone was Sharif, the *koordinator relawan*, or volunteer coordinator. He talked his audience through all the organizing that still needed to be done before election day. The campaign banners needed to be taken down, voter lists had to be checked, and the final few *saksi* recruited. These poll witnesses needed to receive campaign shirts, lunch boxes, and payments of 200,000 rupiah (about eighteen dollars) each—there was some cheering when Sharif mentioned this last point. Everyone was happy by the time Sharif handed the microphone over to Arief. To much acclaim, Arief began by mentioning the latest poll results. According to the campaign's own poll, Arief now stood at 48 percent, with Abdul Syukur, his closest rival, at only 20 percent: "But I am not yet happy, because Syukur has actually gone up 7 percent. We have to continue to work hard in the coming week. We have to continue to approach people, as well as controlling all the voting booths. I want you to report any person who engages in money politics to me. I will give two million rupiah [$180] for every person you catch. . . . We should not lose our base. We are ahead, but we should not now weaken our efforts." Arief ended his speech by promising a goat to coordinators of localities where his vote topped 70 percent of those cast. With that, the meeting ended and the coordinators proceeded to the tables of food that Arief's family had put out. Privately, Sharif said he was content with the meeting. "The solidarity of the team of volunteers is important. They are the mediators between the leader and the people. . . . These people are more important than the political parties. Parties only need people during elections, while the *tim sukses* can maintain contact. We are in constant interaction with the people" (interview, May 26, 2014).

The meeting in front of Arief's house is typical of the sort of coordinating meeting that takes place before every election in Indonesia, and it brought together a group of campaigners who—with a few distinctive twists, such as the garbage collectors—are likewise typical of Indonesian election campaigns. Going by a variety of names, but most commonly known as success teams (*tim sukses*), these organizations resemble the brokerage pyramids used by candidates in many countries. Though success teams vary somewhat in their structure and complexity, their basic function is to connect the candidate, through a chain of intermediary brokers, to individual voters. Success teams can be huge structures, drawing in thousands of brokers. They are always hierarchically structured and geographically arranged, with the best-organized teams running from an apex group of coordinators who assist the candidate, down to neighborhood-level brokers. Ultimately, the key role is played by these grassroots brokers at the base of the pyramid. They are the ones whose job it is to convince voters of the candidate's merits, and they are usually the persons who deliver cash or other gifts to them. These base-level brokers are important because, as many studies of clientelism suggest, appeals made by persons who already have intimate connections with, and influence over, voters tend to be more effective than appeals by strangers. But the intermediary brokers—such as the precinct and neighborhood brokers who assembled in front of Arief's house—are hardly less important because, as we shall see, they are the ones whose job it is to recruit lower down the chain. They ensure whether truly influential, reliable, and effective brokers are mobilized at the grass roots.

In discussing campaign organization in this chapter, we pay particular attention to the loyalty problems that characterize the relationships between politicians and their team members. In a patronage-saturated political environment such as that in Indonesia, where candidates offer material inducements to voters and campaign workers alike, and in which individuals can attain economic and social advantage by attaching themselves to a winner, people working for a campaign are subject to numerous temptations, chief among them being to steal some of the candidate's resources, defect to a wealthier or stronger candidate, or simply to shirk, and so gain the rewards of brokerage while expending little or no effort.

Loyalty problems are particularly severe in Indonesia because of the tenuousness of the links between brokers and politicians. When brokers are linked to politicians through a political party, they know that future rewards for their efforts depend on more than just one electoral victory. If their candidate loses an election, party workers can still use party channels and connections with other politicians from the same party to obtain benefits and access state resources. Such prospects give brokers in party-centered patronage democracies like India or Argentina strong incentives to remain loyal to party candidates, even if their immediate prospects are bad. In contrast, the freewheeling, personal nature of campaign networks in Indonesia does not offer similar prospects of future rewards to *tim sukses* members. If a candidate loses the election, his or her *tim sukses* members cannot expect to be rewarded at all. Their chances of future reward are tied to the success of a single politician. This all-or-nothing logic increases the likelihood of defection and misuse of campaign funds. As we shall see, though candidates worry incessantly about the loyalty of their brokers and devise mechanisms to monitor and discipline them, they lack formal leverage to enforce compliance.

The weakness of parties is also part of the context for the prominence in Indonesia of ad hoc, one-off distribution of private resources during election campaigns, especially in the form of vote buying. When strong parties feature in patronage democracies, they typically operate as a mechanism through which politicians can coordinate their access to and distribution of state resources, in the form of welfare benefits, subsidies, projects, and the like. In Indonesia, only a minority of candidates—incumbents occupying legislative and, especially, executive government posts—can directly access such state resources, with the result that most candidates instead have to provide private gifts to community groups and individual voters. We pay particular attention in this chapter to vote buying—the distribution of individual cash payments—describing in detail how the practice is organized, and showing how candidates turn to success teams to identify recipients and deliver the payments. Though this form of patronage politics is widespread, we also show it is unreliable, with candidates frequently receiving a relatively low return in votes. Even so, candidates feel they have little option but to participate, both given the expectations of voters, and out of fears of being outbid by rivals.

Success Teams as Alternatives to Political Parties

In many countries, clientelist exchange around election times is organized by party machines that are deeply embedded in local communities. Cadres know community members intimately and have a history of performing repeated services for them. Many studies describe how such party machines work in various parts of the world, illustrating the organic connections with voters they can forge at the grass roots. Take, for example, the following explanation of the pattern of Peronist party organization in Argentina:

> The Peronist organization consists of a vast collection of informal, neighborhood-based networks that operate out of a range of different entities, including local clubs, cooperatives, soup kitchens, and often activists' homes. These entities are self-organized and operated. They do not appear in party statutes, are rarely registered with local party authorities, and maintain near-total autonomy from the party bureaucracy. Nevertheless, they routinely participate in party activity, playing a critical mediating role between the party leadership and its base. They recruit new members, distribute patronage, channel local demands, and—most importantly—deliver votes in internal and general elections. (Levitsky 2003, 30)

This description illustrates a crucial dimension of political party organization, yet one that is largely absent in contemporary Indonesia: the use of an extensive network of local party organs to build close personal relationships with voters.

Studies of Argentina's democracy regularly describe how in poor districts party operatives are an important feature of neighborhood life, precisely because they have the capacity to help their neighbors solve everyday problems (e.g., Auyero 2001; Szwarcberg 2015). Through their soup kitchens, their distribution of state-funded welfare benefits, and their ability to mediate with local authorities, Peronist operatives succeed in making themselves nearly indispensable to many citizens. This almost daily grassroots work is, as Levitsky notes, very important during elections. On election day, the Peronist network is capable of turning these everyday favors into votes.

This pattern of machine politics, as we saw in chapter 3, was in the process of developing in Indonesia in the 1950s but was cut short by the trend toward authoritarianism thereafter; it began to revive after the fall of Suharto in 1998 but was then stymied by moves toward more candidate-centered electoral competition. In dramatic contrast to their Argentinian Peronist counterparts, Indonesian political parties today rarely possess extensive networks of grassroots problem solvers capable of delivering voters at election times.

To be sure, as we discussed in the preceding chapter, parties still differ in their mobilizational capacities; parties with closer links to cultural identity categories tend to be stronger. But the overall trend has been for candidates to increasingly look outside their party structures in order to organize their election campaigns. In the expert survey described in chapter 1, about 30 percent of respondents said that party workers played little or no role in the success teams organizing election campaigns in the most recent district-head, gubernatorial, presidential, and even DPRD elections held in their districts; about another 30 percent said that party members made up about half of campaign organizations. And when candidates do rely on parties, they are often disappointed by the lack of organizational and financial strength of local branches. Take, for example, remarks made by one provincial PDI-P candidate in Bantul near Yogyakarta about his interaction with the party's subbranches (*anak ranting*) during the 2014 election:

> They [the local party heads] really hold on to their subbranch as an important part of their identity. But they do not really have a significant [social] role. So they end up at most negotiating with the local community [rather than directing or leading it]. Then, in the end they also ask for money [from me]. Or they come and ask me to pay for party flags in their *kampung*. Then they ask for bamboo poles to put the flags on. Then they ask for money to put the flags up—money for food, or for cigarettes or whatever. Or there's a campaign event and they all ask for T-shirts. Then, after that, they all ask for gasoline money to go to the campaign rally. Meanwhile, the party doesn't have money. It is in

opposition. Yeah, it can steal money here and there, but it's not enough for the grass roots. So the difference with 1999, when everything was done in a spirit of participation and with sacrifice, is that back then there was still some enthusiasm from the grass roots. But now it's the candidate who pays for it all. Back then, people would pay themselves. Back then, people would build things for themselves—now, command posts, flags, T-shirts, all of that, the costs are borne by the candidates. (Interview, Bantul, March 27, 2014)

This is a colorful example, but it is all too easy to encounter similar comments from candidates from across the political spectrum. Candidates all but universally (the Islamist party PKS is the main exception) decry the decline of party enthusiasm since 1999 and accuse party cadres of being unreliable and moneygrubbing. This disillusionment, and the mobilizational weakness it reflects, have arisen largely because parties have been eclipsed by success teams. Success teams in Indonesia go by many names: in our travels around the country we have heard them called *tim pemenangan* (victory team), *tim keluarga* (family team), *tim survey* (survey team), and *tim relawan* (volunteer team), among others. Whatever they are called, success teams are ad hoc networks, set up by individual candidates for the purpose of organizing an election campaign. Such teams vary considerably in size: the smallest, usually formed for village-head elections or elections of district DPRD members, involve only a handful of individuals; the largest, in national DPR or gubernatorial elections, consist of several thousand brokers. But virtually all success teams share a basic pyramidal shape that is dictated by their core function: to connect, through chains of personal connections, a political candidate to individual voters. Accordingly, success teams are usually geographically organized.

When designing a campaign strategy and structure, a candidate and his or her core advisers typically begin by calculating the number of votes they need to secure victory, and then identifying the geographic areas where those votes will be acquired. This involves dividing the electorate up into territories, usually matching the administrative structure used by the government (districts, subdistricts, villages or urban precincts, hamlets (where present), RW (neighborhoods) and RT (sub-neighborhoods), and identifying areas of strength and weakness for the candidate. Areas in the former category might include the candidate's home village or district (depending on the scale), areas inhabited by coethnics or coreligionists, or areas that have benefited from the candidate's past largesse—especially relevant if she or he is an incumbent with a record of delivering pork-barrel projects. Some candidates will calculate that they can win by concentrating on areas of presumed strength alone; others will try to distribute their effort evenly across the electoral district; many use mixed strategies.

Candidates then go about constructing success teams that match their territorial targeting. They start by establishing a core team, usually drawing on close personal friends, relatives, party colleagues, or other associates, and then assigning some of its members specialist jobs, such as financial or media management. This section of the *tim sukses* is often referred to as the *tim inti* or "core team." But the critical jobs at the top are those of coordinators (*koordinator*) of the geographic areas that constitute the uppermost layer in the brokerage structure. Typically, these are district coordinators (in the case of a gubernatorial or DPR elections), subdistrict coordinators (in the case of district head or DPRD elections), or hamlet or neighborhood coordinators (in village-head elections). Sometimes the candidate will also know people who can be recruited as coordinators at lower levels, too; but especially in the larger campaigns, and when trying to seek recruits in areas where the candidate lacks direct personal connections, he or she will need to rely on the higher-level coordinators to recruit people lower down the chain: the district coordinator will recruit subdistrict coordinators, who recruit village coordinators, who then recruit the community-level vote brokers (often called field coordinators or *korlap, koordinator lapangan*) at the base of the pyramid. It is these base-level brokers who then try to enlist individual voters to support the candidate.

Success teams resemble the sort of brokerage pyramids that organize clientelist politics in many countries in which political parties are weak and, especially, where electoral systems favor a personal vote. It should be noted that the type of brokerage pyramid described here is similar to those that have been observed in other countries in which political parties have struggled to institutionalize themselves and assert control over electoral campaigning and patronage distribution. To cite one example, in nearby Thailand it has long been recognized that party candidates rely on networks of electoral brokers known as *huakhanaen* (literally "head vote" but usually translated as "vote canvassers"), such that "finding canvassers, managing them, and channeling money through them are the three key steps to election" (Callahan and McCargo 1996, 382). In one recent study, vote canvassers were "often medium-level government officials, small- to medium-sized shop owners, moneylenders, traders, and monks or religious leaders that are well known to the communities" (Chattharakul 2010, 74). Likewise, in the Philippines, political candidates form brokerage structures that resemble the Indonesian pattern, drawing on diverse family and other personal networks, as well as precinct captains, organizational leaders, and other *liders*, as vote brokers are known in that country: though such networks are often loosely based around a highly localized party, party affiliations are in fact notoriously loose and flexible in that country (Hicken, Aspinall, and Weiss, forthcoming).

Despite informal brokerage structures being quite commonly described in ethnographic accounts, in much of the literature on clientelism—especially that drawing on Latin American experiences—it is assumed that vote brokers are members of parties. In Indonesian campaign teams, party members play a relatively minor role. They do join such teams, and can perform various organizational tasks, just like nonparty *tim sukses* members. Yet particularly during elections for government heads—when candidates are generally supported by coalitions of parties—their role often remains peripheral.

Above all, what distinguishes the *tim sukses* structures from parties is their impermanence. To be sure, many core members will maintain close relations with the candidate after the election, especially if the candidate is successful. In that case, such key supporters often become advisers or assistants to the politician; leading village or neighborhood brokers also maintain ties, hoping for rewards in the form of pork-barrel projects and other benefits. But the team itself invariably dissolves once the election is over. Brokers often complain that candidates forget them, and fail to honor promises to reward them with jobs or projects. The next time an election comes around, even an incumbent candidate will need to build a new success team from scratch, though she or he will usually be able to draw in people who helped in the previous election—provided they have been rewarded in the meantime. And at every election there will be new candidates, seeking to construct their own teams for the first time. Election season is thus always associated with a flurry of organizational activity.

Building a Campaign Team

This type of campaign organization can basically take two forms. On the one hand a candidate needs to recruit a large group of grassroots brokers to execute basic campaign tasks and connect directly with voters. These brokers are assigned the general campaign tasks that Sharif discussed above, such as recruiting polling witnesses, mobilizing their friends and family, distributing campaign material, reminding voters to go to the booth, and so on. As we discuss below, a massive grassroots team is especially important if the candidate wants to distribute cash to voters. On the other hand, a candidate's *tim sukses* also needs to build connections with existing communities and organizations, which often involves cultivation of community leaders and local elites. This distinction partly overlaps with terms that campaign organizers themselves use: in interviews they sometimes refer to the grassroots campaign organizers as the "structural" success team, while calling the community organizations and networks attached to the campaign "functional" groups—a term with New Order origins (Golkar presented itself in those years not as a party but as an organization of "functional"—by which it meant mainly occupational—groups).

This distinction matters because the character of the candidate's relationship with the brokers will differ depending on which approach is emphasized. The structural team members do not differ much from voters in terms of status. They are local operators with time on their hands and some organizational skills. They are often not tied particularly closely by party or organizational link to any candidate, but are willing to sell their services to the highest bidder, do the work as a favor to a candidate they know, or to help a team coordinator with whom they enjoy personal connections. Arief's campaign, for example, used the municipality's garbage program to develop connections with garbage recyclers who doubled as neighborhood and precinct coordinators. They did not receive a salary for this job but were motivated by the hope of receiving future benefits: apart from the goat that Arief promised, such brokers hoped to get access to government contracts, subsidies, or travel money, or simply to be able to keep playing a role in the garbage program.

Each community-level broker is not expected to sway a lot of votes individually. Instead, campaign teams using such a mass strategy endeavor to recruit many such brokers to maximize the reach and effectiveness of the campaign. What then counts is the sum total of the groundwork these workers put in. As one PAN DPRD candidate in Kapuas in Central Kalimantan put it, "In the art of electoral warfare, one person can hold a minimum of twenty-five voters, a maximum of fifty. If they say they've got one hundred, that doesn't make sense anymore. We just use the logic of the family—look at their family ties before you do anything else. The most that is going to be is about twenty-five, thirty people in their immediate family: about five houses" (interview, April 7, 2014). In fact, many candidates put the number even lower than this, with the key being to limit the number of people brokers deal with to those with whom they are truly intimate, so they can be sure of those people's voting intentions and exercise proper influence over them. Brokers who have close social relations with their target voters are more likely to know those voters' preferences, and are thus able to avoid wasting money and effort on voters who prefer rival candidates. They will also be better able to exercise moral suasion to ensure they deliver the promised votes.

In such circumstances, brokers can be distributed with great density through the community. To take one example: As part of a related research project, Aspinall and colleagues collected the broker and voter lists from one candidate who was running for a seat in the DPRD of Blora district in Central Java (see Aspinall et al. 2017). In some villages where the candidate placed brokers, he had one broker for more than one hundred registered voters. But in villages that he considered to be part of his "base," he had one broker for every five voters. In all the villages where we have data for this candidate, there was a total of 122,000 registered voters. He had 490 brokers scattered through these villages, a ratio of one broker to 249 voters. If we take into account that there were many more candidates running for office—this particular candidate had eighty-two competitors—we can see that the competition for such community brokers can be intense. Had all those rivals had the same number of brokers (they almost certainly did not; he was a strong candidate), this would have meant there was one broker for every three voters—and that is without taking into account provincial and national candidates. Given Indonesia's multiple cycles of election over a five-year period—for legislators, presidents, governors, district heads, and village heads—the country's democratization process has generated a considerable demand for brokers with organizational skills and a record of past success at delivering the vote. Such people can easily sell their skills to candidates at election time.

The functional or outreach dimension of campaign organization is somewhat different. This approach involves cultivating the support of influential community notables and leaders of organizations—it is a strategy focused on community-level elites. Such leaders generally do not engage in everyday campaign tasks and are not necessarily seen as active members of a *tim sukses*. Instead, they are drawn into the election campaign because of their assumed influence over the voting behavior of their followers. Thus, one PDI-P DPR candidate in Central Java, speaking of one district where he lacked personal connections, explained: "Well, I don't know the area well there, so I have to choose people who know the area. You need community leaders [*tokoh masyarakat*], people who are influential in the community, such as village heads, community leaders, RT heads, RW heads, successful businesspeople who have lots of employees, and so on" (interview, April 3, 2014). A candidate in a tiny urban electoral district for a district DPRD on the island of Bangka gave a similar explanation, saying that he was drawing in from his neighborhood "all the RT heads, all the community leaders, religious leaders, and people whom I consider to have influence in the precinct" (interview, March 23, 2014).

Apart from such positions, candidates often draw in leaders of formal or informal community-level associations—youth groups (*karang taruna*); women's groups; devotional groups such as *majelis taklim* in Muslim areas or Bible study groups in Christian regions; sports clubs; branches of formal Islamic organizations such as NU and Muhammadiyah or their various women's, youth, and other auxiliaries; ethnic associations (*paguyuban*); *adat* (customary) organizations; and so on. The all-purpose term used in Indonesia for such figures is *tokoh masyarakat*, or community leader, which might also be translated as "notable." In fact, candidates will be on the lookout for *any* socially influential or networked individual, and the variety of such people drawn into success teams is all but endless. We discuss this second dimension of campaign organization—the incorporation of existing organizations and social networks and how their recruitment is often associated with distribution of community gifts, or club goods—more fully in the next chapter. Overall, however, it is worth stressing that no matter which strategy is emphasized, candidates all seek to recruit socially engaged brokers: as part of his doctoral research, Burhanuddin Muhtadi conducted a large survey of brokers in four provinces, and he found that "overall, brokers were highly socially engaged people compared with the general population" (Muhtadi 2018, 176). For example, 50 percent said they were members of *majelis taklim*, compared to 23 percent of respondents in his voter survey, and 34 percent were involved in *arisan* (rotating savings groups), compared to 25 percent in his voter survey.

Election campaigns vary considerably in their relative reliance on the two modes of campaign organization. Incumbents and well-rooted politicians with extensive personal networks can often build a strong structural *tim sukses* while building fewer bridges with existing social networks. As already alluded to, massive structural teams are especially important for candidates who seek to distribute cash to voters, and a large success team is frequently an indication that such a strategy is being planned. Conversely, candidates who lack strong personal networks often depend heavily on the contacts they build with community representatives, and such campaigns often center on club-goods strategies. Most election campaigns, however, rely on both modes of campaign organization, supplementing a structural team with outreach to organizations and networks. Candidates with the organizational strength and resources to build a large structural team can often afford to supplement this strategy by reaching out to established social networks and notables; candidates who lack the former capacity will frequently also be unable to draw on much functional support.

It is also worth noting that cashed-up candidates—especially those running in *pilkada* for *bupati*, mayoral, or gubernatorial posts—often rely on the services of professional political consultants to do all or part of the work normally conducted by the success team. Such firms have experienced a boom since the introduction of direct elections in the mid-2000s (Mietzner 2009; Qodari 2010). Though much attention has focused on the large, well-known national consultancies and polling firms, there has also been dramatic growth of such services in the regions, with academics in local universities and NGOs seeing the rise of direct elections as an opportunity to monetize their skills. Typically, consultancy firms are involved at the early stages of a campaign, often conducting initial surveys in the constituency, with the goal being not only to convince potential nominating parties of the candidate's electability (if the firm is hired by a candidate) or to work out which potential candidates are most electable (if hired by the party), but also to identify and map out areas of electoral strength in the district, advise on possible slogans, and even to work out which voters expect or require payments of what magnitude (Warburton 2016b, 357–358).

The Ground War

A key element of Indonesian election campaigns in the era of the personal vote is the "ground war," a term that candidates use to differentiate their activities from the "air war" of media campaigns and large public events. To be sure, in *pilkada* and even in legislative contests candidates sometimes still hold public campaign rallies, typically featuring singers or other entertainers, in which participants are bused in from outlying regions and paid to attend. Such rallies act primarily as a visible show of the candidate's resources and strength, and are also intended to galvanize core supporters. Candidates, rarely, however, think that such events make a big difference to the mass of voters. Likewise, though wealthy candidates in gubernatorial, DPR, and district-head elections will sometimes expend considerable sums on media advertising, in most parts of Indonesia the limited reach of print media, and even of regionally based electronic media, means that candidates do not place much hope in media campaigns either. Attention is usually focused on the ground campaign.

The starting point in designing a ground campaign is mapping out target areas. In *daerah basis*, base areas, where the candidate is already strong, perhaps because he or she originates in the hamlet, village, or subdistrict concerned, the task will be relatively simple. Some candidates, especially in legislative races where it is possible to win a seat with a relatively small slice of the electorate, will concentrate all, or almost all, their efforts in such areas. The candidate will spend most of his or her time in the base area, hosting community meetings, visiting residents, officiating at ceremonies handing over club goods, distributing mementos, and building up a dense success team structure, often with one team member for every few residents.

In such base areas, success teams often do what they can to prevent entry by rival teams. This will be particularly easy if the local community leaders—the village head, RW or RT heads in particular—are on side, because they will be able to prevent the use of community facilities for meetings by rivals, forestall community-level deals about club goods, and use their moral authority to dissuade community members from working for rival candidates. In such circumstances, success team members often also monitor their neighbors to ensure that members of rival teams are not working among them. As election day nears, and especially on the all-important night before the polling day, groups of men from the success team will often set up guard posts at the entrance points to the village or key streets, ostensibly in order to deny entry to people from other teams bringing cash in for vote buying, but often greatly restricting all movement by residents.

In most races, however, especially those covering larger territorial areas, candidates cannot rely on a personal base area alone. They need to extend their efforts to areas where they lack immediate connections. Typically, they try to penetrate such areas by relying on social network ties—calling in the support of friends, colleagues, or followers they have established relationships with through political, business, family, religious, or other webs. Sometimes, however, candidates have little choice but to go in cold, as it were, and send in advance teams to scout out areas where communities might be amenable to giving their support. The first port of call in such visits will be the local community leaders, especially village, hamlet, and RW and RT heads. Typically, a set of negotiations will take place on what the candidate might offer the community concerned, and then a meeting, funded by the candidate, will be held involving either locals and the candidate or (in larger campaigns) his or her senior team members. Some locals will be recruited into the success team, with the blessing of the community leaders, and the area will be added to the candidate's "base." Where the blessing of senior community members cannot be attained, candidates will either give up on the area, or enter through other network connections—say, via a religious organization, through links with farmers' cooperatives, or sports clubs. We will return to the use of such links in the next chapter. This pattern of mediated access to communities means that many Indonesian election results exhibit a "patchwork" pattern, in which neighboring communities that are demographically very similar return very different results, reflecting differences in network access by competing candidates (Aspinall and As'ad 2015).

Most of the time, candidates try to physically mark their territory, continuing a tradition that was begun in earlier elections when parties tried to designate particular villages or neighborhoods as base areas by swathing them in party flags and, sometimes, painting walls, buildings, electricity poles, and other fixtures in party colors. With the transition to systems emphasizing the personal vote, Indonesian streetscapes and even households are instead plastered with images of candidates. Banners and billboards are placed at strategic locations on street sides, or at entry points into communities, with the hope of increasing candidates' name recognition and providing the impression that they are well organized and funded. Often, such images will incorporate a slogan consisting of a few words about the candidate's character or main concerns, as well as words or images indicating the candidate's ethnic, religious, party, or other affiliation (Fox

2014). As well as increasing name recognition, such materials are often intended to mark the territory as being part of a candidate's base, and so send messages: to residents that there is community pressure to deliver the vote, and to rivals that they should not waste effort there. Likewise, success team members sometimes affix stickers to the door frames of homes they visit, in an attempt to signal to rival teams that the votes of those living inside are already taken.

As for campaigning itself, there are two core modes of connecting with voters in the "ground war," once initial contacts have been established. The first, already mentioned, is small-scale meetings in which the candidate or senior success team members introduce the candidate and his or her "program." A critical goal is to show voters that the candidate is an approachable person whom community members can feel comfortable asking for help should they later need it (Alamsyah 2016; Paskarina 2016). Usually, various snacks, drinks, cigarettes, and other items are consumed at such meetings, all paid for by the candidate. Such meetings can take many forms; the most basic is an informal meeting with community members in a success team member's home. In parts of eastern Indonesia, considerable ceremony attaches to such meetings, including the gifting of items signifying social connection, such as betel or pigs (Rohi 2016); and in places where feasting is central to the creation of social ties, these meetings can themselves be a huge drain on a candidate's finances. In other parts of the country, and depending on the candidate, the meeting will take the form of a religious service or ceremony. Other candidates combine such getting-to-know-you sessions with community service or events—insecticide fogging, medical treatment, community parties, fashion shows, and the like.

Whatever form they take, such meetings often become a forum in which community leaders or members make demands for patronage. Indeed, such meetings put paid to arguments that politicians are always the initiators of clientelist exchanges, instead showing that clientelistic politics is often demand driven (see also Nichter and Peress 2016). We have both attended such meetings in which local notables, or ordinary community members, have openly asked candidates to deliver gifts to their communities. The techniques participants use range from the relatively subtle—such as when they point out that rival candidates have already offered community improvements or made cash gifts in the community—to extremely straightforward requests for cash or other benefits.

To illustrate, one of the most striking examples we encountered occurred at a meeting between two PDI-P candidates (one provincial, one city) and women organized through the women's welfare organization, PKK, in a poor *kampung* in the East Java capital Surabaya, a few weeks before the 2014 election. The candidates spoke for about half an hour, explaining various services they could perform in the community, such as handling the paperwork to enable residents to access a new health insurance scheme. One of the candidates was a local PDI-P power broker; the other was a longtime activist in women's NGOs. The latter talked at length about issues to do with women's and children's rights. The moment the candidates ended their formal speeches, however, one of the women present, who played a record-keeping role for the PKK, opened a book of minutes from an earlier meeting and referred to promises the senior male candidate had made during the mayoral election four years earlier. The women wanted electrification for the RT hall, tarpaulins so they could cover their alleyway while holding their meetings, *sembako*, or foodstuffs, and "recreation," by which the speaker meant a bus trip for the neighborhood women to one of East Java's tourism sites.

A long process of good-spirited but tough negotiations followed, in which the candidates explained the limited nature of their resources and underlined that they would not hand out foodstuffs because doing so could be classed as "money politics" and would so burden them with debt that they would be obliged to participate in corruption should they be elected. The women were willing to compromise on this issue, but on nothing else. One older woman got very upset about the planned trip, stating that this demand was "nonnegotiable" (*harga mati*), and sparking energetic discussion among the women about where their preferred destination would be (the resort town of Batu was eventually agreed upon). The meeting ended on a positive note, with the candidates promising to organize the tarpaulin and electrical connection, and to take them on a trip, before election day. "If we can't do that, I'll ask you not to bother voting for the PDI-P," the male candidate told them in closing. Exiting the venue, the female candidate explained that voters' expectations in this part of town had been changed greatly by the provision to local cadres of small-scale community infrastructure projects that originated from legislators' aspiration funds (a topic we discuss in chapter 7). As a result, she sighed, residents had become habituated to asking for benefits whenever they met politicians.

A second method of connecting with voters goes by the name of "door to door," a borrowing from English. In elections of limited geographic scope, such as those for village head or DPRD II seats, the term is meant literally, and candidates will personally visit residents in their homes, talking about their plans for the area—usually centering on what infrastructure improvements they will deliver—and asking for their "*doa dan restu*" (prayers and blessings), a euphemistic term for political support. The key is again to show the voters that the candidate is someone with an informal and approachable style, who does not stand on ceremony and to whom they can turn if they experience personal difficulties or if they need something for the community. Of course, in higher-level elections, it will typically be impossible for candidates to visit all voters individually, and candidates will instead try to hold a sufficient number of small-scale meetings and *kampung* visits so that their reputation for approachability will spread from mouth to mouth.

In such big constituencies, the job of systematic household visits is typically delegated to success team members. Often, especially when entering unfamiliar territory, the success team members literally do go from door to door; in such circumstances they typically bring with them *cenderamata* (souvenirs), such as paraphernalia bearing the candidate's name and image (key rings, prayer books, stickers, crockery, or T-shirts, for example), foodstuffs (packets of instant noodles, or cooking oil, for example), or other small gifts. Particularly effective are calendars carrying pictures of the candidate. These campaign calendars adorn houses throughout the archipelago long after elections, a visible reminder of the intensity of this kind of grassroots campaigning.

Often, however, especially when a mass structural success team is involved and a vote-buying strategy is planned, the job of talking to individual voters is delegated to grassroots brokers embedded in the communities concerned. They usually do not need to make special visits to the neighbors, friends, or relatives whose support they are responsible for enlisting, but can discuss the candidate's merits in the course of normal daily interactions. That is, if they talk about them much at all: in one survey of grassroots brokers conducted in Central Java, 81 percent of brokers reported spending little or no time talking to voters about their candidate (Aspinall et al. 2015, 13). Brokers relied more on their personal relationships with their interlocutors, and the promised delivery of cash to them, to mobilize the votes.

Vote Buying

We are now in a position to discuss the topic of vote buying, by which we mean the distribution of cash payments to individual voters in the lead-up to an election. In Indonesia, this practice generally goes by the term "dawn attack" (*serangan fajar*) because the payments are often distributed after the dawn prayer on voting day, though in fact they often occur at any time on the few days leading to the vote. While it is certainly true that not all election campaigns in Indonesia involve vote buying, and not all candidates engage in the practice, Burhanuddin Muhtadi has shown that levels of vote buying in Indonesia are high compared to most comparable countries for which survey data are available, with between 25 and 33 percent of voters in the 2014 legislative election, between forty-seven and sixty-two million people, receiving payments or gifts (Muhtadi 2018, 9). The practice has roots in Indonesian history, having been widespread in village-head elections in Java since the New Order period and before (Aspinall and Rohman

2017), but anecdotal evidence suggests that the practice became much more common with the shift to personal voting after the introduction of direct local government heads in 2005 and, especially, of fully open-list PR in legislative elections in 2009.

Vote buying varies across type of election and region. As might be expected from comparative literature on the topic (Schaffer 2007), scale is important: the larger the electorate and the greater the number of voters to whom cash payments would need to be paid, the less likely vote buying is to occur—and when it does happen in larger constituencies, the payments per voter are generally lower in value. It is thus rare for money to be distributed to voters in Indonesia's presidential elections, and when it does happen the funds are usually provided by local political operatives who are trying to impress their superiors with a high turnout in their area, rather than by persons employed directly by the national campaign. In contrast, in legislative elections, as we have seen, open-list PR means that candidates can attain seats by winning a small proportion of the votes cast in a constituency. Especially in district legislative elections, where sometimes it is necessary to win only a few hundred, or a few thousand, votes in order to secure a seat, and where the social distance separating candidates from voters is often narrow, vote buying is particularly common.

The findings of the expert survey support this analysis. Respondents were asked to estimate the proportion of voters who received cash or goods in the most recent elections in their districts. The results (figure 5.1) point to considerable variation across types of elections. In a scale in which an estimate that between zero and 20 percent of voters received cash or goods yielded a score of 2 (a score of 1 would mean there was no vote buying at all), the average score for the most recent presidential election was 2.72, indicating that respondents found the rate of vote buying to be lowest in this variety of election. Respondents estimated the rate as being next highest in gubernatorial and then district-head elections, and believed it was especially common in elections for seats in regional legislatures, with an average score of 5, indicating a range of between 60 and 80 percent of voters receiving payments.

It should be noted that these estimates are much higher than the findings of voter surveys, and almost certainly considerably exaggerate the incidence of vote buying. For example, a national survey of voting-age citizens conducted immediately after the April 2014 national legislative election by the polling institute Indikator Politik Indonesia found that 29 percent of respondents said they had been offered cash or goods in exchange for voting for a legislative candidate in the past (Indikator Politik Indonesia 2014, 31). While social desirability bias on the part of some respondents may mean this figure somewhat understates the incidence of vote buying in such elections, in fact Muhtadi (2018) has closely

DPRD election by district   Average per election type

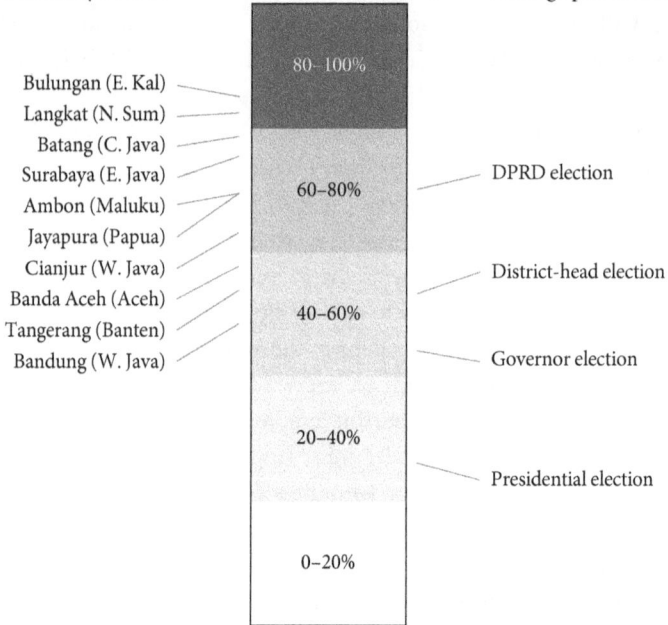

Expert Survey question: What percentage of voters is given money or consumer goods during elections for [district head/governor/DPRD/ president]?

FIGURE 5.1   Estimates of incidence of vote buying

examined the survey evidence and believes the range is 25–33 percent. We therefore strongly believe the experts exaggerated the incidence, being aware of vote buying in their locales but missing the degree of targeting associated with the practice. Despite this discrepancy, the underlying pattern of variation in the incidence of vote buying across types of election is confirmed by general population surveys: in the same Indikator poll, the proportion of voters receiving offers of cash or goods in district-head elections was 13.6 percent, with 11.3 percent saying they had received such offers in gubernatorial elections and only 8.1 percent in presidential elections. The general pattern is clear: the larger the electorate, the lower the rate of vote buying.

At the same time, in areas for which close ethnographic studies are available (see Aspinall and Sukmajati 2016) we also know that amounts paid per voter tend to be lower in national and provincial legislative races than in district competitions, where candidates can often win a seat with just a few thousand, or even a few hundred, votes. It also appears that there is considerable regional variation in the incidence of vote buying, though the considerable subterfuge that surrounds the practice makes definitive pronouncements on this score difficult. On-the-ground studies suggest that the practice is particularly widespread, and certainly most openly practiced in rural areas of Java (Aspinall et al. 2017; Hamdi 2016; Muhtadi 2018; Rohman 2016; Triantini 2016). The expert survey also pointed toward regional variation in vote-buying incidence, as the range of estimates on the left-hand side of figure 5.1 indicates. Yet it should be noted that the geographic variation in vote-buying levels is relatively limited compared to other dimensions of clientelism that, using the expert survey, we discuss in the next chapters. Furthermore, the pattern of this regional variation is also distinctive, as rural Java scores relatively high on vote buying, consistent with qualitative studies. We return to this particularity of vote buying in chapter 10.

The modus operandi of vote buying is quite straightforward and, in our experience, varies little from place to place or between candidates. Candidates usually decide how many voters they will provide with cash in the weeks leading to the election, on the basis of the work conducted by their success team members. In almost all cases we have encountered, the grassroots brokers compile lists (often known by the English-language term "by name, by address") of voters whose commitment to the candidate they have ascertained. They contain minimal information: the name, address, and sometimes the mobile telephone number or identity card number of the voters. These lists are then passed up through the chain of team coordinators to the candidates and his or her core team, who may carry out some checking of the names on the lists, and then use them to calculate how many payments they will make. The money is sent down through the same chain of team coordinators to the brokers, who deliver the payments, typically in a blank envelope, but often with a name card or picture of the candidate attached, shortly before the election. By the time the money is passed on, both the broker and the recipient know what the money is for, and little has to be said, though sometimes the broker will ask the voter to "remember" the candidate at the ballot box, or, in the case of legislative elections, explain how to find the candidate amid the long lists of candidates on the ballot. Various euphemistic terms are used to the describe these payments, some of which express the idea that the money is a trifling amount, while subtly reminding the recipient that even small favors deserve to be repaid (such terms include "breakfast money" or "ice money"). Other terms—such as "tired money" (*uang lelah*)—express the idea that the payment is to compensate the recipient for time or wages lost by going to the ballot booth, a widely held conceit that is used to explain these payments among both givers and recipients (see also Rohman 2016; Tawakkal and Gardner 2017).

Providing payments of this type can be a massive logistical exercise: one national DPR candidate encountered in the course of this research in Central Java was making payments to over two hundred thousand voters, and it took up most of the shelving on a two-by-three-meter wall space to house all his voter lists. The scale of the effort also indicates why it is necessary for some candidates to recruit truly massive success teams (the candidate in Central Java had more than three thousand on his team). In delivering money to voters, candidates are basically trying to make use of their brokers' social ties with the recipients. This is why teams can become so large: in order to minimize wastage of cash, candidates generally instruct their brokers to list only persons whose voting intentions they can be sure of, which usually means a small number in their own and nearby households. As one village-level broker in Central Java summarized their targeting strategy: "We prioritize, number one, family. You can almost certainly rely on your family; let's say you can be 99 percent sure you'll get their votes. Then, second, it's close neighbors or close friends. Only then others; sometimes they are people who are acquaintances, but not all of them" (focus group discussion, August 27, 2014).

However, it should be stressed that this strategy, though potentially very costly for the candidates who pursue it, is no guarantee of success. Candidates who distribute cash payments routinely report a significant gap between the number of payments they hand out and the number of votes they receive: they call this gap their "margin error," yet another English-language loan phrase. For example, a group of nineteen district DPRD candidates for whom data were collected in Central Java distributed cash payments ranging from 10,000 to 30,000 rupiah (about one to three dollars) to between five thousand and thirty-two thousand recipients. But they "wasted" between 86 and 47 percent of these payments: the least successful candidate by this measure distributed ten thousand envelopes but received a little more than fourteen hundred votes (Aspinall et al. 2017). These high rates of wastage are a great source of anxiety for candidates and feature prominently in explanations losing candidates give for their failure. Candidates typically try to build an estimate of anticipated "margin error" into their calculations when distributing cash, but often pick a figure that is too low.[1]

This leakage happens in part because candidates and success team members have few means to monitor or discipline voters. Voting is usually conducted in conditions of secrecy, and surveys routinely show that Indonesians trust the confidentiality of their vote. Some success team members claim that they can judge by recipients' body language, facial expressions, or other behavior whether they have really delivered on their promise to vote for the candidate from whom they received money. Even so, they rarely have any means to punish unreliable voters. Because the cash comes as a one-off gift that will rarely be followed by future benefits—unlike the situation for voters in the slums of Buenos Aires who depend on the help of Peronist party workers to access subsidized food, hospital treatment, and other forms of assistance—brokers typically have little material leverage over recipients. This, again, relates to the limited discretionary control of most politicians over state benefits, which limits their ability to threaten non-reciprocating voters with loss of access. In a country like Argentina, party brokers pay close attention to who participates in rallies and who turns out to vote. As one Argentinian broker warns, a failure to do so might cause people to get "automatically crossed off the list" of party-led distribution of food supplies (Szwarcberg 2015, 62). Such monitoring is made possible by the way in which Peronist brokers are embedded in the social life of urban neighborhoods, an embeddedness that is itself a product of the capacity of the Peronist party to mediate access to state benefits (Auyero 2001). Monitoring voters makes sense only when parties can actually punish disloyal voters: so while vote monitoring is a prominent dimension of electoral campaigning in Argentina (e.g., Stokes 2005; Szwarcberg 2015), we found that the candidates we followed in Indonesia made relatively little effort to monitor the voting behavior of recipients of their gifts.

In such circumstances, brokers have to rely on the weight of their personal relationships, and moral suasion, in the hope that recipients vote for the candidate. Religious appeals often feature: one broker in Central Java explained that he warned voters that they would be "accursed in this world and the afterlife" if they lied about whom they voted for, and that voting for an alternative candidate would make the money they received from him *haram* (prohibited in Islamic law). More commonly, brokers depend on their personal influence over the recipients, for example, explaining that they need the voters to deliver to help them avoid losing face in front of the candidate should they produce a low vote total. More often than not, the expectation of delivery simply arises naturally out of the relationship between broker and voter, especially when brokers deliver cash only to their social intimates: as one broker put it: "I handed out [the money] to my grandchildren, to my nieces and nephews. If it's me who gives it to them, they will be reluctant to break their promise" (focus group discussion, August 24, 2014).

That such moral and personal appeals often fail is, however, not surprising. Sometimes, voters receive payments from multiple candidates, with the result that members of a single household decide to split their votes. Often, it is the brokers themselves who are at fault, by either failing to select recipients carefully, failing to make the case for the candidate, or even failing to deliver the cash at all—a topic we return to below.

If the effectiveness of this particular form of patronage is so limited, the obvious question arises: why do so many candidates continue to engage in it? The most succinct answer we have encountered was given by a PDI-P candidate in Central Java to the researcher Tom Power: "If you give voters money," Utut Adianto explained, "it is not guaranteed they'll vote for you. But if you don't give them anything, you can guarantee that they won't" (Power 2014). Candidates face a dilemma: they know that the payments they distribute at such great personal expense do not ensure victory, but they feel that they will rule themselves out as serious candidates if they do not pay at all.

This paradoxical nature of the payments is also reflected in views expressed by voters. In a series of focus group discussions held in Central Java shortly after the 2014 legislative election, voters frequently stated that while the payments they received did not influence their vote choices, and they supported their preferred candidates on the basis of other considerations—personal connections, respect for the candidate's vision for the district, knowledge of what he or she had done in the past for the village, and so on—they often simultaneously insisted that payments were an utterly normal and expected part of local practice at election time, and that they would be reluctant to vote for a candidate who did not provide them. Even as they denied that most voters were motivated by cash payments, some also had anecdotes about candidates who had refused to distribute cash, and by doing so alienated even their social intimates. For example, one vote broker in Blora district recalled:

> I'll tell you about my village, where there were five [candidates originating from the village itself]. One of them—well nobody at all voted for him. In one polling booth he got only two votes! Only two votes! And that was because he didn't want to spend money. He didn't even want to give out just 10,000 rupiah [per head], or anything. Even though, with us, if there's no money people won't vote. So I think money is very important, even though it's not important. When a candidate gets only two votes, well, that's really embarrassing. . . . Even his own relatives didn't want to vote for him, because they didn't get any money. . . . So the *minimum* a candidate needs to do is provide *sangu* [pocket money—a local term for these payments], sir. That's all. (Focus group discussion, August 23, 2014)

In areas like this, where payments are an established practice, they operate as such a strong social norm that even candidates who run for office without expecting or hoping to win (common in legislative elections, when some candidates stand simply in order to fill out a party list) will often distribute cash because, they explain, it would be humiliating to ask others to vote for them without offering some token of appreciation.

To be sure, candidates use language that mirrors the marketist approach to clientelism, discussed in chapter 2, when talking privately about their strategies—for example, they talk about the "market price" of a vote in a particular constituency, and condemn voters as being primarily motivated by greed (Aspinall et al. 2017). Many voters also accuse other people of being primarily swayed by the size of the payment on offer, though they invariably deny such motivations with regard to themselves. Candidates' actions also reflect a marketist view: for example, candidates often try frantically to match payments being made by their main competitors, often leading to a flurry of additional payments in the final twenty-four hours leading to a vote. No doubt they are at least partly correct, and at least some proportion of voters are willing to be swayed by whoever makes the highest payment.

However, clearly the marketist approach is insufficient for capturing the role played by money in these interactions. For one thing, such marketist language is rarely deployed in regular exchanges between voters, brokers, and candidates: most obviously, nobody uses the term "vote buying" or any close equivalent to describe these transactions. Both voters and brokers strongly reject the notion that what occurs is anything like commercial exchange. Very often, even the expectation of a quid pro quo is merely implicit rather than explicit. In this sense, the culturalist approach to clientelism, discussed in chapter 2, provides a better handle to interpret vote buying. By distributing cash, politicians play on prevailing norms of reciprocity. Though views differ, many participants interpret the circulation of cash during election campaigns within a broader moral logic of gift giving, in which a failure to reciprocate would be considered rude or unseemly. By handing out money, candidates attempt to harness such norms with the aim of obliging a voter to support him or her. In this sense vote buying can be interpreted as an attempt by politicians to impose an obligation on voters. Indeed, some voters spoke about how they resented finding a candidate's envelope on their doorstep because this made them feel *terikat*, or "bound," to the giver. In this sense, there is a strongly ethical dimension to vote buying: in fact, the whole system of vote buying would collapse without ethical underpinnings, given that candidates lack legal or other means to enforce this form of exchange.[2]

Yet we should not overestimate the strength of the obligations generated by the distribution of money. In the expert survey, respondents were asked to estimate the proportion of voters they thought would feel obliged to reciprocate a gift of cash or goods with a vote, and though 38 percent of respondents said that they believed 60 percent or more of such voters in a district-head election would feel obliged, in fact there was a large range in responses, indicating considerable disagreement, and considerable variation across regions, too, with relatively low responses in Jakarta and Central and East Java, but relatively high ones in provinces such as North Sulawesi and East Nusa Tenggara where clan structures play a major role in social life. Informants we encountered during fieldwork also displayed very mixed opinions in this regard. Yes, some voters will admit that they feel bound by a gift of cash, but others will explicitly deny any such

feeling of obligation, something that is also reflected in the relatively low success rate of vote-buying efforts. One way to interpret the fact—to quote again
the broker from Central Java—that "money is very important, even though it's
not important" is that these payments play a role that is akin to being an "entry
ticket" (Aspinall et al. 2015). The gifts of money primarily act as a signal that
candidates must provide in order to be considered seriously by voters on other
grounds. In particular, the gift signals that the candidate possesses sufficient
wealth and social standing to aspire to a significant leadership position, that
he or she possesses a significant group of supporters who are willing to enter
people's homes and speak on the candidate's behalf, and, perhaps most importantly, that the candidate has the desired attributes of being *peduli* (caring) and
possessing *perhatian* (attentiveness) about the needs and aspirations of voters.
Failure to deliver cash payments can easily be read as a signal that the candidate
is *sombong* (arrogant) or *pelit* (stingy) and, should she be elected to office, will
therefore devote her energies to self-enrichment, doing little to help community
members. In this regard, vote-buying practices play on social expectations of
how rulers should properly behave (Piliavsky 2014). Vote buying is a form of
political advertising.

The willingness of many voters to participate in cash exchanges is reinforced
by their skepticism regarding candidates and their campaign promises. Many
voters have very low regard for the politicians they elect, and for the political
class as a whole. They have read media reports about official corruption, and
they often know word-of-mouth reports of malfeasance on the part of the very
candidates they are being asked to support. They also understand from personal experience that politicians frequently fail to live up to the promises they
make to deliver improvements in local infrastructure, services, or living stan-
dards. Voters' willingness to engage in clientelistic exchange is thus conditioned
by the low expectations they have for programmatic delivery. In a political
system based on personalism and rent seeking, many voters feel that it is only
fair if they get an opportunity to benefit personally, even if the opportunity
arises only at election times. Voters thus often express the idea that elections
are "a time for the people to party" (*saatnya rakyat berpesta*)—a play on the
old New Order term whereby elections were described as a people's festival, or
party (*pesta rakyat*). Indeed, some voters claim a higher purpose: as one voter
succinctly put it when asked to explain how people interpreted the meaning of
the cash gifts they received: "People interpret them as a form of revenge money
[*uang balas dendam*], brother. So we can get back at them a bit for the money
we think they'll get through corruption later on. It's very likely lots of people
think of it this way, as revenge money" (focus group discussion, Central Java,
August 25, 2014).

Broker Betrayal and Discipline

One critical problem that bedevils clientelist exchange in Indonesia, and haunts any politician who relies on a success team, is that of securing the loyalty of the brokers. Recent studies of the roles played by brokers elsewhere in the world show that this is a universal problem. As Susan Stokes and her collaborators put it in a recent book on the topic, the "sense that one's operatives in the neighborhoods, towns and boroughs may be 'parasites' and 'traitors'" is "omnipresent, festering in the minds of party leaders from 19th century Britain, to Gilded Age America, to contemporary Argentina or India" (Stokes et al. 2013, 20). Stokes and her colleagues have shown that brokers frequently have interests that diverge from those of the candidates for whom they work: for example, while politicians might prefer to target scarce patronage resources at swing voters, in order to maximize their impact, brokers might have an interest in using these resources to mobilize existing supporters, so as to demonstrate their influence to party leaders and thus encourage them to direct a larger share of patronage resources their way.

But if such problems can arise in contexts in which clientelist exchange is mediated by political parties—such as in the Argentinian and other Latin American cases studied by Stokes and her colleagues—they can be even more severe when parties play a relatively marginal role. Parties have various means to discipline their broker members. As Kitschelt and Wilkinson put it, "We can think of mass party organizations as highly effective group devices for surveillance and mobilization, in which local party bosses closely monitor individuals' conduct" (Kitschelt and Wilkinson 2007, 17). Party members typically have expectations of long careers within their party, and will therefore often be motivated to demonstrate loyalty and reliability to their bosses. If their candidate loses, they can often be accommodated with a job or other benefits located in a neighboring constituency, or provided by a different level of government, or by the party machine itself. Their willingness to defect might also be limited by ideological or other differences with rival parties.

In Indonesia, where electoral machines are more typically ad hoc organizations based on ephemeral relationships among brokers and candidates, we can expect problems of broker disloyalty to be especially severe. In the course of our research, we found problems of broker discipline to be ubiquitous. Virtually every candidate we encountered worried about theft and manipulation by brokers, and they often used a highly charged language of "betrayal" (*penghianatan*) to describe such behavior.

Part of the problem stems from the sort of rewards that brokers expect from candidates. Though a few brokers work simply to help a friend, relative, or some other associate, most expect some sort of material reward for their participation.

For some, their hopes focus on the long-term: they expect that if the candidate wins, they will gain a benefit—access to a patronage job, a government grant, a project, or the like. Brokers who are especially close to a candidate can hope to profit considerably should their candidate be victorious, though they will typically gain nothing if the candidate loses. Brokers typically gain shorter-term rewards as well, but these are rarely great. Most candidates cover their brokers' expenses, make special payments when they carry out particular tasks such as erecting posters or banners, provide small cash gifts when they come to meetings, and give them an envelope containing cash when it is time to hand out money to voters. Only a very few brokers, however, and usually only those who play coordinating roles, can expect to earn a proper salary, or to benefit from the major bonuses that some candidates pay when they win. The combination of tenuous promises of future gain, minimal material rewards in the present, plus responsibility for distributing sometimes significant amounts of resources, creates conditions for the loyalty problems that afflict success teams.

In this context, two major forms of broker betrayal are of particular concern for candidates. One is *predation*, which occurs when brokers expropriate part of the money or other goods that they are supposed to distribute to voters or to brokers further down the success team pyramid. While most candidates tolerate a certain amount of skimming, sometimes they experience massive losses. We both encountered stories in the field of candidates who felt themselves to be victims of massive fraud. For example, one academic who worked for a wealthy mining magnate who made an ill-advised run for local government in South Kalimantan (he was from a minority ethnic group and lost badly) recalled his experiences thus:

> A lot of success team members, whether or not their champion wins, they want to earn an income. A lot of them came out of it with a new motorbike, a new car, renovations to their house, a lot of stuff. It worked like this—they'd get 1 billion rupiah [\$88,000] for their subdistrict, and they kept 700 million for themselves. A lot of them did that. . . . The problem was [the candidate] completely lost control of distribution of money. Lots of people in the network thought "I've got a lot of money here, why on earth would I pass it all on?" One person I know got 3 billion, but he only divvied up a fraction of that. Quite a few took half of the money they received. You just can't monitor this. (Confidential interview, April 14, 2013)

This was a spectacular example, involving a candidate who was exceptionally well resourced; but petty theft is endemic to success teams. Thus, in one survey of voters derived from vote-buying lists in Central Java, only 53 percent of respondents claimed to have received payments, though this was the ostensible reason for their inclusion on the list (Aspinall et al. 2015, 18–19). While some of the negative results may have been the result of social desirability bias, there is little doubt that the finding suggests massive leakage of vote-buying funds.

A second form of broker betrayal is *defection*, which happens when brokers change sides during the course of an election campaign, deserting one candidate for another who offers better material rewards, stronger prospects of victory (and thus future rewards), or both. In *pilkada*, defection is particularly common when a success team member, approached early in a campaign period by one team, realizes later on that another candidate is actually better resourced and/or more likely to win. In such instances, there are good reasons to defect. Particularly for community-level notables like village heads, the imperative to back a winner in a *pilkada* is powerful, given that the notable's access to future community-level projects and other benefits may hinge on supporting a winning candidate. For this reason polling results can be something of a self-fulfilling prophecy, as a bad poll can lead such community leaders to withdraw their support from a candidate and switch to a better-placed rival.

A third, though less common, variant, which we might call *duplicity*, occurs when brokers work for more than one candidate simultaneously, shirking on all or part of the work they have pledged to do for one or more of their candidates. Duplicity is especially common during legislative elections when the supply of candidates far exceeds the number of seats being contested, so that competition for brokers is intense. In such circumstances, candidates struggle to keep track of broker activity at the village level. During the 2014 legislative election, we frequently encountered brokers who were working for multiple candidates, and who relished the opportunity to explain how they were cheating the more gullible among them (Hamdi 2016, 295).

The root of these problems is, of course, that candidates often lack a history of close personal relationships with the brokers upon whose honesty and hard work they so depend. In some cases, a factor accelerating the process is that many brokers are not recruited directly by candidates, but instead themselves approach the candidate, offering their services. Take the following colorful account by a candidate for mayor in one of Aceh's towns:

> Often there are people in the community, say, a group of five, ten people who set out to come to each candidate or team and promise support. One will come to you and say they really like you, and say that, for example, there are a thousand voters in their village and that they can provide you with five hundred votes. That person will then invite you: "Come to the village and see. Send people from your team to my

village!" Then, of course, you will give them some money to cover their costs to get back home, just a little, 20,000 or 50,000 rupiah [two to five dollars]. The next day, the person will return, bringing a couple of other people from the village, community leaders, perhaps a woman leader, or a religious leader. They will say, "I am from hamlet A. I am from hamlet B. We want to work for you." It sounds great. When they go home, you give them money again. Each visit must be converted into money. This will go on for a time, and then, the next step: they will say they want to hold a meeting for you in the village, with a party. Of course, they will need money for transport, for food, drink, and so on. They will be very enthusiastic. Before you know it, you've spent 3 or 5 million rupiah [$265–$440]. Then when you, the candidate, go there, the people will kiss you, they will cheer you, and that's when you are convinced. But on D-day—you don't get one single lousy vote from the village. So someone has organized this. They really show you what we need to win— right in front of your own eyes. But, sorry, they don't do it just for you, they are doing the same thing for all candidates. (Aspinall 2014c, 563)

Candidates can be equally vulnerable when they themselves take the initiative to reach down through webs of social connections to recruit brokers. If they are reasonably well resourced and organized, few will encounter problems in areas where their own social networks are dense. For example, a district DPRD candidate will often personally know many of the grassroots brokers she recruits in her home village. But when candidates want to expand into areas where they lack personal connections, they typically will do so by relying on senior team coordinators to recruit lower-level coordinators, and so on down the chain, leading to a highly attenuated chain of connections linking the candidate to the base level brokers. As one female Golkar member of the Pati district parliament explained: "Not all of my coordinators were recruited through primary ties; a lot were through secondary ties. . . . Primary ties means people I've helped in the past. But secondary ties are when, let's say I've helped Pak Slamet, and then I asked him to look for people for me. My bond [over them] is weaker" (Aspinall et al. 2017, 12). This reasoning explains why family as well as long-standing personal ties constitute valuable political capital. Such primary ties are accompanied by a much stronger sense of obligation, giving candidates more confidence in the reliability of such brokers.

One of us (Aspinall 2014c) has argued previously that the pattern of broker betrayal experienced by a candidate is affected by two main factors: broker assessments of a candidate's prospects of victory, and the amount of resources being pumped through a campaign structure. Brokers who are most interested in future rather than immediate material rewards will be especially attracted to candidates with strong prospects of victory, but concomitantly likely to defect if they believe their candidate is heading for defeat. Brokers most interested in immediate material rewards will be less concerned with a candidate's prospects of victory and more likely to attach themselves to better-resourced candidates from the start, seeking opportunities for predation. The unluckiest combination of all is to be—like the candidate in South Kalimantan noted above—both wealthy and judged as having poor prospects of victory. In such a case, even many brokers who would otherwise be expected to defer expectations of reward will be tempted to make the best of their opportunity and suck as much money as they can out of the campaign.

In the face of such challenges, candidates use various methods to discipline and monitor their brokers. These methods include the mobilization of cultural capital, such as when candidates entrust key positions in their success teams to family members—an extremely common pattern throughout Indonesia— because family members face great social pressure to remain loyal, and will have less doubt about their prospects of reward should their relative be victorious. Candidates also try a variety of technical solutions. One of the most common is the establishment of what are often called "invisible teams" (*tim siluman*), namely groups of campaign workers whose job it is to check whether grassroots brokers have been doing their jobs properly. In practice, this typically means visiting communities and asking brokers' neighbors whether they have heard of the candidate being promoted. Another common method is for candidates to double-check voters—or at least a sample of them—on the lists their brokers prepare, either telephoning or visiting them to confirm that they are committed to voting for the candidate. Others devise various means to insulate their brokers from the money being passed through the team structure. As an example of the latter method, one Hanura candidate in Pati district, Central Java, appointed a special team to distribute his gifts of cash and rice to voters in the days leading to the 2014 legislative election: the grassroots brokers who had identified the voters and added them to their lists were reduced at this final stage to simply pointing out the houses of the intended recipients to the members of this team.

The problem with such technical fixes, however, is that they signal to the brokers that the candidate does not trust them. Doing so can be highly problematic in a system in which candidates are ultimately dependent on brokers' goodwill for their performance. Thus, in the case of the Hanura candidate, during a focus group discussion involving twenty of his brokers, many indicated they were deeply offended by his choice not to trust them to distribute the cash and rice: "All he cared about was how to win; he didn't know how tough it was for us down below"; "He was treating us like puppets"; "Though we had been given responsibility it felt like we weren't trusted." Moreover, the fact that it was strangers who ended up handing over these gifts to the voters, they thought, reduced the gifts' effectiveness, prompting one village coordinator to speak of his own village: "So, if there was a loss there, I don't want to know about it" (focus group discussion, August 28, 2014).

Ultimately, most candidates admitted that they had limited capacity to discipline their brokers beyond relying on the strength of their affective ties with them. Even if their shadow teams caught someone in the act of falsifying a voter list or failing to deliver cash, many candidates were hesitant to confront such a broker directly. At most, they would note the person's identity and make sure that they did not approach him or her to play a role in future election campaigns. An open confrontation would risk alienating that individual and the people in his or her immediate social circles, and could thus lose the candidate a few votes while gaining nothing.

In this chapter we have discussed the pattern of campaign organization that has emerged in Indonesia as candidates responded to the incentives provided by its new candidate-centered electoral system. As we have seen, candidates overwhelmingly favored personal, relatively transient campaign structures called *tim sukses* to connect them with voters and to organize clientelistic exchange. In this respect, politicians in Indonesia differ from their colleagues in India or Argentina, as well as in many other countries, who largely rely on party structures for such tasks. The term "freewheeling" aptly sums up this versatile and relatively uninstitutionalized character of campaign networks found in Indonesia.

This freewheeling form of campaign organization matters, both for the nature of election campaigns and for the character of governance. The absence of strong grassroots networks of political parties has fueled the pervasiveness of retail clientelism: vote buying and other forms of one-off gifting of private resources at election times. Politicians in countries with developed party machines like Argentina or India can use the year-round presence of party representatives in communities to build strong relationships with voters and provide them with access to all sorts of benefits; in Indonesia, party organizations rarely provide much everyday support to voters. This limited capacity to engage in relational clientelism fuels vote buying: lacking sustained interaction, politicians in Indonesia have to rely more on one-off transactions to cement their relationships with voters.

Two additional effects that we have not yet touched upon, but which we elaborate in later chapters, also deserve note. First, the lack of institutionalized campaign structures provides incumbent politicians an electoral advantage, especially in executive races. While challenger candidates need to spend considerable time and resources building their own networks from scratch, incumbents occupying local executive office have control over bureaucratic networks, which they can use as ready-made campaign organizations. We discuss in chapter 9 how politicians pressure bureaucrats to campaign on their behalf.

Second, the freewheeling nature of Indonesian campaign networks makes election campaigns expensive, providing incentives to politicians to engage in corruption once in office. In Indonesia, many politicians spend heavily on vote buying, and virtually all of them need to invest in building their campaign networks and securing the loyalty of their brokers. They typically raise the money for these tasks themselves, without being able to look to a party for financial support; indeed, the parties will often be an additional drain on resources, seeing they often charge candidates a fee for nomination. In other settings, party networks not only provide politicians with sources of funding and a ready-made campaign organization. They also provide brokers with reassurance that their efforts will be repaid in the future, even when elections are lost. The relational clientelism of political parties in India and Argentina can, in other words, keep down campaign costs because the parties' capacity to provide access to state benefits binds both brokers and voters more strongly to them, reducing both the need for gifts and the risks of defection. Campaign supporters in Indonesia lack assurances of future benefits when their candidate loses. This leads, as we saw in this chapter, to considerable problems of defection and betrayal by brokers. Furthermore, as we show in the next chapter, the limited everyday presence of parties requires politicians to expend energy and money building ties with community organizations and social networks. In these ways politicians suffer considerably from the versatile, freewheeling nature of campaign organization in Indonesia.

6

SOCIAL NETWORKS AND
CLUB GOODS

Arief Wismansyah's main campaign office was a spacious bungalow on one of Tangerang's main roads. The building was decorated with a large banner depicting Arief wearing sunglasses and waving a fist. The banner did not carry any party logos, but it did include twenty-four symbols of obscure organizations with names like Garuda, Jaguar, and Arief and Friends. Among these groups were a local fishing club, an organization of factory workers, two botanists' groups, and an association of laundry owners. Others were ethnic organizations for Javanese, Betawi, and Chinese residents. One logo belonged to Kharisma, an association of *ustad*, or preachers, who run local mosques. As it turned out, most of these organizations had been founded for the purpose of supporting Arief's election campaign. Not a few of them consisted of communities that had received subsidies from the municipality over the preceding few years.

The office behind this banner was bustling. Success team members were coming and going, picking up material on their way to campaign events or simply drinking a cup of coffee while discussing the latest political gossip. The place also saw a regular stream of visitors, many of them representing the groups whose logos were on the banner, as well as other organizations. For example, one day, two such visitors were representatives of a local vigilante group called the Communication Forum of the Children of the Betawi (Forkabi). Like many such organizations, Forkabi combines community patrolling and neighborhood security with a range of extortion rackets, sometimes relatively benign (I. Wilson 2015). The Forkabi visitors were concerned about the upcoming election. Arief's opponent, Abdul Syukur, was a former head of Pancasila Youth (Pemuda Pancasila). This vigilante group was Forkabi's chief rival for control over territory in Tangerang and, hence, income. Both groups competed to make money from controlling street parking and from providing security at local factories. The Forkabi representatives were worried that if Abdul won, the Pancasila Youth might take over some of these activities. Their discussion with the head of Arief's success team revolved around the particular favors Forkabi would get from Arief, such as control over more parking lots, if they supported his campaign.

Later in the afternoon Jon, a representative of a local martial arts (*pencak silat*) group, also dropped by. As he later stated in an interview, he hoped the government would provide him with a training facility. In return, Jon said, his organization could be turned into a powerful campaign machine: "People believe in me, so if I say something, people will follow. We are a very disciplined organization. There is one line, one commando. If the leader says something, everyone has to follow."

In this chapter, we discuss another response of politicians to the mobilizational weakness of parties: namely, how politicians involve a wide range of social networks in their campaigns to help connect them with voters. We show that the weak mobilizational capacity of parties generates an intensive, albeit short-lived, politicization of social life around election time. Deprived of regular, more institutionalized channels to connect with voters, politicians see preexisting social networks as useful political tools and try hard to bind such networks to their campaigns. We mentioned above some of the community organizations that Arief drew upon, ranging from a fishing club and ethnic associations to a local vigilante group. This is just a small selection of the wide range of networks and organizations that play a role in Indonesian elections. Almost every type of social network can be turned into political capital: not just obvious examples such as family networks, farmers' associations, labor unions, market traders' organizations, and religious congregations, but also such groups as football clubs, martial arts associations, cooking groups, fan clubs, hiking groups, maternal welfare organizations, pigeon fanciers, and so on. In effect, politicians draw on any kind of "trust network"—any network in which members can make claims for the attention or aid of others (Tilly 2005, 4). Such networks can constitute political capital, because the obligation, intimacy, and social control they generate help facilitate clientelistic exchange.

Much campaign activity consists of frenzied deal-making among candidates, their success team coordinators, and representatives of such social networks. After engaging in sometimes sophisticated efforts to identify the strongest networks, politicians seek to piggyback on the social capital and influence of these networks' leaders, who in turn see election campaigns as an opportunity to ingratiate themselves with power holders and earn money and resources for themselves and their members. As a result, community-level notables, typically known in Indonesia as *tokoh masyarakat* (community leaders), play a crucial brokerage role in elections.

As we delve into the challenges of such deal making, we highlight an important feature of Indonesian elections: the provision of community gifts, ranging from sound systems and repairs for mosques and churches, to road paving, street lighting, or irrigation for villagers; ambulances, garbage trucks, firefighting water pumps, and mosquito fogging for urban localities; uniforms and courts for sport clubs; carpets, tents, and cooking equipment for women's groups; livestock, fertilizer, and hand tractors for farmers' cooperatives; and so on. In the literature on political clientelism, such gifts are often called "club goods" because they confer a benefit to a bounded collective rather than simply to individuals.[1] In Indonesia, club goods are an extremely prominent part of election campaigns, with candidates often investing even more of their financial resources in this form of exchange than they do in individual gifts and vote buying. Unlike in many electoral contexts, where such club goods are often provided through government budgets (and are often known as pork-barrel spending), in Indonesia these collective gifts are often provided privately by candidates. Despite the ubiquity of these gifts, however, we will see that this form of patronage politics is far from being a guaranteed method of delivering votes, and is as problematic as individualized vote buying, not least because many recipients of such collective benefits might decide to simply free ride, enjoying whatever facility the candidate provides but nevertheless voting for someone else. As a result, candidates often expend much energy trying to lock in the support of as many influential community-level notables as they can find. The best-resourced combine such collective gifts with more individualized forms of patronage such as vote buying.

The Quest for *Massa Riil*

In part, politicians rely on existing social networks and organizations and their leaders for the same reason they build success teams: they are seeking access to voters under conditions in which, for structural and institutional reasons explained in previous chapters, they cannot rely on political parties to perform this task. When politicians rely on existing social networks and their leaders, they are outsourcing their electoral efforts and using them as a short-cut to reach a mass audience, rather than relying on success teams they build from scratch. Indeed, these two tasks tend to be two sides of the same coin—as we pointed out in the preceding chapter, sometimes candidates refer to their attempts to co-opt existing networks and leaders into their campaigns as the "functional" aspect of their success team.

However, there are also deeper reasons why candidates turn to social networks and their leaders, reasons that go to the very heart of the politics of clientelism, and which we have already touched on in previous chapters. Clientelistic politics is bedeviled by a problem of trust. As we have seen, clientelism implies *contingent exchange*: the politician provides a material benefit to the voter, who, it is understood by both parties, provides his or her vote in exchange. But, as we have seen, in conditions of ballot secrecy it can be difficult for politicians to enforce this exchange, or even to know whether the individual voter has complied with his or her side of the bargain. Social norms of reciprocity can help, but so too can outsourcing the deal to brokers who play leading roles in social networks. If the politician cannot monitor the compliance of individual voters, it often *is* possible to monitor the compliance of a voter bloc, especially if that bloc is organized territorially: if a candidate makes a deal to provide, say, street lighting for a village but then gets very few votes there, he or she will be able to know that the deal failed (Holland and Palmer-Rubin 2015).

But more important still, if the critical problem bedeviling clientelist exchange is one of trust, we know from the literature on social capital that social networks generate trust between their members because of the regularity of their interpersonal interactions (Fukuyama 1995; Putnam et al. 1993). That is another reason why cohesive social networks are the target of campaigns: these social connections generate trust, interdependencies, and a sense of obligation, all of which reassure politicians that the gifts and clientelistic favors that they provide will actually be reciprocated with votes when it comes to polling day. When politicians try to mobilize voters by way of the social networks that play an intimate and important role in voters' lives they are, in effect, trying to "hijack" the social trust generated by these networks (Rohi 2016) and to make use of the obligations they impose on participants.

Of particular interest, from the viewpoint of a politician, therefore, are the influence and status that a social network confers on its leaders. A voter who is offered some benefit by a political candidate may feel little obligation to repay that candidate with a vote if few preexisting social ties connect the two. But if the candidate delegates the act of persuading the voter to a leading figure in a social network that is meaningful for the voter, and if the person making the appeal is somebody the voter respects and even depends upon, it is much more likely the voter will feel a greater sense of personal obligation to adhere to the deal. In this sense, the character of election campaigns will closely match the character of social life, as political success is to a certain extent premised on capacity to connect with social networks that are useful and meaningful to voters (Berenschot

2015a). Accordingly, whichever leaders and networks structure social life will generally be reflected in the patterns of election campaigning—in clan-based societies such as in Central Asia, clans become central to the organization of political campaigns (Collins 2006); when communities are based around "big men" and *wantok* groups, such as in Melanesia, these are the brokers and networks politicians turn to (Wood 2014); and so on.

Indonesian society is marked by unusually dense organizational life: according to the World Values Surveys from 2005 to 2008, for example, while the average number of organizational memberships per respondent worldwide was 1.69, in Indonesia, it was 2.55; worldwide an average of 62.6 percent of respondents stated they were members of an organization, while in Indonesia the figure was 83.8 percent (Lussier and Fish 2012, 74). This organizational complexity comes to the fore at election time as a plethora of professional, ethnic, youth, and, especially, religious organizations are targeted by politicians. Among the sites of intense politicization are the mass-based Islamic organizations such as Muhammadiyah and NU, for which Indonesia is famous. But Indonesia also becomes especially energized at the micro-foundations of everyday life: among the numerous neighborhood-level organizations such as women's PKK groups, RT and RW bodies, *karang taruna* (youth groups), *arisan* (communal saving clubs), as well as grassroots devotional organizations such as *majelis taklim* (Islamic study groups). Such organizations, many of which formed part of the New Order's apparatus of community-level surveillance and control, have largely escaped the attention of political scientists, instead having been the subject of numerous anthropological studies down the years (e.g., Guinness 2009; Newberry 2006). Yet at election times they emerge into their own, being targeted in most of the "ground wars" organized by candidates and revealing Indonesian society in a new light: as a place where grassroots community-level organizations matter most to citizens and form the foundation of the country's political life.

However, the great range of opportunities for networking that such dense organizational life presents means that Indonesian politicians themselves sometimes have to resemble anthropologists, working hard to map local social networks and identifying local leaders who actually wield influence over their members. Though many politicians will already be connected by organic social ties of their own to various community groups and networks, the fact remains that a mistaken assessment can be costly. At election time, candidates are besieged by various kinds of brokers who promise to deliver votes in exchange for "operational" or "transport" money. This can be a lucrative business for some social leaders. As we saw in the preceding chapter, some such proposals are simply fake. For example, some enterprising brokers present themselves as the chairperson of a serious-sounding NGO while in fact being the only member. Others go around collecting signatures and copies of identity cards from their neighbors to prove their influence. One of us even came across one broker who went at night to cemeteries to note down the names and birthdays on the graves, and then handed them over to politicians as proof of his access to a large pool of voters.

Aware of these challenges, candidates and their campaign teams spend much time and energy checking the actual influence (termed *massa riil* or "real masses") of community leaders. Not infrequently, candidates go as far as employing a survey agency for this purpose. As Pak Rahmat, the head of Arief's campaign organization in Tangerang, explained,

> When we do a survey about the popularity of our candidate, we also ask, "In this precinct, who is the leader here, who is a *panutan* [role model]? And we ask the same thing via our network. If people say that the leader is Edi, and our people know him, then we put him on top of our list [of people to approach for help and with offers of patronage]. We look at the *massa* someone has. There are those who have real support, but if an organization comes that has just been established and asks for a lot [of money], then we have to weigh the proposal. We have to detect whether they really have strength. (Interview, August 15, 2013)

Community leaders are aware that their chances of making a good deal with a politician depend on their capacity to show their influence over voters. It can be argued that a lot of local organizational activity in Indonesia's districts, especially as an election nears, occurs for the purpose of demonstrating the *massa* of an organization and its leaders. Meetings, demonstrations, cultural events, and membership drives all serve as manifestations of the strength and cohesiveness of a particular network or organization. For example, in a multiethnic city like Tangerang, one can readily see various ethnic organizations stepping up their activity as an election draws near. Communication forums (*forum komunikasi*) of Florenese, Balinese, Madurese, ethnic Chinese, Betawi, and the like start to organize cultural events with politicians as honored guests. Most of these organizations do not actually play a big role in the everyday life of their members. But given how such organizational strength can be traded for money or other favors from the local bureaucracy, such activity can be worth the effort. Leaders can profit directly, and we encountered many leaders of ethnic and other organizations taking money in return for endorsing a politician. But for ordinary members of, say, a forum of Batak migrants, it makes sense to support the claims of such leaders, because if the group benefits, it is possible the individual members will also gain some share of the benefit; at the very least, they will be able to enjoy the social events and parties that the politician's donation will fund.

Such organizations operate like vote-pooling devices, not unlike the election clubs that once operated in many US cities (Banfield and Wilson 1963; Scott 1969): if an organization can convey a credible promise to a politician that it can offer a sizable number of votes, it can increase the likelihood its members will gain benefits. Such dynamics constitute another reason why clientelism boosts the salience of social identities: such identity-based networks are useful not only for politicians, but also for voters who want to maximize their capacity to trade their votes for money and state benefits (see Berenschot 2015a; Chandra 2004). In this way clientelistic politics fuels identity politics.[2]

Varieties of Networks

Yet despite Indonesia being one of the most complexly multiethnic societies in the world, the political importance of ethnic identities is muted (Aspinall 2011). There is much variety across the archipelago, to be sure. In many places, ethnicity plays an important role in political strategizing and everyday political discussion. In a few places, especially where there are two or three large ethnic groups, elections can resemble zero-sum contests for control over political office and the patronage resources that come with it. The typical pattern, however, is that during district-head or gubernatorial elections in multiethnic regions, the candidates make sure they choose a running mate from another ethnic or religious group to maximize their appeal. And candidates often spend considerable effort to obtain the support of multiple ethnic associations or leaders of ethnic groups. Compared to the state of affairs in India or many countries in Africa, the political role of ethnicity is highly fluid; it is also much less conflictual than it was during the transition from Suharto's rule, when violent communal conflicts broke out in a number of locations around Indonesia. Parties and candidates rarely present themselves as a candidate of one ethnic group, and politicians are generally reluctant to adopt divisive discourses that emphasize us-them divisions. In part this is because of the availability of a host of cross-cutting social networks that can also be instrumentalized politically: religious organizations, neighborhood associations, trade networks, labor unions, farmers' groups, sport clubs, hobbyists, and so on. Ethnicity is merely one among many different social networks around which politically useful networks are organized.

To capture this variety of networks and the different ways in which they are drawn into politics, it is useful to distinguish between *networks of affect* and *networks of benefit*. This distinction is primarily a heuristic device, insofar that the distinction between the two categories often breaks down in practice; but it is helpful for describing a slow, subterranean shift in the character of election campaigns: we feel that community brokers whose influence is based on cultural capital are gradually being replaced by community brokers whose influence is based on a capacity to provide members with material benefits.

Many of the networks targeted by politicians might be thought of as being primarily, at least ostensibly, *networks of affect* in that they are primarily defined in terms of religious, cultural, or similar identity-based terms, and because their basic functions are primarily social. The influence and standing of leaders of such networks rests largely on the cultural capital they accumulate: specialist religious learning, family status, perceived traditional wisdom, skill or experience in a sport or similar activity, and so on. In contrast, *networks of benefit* serve purposes directly linked to the income-generating, employment, or other material needs of participants. Most obvious here are networks that are themselves based around livelihoods—relations between employers and employees, wholesale traders and suppliers, foremen and plantation workers, funders and farmers' cooperatives, and so on. Other examples are the many neighborhood associations and networks that populate the foundation of Indonesia's associational life.

The prime example of networks of affect are religious organizations, which historically have played a very important role in Indonesian politics. The ubiquity of religious organizations at the community level—mosques, prayer halls, religious schools, prayer groups, Sufi brotherhoods, Bible-study organizations, choirs, and so on—plus the fact that religious leaders obviously exert influence over their followers, explicitly guiding them on matters of morality and social behavior, makes religious groups prime targets for politicians seeking access to *massa*.

Dating back to the 1950s, religious clientelism has been an important feature of Indonesian political life. The so-called *aliran* pattern of socioreligiously aligned political parties was sustained in part by the provision of a flow of patronage goods to the religious leaders, schools, and associations that constituted their base (for an analysis of the patronage politics of Nahdlatul Ulama in the 1950s and 1960s see Fealy 1998). As we saw in chapter 3, even during the New Order, government officials campaigning for Golkar during that regime's regular but tightly controlled elections routinely cultivated religious leaders with donations to help their educational, devotional, charitable, or other activities.

When the transition to democracy took place, a number of Islamic political parties arose that sought to revive the 1950s pattern of religious clientelism. These Islamic parties remain important, together consistently winning around one-third of the vote in legislative elections. Socioreligious identity still represents a major cleavage that structures Indonesia's party system. However, several developments have encouraged growing de-alignment of party and religious organization, and opened up religious networks to competing patronage politicians. There has been a complex process of splintering and reformulation of the Islamic parties themselves; nationalist parties have seen they can benefit electorally by incorporating religious appeals and reaching out to religious networks; most importantly, the candidate-centered nature of much electoral competition means that most politicians can readily forge personalized links, either directly or via brokers, with religious groups.

As a result of these trends, religious communities, institutions, and networks have become sites of complex political contestation. Such contestation is visible in apex organizations, whose national congresses routinely feature competition between leaders linked to rival national parties, leaders, or factions that have an eye on the political benefits to be attained by gaining influence in such organizations—developments that have meant that vote buying has begun to feature in the national congresses of Nahdlatul Ulama (van Bruinessen 2010; Fealy 2015). More important for our purposes, atomized patterns of electoral deals and alliances with religious organizations and communities occur at the grass roots. To stick with Nahdlatul Ulama for the moment, during a legislative election in NU heartland areas, it is often possible to find multiple *pesantren* headed by different *kyai* within a single subdistrict who endorse candidates from rival parties, while leaders of NU mass affiliates like Ansor and Muslimat in the same subdistrict may be running success teams for yet other candidates. Though PKB remains the strongest party in the traditionalist milieu, its hold over NU leaders and their *massa* is far from monopolistic, and it fluctuates considerably. In some places, a particularly influential *kyai* may be able to rally most local NU notables and their followers behind a single candidate, but the norm is closer to a free-for-all, with multiple parties and candidates all trying to leverage their individual connections with *kyai* and grassroots NU leaders for their own campaigning purposes (Rubaidi [2016] hence argues that fragmentation and clientelistic politics are eroding *aliran* identities). Patterns are similar in areas inhabited by other faith groups. In majority Christian areas, such as North Sulawesi, for example, virtually every candidate will try to reach voters by making connections with different churches, congregations, preachers, youth groups, choral clubs, and whatever other religious access points he or she can reach.

The result is that "religious politics" frequently occurs in a distributive rather than ideological mode, with candidates promising to help the immediate needs of the group concerned, rather than emphasizing how they will deliver on cherished long-term social goals. One sign of this pattern is the ubiquitous gifting of club goods to religious congregations and organizations at election times. Throughout the country, community-level religious groups host repeated visits by political candidates and are showered with gifts of various kinds, whether for the group itself (for example, a sound system or mats for a prayer group) or for individual members (prayer robes, mats, or *sarung* are common as gifts for members of Islamic groups, Bibles for Christians).

Another example of a network of affect is an ethnic community. In some parts of the country, customary leaders (*tokoh adat*) or elders possess considerable influence over their communities by virtue of their family status or community role. Various ethnic groups throughout Indonesia have traditional leaders with names like *damang* (the Dayak in Kalimantan), *punyimbang* (Lampung), or *penghulu* (Minangkabau), who have historically performed community roles like settling disputes, officiating at rituals, and representing the community to outsiders. Often, clan (*marga* or *fam*) leaders play similar roles. In some parts of the country, especially in more remote, economically backward, and agrarian parts of the east, they are particularly sought out as vote brokers, because politicians sometimes believe that they can deliver bloc votes. In such places, candidates often invest great resources in approaching such leaders in a culturally appropriate manner, making use of kinship ties to forge initial connections, providing appropriate cultural gifts—which, in non-Muslim parts of eastern Indonesia, are often pigs—and introducing themselves to voters through traditional ceremonies officiated by *adat* chiefs. Even so, despite the revival of *adat* in post-Suharto Indonesia (Davidson and Henley 2007), the influence of such leaders is, by and large, declining. Processes of social change—economic and social mobility, migration, competition from local state representatives—are robbing these leaders of influence.

Somewhat different are the ethnic associations, often known as *paguyuban* or *forum komunikasi*, that represent migrant groups in ethnically diverse areas of Indonesia, such as Tangerang. Such organizations often sponsor cultural events and community gatherings, and they sometimes play a self-help role, assisting, for example, when community members experience a death in the family or other hardship. However, as already noted, heading such a group can also be a lucrative source of income at election time, because candidates are often eager to seek the endorsement of such organizations as a signal to the ethnic group concerned that they are sympathetic to their concerns. Association leaders can often simply sell such endorsements for cash, leading to a proliferation of such groups during the *reformasi* period. Candidates connect with such organizations to build an image as a defender of a particular ethnic community, while members of this ethnic group use such ethnic associations to build ties with influential politicians and bureaucrats. In such circumstances, it can be argued that ethnic communities are turning more and more into networks of benefit rather than affect.[3]

Such clientelist behavior by both religious networks and ethnic communities is a striking feature of election campaigns throughout Indonesia. In our expert survey, respondents were asked to assess the capacity of various types of leaders and organizations to influence voting behavior. In the perception of the 509 political observers surveyed, religious leaders were judged as retaining a strong reputation for being able to deliver votes, being placed equally first in their influence alongside community-level state representatives, such as village heads and neighborhood (RW) and sub-neighborhood (RT) heads. These two groups were followed closely by *adat* leaders and ethnic organizations. Party workers came in at fifth place.

The high level of influence seen as being exercised by figures such as village heads is significant. This pattern of linkages between voters and community-level government representatives is a good example of a *network of benefit*, in the sense that the influence of such local community leaders over voters is largely based on their capacity to provide benefits to voters—in this case access to prized state benefits. As we explore in greater detail in the next chapter, these officials provide citizens with the letters, identity cards, and endorsements they need to access public health and other services. They often also exercise informal influence over the allocation of cash transfers, subsidized rice, or other benefits, and negotiate on their citizens' behalf in dealings with outside authorities, such as police or land title officers. At the same time, such village and neighborhood leaders often enjoy a strong level of community approval and endorsement: they are elected, often play a critical role in mediating disputes and making decisions on behalf of their communities, and, at least in most places, conduct their affairs in a consultative mode, officiating at community meetings where local problems are talked through and resolved.

Such community-level state representatives thus powerfully combine cultural capital, based on their legitimacy as elected community leaders, with the sort of problem-solving capacity that brokers working for Indian or Argentinian political parties often rely on when mobilizing, giving them relatively strong influence over citizens at election time. Their capacity to solve everyday problems and the generally high levels of community support they enjoy lend these leaders local influence, which makes them attractive to politicians. Political candidates frequently state that village heads, as well as RT and RW heads, are the best people to recruit into success teams, precisely because of the authority they wield in their communities and, therefore, their ability to deliver votes.

To be sure, working through community leaders is far from being foolproof: community politics are often fractious, and not all community leaders will have the authority to deliver on their promises of votes. Ahmad Zainul Hamdi, writing about Madiun in East Java, notes that deals mediated by community leaders and involving the gifting of club goods by candidates often fail to deliver votes if there is significant disunity among local leaders:

> For this strategy to work, the candidate would work closely with both informal community leaders and formal leaders (such as the village, RW and RT heads) in the location. If they reached a deal to "guarantee" the votes of that location for the candidate, the candidate would then try to "quarantine" it from rivals by targeting it with donations or assistance packages of some sort—typically funds for road repairs or other infra-structure, money for the mosque or *musholla*, or other club goods. The logic was that this assistance—and the endorsement of the community leaders—would win local residents over to the candidate, and that those local leaders would then be reluctant to open access to their community to rival candidates. This strategy would come unstuck, however, if any significant leaders in the community concerned opposed the deal, or had conflicting loyalties. (Hamdi 2016, 288)

Another salient example of networks of benefit are those generated by eco-nomic activity, such as trade networks or work-related networks. For example, we noticed during our research that various types of commodity buyers (from rubber to cloves to coffee) were often solicited to join election campaigns. Such traders roam their districts to buy these commodities directly from farmers, which not only gives them access to many voters but also generates dependencies that can be turned into political leverage. In coastal communities, likewise, boat owners and money lenders have the authority to simply order their crew or subordinates to vote for the candidates of their choice (Haryanto 2017). Similarly, we noticed that many campaigns made efforts to enlist the support of big employers such as man-agers of plantations, factory owners, or contractors. Job security in these sectors is often precarious, as particularly plantation and construction workers can easily be dismissed. At election time, managers can exploit this vulnerability by instructing their workers to vote for their preferred candidate, adding a veiled threat that a failure to do so might have dire consequences. As these industries often depend on either government budgets or regulatory approval, their managers face strong incentives to engage in such manipulation of voting behavior.

Gift Giving as Network Building

Once the most important social networks and community leaders in the con-stituency are identified, how do candidates and their campaign teams incorpo-rate them in their election campaign? One perceptive informant, a customary leader in Lampung, regularly approached by politicians, answered this question thus: "In my perception, there has to be a relationship [which can be formed] in three ways: through friendship, family-clan relationship, or through gifts. It is important that people feel a connection with a politician. When there is no relationship, some gift has to be given to establish the bond" (interview, September 16, 2013). It certainly is possible to observe these three types of ties between politicians and leaders of social networks, though the list is far from definitive, and religious, ethnic, and other ties can also be used by a politician seeking to establish connections.

Ideally, a candidate will already have strong personal networks before entering the political arena. For candidates with backgrounds in large and important families and clans, such networks often come naturally, as they do for those who are already deeply embedded in bureaucratic or religious organizations. Others will need to spend considerable energy cultivating networks before embarking on a political career. For example, such prospective politicians might endeavor to become the chairperson of professional associations or sporting clubs, make donations to sports clubs or religious organizations, or patronize cultural events and ethnic associations. Accordingly, the curricula vitae of Indonesian politicians frequently contain dozens of organizational affiliations.

In fact, the list of network opportunities is almost endless. We came across ingenious examples in our fieldwork. For example, one member of a district parliament in Central Timor observed at the start of his political career that successful politicians over the long term are those who are "smart at binding their constituents to them." So he spent about 1 billion rupiah [$88,000] to set up a rice-hulling plant at the back of his house and to buy fertilizer, which he distributed for free to several hundred farmers in his electoral district. They pay him back in the form of a sack each of unhulled rice at harvest time, and he mills their rice for free at his home, keeping the rice dust, which he sells as pig feed, and reinvesting the profits in more fertilizer, forming a sort of revolving fund through which the farmers keep coming back to him for fertilizer each planting season. He also engages in other forms of munificence and public service: "If someone dies, I take care of it, right to the grave—no charge. . . . People want to build a house? I give sand, at a cost of about 1 million rupiah [eighty-eight dollars] per house." Every day, he says, people start coming to his house from 7 a.m.: "A sick child? I give them an envelope. Someone is bereaved? An envelope. Need held building a church? I help." He is particularly keen on helping churches: "When people go to the church now they'll look at it and remember me, and pray for me."

A striking aspect of this story is how this politician, though lacking personal experience in the agricultural economy, chose a role for himself that might almost have been lifted straight out of the literature on classical agrarian clientelism, as if he instinctively knew that the vulnerability of subsistence farmers made them particularly susceptible to clientelist appeals. But setting aside this aspect of the story, and the unusual forethought that went into the plan, such purposive network and reputation building, and the cultivation of a personal reputation as a social benefactor, are typical of the new patronage politicians who have become established in post-Suharto Indonesia. Long-term efforts at building social networks or forging ties repay themselves as election day nears: they potentially mean that the politician concerned needs to spend less money on handing out gifts.

But when the constituency is large, when politicians lack preexisting ties, or when competition is especially fierce, candidates will also typically need to spend considerable time in the immediate lead-up to an election in acquiring the support of networks, organizations, and community leaders who are new to them. Generally speaking, this process of obtaining support from a community and its leader goes through two steps.

First, usually after initial contacts and preliminary negotiations mediated by success team members, a candidate will seek the endorsement of a *kyai*, priest, village head, or other figure who occupies a respected role in a particular network or community. Candidates can attain such endorsement in various ways. Sometimes, it is enough simply to *sowan* (make a respectful visit) to the home of the leader—especially if the person concerned is a locally revered religious leader—and receive his or her endorsement, which is often expressed obliquely, and then let his or her followers know about it. Of course, it is preferable for the candidate if the leader states that endorsement explicitly, at a religious service or other function attended by the candidate. If the leader concerned is a village or neighborhood head, or the leader of an occupational or ethnic association, support will generally be expressed openly at a community meeting or in informal discussions with leading community figures. Such endorsement does not come for free, in the sense that the candidate will frequently present a gift of some sort, often a cash payment, to the leader concerned. Doing so is often not viewed as being untoward if the broker is a religious leader, given that presenting donations can be a standardized interaction between a follower and a religious leader, and given that many preachers earn their primary incomes from appearance fees. Voters can be resentful, however, if they learn that a village head or other community leader receives a private payment, suspecting that their votes are being sold off above their heads. Even so, such payments to community leaders are common.

Second, to cement this support the candidate typically donates club goods to the institution or group associated with the leader. The classic form is funds or building materials (cement, bricks, water tanks, corrugated iron, etc.) to help with the construction of a house of worship, religious school, orphanage, or other physical infrastructure, if a religious network is being targeted. When the deal is made with village or neighborhood leaders, the gifts are typically small-scale community infrastructure: construction of or repairs to bridges, meeting halls, irrigation ditches, village roads, lighting, sports fields, and the like, or sometimes support for community services such as fogging, ambulances, or garbage collection. Such gifts are in fact something of a cliché of modern Indonesian political campaigning: touring the countryside after an election campaign, one can see in almost every village the new tiles, domes, water tanks, and other improvements on local mosques, and villagers can often point out which roads have just been asphalted, which drains have been dug out, where the new wall around the graveyard is, and so on. Equally common are donations in cash or kind to a group or organization. The gift can be anything that helps the organization in its daily activities, ranging from a sound system or rugs for a prayer group, to new goal posts and footballs to a soccer club, crockery and cooking equipment to a women's communal savings group, fertilizer and seeds to a farmers' collective, to new pylons or nets for a fishers' cooperative.

All kinds of community leaders, but especially religious leaders, need to be cautious when accepting such gifts. Significant social stigma can attach to a religious leader who is seen as involving himself or herself too deeply in the "dirty" world of politics or who is seen as pursuing material goals at the expense of spiritual ones. As a result, *kyai* and other religious leaders who receive club goods (let alone individual gifts) from a candidate will often be reluctant to issue an explicit endorsement or directive to their followers to support the candidate. Instead, the leader's endorsement is typically expressed indirectly, such as when the religious leader appears with the candidate at a rally and recites the opening prayer. In turn, the political candidates who provide club goods to religious networks frequently present such gifts as *sedekah* or *amal*—religious charity—often stating explicitly that no *pamrih* (expectation of personal gain) is attached to the gift. Thus, even though everybody will understand the electoral context in which the gift is presented, typically enough ambiguity surrounds it for at least some recipients to feel no obligation to repay with their votes. The great density of religious organizations and networks in Indonesian society makes them very attractive for politicians, especially for a neophyte who feels that a reputation for piety and a connection with a religious network translate to a good chance of being elected. But the ambiguous nature of religious gifting, and the intense competition there is for the loyalties of religious networks, often undercut effectiveness in delivering votes: candidates who reach out through religious networks often lose (Aspinall and As'ad 2015; Ismanto and Thaha 2016).

Perhaps not surprisingly, candidates we followed often professed a preference for dealing with community leaders like village, RW, and RT heads instead. Such people are vote brokers par excellence in Indonesia. The deals they make have the advantage of generating more explicit forms of support. Indeed, it is very often the village, RW, or RT head who makes the approach to the candidate, knowing that election time represents an opportunity to extract benefits from politicians and obtain needed community infrastructure. One particular advantage that such strategies have is that they are explicitly transactional. Unlike with donations to religious leaders, little ambiguity will surround a donation of infrastructure to a village or urban community at election time. In fact, candidates will often draw up a written "political contract" (*kontrak politik*) that details precisely what it is they promise to deliver to the community concerned in exchange for support (Sulaiman 2016, 63–64; Rohi 2016, 380). As noted above, village, RW, or RT heads are used to dealing with their communities in a consultative mode, and they often exhaustively talk through the deals they strike with politicians, if not with all members of the community then at least with community leaders, explaining the benefits and the need for the community to unite behind the candidate concerned, and delegating to leading individuals the task of mobilizing votes.

A large proportion of these club goods are funded privately by candidates. First-timers have little option but to pay for them personally. But if the candidate is an incumbent, a cheaper strategy is to use state resources. When they can, elected parliamentarians and local executive government heads direct government budgets—such as infrastructure projects or the so-called aspiration funds allotted to them—to targeted communities, which they then draw into an ongoing clientelistic relationship. We discussed in chapter 5 how Tangerang's deputy mayor used a garbage program to build local garbage-collection groups, which subsequently helped his election campaign, and we look at the use of such resources in greater detail in the next chapter. For present purposes it is important to note that one result of this dynamic is that many local government programs acquire the character of network building: while having various attractive formal goals—from garbage disposal to health education and from rural development to youth training—the unstated political aim of many such programs is to build networks that can help the candidate who provided them ensure his or her reelection. If politicians manage to implement these programs in such a way that recipients get the impression that their access to the benefit is due to a politician's personal intervention, the result can be electoral rewards.

Take for example the reelection strategy of Irwan Setiawan, a member of the closest thing Indonesia has to a puritanical Islamist party, the PKS, in the East Java provincial legislature. Irwan, who represents a largely rural seat in the very east of that province, is a former campus religious activist, and not even a native of East Java. In 2009, he was first elected by relying largely on the party's cadres and its Muslim Brotherhood–inspired networks to organize his campaign. His votes were almost all in urban areas, or, as he put it, "from voters who watch television and read newspapers and get their political information that way." By the time of the 2014 election, his support base was significantly transformed, with much of it now located in rural parts of his electoral district, and consisting of people who were culturally far different from the rather austere urban support base he relied on in 2009. His strategy had also shifted dramatically, from religious appeals to targeting networks of benefit using livelihood projects.

As a member of East Java's legislature, Irwan had access to "aspiration funds"— a type of fund that legislators can direct toward favored purposes in their constituencies (see chapter 7)—to the tune of 4 billion rupiah [$350,000] annually. Using these funds, he was able to help between 100 and 150 village cooperatives or groups per year. He forged his initial relations with beneficiaries during his official study tours to the constituency (a few hours by car from Surabaya, where the provincial parliament is located, and where he spends most of his time), with these visits taking place three times a year and allowing him to meet about a thousand people on each visit. At community forums, local *tokoh masyarakat* would express their "aspirations" to him—for road construction, livestock projects, agricultural assistance, school buildings, and the like. A particular favorite of Irwan's was providing goats and cattle to farmers' cooperatives, both for what he saw as the livelihood benefits the recipients experienced, and for the gratitude these grants evoked.

As a result of his efforts in delivering these government-funded small-scale projects and benefits, his support base penetrated deeply into rural areas over the course of his first five-year term, during which he would visit even remote mountainous areas on his motorcycle. After establishing initial contacts he would maintain communication with grant beneficiaries both through electronic communication and through repeat visits: "We maintain the groups we've helped." During the 2009 campaign, he visited only ten to fifteen subdistricts in the electoral constituency; in 2014, months ahead of the election, he was able to say he had visited them all, more than sixty in total. He also built a success team, outside his formal party structure, that aimed to place village coordinators in three hundred villages, an achievement that was itself a "product of all the communication I've been doing over the last four years." These village coordinators and the polling booth witnesses they would recruit were in turn almost all from groups he had helped, though some were individuals who hoped he would help them in the future. The attraction of such programs for elected politicians should be obvious: they can reduce their own expenses while using government budgets to increase their reelection chances. In the next chapter, we look in greater detail at how such patronage dynamics are transforming the delivery of public services in Indonesia.

These exchanges between community leaders and candidates, however pragmatic they seem, are more than just straightforward transactions. We highlighted in chapter 2 the contrast between marketist and culturalist approaches to political clientelism, and pointed out that the effectiveness of clientelistic practices often stems from prevalent norms and expectations. These community gifts illustrate this observation: even while such gifts may be strategic and targeted, politicians actually possess few ways to ensure that gifts are transformed into votes. In continuing to hand out such gifts, they are trying to do more than just purchase support. Similar to how we described cash payments in the preceding chapter, club goods can serve as signals to voters that a candidate possesses certain desirable attributes, especially that he or she is truly "caring" (*peduli*) and has the ability to deliver community improvements. Accordingly, some candidates describe community donations as an "entry door" (*pintu masuk*) into a community where they lack connections: even if the gifts do not guarantee votes, they help demonstrate the seriousness of a candidacy. Furthermore, as anthropologists studying gift giving have repeatedly emphasized, community gifts also serve to build and solidify social relationships (e.g., Björkman 2014). As the customary leader from Lampung quoted above mentioned, gifts serve to "open the relationship." Ad hoc gifts help to build connections with voters in the absence of other means—for example strong grassroots party networks—of doing so.

The Limits of Club Goods

Despite the perceived indispensability of community gifts, post-election interviews with politicians are often full of complaints about them. There is a common view among candidates and brokers in Indonesia that club-goods strategies are insufficiently effective on their own to bind voters to candidates. Take, for example, this comment by a Gerindra candidate running for a seat in East Java's provincial parliament, when asked whether it was still an effective electoral strategy to rely on the brokerage of *kyai* or other influential community leaders:

> No, that's really changed. Now, no candidate wants to trust the *kyai*. They'll take the money and eat it up themselves, and won't necessarily get their followers to vote for you. Now the trend is that if you want to use money, you must do it by name, by using KTP [ID cards]. It's no longer good enough [for a broker] to just claim a mass following of five

> thousand people, because a lot of those people won't vote the way [the broker] tells them. It's often just a claim. But if [the broker] hands over [the voter's] ID cards to the candidate, at the very least that is more of a guarantee than just approaching community leaders. . . . If [brokers] can't give you the [photocopies of] ID cards, that means they are not working seriously for you. Because ID cards are in people's houses [so they are evidence that brokers have been talking directly to voters]. (Confidential interview, March 6, 2014)

Another example is a comment by a broker who worked for an unsuccessful PAN provincial candidate in Central Java:

> He gave them so many cows, and they didn't vote for him. It was all a useless waste. He gave away so many cows I lost count. . . . He gave donations for the *musholla*, for streetlights, for *sedekah bumi*, for *tayub* [local cultural festivals], all sorts of things, but yeah, on D-day they voted for some other guy. Because on D-day he didn't give them enough money. It's much more effective to give it on D-day. If you want to fight, you've got to fight for real. You've got to . . . what do you call it? . . . You've got to be pragmatic. (Focus group discussion, August 21, 2014)

The same broker noted that the candidates he had been supporting had delivered many projects to their target constituencies, but on voting day it counted for little in the eyes of voters who reacted to cash payments as if "a long dry season was extinguished by a sudden rain."

In the context of such disappointments, it is not surprising that, in the days and weeks following elections, the Indonesian media often carry stories of candidates who are angered by the poor vote they received in a particular community they had targeted with club goods. Driven by a sense of betrayal, such candidates then take action to withdraw their gifts—pulling out water pipes they have installed, taking down streetlights, or even ripping out tiles from mosques. Politicians' own expressions of disappointment are frequently accompanied by descriptions of the voters' selfishness (a favorite theme of Indonesian politicians) and their shortsighted preference for individual rather than communal forms of patronage.

The frustration is partly due to the shaky foundation of these transactions. One problem is that their electoral effectiveness depends to a great extent on the influence of community leaders over their followers. Levels of trust in the authority of particular categories of community leader vary greatly across Indonesia. While in certain areas the advice of local notables carries much weight—for instance in the clan-based societies of Papua, and other parts of eastern

Indonesia—in many other areas economic development, the growth of complex media landscapes, digital communication, education, and migration are loosening ties between established community leaders and citizens and generating more atomized patterns of social relations. Increasingly, ordinary voters have access to multiple sources of information and political authority. For example, while many residents of urban areas may still be attached to a local religious preacher, such areas are typically thickly populated by religious networks, so that multiple religious activities will be within easy reach, with yet more sources of religious advice and guidance available through electronic and digital media. Access to competing sources of religious authority does not necessarily make people more skeptical of political advice offered by their local preacher, but it inevitably contextualizes it and makes it seem less portentous than it would be if that preacher was the sole religious leader accessible on a daily basis.

Another source of these complaints by politicians is a basic free-rider problem that besets club-goods strategies. Even if a voter receives some benefit from a club good as a member of a collective, she may feel that other beneficiaries will repay the giver with their support, freeing her to support some other candidate. Political operators in the field are all too aware of this problem. Take for example the following comments made by a village-level vote broker who had been supporting a Golkar candidate in Central Java:

> Well, it is a fact, there was one place where Pak R. from the national DPR helped them by getting them an asphalt road, but he lost to I. S., who was distributing 10,000 rupiah [about 88 cents] a head. If you think about it logically, if you are asphalting a major road, how much money would that cost, compared to just 10,000 rupiah? But people think simply here. They think, "Well, who is it that enjoys the road? It's not just me, is it? So I may as well take this [money]." . . . So, just think, if every person [in the village] contributed 100,000 rupiah each to build a road, even that wouldn't be enough; but 10,000 rupiah—which is just enough to buy a bowl of meatball soup—could defeat that gift. (Focus group discussion, August 25, 2014)

The conclusion of these and many other candidates interviewed before and after the 2014 election was that the most effective electoral strategies do not rely on club goods or individualized vote buying in isolation, but in combination. The most effective candidates are those who cultivate a target area and "open the door" with club goods of various kinds, but who then follow up those efforts with individual vote buying or gift giving as election day nears. Often candidates talk about their club goods as either an "entry door" or a way to "open the road" (*membuka jalan*), while the payments are a way to "bind" (*mengikat*) the voters to them. Little wonder that elections are such an expensive business for candidates.

We have argued in this chapter that the weak mobilizational capacity of political parties in post-Suharto Indonesia generates intense politicization of nonparty social networks at election times. As candidates need to look elsewhere to develop means to connect with voters, they try to incorporate a wide range of social networks into their campaign efforts. Providing various kinds of gifts is a near-indispensable means to build such relationships, particularly where none existed before an election season. This logic accounts for why provision of club goods constitutes such an important aspect of election campaigns in Indonesia: in contrast to countries with strong party networks, like Argentina or even India, in Indonesia politicians generally have to build their own networks. The resulting need to engage in ad hoc deals with community leaders contributes considerably to the cost of election campaigns.

This kind of political instrumentalization has important consequences for the nature of governance in Indonesia. As well as adding to the personal expenses that candidates rack up while running for office, and increasing their incentive for engaging in corruption, the need for network building also shapes the character of government programs. As politicians have become increasingly aware that their chances of getting reelected hinge on establishing connections with local social networks, they have turned to using government programs to forge such networks. Virtually every politician wants to be like Irwan Setiawan, the PKS legislator from East Java discussed above, who used the power of office to distribute government grants and so expand his personal network throughout his electoral constituency. We discuss how Indonesian government programs are increasingly being used for such electioneering purposes, and the consequences for governance, in the next chapter.

Part 3
DISCRETIONARY CONTROL

7

GOVERNANCE AND PUBLIC SPENDING

Pak "Toguh" seemed an odd choice as the deputy head of Arief's election campaign. Arief had given him the responsibility of building the grassroots network of his success team. Retiring just three months before the elections, Toguh had been the head of the municipal department in charge of garbage collection and city beautification. In India or Argentina such a person would likely be an anonymous bureaucrat, buried in the offices of the municipality, rather than a budding political operator. Why would Arief rely on such a person to set up his campaign network?

Arief's choice makes sense if we consider how skillfully Pak Toguh had used his position to build a network of dependents throughout the city. Toguh had been in charge of a municipal garbage program called "making a thousand garbage banks." Under the banner of promoting recycling and waste management, Tangerang municipality had set up garbage recycling groups. Toguh ordered his staff to hand over garbage they collected to these garbage banks. Tangerang's many factories also produced a steady stream of garbage. Some of these factories, wishing to remain on a good footing with the municipality, also heeded Toguh's request to allow the garbage banks to process their waste. These policies provided a valuable opportunity: throughout the city about six hundred people found jobs as waste sorters, earning a livelihood by selling the plastics, metals, and paper they extracted from the garbage. Their work was overseen by about one hundred garbage bank coordinators.

Pak Toguh had managed this program. An outspoken man with an authoritative demeanor, he had realized from the outset the political value of his program:

"I managed these programs, they were our advantage. The people in these networks of education and garbage, they were drawn into the campaign. The program was not only about, for example, informing people about garbage; it was also to connect people to us. . . . There has to be a *link* with the future leader, they have to connect, right? They feel enthusiastic about working because they hope there will be a leader who will make sure that the programs they work in will function well. The community was ready to support us" (interview, November 14, 2014).

As Toguh described it, he built up Arief's campaign network by drawing on the connections that grew out of the garbage program (and similar educational and health care programs). The benefits that the waste sorters derived from the program generated a sense of loyalty and obligation to the officials who had provided them. The workers wanted to keep their valuable new jobs, motivating them to enlist in Arief's campaign team. As Suhaimi, one of the garbage bank managers, explained during a campaign event: "Our organization just worked together with the government. But I told them [the garbage sorters] 'How about the future of our city? We should not elect the wrong candidate. Our current leader [Arief] does not just make promises, his work is proven.' So we linked up [with the campaign] to make Arief win."

Tangerang's garbage program is an example of how incumbent politicians can use their positions to cultivate support and gain electoral advantage. As such, Arief's use of the garbage program does not differ much from, say, the way in which Peronist politicians in Argentina use local maternal support programs (Auyero 2001), or how Indian municipal councilors turn government funds for improving basic amenities into electoral assets (Berenschot 2010). But at a subtle level, there is an important difference. Arief's campaign asset was not just the garbage program, but also the loyalty of the bureaucrat—Pak Toguh—who had managed it. The selection of the beneficiaries of the program and thus the distribution of its benefits did not rest in the hands of party cadres. This selection was at the discretion of a bureaucrat, which was the reason why Arief gave Toguh such an important position in his campaign team. Toguh could readily transfer the authority he had gained as the dispenser of the garbage program to his role as campaign organizer.

In chapter 3, we discussed how Indonesia built a state-centered form of patronage politics during three decades of the New Order regime. Military officers, bureaucrats, and their business allies benefited from an inward-looking system of patronage distribution in which rents circulated mostly among elites. In subsequent chapters we discussed how political parties were sidelined in election campaigns in post–New Order Indonesia, with candidates instead relying on nonparty social networks for their campaigning purposes. We explained this relative marginality of parties by emphasizing the role of Indonesia's candidate-centered electoral rules, and by pointing to the legacy of the New Order's patronage system.

In this chapter, we discuss the nature of governance and the provision of public services in Indonesia, focusing particularly on the ongoing struggle between bureaucrats, parties, and politicians for control over patronage goods. In doing so, we explore a further aspect of the legacy of the New Order by pointing to the relatively limited control that political parties are able to exert over the distribution of state patronage resources, such as budgets, programs, and benefits. Instead, it is primarily state representatives—by which we mean both elected local officials and civil servants—who exercise such control. They are the ones who can use state resources—such as welfare programs, development funds, and government contracts—to influence voting behavior. While in many patronage democracies the clientelistic distribution of state resources is organized through party networks, in Indonesia it is more often facilitated by persons anchored in elected and career positions in the state apparatus. Despite many efforts, parties have been unable to fully wrest control of state patronage resources out of the hands of such officials. In contrast to party-centered patronage networks in countries like Argentina and India, patronage networks in Indonesia remain state centered.

However, the nature of Indonesia's state-centered patronage networks has changed dramatically since the New Order years. For one thing, state representatives, as understood here, come in two main varieties. First, unlike in the New Order period, the apex leaders at each level of executive government are now elected. At the community level these elected officials are village heads and, beneath them, neighborhood and sub-neighborhood heads, who are officially nonpartisan and are not nominated by parties. Higher up the chain are the *bupati*, mayors, governors, and their deputies, who exercise much control over government budgets in the new decentralized Indonesia and, as we saw in chapter 3, are typically nominated by parties but often enjoy only weak relationships with them. As we shall see, elected officials at every level have an interest in using the resources they control for their own electoral purposes. A second group of state representatives is bureaucrats. Civil servants retain significant residual authority over the allocation of many state programs. Particularly important are the *lurah* (heads of urban precincts, the unelected urban equivalents of the rural village heads) and *camat* (subdistrict heads), as well as the heads of various government bureaus (*dinas*) or work units (*satuan kerja pemerintah daerah*) in the regions. Also trying to access state patronage resources are the more clearly party-aligned politicians located in Indonesia's legislatures, where their powers to approve budgets and interrogate executive government heads also provide them with access to state resources, though with less personalized control than exercised by other state representatives.

Though patronage distribution networks remain state centered, in other respects they have changed considerably. Under Suharto's "franchise system" (McLeod 2011), patronage networks were organized in an orderly pyramid, with clear hierarchies that reduced competition. Politics in the post–New Order period is characterized by a fragmentation of points of access to patronage resources and constant battles to control that access. Fragmentation is largely due to democratization and decentralization, with democratization giving greater powers to elected officials and institutions (notably legislatures) to influence budgeting, and decentralization pushing government funds and programming down to the districts, villages, and local agencies. Various anticorruption reforms have tried to place budgetary allocations beyond the discretionary control of officials, but elected politicians and low-level state representatives alike subvert such reforms and devise new discretionary funds. As we shall see, programs that are formally supposed to be allocated on the basis of transparent procedures— whether these be fair tendering processes or selection of welfare recipients on the basis of need—are often diverted for clientelistic and rent-seeking purposes.

In this chapter, we substantiate these arguments by examining the distribution of three categories of state benefits: welfare programs, development funds, and government contracts. Our aim is not to provide a comprehensive overview of the relevant policies and procedures. Rather, we aim to identify how and by whom these benefits are distributed in practice. Drawing both on our fieldwork and the expert survey, we examine the extent to which political actors manage to circumvent formal distributive procedures and put state resources to clientelistic use by making access to them contingent on political support. We also discuss the influence of politicians, state representatives, and parties over the provision of these state benefits, exploring who it is, exactly, who controls their actual distribution.

Welfare Programs

In recent years, political scientists working in many parts of the world have drawn attention to how social welfare programs, such as those providing subsidized food, medicine, or other benefits, or conditional or unconditional cash transfers, can get hijacked for clientelistic purposes by ruling political parties (e.g., Calvo and Murillo 2004; Nichter 2014). In fact, party-mediated clientelistic provision of social welfare services has a long history in many parts of the world. As we made clear at the start of this book, in both Argentina and India local party representatives are active intermediaries between citizens and state institutions. In Argentina's *unidades básicas* (basic units) and India's "roadside offices," party representatives—referred to as *punteros* in Argentina and "party workers" in India—engage in almost round-the-clock efforts to help neighbors solve everyday problems. Frequently, this help involves mediating access to state benefits. Auyero (2001) describes, for example, how in Argentina state welfare benefits—from powdered milk and packaged food to subsidized medicine and municipal jobs—are often distributed through local branches of the Justicialist Party. Similarly, Indian politicians and party workers use their control over bureaucrats to provide loyal party supporters with access to public services like school admissions, hospital beds, and street lighting (Berenschot 2010, 2011a).

Not coincidentally, in both Argentina and India the organization of election campaigns lies largely in the hands of these local party branches. Auyero (2001, 117) describes not only how effective these *punteros* are as vote mobilizers, but also how this capacity is premised on their everyday role as intermediaries between state institutions and citizens: "In the act of getting help, problem holders become increasingly ensnared within the Peronist web. . . . Party agents generate a network of obligation through their service activities; people are said to repay these obligations by voting as they are told." In India, meanwhile, party representatives deliver votes by building a capacity to deal with the state bureaucracy: "Party workers . . . take issues, complaints, problems of people around them . . . to politicians and state officials, and . . . make use of their political backing to deal with the bureaucracy. In this way, the support of politicians lends both party workers and social workers status and authority in their neighbourhoods" (Berenschot 2011b, 114; see also Auerbach 2016; De Wit 2016).[1]

What are the Indonesian equivalents of the Peronist *unidades básicas* and India's roadside offices? The closest approximation is the *kantor desa*, or village office, of village heads and their staff, and perhaps the houses of the RW and RT heads. These community-level functionaries are simultaneously elected officeholders and the lowest rungs in the Indonesian state and its growing welfare machinery. They are the people who strike the deals with higher-level politicians and bureaucrats when community members need to get drainage repaired or potholes filled, they write the letters people need to prove eligibility to welfare programs, and they are the ones who negotiate with the police when a villager gets in trouble with the law. For example, these base-level state functionaries provide the needy with the all-important SKTM (*surat keterangan tidak mampu* or "letter indicating poverty") that can provide recipients with access to district-level welfare programs. The village heads and, below them, the RW and RT heads are also the persons to whom citizens turn in order to obtain an identity card, register a birth or the sale of land, or get help obtaining medical treatment or admission to a school. Government employees will often ask for an introduction letter (*surat pengantar*) from such community officials as the first requirement to get the requisite bureaucratic processes going. Village heads are, together with their urban equivalents, the unelected *lurah*, and the RW and RT heads, still entrusted with implementing a wide range of basic programs, from the management of garbage collection to the organization of various welfare and health care programs. Elected by their neighbors, they operate as the interface between Indonesian citizens and the state (Kurasawa 2009).

The offices and homes of these community-level officers are not decorated with banners of political parties. Indeed, formally speaking, none of them are allowed to be party members (one legacy of the "mono-loyalty" enforced by Golkar was that in the post-Suharto period political reformers were keen to ensure the political neutrality of the state apparatus and insulate it from party politics). Yet Indonesian politicians are well aware of the importance of these low-level state functionaries in their communities, and try to draw them into their campaign teams. But they do so as individuals, by way of personalized networks and success teams, rather than through party structures. The political parties themselves hardly concern themselves with day-to-day delivery of government services. In fact, observers of Indonesian politics regularly make remarks such as "On the local level, party activities are almost non-existent outside election times" (Tomsa 2008, 41; see also Tan 2006; Mietzner 2013b). The offices that political parties maintain in district or provincial capitals do not see the hustle and bustle of their Argentinian or Indian counterparts. Party offices often give an impression of desolation, being staffed by one or two weary doorkeepers who seem unaccustomed to receiving visitors. Especially at the subdistrict level and below, they are often phantom offices—addresses given to the election commission for the party registration process, but rarely if ever used for party activities.

The relative absence of political parties between elections is not, as many Indonesians believe, simply due to laziness. The main reason that these offices are not as lively as the Peronist basic units or India's roadside offices is structural: Indonesian parties have less to offer. They do not possess the discretionary control over welfare benefits that their Argentinian or Indian counterparts enjoy. As a legacy of the restricted role of political parties during the New Order period, community-level state officials still have much more influence over the distribution of welfare benefits. As a result, the private homes of these individuals, along with the village office, are the most bustling places in the village, with a constant stream of visitors seeking letters, assistance, or advice.

Village, RW, and RT heads have played the main mediating role between citizens and the state since the New Order period, as we noted in chapter 3, but since the downfall of Suharto they have had even more to offer to their neighbors. Indonesia's central government has introduced a slew of national welfare programs such as subsidized rice, direct cash transfers, a conditional family subsidy program, and a family welfare saving program. In addition, both national as well as local district-level governments have adopted programs of subsidized education and health care. Together, these programs have reached many millions of households.

Officially, these programs are distributed according to need. Beneficiaries are identified in various ways. Typically, recipients of district-level welfare or health care programs need to obtain an SKTM through the village head or *lurah*, sometimes with help from a community health worker as proof that they are really poor and deserving of support. For national programs, this discretionary power of local state representatives is, at least on paper, more limited. The beneficiaries of the subsidized rice program, the unconditional cash transfers, and the new national health insurance scheme are selected through surveys, carried out by staff of Indonesia's Central Statistics Agency (BPS). These surveys assess households according to various indicators of poverty—ranging from income and expenditure to the absence of a refrigerator, sealed floor, or motorcycle in the household—to ensure proper targeting. Furthermore, the unconditional cash transfers are distributed through post offices, further limiting the role of state representatives.

Yet access to these welfare programs is often perceived to be highly political. It seems that local state representatives at least sometimes make access to these programs contingent on political support or personal connections. According to a campaign organizer from Tangerang city, district-level welfare programs especially lend themselves to being used for clientelistic strategies: "The subsidized rice program is a program from the national government. When someone is poor, they will get it, even if they did not vote for the mayor or someone else. But if it is a local program, this rarely happens. He [the RT head] will then see a relationship [between the program and] the previous election. He is going to prioritize the voters [who supported the mayor] in the previous election" (interview, May 26, 2014).

In our research, observers from outside Java were especially likely to feel that politicization of access to welfare programs went further, as did this villager from North Lampung: "Programs like subsidized rice and the direct cash transfer, they are already cut from above. But whatever reaches the village, the village head will distribute it to his family and in-laws. . . . These programs should go to poor people, but in reality they do not get it. People with a nice car and a big house can get it. Why? Because if you have no family or close personal relationship with them, they will forget you. The village head will consider: 'Will I get a benefit from him, will he be of use to me?' People like that will get the benefit" (interview, February 4, 2014).

Such an observation suggests that village, RW, and RT heads sometimes suc-ceed in manipulating the selection of welfare recipients to benefit supporters and acquaintances. Indeed, one study on the implementation of welfare programs across Indonesia concluded that "village heads utilized both Raskin [subsidized rice] and BLT [direct cash transfer] programs to reward people who voted for the village heads in the village-head elections and to keep their political loyalties for the next village-head elections" (Mulyadi 2013, v).

Many of the observers in our expert survey agreed with this observation, although not everywhere. In fact, this topic elicited a highly varied response (see figure 7.1). Experts especially in Surabaya (average 1.92 on a scale of 1 to 5) but

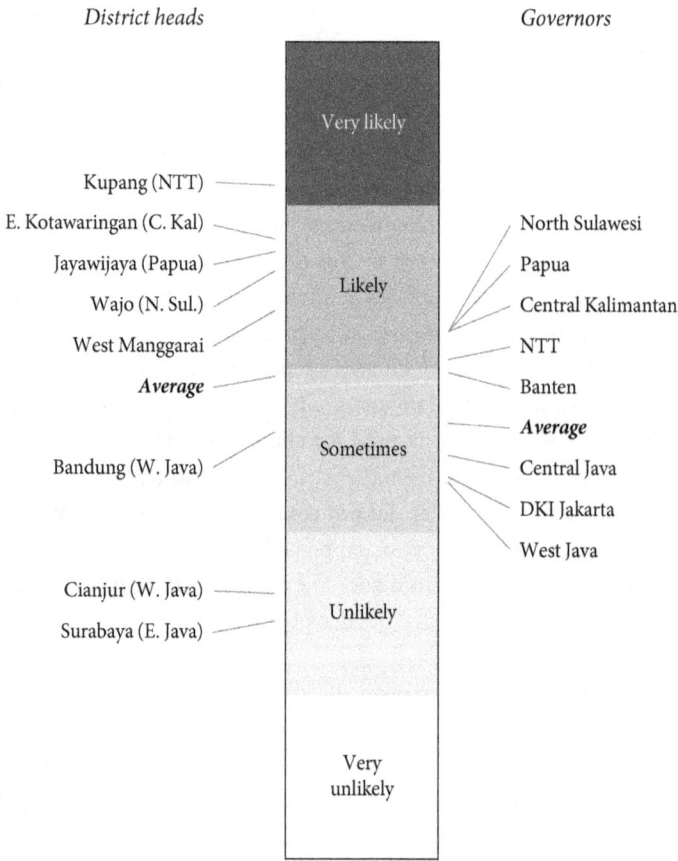

District heads   Governors

Very likely

Kupang (NTT)

E. Kotawaringan (C. Kal)   North Sulawesi
Jayawijaya (Papua)   Papua
                           Likely
Wajo (N. Sul.)   Central Kalimantan
West Manggarai   NTT

Average   Banten
                                                  Average
                           Sometimes
Bandung (W. Java)   Central Java
                                                  DKI Jakarta
                                                  West Java

Cianjur (W. Java)   Unlikely
Surabaya (E. Java)

Very
unlikely

Expert Survey question: In your estimation, when implementing welfare programs (such as handouts of cash and rice, or subsidized health care) after elections, how likely is it that local government representatives (such as village heads, RT heads, or *lurah*) prioritize people who voted for their preferred candidate for district head [governor]?

FIGURE 7.1 Welfare programs as political rewards

also elsewhere in Java (and Aceh) felt that voting behavior did not really influence the manner in which village heads and RW/RT heads implemented welfare programs. Yet respondents in more rural and remote locations in Kalimantan, East Nusa Tenggara, and Sulawesi felt local state representatives were very partisan in their functioning, with Sumatran districts scoring somewhere in between. Particularly in Kupang, the average answer (4.69) could hardly be higher.

Such high scores, particularly in east Indonesia, are somewhat puzzling, given the use of standardized surveys to select recipients for the national programs. It might be that people perceive distribution of welfare programs as being manipulated by village elites either because of New Order memories or because these elites have an interest in maintaining that perception, while the scope for manipulation is actually limited. Yet evaluative reports on these welfare programs do suggest that they are marred by considerable targeting errors. An early assessment (in 2002) of the subsidized rice program found that of all beneficiaries, only 53 percent belonged to the targeted poorest income group (Hastuti and Suryahadi 2007, vii). A World Bank assessment of a new national health insurance scheme found in 2010 that only 47.6 percent of the beneficiaries were actually poor, while as many as 20 percent belonged to the highest income groups (Harimurti et al. 2013, 12). Such assessments also recorded widespread complaints about perceived unfairness in the selection of beneficiaries (Dwicaksono, Nurman, and Prasetya 2012, 27).

Evidently, the survey methodology employed by the Indonesian government is not watertight. While BPS enumerators are supposed to collect their data independently, in practice they often limit their visits to the house of the village head, where they jointly fill in the forms about each household in the village. It seems likely that the status of village, RW, and RT heads, as the go-to persons for information, lends these local state representatives considerable leeway in influencing the final selection for national programs. This influence is even more pronounced for district-level welfare programs, where village officials are often directly tasked with the selection of beneficiaries.

While thus differing in degree across Indonesia, such observations suggest that access to welfare benefits remains highly mediated. Prevalent social norms, personal interests, including electoral interests, and habits carried over from the New Order all discourage local state representatives from implementing government programs in a purely impersonal manner. As a result, the quality and character of personal ties of family, friendship, and neighborhood continue to affect the capacity of citizens to deal with the Indonesian state. For citizens for whom formal laws and procedures are largely irrelevant, cultivating clientelistic ties with village or neighborhood elites constitutes a much more reliable, and familiar, strategy for assuring access to a state grant, medical treatment, or school admission than relying on formal procedures alone. In such circumstances, feeling a sense of obligation to the gatekeeper who facilitates such access is hardly a burden, and repaying it by such a minor act as following his or her advice about whom to support in a legislative or *bupati* election serves as reassurance of continued access. Indeed, for most people living with a fragile livelihood and unpredictable state institutions, nurturing clientelistic ties with village heads and other community leaders is one way to gain some sense of security.[2]

As a result of such dynamics, the implementation of welfare programs often gets entangled in village-level politics. As village heads, as well as RW and RT heads, are elected, they can be tempted to use these programs to reward followers and to (threaten to) punish families who support opposing candidates. Power struggles between village elites can be bitter, and village-head elections can be expensive and high-stakes, with extensive vote buying (Aspinall and Rohman 2017). In such a context, controlling the spigot of welfare programs can be a useful political tool for a village head—though acting in a way that is seen as unfair can also backfire when standing for reelection. Providing access to welfare programs and other services can also help these community-level officials accumulate the social debts that enable them to play an important role as vote brokers in election campaigns. Party leaders, higher-level elected officials, and candidates know very well that these community officials have the greatest social and political influence at the grass roots, which is why they try so hard to draw them into their success teams. To facilitate this process, incumbent *bupati* or legislators often cultivate village heads with projects and other benefits, and clientelistic relationships often grow between them (Paskarina 2016). In sum, while social welfare programs nurture clientelistic relationships linking politicians with ordinary citizens, these relationships typically grow outside of party structures and are instead mediated by community-level state representatives.

Even so, we should be open to the possibility that this situation might gradually change. While conducting our research, we came across indications that politicians and party members were starting to offer themselves as alternative intermediaries in securing public services. The recent extension of subsidized health care and other programs offers opportunities for political actors to earn local gratitude and fame by helping people overcome the practical administrative hurdles involved in accessing these services. For example, during the 2014 legislative election, one of us (Aspinall) observed PDI-P workers in East Java's capital city, Surabaya, offering to arrange to do the paperwork and fee collection for *kampung* members to help them participate in the national health insurance scheme, while also offering to negotiate various *kampung* improvements with the city government. In many parts of the town, local RW and RT heads were members of the PDI-P. In Jakarta, too, observers have described district and provincial parliament members engaging in efforts to help their voters to access the subsidized health care program and other government services, even if they mostly do so by forming personalized teams rather than relying on party networks (Dewi, Hajanto, and Purba 2016; Hanani 2016; Berenschot, Hanani, and Sambodho 2018). While such developments are a recent trend and seemingly limited to a few areas, they are reminiscent of the way Indian and Argentinian party workers operate, and might be pointing toward the emergence of party-based machine politics.

Still, for the time being, when Indonesians want to access state services, most turn first to their RT and RW heads, their village heads, *lurah*, and other community-level officials. Because such officials exercise discretionary control over the distribution of the kinds of state benefits—welfare payments, health care, education—that matter to voters, and because they can help them with the paperwork needed to access such benefits, they accumulate influence, gratitude, and social debts, making them highly influential vote mobilizers. As we mentioned in chapter 6, the political observers in our expert survey considered community officials (together with civil servants) to have the greatest capacity to sway votes, just above religious leaders. Similarly, when the survey organization Indikator Politik Indonesia in a nationally representative survey asked respondents whose advice they follow in political matters, the largest group of respondents (27 percent) indicated that they were influenced by the voting advice of village, RW, and RT heads.[3] The influence of such public officials on voting behavior contrasts sharply with Indian experiences. When India's large National Election Survey asked "In deciding whom to vote for, whose opinion mattered to you most?" state representatives were not even offered as an answer category. According to Indian respondents, the opinion of family members and local political leaders are most important when deciding their vote. Significantly, 62 percent of Indian respondents reporting the party mattered more than the candidate when deciding their vote.[4]

Findings such as those revealed by the Indikator survey are reinforced by our qualitative fieldwork. Our informants often linked the political influence of village heads and other community officials to their capacity to shape the distribution of state benefits. As a resident of Tangerang (Banten) remarked, "When the RT head distributed the voting ballots, he says 'please vote for this one.' We just listen and smile, [because] he is the one who distributes this card [for access to welfare services] to us." Or, as a voter in Lampung put it: "We take money from all [the candidates], but we usually vote for the one close to the RT head. Because he is close to us, and he manages things for us. We need to ask for his help."

Development Funds

The allocation of government budgets to improve community facilities—roads, bridges, schools, electricity connections, and the like—do not lend themselves to clientelistic exchange in the same way as welfare programs targeting individuals. Whereas access to welfare programs can be made contingent on individual voting behavior, the same is not possible for public infrastructure like bridges or schools, which can be used by anyone, regardless of whom they vote for. Such items are called "club goods" precisely because they are awarded to a community rather than an individual. That does not mean, however, that such benefits cannot be awarded in a clientelistic manner. On the contrary, we saw in chapter 6 that club goods are an important medium of exchange in Indonesia's patronage democracy. The allocation of budgets to improve public infrastructure and basic amenities—we will call them development funds here—can be made clientelistic when politicians award these funds to a particular locality as a reward for past or future electoral support.

Development funds have long been critical to politics in Indonesia. The New Order regime made development its central goal, using it to justify repression of opponents. The regime's performance legitimacy depended on its ability to deliver sustained improvement in community-level infrastructure. Under the New Order, control over development budgets was centralized in the bureaucratic hierarchy. The relevant ministries in Jakarta established development priorities and rolled out programs in a uniform manner across the archipelago. As we saw in chapter 3, the bureaucracy used these budgets to maintain political loyalty. Compliant villages that recorded high votes for Golkar were rewarded with projects, giving village elites strong incentives to suppress community unrest.

In post-Suharto Indonesia, too, infrastructure remains a central concern of ordinary citizens and politicians alike, with voters often judging politicians harshly in terms of their ability to deliver improvements in public utilities such as electricity, roads, and irrigation. But there have been important changes in the way that development funds are allocated, with two key processes reshaping spending patterns.

First, a major thrust of Indonesia's reform process has been the downward distribution of development funds and the authority to determine how they are spent. Decentralization laws, in force since 2001, oversaw a massive transfer of public expenditure to the districts, while a village law passed in 2014 similarly transferred funds to the villages. At the same time, provincial governments and national government departments retain their own budget lines and spending priorities, giving rise to a complex institutional map. Critically, bureaucrats remain central players in the management and allocation of development funds.

Unlike at the national level, cabinets are not formed in Indonesia's provinces or districts, so there are no party-affiliated ministers with control over departmental budgets. Instead, career bureaucrats head the local government agencies and determine how their budgets are spent—under the direction of the elected local government heads and, more or less, in accordance with national guidelines.

Second, elected executive government officials at all levels, as well as legislators, face strong incentives to make use of development funds for their own electoral benefit. Elected local government heads—especially *bupati* and mayors—are key players, but legislators have also been demanding more say in deciding how development funds are allocated. Overall, while rules and programs direct state officials to use universalistic criteria and planning priorities when allocating development funds, political imperatives create contrary incentives to instrumentalize such funds for clientelistic exchange. The outcome is a complex, hybrid system.

As a result, development spending decisions are made in a much more fragmented institutional landscape, with more dispersed control, than during the New Order period. The old bureaucratic development planning mechanisms survive, in modified form, but they are now overlaid by a multiplicity of agencies at the various levels of government, with multiple opportunities for bureaucrats and elected officials to have input. Formally speaking, decision makers in the various agencies are constrained by planning procedures and development priorities, which often come in the form of complex guidelines and formulas about how to allocate their funds, typically directing them to prioritize spending in areas of greatest need. In practice, the complexity of planning processes means that numerous officials can exercise discretion in allocating funds as they see fit, while often needing to compromise with other actors.

The end result, if viewed from the perspective of a village head on the lookout for development projects for his or her village, is massive multiplication of potential avenues for lobbying (*melobi*). The most important local decision maker will almost always be the *bupati* or mayor, given the importance of the districts in Indonesia's new decentralized mode of governance. But if the village head fails there, other potential targets at the district level include senior bureaucrats at the local development planning agency and relevant local government bureaus, such as public works, the subdistrict head (*camat*), or legislators in the district parliament. Enterprising village heads can also pursue connections to the equivalents of these officers and agencies in the provincial, or even the national, government. And if he or she lacks the right connections to get a hearing, there will always be plenty of people offering their services as intermediaries and project brokers. There are thus multilevel and ever-shifting opportunities for lobbying and access.

Elected politicians try to use their control of regular district development funds for their own political purposes. Incumbent district heads often use project funds to shore up support in villages where they received votes in the past, or where they enjoy particularly strong links to village heads or other community-level brokers. Even so, in contrast to other forms of clientelism discussed in this chapter, the direct exchange of development projects for votes appears not to be a ubiquitous pattern. In the expert survey, respondents were asked whether villages or neighborhoods that had not voted for the district head could still receive funding from the district government to improve basic amenities: 45 percent of respondents answered that such funding remained "likely" or "very likely" (with a further 37 percent answering that gaining funds in such circumstances just "required extra effort").

Part of the explanation for this outcome is the complexity of the development funding framework already described. Given the multiplicity of access points, even a village head closely identified with a losing candidate will often be able to lobby other district government officials, notably the *camat* or bureau heads, as well as legislators, and pursue options in higher levels of government too. And an incumbent district head will often have at least a few supporters in most villages, including ones where he or she did not win the vote: informants sometimes say that for a village to receive development projects it can be more important to have a few members of the *bupati's tim sukses* there than to win the village en bloc. Team members can invoke their campaign efforts to pressure a district head to deliver projects (though, as we shall see below, often it is the contract funds and skim-offs, rather than the actual development activity, that are really at stake for such people). It is rare that a district head will be so lacking of supporters within a particular community that he or she will want to punish it by withholding all development funds.

The perception that voting behavior matters little for access to development funds might also have been fueled by attempts of Indonesia's national government to sidestep district governments and promote participatory development planning. More or less coinciding with the democratization period, the Indonesian government, together with the World Bank, funded a massive village-development program that in its best-known iteration was called the National Program for Community Empowerment, PNPM (Gibson and Woolcock 2008; Guggenheim 2006; Li 2007, 230–269). Dubbed the world's largest community-level development project, PNPM operated largely autonomously of established bureaucratic and political networks. Independent facilitators organized village consultations to decide on the roads, bridges, schools, or other projects that should be funded, with the funds then being transferred directly to village accounts. This design served to reduce the dependence of villagers on bureaucratic networks in the district government. On the other hand, it also created a new layer of rural brokers, with the PNPM facilitators in many cases building up strong local reputations that subsequently allowed many of them to either engage successfully in electoral politics as vote brokers or to run for office themselves, either in local parliaments or as village heads.[5]

Meanwhile, village heads are gaining greater prominence in grassroots development because the PNPM program was not renewed but was instead rolled into new funding arrangements under the new Village Law of 2014. Under this law, large grants are being transferred directly to the villages. Development decisions are supposed to be participatory, but the real power will lie in the hands of the village head and the village apparatus. This law will raise the profile of the village head and likely drive up the intensity and costs of village elections. As the law awards budgets and considerable discretionary power directly to village heads—required by law to be nonpartisan—the losers are political parties and their representatives in the district assemblies.

Meanwhile, the inconveniences of using the regular development budget for electoral purposes has led to a ballooning of certain categories of expenditure that have little other function than patronage. Particularly prominent are grants—called *hibah* ("gift") and *bansos* (*bantuan sosial*, or social assistance)— to social organizations. Such grants are supposed to be given to organizations, institutions, communities, or individuals in need, but the formal criteria for awarding them are so lax that district heads and governors have great freedom to award them to groups that have supported them at election time, or whose support they want to court.[6] The Indonesia Budget Center noted, for example, that Fauzi Bowo, the former governor of Jakarta, directed much social assistance to the Betawi Brotherhood Forum (FBR)—a local ethnic militia—that supported his election campaigns in 2008 and 2012 (Nilawati, Jaweng, and Darwanto 2013). In East Java, the traditionalist Islamic organization Nahdlatul Ulama is virtually flooded with *bansos* grants from district and provincial governments, especially in the lead-up to elections. Throughout the country, governors, mayors, and *bupati* routinely provide *bansos* and *hibah* grants to religious groups, preachers, houses of worship, schools, social enterprises, and a plethora of other groups for naked campaigning purposes. Numerous observers have pointed out that there is often a spike of *bansos* and *hibah* spending in the year leading up to a local government-head election (see for example JPNN.com 2011).

In fact, quite often the recipient organizations do not have a track record in the relevant field, or even members. The weak rules governing these grants make them an easy target for corruption and misuse. *Tim Sukses* members sometimes cash in on the success of their candidate by forming their own social organizations, enabling them to claim some of the social assistance budget. In some cases, the incumbent governor or district head organizes supporters to form front organizations, with *bansos* and *hibah* grants then becoming a means to recycle money from the government budget back into the pocket of the incumbent, who can then use it to fund vote buying, other patronage purposes, or personal enrichment. The terms *ormas tidak jelas* (unclear social organization) and *organisasi fiktif* (fictitious organization) have come into use to describe organizations that are purpose-built for receiving such funds. In yet other cases, the recipient organizations are genuinely needy but receive only a fraction of the funds that the official budget documents say they have been provided with, with the rest getting diverted back to the local government head. Not surprisingly, such practices have come under scrutiny from reformers and law enforcement agencies. Indonesian newspapers have reported on many egregious cases of abuse, and numerous local government heads and bureaucrats around the country have been prosecuted for corruption and manipulation in such cases.

Even so, as figure 7.2 shows, the local observers in our expert survey considered this practice to be very common, particularly in districts in Kalimantan, East Nusa Tenggara, and South Sulawesi (especially Makassar). They believed governors were most likely to use these budgets in this way in Banten and South Sulawesi—also the two provinces where political dynasties have struck the deepest roots. They considered these practices much less common in districts and provinces in other parts of Java, as well as districts in Aceh.

Once politicians realized how useful these grants could be for fueling election campaigns and repaying favors, their size ballooned. In 2014, the amounts budgeted for *hibah* and *bansos* amounted to 2.6 percent of the total budget of district governments and a massive 16 percent of the budgets of provincial governments. At the provincial level these budgets increased almost fourfold over six years, from an average 290 billion rupiah ($26 million) per province in 2008 to 1.1 trillion rupiah ($97 million) in 2014.[7] In contrast, while the size of social assistance budgets of district governments also increased considerably, their share of total budgets decreased from 4.1 percent in 2008 to 2.6 percent in 2014. Presumably, the greater magnitude of such funds in the provinces reflects the fact that, under Indonesia's decentralization framework, most of the regular development budget is funneled through the districts, meaning that it is in the provinces that politicians feel the greatest need for specialized patronage funds. In any case, such increases represented a massive expansion of resources available for patronage purposes.

What about legislators? Legislators in the districts and provinces have less discretionary power over budgets than do local government heads, but they do enjoy considerable bargaining power, because legislatures must approve government budgets, and have authority to monitor and investigate implementation

Discretionary grants   *Government contracts*

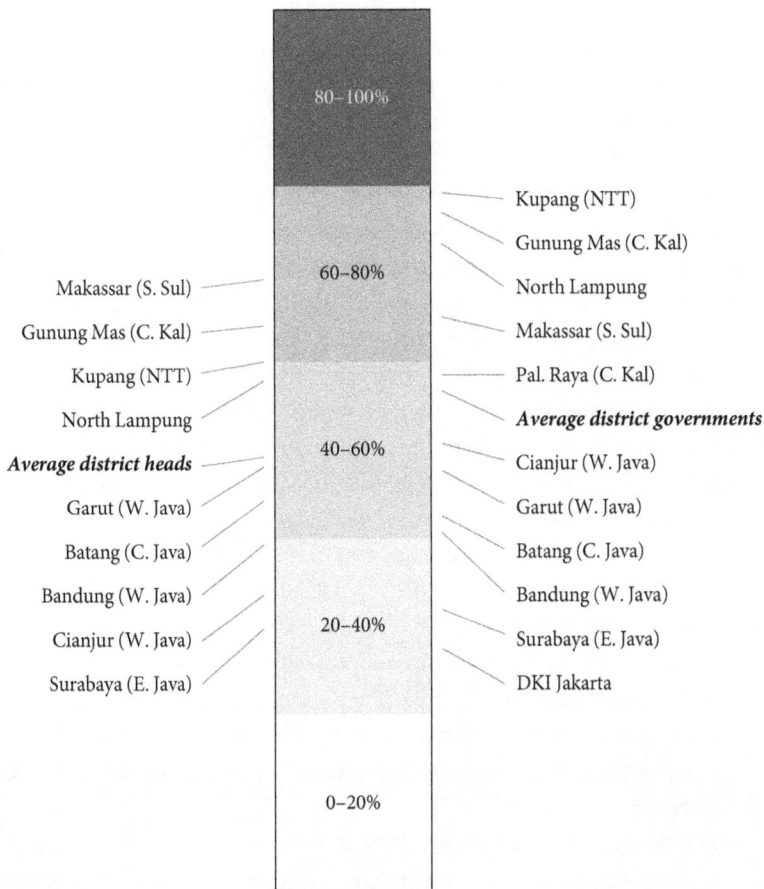

FIGURE 7.2 Discretionary grants and government contracts as political rewards

Expert Survey questions:

Left column: In your estimation, of the *hibah* and social assistance budgets of the district government, what percentage is used by the sitting district head to reward supporters for their campaign efforts?

Right column: In your estimation, of all the major contracts that the district government awards, how many go to companies or businessmen that have supported election campaigns of ruling politicians (*bupati*, governor, members of DPRD) during elections?

of government programs, which can be potentially embarrassing for the regional government head. Sometimes legislators use this power simply to extract payments from executives: for example, a corruption investigation in 2016 revealed that the government of North Sumatra Province typically paid "gavel money" of between 1 and 2.5 billion rupiah ($88,000–$221,000) to each member of the provincial legislature simply to pass its annual budget. As the governor told the corruption court: "If we don't pay the gavel money, they won't deliberate on the budget, your honour" (Talib 2016). We will see in the next section that legislators often also use these powers to gain access to contracts and other concessions.

Since 2009, under the stimulus of the transition to open-list PR, Indonesian legislators have been increasingly keen to use their leverage to find ways to direct development funds toward their constituents in order to boost their personal votes. A new category of grants known as "aspiration funds" (*dana aspirasi*) has been the result. Known in many countries as constituency development funds, these are an Indonesian version of pork barreling in which legislators are granted access to designated funds for use in their electoral districts. In Indonesia, legislators do not directly control these funds (they do not flow into an account where the legislator has sole authority to release payments). Instead, each legislator is typically assigned an annual allocation of funds—ranging from 5 billion rupiah ($440,000) in East Java and Aceh Provinces down to just 100 or 200 million rupiah ($8,800–$17,600) in some district parliaments—for which he or she can endorse projects or *bansos* transfers with the relevant local government bureaus. In practice, this means that the legislator typically has discretion over the awarding of his or her allotment of grants. They are called "aspiration" funds (in fact the names vary somewhat from place to place) because the idea is that legislators authorize payments that satisfy the "aspirations" of their constituents for needed development programs.

In reality, legislators who have access to aspiration funds use them for electioneering purposes. During research we conducted in 2014, all around the country the modus operandi was remarkably similar. Sitting legislators would direct their aspiration funds to small-scale village or neighborhood infrastructure projects, using them to lock in the support of village heads and other local notables. Or they would direct them in the form of grants to organizations—micro-enterprises, farmers' cooperatives, neighborhood youth groups, religious organizations, and so on. In both modes, the grant beneficiaries would join the candidate's success team, and in some places candidates constructed their teams by almost exclusively relying on former grantees. In this way, these grants are transformed into an important electoral asset: as one study concluded, "almost all informants agreed that aspiration funds helped make incumbent candidates virtually unbeatable" (Mahsun 2016, 135). In fact, this is not always the case: voters are sometimes disappointed with an incumbent for having been insufficiently generous with his or her grants—especially given that corruption and "leakage" are just as rife in aspiration fund projects as they are in *bansos* grants.[8]

Moreover, nonincumbents can also promise to direct their future aspiration funds toward brokers, groups, or communities—and sometimes sign written contracts promising to do so. In this way, they try to counter incumbency advantage.

Not all local legislatures have such funds. Their take-up has been uneven across the country, with aspiration funds often being introduced in response to some particularly heated moment of contestation between the legislature and the regional head. Public pressure has prevented them from being adopted at the national level. Having witnessed how useful such funds are for district and provincial assembly members, members of Indonesia's national DPR have made repeated attempts to get aspiration funds of their own. In June 2015, the DPR adopted a proposal to allocate 20 billion rupiah ($1.77 million) as constituency funds to each of its 560 members. After a public outcry, the government ruled this out but granted a more modest program of funding of 150 million rupiah for "aspiration houses" for each national parliamentarian.

But national or local legislators who lack access to aspiration funds have other ways of squeezing development funds from the state budget for their personal electoral purposes. All legislators sit on parliamentary commissions that are paired with several ministries and agencies at the national level and the equivalent local government work units in the provinces, districts, and municipalities. Legislators on these commissions have the job of scrutinizing the work of these partner government agencies, including by investigating the projects they run, looking into their budgets, and drafting and debating relevant legislation. They typically develop close working relationships with their executive counterparts and can use this influence to extract patronage. This typically comes in the form of bribes, such as when they extract fees in exchange for passing a law or regulation that is desired by a particular ministry or agency.

But legislators, especially since the introduction of open-list PR, are also keen to influence executive government bodies to direct projects toward their constituencies, so they can claim credit for bringing home these benefits. Thus, when negotiating a piece of legislation through the house, or when discussing a ministry's program, legislators often make deals to ensure that partner agencies allocate projects in their constituencies. They then make sure they are present at the public launch of the project concerned. Partly as a result, there is competition between legislators to sit on the most "wet" commissions such as those dealing with public works. For example, a DPR member in Central Java explained how he moved, at his own request, from Commission III, which deals with the police, prosecutors, the KPK (Corruption Eradication Commission), and other bodies, which this legislator dismissed as "just elephants." Though Commission III was the best fit with his professional background (he was a retired police officer), he was unhappy there: "The people don't like it. You can't bring the results home. The police chief, the KPK, offer no programs" (interview, Pati, April 3, 2014). He eventually moved to Commission IX, which dealt with health and manpower, and "felt lucky" as a result because he was able to access various government programs through this link: for example, he distributed several hundred LPG tanks to constituents, which were provided to him by the Ministry of Manpower and Transmigration. For similar reasons, Commission V, which deals with infrastructure, is particularly popular with legislators.

As we explained in chapter 3, Indonesia's legislatures are domains of party politics: only party nominees can be elected to them. There is evidence of some cooperation along party lines in sharing access to the patronage resources that come through legislative office. For example, Mahsun (2016, 131–132) notes that incumbents sometimes direct a proportion of their aspiration-fund projects to help co-partisan candidates who are contesting for the first time. Members of national parliamentary commissions likewise sometimes lobby partner agencies to direct some of their programs toward co-partisans running for seats in different constituencies. Overwhelmingly, however, legislators seek such funds and projects for their personal electoral purposes and distribute them to beneficiaries who join their personal success teams. It is no coincidence that the rise of aspiration funds coincided with the move toward open-list PR: the incentive to build personal connections between legislators and constituents drove the expansion of this mode of patronage politics. Thus, although legislative office—for which party membership is a precondition—has grown in importance as a site where development funds are converted into patronage, this move has not been accompanied by a rise in the importance of party networks.

Two conclusions stand out from this short overview of the manner in which development funds are allocated in post-Suharto Indonesia. First, the discretionary power of state officials remains considerable. Compared to our Indian and Argentinian counterexamples—where people regularly turn to party brokers to obtain such funds—Indonesian civil servants and village heads have maintained much of their previous influence in deciding who gets access. The influence of the latter group will expand as the Village Law comes into effect. Second, democratization and decentralization have fragmented control over government budgets. Multiple actors—civil servants, elected officials at all levels, and legislators—struggle to influence the distribution of funds. The system resembles one with multiple players in which all important actors get a share.

However, so far we have only discussed the use of development funds to reward groups of supporters with, for example, a road or a renovation of a mosque. An equally important question is: who gets to build that road or renovate that mosque? That is the question we turn to next.

Awarding Government Contracts

Development funds are important not only because they can generate political support among ordinary voters, but also because they can generate rents—in the form of construction or procurement contracts—for political operators and elites, which can be used to bind together campaign teams, reward campaign donors, and build political careers. In other words, development funds are a source not only of pork, but also of corruption (Samuels 2002). Indeed, it is not too much of an exaggeration to say that awarding and obtaining contracts for government projects, or *proyek*, is the lifeblood of Indonesia's local politics, so much so that we might think of Indonesia as a "project state" (Aspinall 2013a; Li 2016). Political operatives routinely reward allies, funders, and cronies with projects, and an informal economy of skim-offs and illegal fees surrounds the awarding of such projects—so much so that local contractors, politicians, and civil servants can usually reel off without a moment's hesitation the going rate of informal fees that must be paid to obtain projects from the various government bureaus. They also know exactly how these fees are divided between the civil servants, politicians, law enforcement officers, and other actors who get a share.

The chance of being awarded *proyek* motivates many *tim sukses* members to devote their energies to election campaigns. Likewise, the expectation that they will be able to receive sizable kickbacks once they are in power emboldens political hopefuls to run for office; in many parts of Indonesia virtually every member of the local parliament will either have a background as a construction contractor or have a set of favored relatives and cronies who are in the construction business. Civil servants, for their part, can afford to pay large bribes to be promoted to a wet department like public works in the expectation of repaying their investment with the future bribes they will receive. Complex arrangements for sharing out illegal fees and skim-offs surround the system for awarding projects—with some share typically being passed upward, to the bureau heads and regional government head, and some making its way sideways, to potential veto players such as the police, prosecutors, legislators, inspectors, and even competing contractors. In this way, *main proyek*—"playing projects," the euphemistic term for the creative ways that are used to derive an income from government projects—is central to the careers and livelihoods of a wide range of people, from *tim sukses* members and politicians to contractors and civil servants.

Yet while expensive election campaigns have increased the pressure to "play" with projects, democratization has also led to the adoption of policies and procedures aimed at curtailing this form of corruption. During the New Order, the government awarded contracts in a highly opaque and corporatist fashion, with only contractors accredited by state-sanctioned associations allowed to bid. Accreditation depended not just on past performance but also on support for Golkar and willingness to share the proceeds. This meant that available projects were generally divided more or less evenly—there were quotas for each member company (Buehler 2011)—within an artificially limited group of contractors. While collusion and corruption were rife, the process of awarding these contracts was relatively regularized in the sense that insider companies were assured a steady stream of contracts, and it was relatively clear who should be bribed with how much.

After *reformasi*, the government introduced various reforms to curtail this obvious source of corruption. Presidential Decree no. 80 of 2003 on public procurement aimed to make bidding processes more open and transparent. This decree, and its subsequent elaborations, such as Presidential Regulation no. 54 of 2010, laid out procedures for public procurement that promote competition. Local governments were now required to publicly invite tenders for all contracts valued at over 100 million rupiah, rising to 200 million in 2012, curtailing the process of "direct appointment" for contracts, which had allowed government officials to give contracts to whomever they pleased. Bidding processes were now managed by specially trained bidding committees tasked with ranking submitted bids on the basis of price and quality. The combination of highly specified sets of selection criteria with various transparency measures—such as adoption of electronic "E-procurement" systems—was intended to curtail collusion between bureaucrats and contractors.

Yet pressure to circumvent this system is intense. As election campaigns have become more expensive, they have increased incentives for politicians to find ways to derive funds from the awarding of contracts. Politicians can recoup their campaign costs from bribes they receive in exchange for projects, or they can direct contracts toward their financial backers and allies. Capacity to award projects to preferred companies helps them to recruit and motivate members of their *tim sukses*.

The combination of a continued imperative for misuse and the new regulatory framework has produced a set of practices that fuse almost obsessive focus on the letter of formal procurement procedures with gross violation of their spirit (Aspinall and van Klinken 2011; Tidey 2013). One such practice is the manipulation of the specifications (the "*spek*") for a tender. For example, *spek* can be so narrowly formulated that only the preferred company—such as the contractor who made contributions to the *bupati*'s election campaign or who is a relative—can qualify. Another widely used trick is the subdivision of one big project into several small ones, so as to avoid the tender procedure altogether. Competing firms can be induced (or paid) to withdraw their bids, or to submit uncompetitive bids. Another option is to discover minuscule administrative faults in submitted bids, which can lead to the cancellation of bids from non-preferred companies, or at least an opportunity to extract a higher project fee. "Markups" are also common, in part to cover the cost of such fees. Markups occur when politicians, bureaucrats, and the successful contractor cooperate to increase the cost of the contract, enabling these three groups of actors to divide the spoils; underspending on the project—for example laying a thin layer of asphalt on a road—has the same effect (Buehler 2011; Aspinall and van Klinken 2011; Savirani 2014; Tidey 2013).

Most people agree these work-arounds are quite effective. Despite the adoption of new procurement procedures, the political observers in the expert survey considered politicians to be successful in directing government contracts to campaign supporters. A large majority—73.3 percent of those surveyed—estimated that authorities direct at least 40 percent of all big government contracts in their region toward the backers of politicians. The most common estimate—made by 28.9 percent of respondents—was that between 60 and 80 percent of such tenders were won by companies that had supported a ruling politician. Significantly, most respondents felt that this practice of awarding government contracts to campaign supporters had become more prevalent over the preceding ten years: most (68.7 percent) answered that this practice was "more" or "much more" common than it was ten years earlier, while only 8.3 percent saw a decline (22.6 percent saw no change). While we need to interpret such high percentages in the light of a broader disillusionment with official politics, these responses suggest that politicians have been quite successful in finding ways around the reformed procurement procedures. At the same time, there was significant regional variation, similar to that witnessed with spending on *bansos* and *hibah*: see figure 7.2.

Manipulation of tender processes requires coordination between politicians, civil servants, and contractors. Procurement procedures lend civil servants—particularly those on the bidding committees—much control. In order to award a contract to a campaign donor or a family member, politicians need the support of the relevant bureau heads and members of the bidding committee in order to, for example, manipulate the project specifications, smooth out administrative hurdles, or include fake bids. Furthermore, these different actors need to cooperate closely to prevent accusations of corruption, and, where possible, neutralize threats from investigatory and law enforcement agencies. Disgruntled participants who feel cut out can be dangerous. Practically, this generally means that money obtained as project fees is widely shared between politicians and bureaucrats of different ranks, giving everybody a stake in hiding the dirty linen.

While the key actor in this system is generally the regional head—he or she ulti-mately has responsibility for appointing and transferring civil servants—DPRD members also play a role, and, as we saw in the preceding section, their power to withhold approval for the regional budget, and to investigate or obstruct the work of government agencies, gives them considerable bargaining power. This power is an important incentive for civil servants (particularly bureau heads) to maintain good relations with DPRD members and to be receptive to their requests for favors, including projects for them or their business allies. Indeed, in most places, the system of mutual favors is well established, with legislators able to insert special projects into regional government budgets.

A conflict that erupted in 2015 between Jakarta governor Basuki Tjahaja Pur-nama, commonly known as Ahok, and the city's legislative assembly sheds light on how this cooperation between DPRD members and civil servants works. In early 2015, members of Jakarta's legislative assembly tried to include additional proposals worth a total of 12.2 trillion rupiah ($108 million) into Jakarta's bud-get for 2015 after this budget had already been approved and finalized. A new e-budgeting process brought these last-minute additions to light. Having noticed the discrepancy between the approved budget and the final version, Ahok ordered civil servants not to include any last-minute proposals from DPRD members. His instruction prompted dismay and anger among legislators. Claiming that these items were for "the aspirations of the public," DPRD members threatened to hold a public inquiry and impeach the governor. Thus piqued, Ahok decided to scrutinize the previous 2014 budget. He identified various *dana siluman* (invis-ible funds)—budget items that were unclear, not called for, or double budgeted. Electricity generators and 3-D printers had been purchased for schools that had not asked for them, an expensive but unknown book trilogy about Ahok's life had been commissioned, and various infrastructure works were budgeted and had, on paper, been executed but either did not exist or had been funded through multiple budget lines (*Tempo* 2015).

Ahok helped to expose how such shadowy proposals by DPRD members make their way into the official budget. Strategically located civil servants had helped to enter these additional proposals of DPRD members in the already approved bud-get. Subsequently these or other civil servants in on the plot also influenced the ten-dering procedure, ensuring that companies put up by DPRD members would win the relevant tenders. Many of the winning companies were shadowy front compa-nies, registered at an office located fifty meters from the DPRD building (Persada et al. 2015). According to Ahok, this collusion between DPRD members and civil servants had been going on for years: "This is a tradition between the adminis-tration and the councillors, to compromise and cooperate to misuse the money" (Wardhani and Halim 2015). While DPRD members had no formal relations with civil servants, who were formally responsible only to the governor, the two groups had been able to establish lucrative forms of cooperation, aiming to swell departmental budgets, extract kickbacks, and scoop up misappropriated funds.

The episode left the impression that the governor had rather limited control over the Jakarta budget. Ahok started to complain regularly in the press about the "strange budgets" of several departments (Aziza 2015), illustrating the relative autonomy that civil servants still possessed, even in Indonesia's capital. By engaging in strategic coalitions—in this case with DPRD members—senior civil servants had maintained some of the discretionary power over budget allocations that they had during the New Order, to the dismay of an elected reforming governor.

At the same time, cooperation is not always guaranteed, and competing alliances over project allocation can lead to messy and heated politicking, which not infrequently leads to delays in executing projects. As a detailed insider study in Pekalongan (Central Java) reveals, tender processes often generate tension between civil servants and politicians:

> The newer contractors mainly focused on developing such ties with politicians, while the senior builders made use of their connections to administrators. The latter do not necessarily offer administrators electoral support, although some of them do cultivate these contacts for launching a political career. Rather, they offer lucrative kickbacks [to the civil servants] and, occasionally, support to secure a promotion. In this way, politicians often back a different contractor than the administrators. Project allotments take the form of negotiations between them, with the mayor as the final "referee." (Savirani 2014, 138)

Savirani's description is suggestive of subtle distinctions of power, with established contractors concentrating on working with bureaucrats, while arrivistes seek political connections as a shortcut to success. It is possible that there are also gradual changes in this balance of power, with elected politicians becoming increasingly influential in project allocation. But such descriptions also illustrate that politicians have not yet succeeded in dominating this process. Procedural regulations lend some civil servants a central role in tender processes. These civil servants have their own interests: critically, they need to recover the money they spend on getting promoted, sometimes with the hope of acquiring the kind of wealth that might enable them to launch their own political careers. Thus, while democratization has enabled politicians to gain more control, governance reform has strengthened the civil servants, whose cooperation is necessary if the politicians are to use project funds for political purposes. The upshot is that, in order to control the allocation of government budgets, politicians face strong incentives to select and promote loyal civil servants who are willing to heed their directives—a topic we return to in the next chapter.

These sketches of patterns of control over the distribution of three types of state benefits—welfare programs, development funds, and government contracts—suggest that, in comparison to our Argentinian and Indian counterexamples, the capacity of party networks to manipulate the distribution of state benefits in Indonesia is relatively limited. We have discussed how, unlike in Argentina and India, citizens in Indonesia rarely address themselves to party representatives to gain access to welfare benefits, to do official paperwork, or to improve basic amenities in their neighborhoods. As so much discretionary power remains in the hands of state representatives, citizens lack incentives to frequent party offices. Instead, most Indonesians go to their neighborhood or village head to get the help they need.

Furthermore, the kinds of resources that politicians do control do not necessarily serve to strengthen the bonds between parties and voters. Indonesia's democratization process has enabled politicians to get their hands on a widening range of resources, like constituency development funds and social assistance grants. Elected government heads exercise great control over local development budgets and projects, but legislators, too, can intervene in tendering processes and can "play," to a certain extent, with the budgets of district governments, typically by way of negotiations and deals with civil servants and district heads. Such deals, especially those for aspiration funds, allow politicians to deliver pork-barrel projects to voters in their constituencies.

Overwhelmingly, however, the beneficiaries of these resources are a rather limited political class of contractors, *tim sukses* members, and other political players. While the awarding of government contracts enables politicians to fulfill election promises to campaign supporters and donors, such practices rarely build wider gratitude and loyalty to politicians and their parties. On the contrary, they often fuel resentment about manipulation and corruption, contributing to voter disillusionment with party politics.

Overall, the state-centered nature of patronage networks in Indonesia provides us with a deeper explanation for the patterns of election campaigning we have explored in earlier chapters. The limited role of political parties in campaigns, and the reliance by candidates on miscellaneous social networks, can be attributed in part to the relatively strong discretionary control that bureaucratic actors still exercise over state resources. This discretionary control is a heritage of the New Order. While elected government heads and DPRD members are gradually chipping away at bureaucratic dominance, political parties have been less successful. Parties in Indonesia are caught in a bind: the limited discretionary control they exercise over state resources limits their influence over voters; the resulting weak mobilizing capacity in turn discourages political actors from rewarding parties with greater control. Instead, as we explore in the next chapter, politicians rely heavily on bureaucratic networks during election campaigns.

8

BUREAUCRATS AND THE POWER OF OFFICE

Pak Rahmat felt proud. As the head of Arief's campaign team, he had succeeded in winning a convincing electoral victory. On August 31, 2013, Arief won 47.9 percent of the vote, with Abdul Syukur taking only 25.8 percent. When discussing this result, Rahmat was not shy about attributing this success to superior campaign organization. But, he argued, control over local bureaucrats had also been important: "In Indonesia, people know that the bureaucracy, the civil servants, are capable of garnering votes. So all candidates usually compete to get support from the bureaucracy" (interview, March 13, 2014).

However, within a few weeks of the victory, Rahmat began to experience the downside of Arief's support among civil servants. He was besieged with requests: "I get so many phone calls. And when I get to my office, there are always people waiting for me. Even in the evening they wait in front of my house. They are waiting because they want to get a position. Wherever I go, they chase me!"

These supplicants knew that Rahmat was engaged in near-daily discussions with Arief over *mutasi*, or transfers of bureaucrats. To deal with the flood of requests for such transfers, Rahmat had to be just as methodical as he had been about the organization of the campaign. "I only like such requests when I have met this person before, during the campaign. [To know] if someone is a loyalist, we made a list [of those] who really helped us. If someone enthusiastically promoted Arief, we put that in our database." Yet Rahmat denied that such support would be the sole criterion for promotion: "There have to be clear criteria. We shouldn't demote or neglect a capable person just because they supported Abdul

Syukur. We need to look at the functioning [of the person]. However, when their capacities are similar, we prefer to give [our supporter] the promotion."

One of the hopes underpinning Indonesia's reform was that decentralization and the introduction of direct elections would serve to make the bureaucracy more accountable and responsive to the needs and wishes of citizens. Political power under the New Order was highly centralized, and Indonesia was described as a "bureaucratic polity" (Jackson 1978). During this period, a bureaucratic career was extremely secure: so long as a civil servant supported Golkar and pleased his or her superiors, he or she could serve out a full career, enjoy many opportunities for rent seeking, and retire comfortably. As promotions were largely based on seniority, bureaucrats had few incentives to perform. The saying *rajin malas pendapatan sama* (the diligent and the lazy get the same salary) summed up the incentive structure within the civil service; the phrase *asal bapak senang* (as long as the boss is happy) described the workplace culture: loyalty to one's superiors was more important than performance for career advancement.

Democratization and decentralization were supposed to change all this. Those who designed the new policies hoped the reforms would provide elected officials with incentives to adopt a merit-based system for bureaucratic promotions and, in this way, turn the self-absorbed and corrupt bureaucracy of the New Order into a more responsive and effective civil service (Luebke 2009). In this way, electoral incentives would work their way through the system: by providing politicians with a reason to improve the provision of public services they would stimulate them to build a high-quality bureaucracy.

It is certainly correct that bureaucratic reform has been a priority of successive post-Suharto governments. One of the earliest reform measures of the post-Suharto period was the separation of the bureaucracy from Golkar, which had been the authoritarian regime's electoral machine, and the formal proscription on civil servants' engaging in politics. Spurred on by foreign donors as well as public pressure, new laws—such as Law 43/1999 on civil service, Law 32/2004 on local governance, and, most recently, Law 5/2014 on bureaucratic reform—have been adopted to establish a more merit-based system of appointing and promoting civil servants. These laws outline new performance appraisal instruments, establish a civil service commission tasked with overseeing recruitment of top-echelon bureaucrats, and pave the way for appointment of outsiders to bureaucratic positions. Some local politicians have displayed a similar commitment to bureaucratic reform. Over the now almost two decades of *reformasi*, local politicians like Gamawan Fauzi (Solok, Sumatra), Rustriningsih (Kebumen, Java), and Joko Widodo (Solo, Jakarta) have adopted measures like "fit-and-proper tests" to discipline the local bureaucracy (Choi and Fukuoka 2015). Some politicians, such as Jakarta's governor Basuki Tjahaja Purnama (Ahok), or Aceh governor

Irwandi Yusuf, made themselves popular by engaging in unannounced spot-checks and publicly scolding underperforming bureaucrats.

This chapter discusses the evolving relationship between bureaucrats and politicians. We advance three main arguments. First, we suggest that, contrary to expectations—and partly contrary to Indonesian law—bureaucrats remain key political actors in regional Indonesia. Bureaucrats built up a large stock of social influence under the New Order, and they retain considerable prestige in local societies, especially in parts of the country where the private sector is underdeveloped. As we discussed in the last chapter, bureaucrats also retain relatively large discretionary control over distribution of state benefits. As a result, they wield significant mobilizational power at election times. Many civil servants are actively involved in election campaigns of, particularly, district-head and governor candidates. Equally importantly, they continue to provide many of the leading candidates for senior elective office in the regions—especially executive government posts—reflecting the financial and political capital that holders of key bureaucratic office can accumulate over their careers.

Our second main argument flows from the first: democratization—particularly direct elections—has overall not fostered a more merit-based bureaucracy. On the contrary, in most of Indonesia, democratization has intensified politicization of the local state apparatus. Incumbent regional heads have strong incentives to cultivate loyalty among civil servants in order to benefit from their capacity to generate support and votes. Yet that loyalty can no longer be taken for granted: while senior bureaucrats have incentives to support the incumbent, disgruntled or ambitious functionaries lower in the hierarchy can support a challenger with the hope of making a career leap. In such a context, civil servants who opt to remain neutral during election campaigns—which is what they are supposed to do, according to the law—still experience considerable anxiety at the prospect they might lose their position to supporters of the winning candidate. The result is that, despite reforms aimed at professionalizing recruitment and promotions, performance still counts for less than cultivation of contacts for a successful bureaucratic career.

Third, and finally, we bring together our observations from this and the preceding chapter to explain two important features of local politics in post-Suharto Indonesia: the great frequency with which former bureaucrats win elections as regional heads, and the advantages enjoyed by incumbents in these races. In key respects, post-Suharto Indonesia remains a democratized bureaucratic polity, where the rise of elections, political parties, and civil society has failed to dislodge civil servants from the position of political dominance they built up in the regions during the Suharto period. The continuing politicization of the bureaucracy, the social weight and influence that civil servants still enjoy, and, critically, the high degree of discretion they still exercise over distribution of patronage resources combine to give bureaucrats and incumbents structural advantages during local elections. As a result, civil servants remain the key actors in local politics, to a degree that is unusual in democratic systems. We illustrate this point by a comparison to India, where analysts regularly invoke an "anti-incumbency factor" to interpret election results. In Indonesia, incumbents have much greater success. To develop these arguments, we begin by illustrating clientelistic exchange relationships between politicians and bureaucratic actors in an electoral race in North Lampung. In this rural district, the unpopularity of the incumbent district head caused anxiety among local bureaucrats, while great rewards awaited those who backed his ultimately successful challenger.

Anxiety in Lampung

The interview was a highly uncomfortable failure. Taufik had taken one of the authors (Berenschot) to meet Afrizal, his former boss at the fisheries department of North Lampung's district government. Because Afrizal had been a civil servant since 1989, the goal was to talk to him about the changes he had experienced since direct elections of district heads were introduced in 2005. But it was clear that Afrizal did not want to talk—despite previous reassurances by Taufik that this senior civil servant was a close friend and very knowledgeable. Seated on his flowery sofa, Afrizal put on a fixed smile that suggested he was entertaining his visitors only out of politeness. His answers to questions were staccato, brief, and unilluminating: "The difference is that now civil servants are more often removed from office," and "It is a risk to take sides during elections. Civil servants should be neutral during election campaigns; that is the right thing to do." No amount of prodding could bring him to elaborate or explain what he meant.

The interview became even more uncomfortable when Taufik—at thirty years old, about twenty-five years younger than Afrizal—began to disparage his older colleague for his unwillingness to talk. "Come on," he said, "don't be so rigid. You are not being serious." Then he heightened the discomfort by speaking over Afrizal's head: "His answers are too closed. He is being defensive and afraid because of his position. We can leave if you like." After a brief and uncomfortable discussion, it began to become clear what Taufik had meant when he mentioned Afrizal's fear for his position when, standing outside, Afrizal despondently mentioned to his foreign visitor that "the house is for sale; you can buy it if you like."

It turned out that the visit had helped Taufik to rub salt in Afrizal's fresh wounds. After the previous incumbent *bupati* had lost the election and the new *bupati*, Agung Mangkunegara, had been installed, the tables had been turned between Taufik and Afrizal. The change had led to Afrizal losing his position as vice-head of the fisheries department. He had been *dinonjobkan*—literally "non-jobbed," or removed from office. While civil servants cannot be fired in Indonesia, except in cases of gross violation of their duties, they can be removed from their posts without being reassigned. While the affected bureaucrat still draws a salary, the removal means considerable loss of income from the perks, bribes, and allowances that typically constitute the lion's share of a civil servant's earnings. And Afrizal did not only lose the means to pay for his house. "This was his car," Taufik explained while driving back to the town center, "but somehow he lost his position and had to return the car. Then I got this car." Taufik had recently got a big promotion: from being a mere staff member he had been made subdivision head of the fisheries department. As Taufik recounted his recent success with glee, it became obvious that the whole visit had been engineered to show Afrizal that Taufik was now using the office car.

A few months earlier, Taufik had been full of anxiety. In the weeks leading to the district-head election in North Lampung, Taufik was anxious about who would win. He had been openly supporting the challenger Agung, and was worried that his career would suffer if Agung lost. He lamented how most of his colleagues supported the incumbent, Zainal Abidin, to protect their jobs. When Agung actually won the election, Taufik's anxiety did not end immediately: in his last two months in office, Zainal effected a big transfer of civil servants, a practice referred to as *rolling pejabat*, or the "rolling of officials." This "rolling" was perceived as an attempt to reward and punish bureaucrats for the level of support they had given Zainal in the election campaign. Taufik was sent to a remote village, twenty kilometers from the district capital.

But his exile was brief. After Agung took office, he quickly brought Taufik back to the district capital and made him subdivision head. As Taufik drove his newly acquired official car to the house of another colleague, he seemed happy about his decision to prioritize politics over his administrative duties:

> I do not put too much effort into showing [my superiors] what I am capable of [in the office]. That is not effective. Many people can work well. But if I was not active in politics, I would not have got a promotion. Your career can develop through political involvement, not through working. Take the example of Pak Afrizal. While he can work well, he was still dumped, because he failed in the political work. Throughout the coming five years, while they [i.e., Agung and his deputy] remain in

office my career will be good. After that, I have to make another effort
[i.e., during elections] or I could be dumped too. Now I can give orders
to Afrizal, though he used to give me the orders. He is my senior, and I
now give him orders. (Confidential interview, June 30, 2014)

Taufik's strategizing, and particularly his delight, need to be interpreted in the
context of the considerable sums of money that civil servants normally must pay
to ensure promotion or a transfer to a wet position. The purchase of bureaucratic
office remains a common practice in post-Suharto Indonesia. During the New
Order, such fees were already the norm, but research suggests that they continued
to increase in the post–New Order period. According to one account (Kristiansen
and Ramli 2006), which drew on interviews with sixty junior civil servants in
West Nusa Tenggara Province, payments averaging just over 27 million rupiah—
or twenty-seven times the monthly starting salary for civil servants—were made
in order to join the civil service. In another survey of civil servants early in the
reformasi period, "some 56% of officials said that personal or family connections were a factor in their recruitment decision, while one in eight admitted
to payments or gifts as an inducement to get the job" (World Bank 2003, 103).
In early 2017, a Corruption Eradication Commission investigation into graft in
Klaten district in Central Java revealed that the bupati had been raking in fees
ranging from a low of 5 million to 15 million rupiah ($440–$1,320) for postings to administrative jobs in local health centers, through fees in the range of
75 to 125 million rupiah ($6,600–$11,000) for such posts as elementary school
principal, up to 400 million rupiah ($35,000) to head certain local government
bureaus (Puspitasari 2017).

The result of this system is that civil servants are routinely appointed to
posts for which they lack the required qualifications or skills, or transferred
to departments where there is no real need for them. Performance apprais-
als often have little real impact, and promotions still require sizable bribes.
On the basis of interviews with civil servants, another study (Blunt, Turner,
and Lindroth 2012a, 215; see also 2012b) came to a stark conclusion about
bureaucratic appointments: "What matters is who you know, what and who
you pay, and to whom you pledge loyalty, [while] initiative, excellence and
results matter little."

The levying of informal charges on would-be bureaucrats, and on those seeking promotion, generates a strong incentive for bureaucrats to engage in corruption once they are in office, and there is generally a direct correlation between the
size of the fee levied and the wetness of the post on offer. At the same time, the
high cost of office is integrally connected to politics. Incumbent regional government heads often levy such fees on bureaucrats as one way of funding their own

election campaigns. By the same token, offering political support to a regional head can be a means for bureaucrats to circumvent, or at least minimize, their outlays on career advancement. As Mungiu-Pippidi (2015, 8) notes, corruption is often a "counterbalance," or an alternative to other forms of favoritism, such as those based on clan, ethnicity, or political connection. Helping a would-be *bupati* to win office by supporting his or her election campaign can thus be one way to gain a promotion to a key post without making a costly financial outlay. Fees for promotion can be much reduced or, according to Taufik, even waived, if a civil servant actively and effectively supported the district head's election campaign. However, taking such a step is a calculated gamble: supporting a losing candidate can stymie one's chances of promotion. Civil servants thus need to assess the candidates very carefully.

Such assessments are rarely unencumbered. In a small district like North Lampung, many civil servants have family ties to one of the candidates, which, whether they like it or not, effectively associate them with that person. Furthermore, senior civil servants with structural positions (*pejabat*) within the district bureaucracy are often tied to the incumbent by shared careers, mutual favors, and sometimes even joint business dealings—as well as a lot of dirty laundry. These civil servants face the highest risk of being transferred or, worse, being non-jobbed if the incumbent loses office. Not infrequently, such senior bureaucrats have to pay bribes to secure their existing posting if a local government head loses his or her position. This situation generates anxiety, and nostalgia for old certainties. As one of Taufik's colleagues, another senior bureaucrat in North Lampung's fisheries department, put it,

> During the New Order, there was no internal conflict because everybody supported Golkar. Then, to get a promotion, the support of your bureau head was enough. He issued a letter, and the [district head] signed it. Now if the bureau head wants to promote someone, it is not guaranteed that the district head will agree. Because it depends on [this person's] political activities. If a civil servant does not support and vote for the winner, that's a problem, and it's dangerous. You can lose your position. What emerges is chaos and confusion if a new [district head] comes in. What happens is that people are often not used any more, they are non-jobbed.

In the course of our research, we regularly encountered civil servants who complained about the anxiety that direct elections had brought. While their careers had been predictable during the New Order, now they faced risks of losing income and status if they were responsible for, in Taufik's words, "a failure in the political work."

Politicized Bureaucracies

A merit-based system of recruiting and promoting civil servants was one of the promises of Indonesian reform. It is not only that new regulations early in the post-Suharto period were supposed to depoliticize the bureaucracy, requiring bureaucrats to be politically neutral. Also, as noted above, it was widely expected that electoral incentives would stimulate politicians to strengthen the capacity of local bureaucracies. Because voters would evaluate their district heads, mayors, and governors on the basis of the quality of local public services or the effectiveness of government programs, so this argument went, such politicians would have incentives to appoint people with the capacity to implement such programs.

These expectations have proved not to be entirely unrealistic: elections, along with the widening of press freedoms and the strengthening of public debate, have generated more pressure on politicians and public officials to perform. In particular, as we have noted, the shift to direct elections has been associated with a rise of health, education, and other welfare policies at the local level (Aspinall 2013b, 2014a), even if many assessments suggest that the actual improvement in these services has been limited (Schultze and Sjahrir 2014; Skoufias et al. 2014) and local governments still spend a disproportionate share of their budgets on bureaucratic salaries and travel (Sjahrir, Kis-Katos, and Schulze 2014). Everywhere we have visited in regional Indonesia, meanwhile, voters and politicians alike pay great attention to the quality of public infrastructure and often make harsh judgments of leaders they believe fail to deliver improvements. While voters often tolerate some level of corruption and inefficiency, they often vote out leaders whose corruption they believe to be excessive (Mietzner 2006). All in all, directly elected politicians thus do face incentives to select and promote civil servants on the basis of their proven capacity to improve delivery of public services and so improve their own reelection chances.

Yet both our fieldwork and our expert survey suggest that democratization did *not* succeed at fostering meritocracy. On the contrary, as the North Lampung case suggests, democratization and particularly the advent of direct elections seem to have fostered a new form of politicization of local bureaucracies. In the course of our research, throughout the country we consistently heard stories about district heads filling strategic posts in the bureaucracy with political allies, and exiling troublemakers and recalcitrants to remote regions, uninviting posts, or non-jobs. Almost any public servant in a regional government can share stories of unqualified persons being appointed to key positions—a high school teacher suddenly ending up as the head of the public works bureau, for instance—because of the support he or she offered a victorious contestant in an election, or as a result of some other personal connection. In one district of Lombok, for example, locals talked wryly of the "*birokrasi sampi*," where *sampi* means cow, but was also one of the acronyms that Indonesians so love, this time for *saudara, anak, mertua, ipar* (relatives, children, and in-laws), because such people were a core part of the incumbent's campaign team. The experience in North Lampung was similar. The incumbent district head (and Taufik's boss) engaged in a massive transfer of bureaucrats. During this wave of transfers—a *rolling*—civil servants who supported his opponent were transferred to remote locations, while his supporters received last-minute promotions. When, a few months later, his opponent took office, he initiated another *rolling*, which led to Taufik's stellar promotion. Newspapers, too, frequently contain stories of mass transfers of staff members in the immediate lead-up to a *pilkada*, or in its aftermath. In Lombok again, one regulation-minded local bureaucrat called such waves of transfers the "disease of post-*pilkada* local politics" (interview, December 16, 2011).

In making such transfers of career bureaucrats, local government heads have benefited from the regulatory framework created under decentralization in which, at the district level especially, they had all but unfettered authority to move public servants around between jobs. In 2014, a new civil service law imposed formal limits on this ability. For example, the law established a new civil service commission with authority to oversee recruitment and promotion of senior civil servants, both in Jakarta and the regions, to ensure adherence to due process and meritocratic principles, and to override senior appointments and transfers that ignored them. The law also gave greater authority to regional secretaries—the most senior civil servant in any district or province—in determining bureaucratic promotions and transfers. Furthermore, a subsequent instruction from the Ministry of Administrative and Bureaucratic Reform (circular no. 02/2016) forbade district heads and governors transferring civil servants until six months after their inauguration as regional head.

Most of our field research was conducted before this law came into effect, or early in its implementation, and we did not observe any significant impact. Throughout our period of fieldwork, government heads were generally considered to have full discretionary authority in arranging transfers and promotions. Since that time, the commission has issued several hundred directives overruling transfers and promotions of civil servants in the regions, including a large wave that followed the local elections in 2015. Even so, one member of the commission herself acknowledged that it had limited capacity to directly monitor and intervene in any but the most strategic posts in most regions, especially remote ones. It was often difficult even to ensure that promotions committees were filled by qualified people in such locations—let alone by people who were not allied to the local government head (Ida Mokhsen, interview, October 11, 2016). It is thus far from clear that this reform will have a long-term impact on inculcating meritocratic principles, rather than simply adding an additional layer to the already thick sedimentation of laws and regulations that local government heads and bureaucrats have long proven adept at avoiding.

In contrast to the great discretion they have enjoyed over promotions and transfers of individuals who are already members of the civil service, local government heads have had less flexibility when it comes to recruiting newcomers into civil service jobs. Civil service jobs are a critical patronage resource in many countries, but Indonesian local government heads have much less control over recruitment than do politicians in some countries (Grindle 2013). To enter the civil service, recruits have to pass a competitive exam, managed by the Ministry of Administrative and Bureaucratic Reform. Furthermore, this ministry also determines the number of permanent civil service jobs that each local government can provide. This system is not watertight. One report finds that examination results are regularly falsified for the benefit of the highest-paying contestants; sums of up to 120 million rupiah (about $11,000) are regularly paid to pass the test (Blunt, Turner, and Lindroth 2012a). Even so, generally speaking, this system of entrance examinations and quotas limits the influence of government heads to offer permanent civil service posts as patronage rewards to supporters. In response, regional heads frequently instead offer low-paying casual (*honorer*) positions, which do not require civil service examinations and are thus available to be offered on a more discretionary basis. Unsurprisingly, as a recent study finds, politicians regularly use such positions—especially as casual teaching assistants, or *guru honorer*—to reward political supporters (Pierskalla and Sacks 2015; see also Rosser and Fahmi 2016).

The expert survey throws light on the extent of enmeshment of bureaucratic and electoral politics across Indonesia. The 509 political experts surveyed were asked what percentage of higher-level civil servants received their positions as a reward for supporting a candidate in an election campaign. Even if we take the likelihood of some exaggeration into account, the expert perceptions confirm our observation that direct elections have entrenched politicization of district and provincial bureaucracies.[1] Fewer than 1 percent of respondents said there were no political appointments in local bureaucracies, while the largest group (32 percent for districts, 27 percent for provinces) felt that 60 to 80 percent of senior appointments were due to the support those concerned had offered to a candidate during a campaign (the question did not specify which candidate, but we can infer that in most cases this would be the incumbent regional head). More than half of all observers estimated that 40 percent or more of all senior bureaucrats were awarded their promotions in this way. We also asked the experts to assess whether the chances of getting promoted depended more on a bureaucrat's capacity to perform his or her duties or on loyalty to elected politicians. Only

10 percent of experts believed capacity was more important than loyalty in district governments. In contrast, 61 percent felt that loyalty was more important; 29 percent considered both equally important. The answers were roughly similar for provincial bureaucracies.

Respondents were also asked to assess to what extent district and provincial bureaucrats actively supported candidates during elections. Given the fact that this is forbidden by law (article 80 of Law 32 of 2004 on Regional Government states that "civil servants . . . and village heads are forbidden from taking decisions or engaging in behavior which benefits or disadvantages candidates during the campaign period"), such campaign support is surprisingly common: most local observers estimated that 40 to 60 percent of senior district bureaucrats had participated in election campaigns for district head, governor, or both.

Once again, the pattern of regional variation was striking: in cities in Java like Jakarta and Bandung, respondents on average estimated that only 25–50 percent of senior civil servants were involved in campaigning; in some outer-island locations such as Makassar, Samarinda, and Jayawijaya all or almost all experts believed that between 75 and 100 percent of bureaucrats engaged in politics in this way. Moreover, positive answers to this question correlated strongly with positive answers to the above-mentioned questions about patterns of bureaucratic appointments, suggesting that in areas where respondents felt civil service appointments were more likely to be politicized, civil servants were more likely to participate in election campaigns. We return to these patterns of regional variation in future chapters.

These findings suggest that article 80 of Law 32 of 2004 would be placed very high on the crowded list of most commonly violated Indonesian legal provisions. Respondents felt that it was less common for bureaucrats to campaign during presidential and legislative elections. This makes sense when we remember that it is district heads who exercise most control over local bureaucratic posts: the more control elected officials exert, the more likely civil servants are to support their election efforts. The president is far removed from the lives and career paths of most civil servants, while local legislators, too, have no direct say in their employment paths—a point we return to below.

Mobilizing for Elections

What form does the support of civil servants take during electoral contexts? Part of the answer to this question is implicit in our account of the state-centered nature of Indonesia's patronage networks in the last chapter: because civil servants exercise so much control over patronage resources, they can play an influential role as vote brokers within their own social and professional networks. They have influence because, in Indonesia's state-centered patronage network, civil servants (along with elected community officials like village heads) control access to the government services that people need. They are gatekeepers not only for the new cash transfers and welfare services, but for all manner of public services. At the community level, teachers and school principals control the education that many parents see as being so important for their children to achieve upward social mobility. The local health workers are the ones who make first-line decisions about whether patients will be checked by a doctor and whether they will receive subsidized health care (Berenschot, Hanani, and Sambodho 2018; Hanani 2016). Though such services are in theory provided according to universalistic rules and criteria—and are supposed, increasingly, to be free of charge—in practice they often involve informal fees and favoritism. It can pay off for ordinary people to cultivate close and respectful personal ties with the people who offer such services, which might extend to following their advice on voting day.

A little higher up the bureaucratic hierarchy, individuals like the *camat* or the officeholder in the subdistrict public works or agricultural extension service do not so much control direct access to basic services for ordinary citizens, but they have their hands on the spigot of government projects, grants, licenses, and subsidies that wealthier community members want to access. Such mid-ranking bureaucrats thus have the capacity to influence the political choices of influential community leaders who can then bring their own clienteles behind a favored candidate. These bureaucrats can also disproportionately direct resources they control to locations where their candidate is trying to gain votes. Though civil servants cannot be formally enlisted into success teams, given the legal proscription on their political engagement, in fact their involvement is often quite openly on display during election season. It is not unusual to see civil servants helping to prepare campaign events, or to meet them doing the rounds, going from house to house to canvass on behalf of their candidates. Pak Solikhin, the head of the campaign team of incumbent Zainal Abidin in North Lampung, was quite explicit about why his election campaign could count on the support of both civil servants and community-level state officials:

> The incumbent *bupati* makes use of his civil servants, from his civil servants to the village heads. They become part of his campaign team. The bureaucracy should be apolitical, but they are manipulated by the incumbent. Particularly the *pejabat* [senior officials], the department heads, the section heads, subsection heads, the *camats*, they are all co-opted. The village heads often also want to join [the campaign] because of the money that they get from the government structure. . . . And civil

> servants, for their part, want to support a candidate with the expectation that if their candidate wins, they will get promoted. There is an exchange of favor between candidates and the bureaucracy. (Interview, May 21, 2013)

Indeed, this form of electioneering can be highly organized. On another occasion, in East Nusa Tenggara Province, an NGO activist who described himself as a "political consultant" and was clearly very experienced in the closely related worlds of brokering projects and organizing election campaigns, described the process by which an incumbent district head could mobilize the bureaucracy to support his or her reelection. He was obviously describing an election he had been involved in not long before, in a rural district not far from the provincial capital Kupang, though he spoke in hypothetical terms. As he put it, for an incumbent standing for reelection in this province, the first step is to make a "political contract" with his or her "shadow cabinet"—senior civil servants, notably bureau chiefs, subdistrict heads, and school principals. Then, he said, it is simply a matter of setting vote quotas. He started reeling off numbers:

> Let's say each *camat* is required to deliver 200 votes. There are 24 of them [in this district]. Twenty-four times 200 is 4,800 votes. Each school principal, there are 491 of them, let's say just 100 of them are required to deliver 150 votes each, that's 15,000 votes. Then you look to the village secretaries and village heads. It's actually easier to pressure the village secretaries because they are civil servants [while village heads are elected]. There are 177 villages, let's expect 50 votes from each of them [in each village], that's 17,700 votes. Then the heads of bureaus—let's count just the heads of the public work bureau in each subdistrict, that's 24 times 100, that's 2,400 votes. (Confidential interview, September 10, 2013)

He worked this all out, and it came to just a few thousand votes short of the vote total actually won by the incumbent concerned. The few thousand votes not accounted for this way were gathered through family, business, and other connections, he explained. As for how these various civil servants had campaigned, some had done the work personally, going door to door, others had mobilized their followers, and others had distributed money—their own money—to voters: "He [the incumbent] didn't buy votes. It was the *camat* who did it for him." It was worthwhile for such people to invest their own time and money in such an effort: "What's the price of a hundred votes in exchange for retaining your position as *camat*?" (confidential interview, September 10, 2013). One of the losing deputy *bupati* candidates in this election confirmed this account, describing elections in this part of the province as a "conspiracy of civil servants." He noted that the remoteness and poor infrastructure of the district made this tactic especially effective: "The public servants are traumatized about being transferred to remote locations. It's a serious problem; roads are so bad in [this district]. There are places you can be sent [if you get on the wrong side of the *bupati*] from where you cannot return at all during the rainy season. Then, if that happens, your local connections and connections in the government are all broken. It hurts your career. They are really scared about getting stuck somewhere in the interior, and that they'll then end up finishing their careers there" (Vincent Bureni, interview, September 7, 2013).

Before we move on, we should emphasize that in this chapter we almost exclusively deal with elections of local executive government heads, rather than those of legislators. Local government heads wield direct authority over civil servants in their jurisdictions. Accordingly, they have the greatest ability to bend the civil service to their will at election time. Compared to regional government heads, legislators are bit players in the patronage system: their input into the budgeting and legislative process enables them to forge rent-seeking alliances of convenience with civil servants, sometimes even behind the back of the regional government head (as our discussion of Governor Ahok in the preceding chapter showed). But they do not have the power to single-handedly advance or freeze a civil servant's career, and therefore they lack the leverage to mobilize the bureaucracy en bloc for electoral purposes. To be sure, occasionally, legislative candidates are themselves relatives, clients, or allies of a sitting regional government head or a senior civil servant, and such officials can often mobilize extensive bureaucratic support on such candidates' behalf at election time (Sumampouw 2016). But such individuals are the exception that proves the rule, and as indicated above, our expert survey showed that civil servants participate at a lower rate in legislative elections than in regional head elections. Most legislative candidates, including incumbents, have to compete for the support of civil servants, just as they compete to recruit other vote brokers. Many can rely on the support of a few friends, clients, or allies who are bureaucrats, but bureaucratic mobilization cannot be the centerpiece of their strategy.

Pathways to Power

The discretionary control that civil servants exercise over state resources and the related capacity of bureaucratic networks to deliver votes have two important effects on the outcome of elections: candidates for political office often have bureaucratic backgrounds, and incumbent government heads are advantaged. We discuss these two effects in turn.

The factors that make civil servants such excellent vote brokers also equip them to compete for power themselves. It is not simply that they control the government services and resources that citizens need, and carry social weight as a consequence of being among the best-educated and highest-status individuals in their communities. They also possess private wealth that adds to their influence, and which they can use to finance election campaigns. The source of this private wealth is, of course, public office itself. Being a civil servant provides many opportunities for rent seeking and personal enrichment. These opportunities begin with small-scale extraction, such as handing in fake or exaggerated receipts for travel expenses or demanding irregular fees for school enrollment or paperwork, but get progressively more lucrative as officials move up the hierarchy, with senior bureaucrats able to rake in large fees by manipulating budgets, marking up procurement costs, levying imposts on their subordinates, taking payoffs for issuing government contracts or licenses, and so on.

Obviously, different government jobs provide different opportunities, reflected in the common classification of "wet" and "dry" positions, but the upshot is that senior bureaucrats—especially those who, over the course of their careers, have had the personal resources and connections to move up through the wettest bureaus and posts—are often among the richest people in their districts, owning serious investments in local plantations, fish ponds, mining operations, real estate developments, or whatever economic activities flourish in their locale. Such private wealth, and the state-business networks forged over the course of a bureaucratic career, provide them with the resources to launch political careers of their own in the new democratic Indonesia.

This background allows us to understand a remarkable feature of post-Suharto Indonesia: the ability of bureaucrats to maintain their dominance in local politics, despite democratization. Under Suharto, as we have seen, Indonesia was commonly understood to be a bureaucratic polity. The political dominance of bureaucrats was obvious. Early in the New Order, a large majority of governors, *bupati*, and mayors were military officers; their numbers declined gradually over the course of the New Order, but the winners were civilian bureaucrats, rather than outsiders. As Malley (2002, 107–108) explains, "the percentage of victorious candidates from the armed forces declined during the 1980s to about 40 per cent, the others were drawn entirely from the bureaucracy." A remarkable feature of post-Suharto Indonesia is that persons with bureaucratic backgrounds continue to dominate such posts, but now do so by winning competitive local elections. Indeed, with only a little exaggeration, we might think of post-Suharto Indonesia as representing *a democratized bureaucratic polity.*

Several studies have demonstrated that civil servants have been prominent players in local government-head elections. For example, an analysis conducted by Mietzner of fifty *pilkada* in the first round of such elections in 2005 showed that "the strongest group in the field of nominees was that of the career bureaucrats, who made up around 36 percent of all candidates. . . . These key bureaucrats controlled large financial resources, had extensive networks in business and civil society, and had the advantage of high name recognition" (Mietzner 2010, 178). A study by Buehler (2010, 275) indicated that of all gubernatorial candidates between 2005 and 2008, 26.4 percent had a background in either the bureaucracy or the police. Another 43.2 percent were either incumbent governors, deputy governors, or former previous district heads—many of whom were themselves former bureaucrats. In Buehler's sample of 132 such candidates, not a single one was classified as a party cadre.[2] In a later study, which assessed district head elections held between 2005 and 2013 in the three provinces of Banten, West Java, and South Sulawesi, Buehler also found that bureaucrats were the major source of candidates, but most candidates had served in the local bureaucracy rather than having spent time in Jakarta, as had often been common under the New Order:

> A "typical" career of a candidate competing in the latest round of direct elections starts as a village head or with an entry level position in the local bureaucracy in the early 1980s. He then continues as a sub-district head (camat) through the 1990s. Various stints in higher echelon posts in the local bureaucracy follow towards the end of the New Order, from where he eventually makes a bid for the top executive post. Heads of the local Revenue Office (Dinas Pendapatan Daerah), the Public Works Office (Pekerjaan Umum), the Office of Staff Administration (Kepegawaian) as well as the post of District Secretary (Sekretaris Daerah) seem to be particularly common launching pads. Arguably, rent-seeking opportunities in such so-called "wet" posts abound and may therefore allow office holders to amass the vast amounts of money they need to run as district head or mayor. (Buehler 2013)

Our own assessment of 269 local elections held in 2015 confirm these conclusions. As table 8.1 demonstrates, of the 695 candidates running for governor, *bupati*, and mayoral positions, the largest group (26.8 percent) were bureaucrats (this figure excludes incumbents and deputies, a proportion of whom would also have had prior bureaucratic careers). After incumbents, civil servants constituted the group that most often won these elections (fifty-one times), while their success rate was actually just below average.[3]

The conclusion is obvious: even though *bupati*, mayors, and governors are now selected by open elections, in many ways these positions remain what they

TABLE 8.1   Backgrounds of 695 candidates in 223 regional head elections, December 2015

OCCUPATION	ALL MAIN CANDIDATES	OCCUPATION (IN %)	WINNING MAIN CANDIDATES	SUCCESS RATE (% WINNING)
Incumbent	109	15.7	69	63.3
Deputy	62	8.9	21	33.9
DPRD/DPD	129	18.6	41	31.8
Civil servants (incl. retired)	186	26.8	51	27.4
Business	175	25.2	31	17.7
Other	31	4.5	9	29.0
Unknown	3	0.4	1	33.3
Total / average	**695**	**100.0**	**223**	**32.1**

have always been in post-independence Indonesia: the apex position in the local bureaucracy, and the dream job of ambitious local civil servants. Political competition has opened up in post-Suharto Indonesia, but it frequently takes the form of competition between bureaucrats.

In noting this pattern, we should stress that it appears to be unusual internationally, and a marker of Indonesia's state-centered pattern of patronage distribution, and of the legacy of its period as a bureaucratic polity. It should also be interpreted in the light of the limited control that political parties exercise over the bureaucracy. Returning to our touchstone comparisons of India and Argentina, in these countries political parties have much more capacity to manipulate how state resources are distributed, so it is the parties that accrue much of the credit for provision of public services and welfare. As a result, in these patronage democracies local civil servants are generally not important political actors.

Available studies on the backgrounds of local government heads in both countries suggest that the pathway from professional civil service to politician is relatively rarely taken. In Argentina, an analysis of provincial governors, who are directly elected and whose power "is based on patronage, pork-barrel politics, and clientelism" (De Luca 2008, 191), shows that the large majority had previously held posts such as national deputy, provincial minister, provincial party president, and national senator—posts that indicate that most had built long careers as professional politicians and had risen to authority through the country's party system. Civil servant did not even rate as a separate category in De Luca's analysis, which concludes that "governors' political careers are strongly underwritten by the political parties that back them" (De Luca 2008, 212).

A similar picture arises when we look at Indian politicians. The comparison is somewhat problematic, since in India there are no direct elections of government heads. Politicians compete for seats in parliaments and municipal councils— which subsequently elect executive politicians such as chief ministers or city mayors. While keeping this in mind, the contrast is striking: Jaffrelot and Kumar (2009) show that these members of legislative assemblies (MLAs) in India (which include the subsequently appointed government heads) hardly ever have bureaucratic backgrounds. In Uttar Pradesh, for example, only 3.4 percent of MLAs are listed as originating from "other" backgrounds, a category that includes "government service," along with housewives (Zerinini 2009, 50). As chief ministers, the Indian equivalent of Indonesia's provincial governors, are also members of legislative assemblies, we can assume that they also very rarely have bureaucratic backgrounds.[4] Similarly, a study of the backgrounds of legislators in Argentina concludes that "the career paths of Argentine Chamber deputies during the post-1983 period are extremely party oriented. Virtually all deputies arrive to the Chamber having previously occupied an elective, appointive (in a national or provincial executive branch), or party post. [There is a] very strong link between the careers of legislators and their relationship with their party" (Jones et al. 2002, 658).

The comparison becomes more interesting still when we consider that it is relatively rare for members of Indonesia's legislatures to have bureaucratic backgrounds. For example, in the 2014–2019 national parliament, only 32 of the 560 members could be identified as former civil servants, and only an additional 8 members had backgrounds in the police or military, making a total of only 7.2 percent of the national parliament with backgrounds in government service.[5] This figure, comparable to that in India, is suggestive of the sharp disjuncture between the powers of legislatures and of executive governments in Indonesia's patronage democracy. The key power holders in Indonesia's system of decentralized government—and the chief controllers of the government resources that flow through the system—are heads of executive government, as we have seen. As a result, it is to be expected that senior bureaucrats in a region, who are themselves major patronage wielders, will aspire for the peak position in the local government apparatus as *bupati*, mayor, or governor. Winning such a post puts them in command of the entire government budget and provides many opportunities for rent seeking.

In contrast, a seat in the legislature offers access to what are essentially side payments, in the form, for example, of the "gavel money," aspiration funds, and opportunities for profiting from contracts and projects of the sort we discussed in the preceding chapter. Such opportunities, while no doubt representing a cornucopia of state patronage to legislators who arrive in an assembly from a background in the private sector, typically pale in comparison to what is available to senior bureaucrats such as bureau heads or regional secretaries. Accordingly, legislatures are often arenas in which outside actors can gain access to government patronage resources and are often populated by private businesspeople, as well as lawyers, other professionals, former village heads, and, of course, professional party politicians, as well as junior family members of senior civil servants or regional heads. An account produced by the University of Indonesia research institute, Puskapol, after the 2014 election revealed that 59 percent of the DPR members had backgrounds in business and the professions (*Republika* 2014). Senior retired civil servants themselves often view a seat in the legislature as a step down in their career progression, especially if it is in the district where they served rather than involving a move up into the provincial or national legislature.

Incumbency Advantages

The second major consequence of the importance of bureaucrats (and of community-level state officials such as village, RW, and RT heads) in election campaigns is that they are in a position to confer advantages on incumbent heads of local government in their reelection efforts. Certainly, it is widely believed in regional Indonesia that incumbent district heads and governors are likely to win elections (though term limits of two five-year periods in office cap these efforts), and there has been a new trend of uncontested elections involving incumbents, which seems to support this view (Lay et al. 2017). Throughout the country, our informants often told us that the control of incumbents over local bureaucracies explained their victories. For example, a district chairperson of PDI-P in Lampung claimed, "If there is an incumbent [standing for election], then he or she should be able to win because [the campaign] is already made easy for them in so many ways" (interview, May 20, 2013). A DPRD member from Tangerang agreed: "It should be different, but in reality people [candidates] use the government apparatus to win support. You can win with the bureaucracy because they are directly in contact with people. So the incumbent candidate tends to win elections" (interview, December 2, 2013).

Our discussion of election campaigns so far provides several reasons why incumbents might have advantages. Let us mention three. First is the support of the bureaucratic apparatus itself. As we have explained, civil servants often support incumbent heads of government in order to safeguard their jobs, providing incumbents with a ready-made campaign network. Other candidates have to spend time and money building a campaign infrastructure; incumbents can lean on the hierarchy of bureau heads, *camat*, village heads, and so on. Not only does this infrastructure extend into the remotest villages; it exercises considerable influence over voters.

A second incumbency advantage is control of state resources. Mindful of the need to secure reelection, many incumbents develop creative strategies to direct state budgets and other benefits to supporters. Social assistance funds, garbage programs, scholarships, infrastructure projects, or budgets for public services: almost everything that local governments hand out can, if managed well, be distributed in a way that suggests the recipients should reciprocate at election time. We have highlighted many examples in this book, but it is worth noting that sometimes this distribution of state benefits takes a form that is not too dissimilar to vote buying, as when government officers distribute social assistance in the form of packets of free medicines, oil, soap, or other basic commodities. Frequently, such packages are labeled with the picture and name of the district head, not unlike the envelopes and consumer goods that candidates hand out during elections.

A third advantage is that incumbents can use government programs to maintain public visibility. Most of the advertisements or banners that local governments produce carry a picture of the district head or governor, often with his or her deputy. As there are government campaigns for many causes—from encouraging people to pay tax to promoting hygienic behavior or interreligious harmony—there are plenty of opportunities to use government budgets to publicize incumbents. Ambitious bureau heads also often try to ingratiate themselves with their superiors by putting up banners or buying newspaper advertisements to congratulate the incumbent on this or that achievement. The effect is that a district or province gets blanketed with banners, posters, and newspaper advertisements that portray the incumbent in a positive light.

To what extent do these advantages affect election results? To see whether incumbent district heads and governors are indeed more likely to win elections, we collected the results of 223 elections for *bupati*, mayors, and governors that were held on December 9, 2015.[6] As Indonesia's election system allows district heads and governors to be reelected only once, incumbents competed in only 109 of these elections. In table 8.1 we presented the background of all candidates in these races; table 8.2 analyzes the winning candidates in these contests, with the first column showing the percentages of winners in all elections, and the second column considering only races in which an incumbent was competing.

The results in table 8.2 provide further evidence to support our arguments about the state-centered nature of Indonesia's patronage democracy. The high success rate of incumbents, at 63 percent, suggests that incumbents do have considerable electoral advantages, though they are not overwhelming. An earlier study (Mietzner 2010, 183) found a similar success rate of 60 percent for 103 elections held between 2005 and 2009. Mietzner interpreted this as a healthy sign and an indication of the "declining importance of incumbency." In fact, it appears that the incumbency advantage of sitting regional heads has become an established feature of Indonesian elections.

TABLE 8.2   Backgrounds of winning candidates in local government elections, December 2015

OCCUPATION	BACKGROUND OF WINNER (ALL RACES)	SHARE OF WINNING CANDIDATES (%)	BACKGROUND OF WINNER (ONLY WHEN INCUMBENT RUNS)	SHARE OF WINNING CANDIDATES (%)
Incumbent	69	30.9	69	63.3
Deputy incumbent	21	9.4	6	5.5
DPRD member	41	18.4	8	7.34
Civil servant (including retired)	51	22.9	13	11.9
Business	31	13.9	11	10.09
Other	9	4.1	2	1.83
Unknown	1	0.4	0	0
Total	**223**	**100.0**	**109**	**100.0**

It is noteworthy that this incumbency return rate is significantly higher than that enjoyed by legislators. Unfortunately, we lack data from across Indonesia's regional legislatures, but we compiled figures on the 2014 national legislative election and found that of the 501 DPR members who chose to re-contest their seats—90 percent of sitting legislators—231 persons, or 46 percent, were reelected. This lower return rate reflects both the greater competitiveness of legislative races and the greater difficulty that DPR members have in controlling patronage resources.[7] As we have explained, legislators can certainly access resources as a result of the budgetary and legislative bargaining power they wield, but they lack the direct control enjoyed by regional heads. We also tried to measure whether membership in a wet parliamentary commission significantly improved a legislator's chance of reelection, given that, as we have explained, membership in certain commissions improves legislators' chances of accessing resources. It is difficult to draw definitive conclusions on this score, because many DPR members move around between commissions over the course of a parliamentary term. Even so, it is potentially significant that some of the highest rates of return were in resource-rich commissions, notably Commission V (which covers areas such as transportation, public works, and telecommunications), with thirty members returned, while some of the lower rates of return came in commissions such as Commission II (internal affairs, agrarian matters, and internal affairs) and Commission VIII (religion, social affairs, and women's empowerment), with ten and thirteen members returned respectively.

In our two comparative cases, India and Argentina, the success rates of incumbent legislators are even lower. Quantitative studies of Indian election results show that in local elections, incumbents are at a considerable disadvantage (Uppal 2009), with about 70 percent of incumbent assembly members *not* reelected between 1989 and 2007, a figure that includes those who did not get party support to run for reelection (Manor 2010, xvi). Thus, while in Indonesia incumbency is often proposed as a reason for electoral success, the "anti-incumbency factor" is a recurring feature of analyses of Indian politics to explain the regular electoral *failure* of incumbents (e.g., Nooruddin and Chibber 2008; Uppal 2009). The success rate of incumbent politicians in Argentina is even more dismal; one study found that during 1989–1999 the reelection rate of members of Argentina's chamber of deputies varied between 15 and 24 percent (Jones 2002, 166–167). This very low reelection rate is partly due to the control that parties exercise over candidate selection and their tendency to deny sitting parliamentarians the opportunity to run for reelection (Jones et al. 2002).

Returning to local government-head elections, our assessment of incumbency advantages gains depth if we look at the backgrounds of other winning candidates. As already noted, one remarkable aspect of the results depicted in tables 8.1 and 8.2 is the regular electoral victories of (retired) civil servants. The first columns of table 8.2 show that in our sample, 23 percent of all elected district heads and governors came to these posts from positions as senior bureaucrats. If we add the number of successful incumbents and deputies, that means that 63 percent of all successful candidates had backgrounds as senior local government functionaries. Narrow the focus further to only elections where incumbents could compete (the last two columns of table 8.2) and this percentage reaches a stunning 81 percent.

The conclusion is clear: candidates who have exercised some degree of control over local bureaucracies are remarkably successful in these elections. Conversely, candidates from outside the local government apparatus stand little chance of being elected. In our broad "other" category of successful candidates we counted only nine doctors, activists, and university lecturers. Even persons who list their professions as business (remembering that many of the civil servants and government heads will have business interests on the side) were unsuccessful, with a success rate of only 18 percent, far below the success rates of civil servants and members of local parliaments. The limited number of electoral victories by candidates lacking local government backgrounds suggests that incumbency advantages accrue not only to ruling politicians, but also to other actors who have exercised some degree of control over local bureaucracies. Indeed, the three incumbency advantages we outlined above would also benefit—albeit to a lesser extent—senior bureaucrats, deputy district heads, and deputy governors.

These results imply that the fiercest electoral challenges to incumbent regional heads in Indonesia tend to come not so much from populist outsider candidates, but from insiders within local government offices. When incumbents are defeated, they are most likely to lose to their own deputies, or to senior bureaucrats who

have served under them. Indeed, our informants often added this very qualification to their comments about the power of incumbency. Thus, the PDI-P leader
from Lampung quoted above as being so adamant about the strength of incumbents added that "there is a chance that an incumbent loses if he or she loses the
support of the bureau heads. They can lose if they are too greedy. If the incumbent takes too much profit and is not good at sharing, then [bureau heads] will
not support the candidate." The DPRD member from Tangerang agreed: "The
incumbent candidate tends to win elections, except when there is no harmony
[within the bureaucracy]. When [the incumbent] does not take care of people,
does not give opportunities, or is too strict, then he or she can be sabotaged."

Incumbents have advantages in many democracies, but especially those based on
patronage. By definition, politicians who hold office have more control over state
resources than those who do not. Yet not all ruling politicians can monopolize
state resources to the same extent. The key variable here is whether, and to what
extent, elected politicians need to share this control with other political actors.
The conclusion of these last two chapters is that while control over state resources
is becoming increasingly fragmented in Indonesia, much of this fragmentation
is still occurring *within* local bureaucracies. Political parties are just starting to
develop their capacity to affect the distribution of patronage goods.

We should certainly not understate the effects of the fragmentation that has
occurred. There has been growing competition within government, with various
actors struggling to control government funds and projects. This struggle has
different dimensions: on the one hand members of legislatures and party bosses
try to wrest access to budgetary resources, projects, and other side-payments away
from executive government heads and bureaucrats. On the other hand, much
competition is between officials and bureaucrats inside government offices.
Such internal competition often has negative effects for the quality of local governance, because fights over, say, the awarding of government contracts cause
delays and waste.

The limited control political parties and other non-state actors wield over the
bureaucracy constitutes an important reason why campaign networks in Indonesia are so transient and freewheeling. Because party networks struggle to control
state resources, they also struggle to build grassroots networks capable of mobilizing voters, a task bureaucratic networks are often better able to perform. This
pattern, we have shown in this chapter, has important consequences for electoral competition, making bureaucrats prominent as candidates and victors, and
advantaging incumbents. In turn, the electoral prominence of the state apparatus
constitutes an important reason why politicians continue to promote loyal rather
than capable bureaucrats. These factors point toward a considerable challenge

that Indonesia's democratization faces: Indonesia is becoming a democratized bureaucratic polity, in which power remains concentrated in the bureaucracy, and outsider candidates are at a considerable disadvantage. This is an important obstacle, both to strengthening democratic accountability and to improving the functioning of local governments.

Part 4

COMPARING ACROSS INDONESIA

9

CAMPAIGN FINANCING, BUSINESS, AND THE PUBLIC SPHERE

So far, we have painted a picture of the general pattern of clientelistic politics in Indonesia. Though we have touched on regional variations, our focus has been on identifying core features that characterize clientelistic politics in the country as a whole: candidates' use of nonparty networks to organize their campaigns, their reliance on community leaders and brokers, the state-centered nature of patronage networks, and the continuing political prominence of civil servants. Such features have been shaped both by legacies of authoritarianism and by the electoral institutions adopted by the new democratic Indonesia. These factors apply nationwide.

But Indonesian politics are not monolithic. Over the last decade or so, just as the new pattern of freewheeling clientelism has bedded down, challenges, variations, and alternatives have also emerged. In particular, members of a new breed of local government leaders have won elections in some areas by presenting themselves as anticorruption reformers, not beholden to established oligarchs and bureaucratic networks, appealing directly to voters through the media, and winning elections on the strength of personal image rather than patronage. The most prominent such local politician was Joko Widodo, or Jokowi, the reforming mayor of the Central Java town of Solo (2005–2012), who went on to win election as governor of Jakarta in 2012 and as Indonesian president in 2014, a figure who has prompted much scholarly interest (Luebke 2009; Mas'udi 2016; Mietzner 2015). Beyond Jokowi and his ilk, scholars have pointed to other variations in both the character of election campaigns and relations of politicians with local business elites. In one important study, Ryan Tans (2012) compares elections in several districts in North Sumatra province, arguing that different types of coalitions compete for local power (he characterizes these as political mafias, party machines, and mobilizing coalitions). Luky Djani (2013) has explained why corrupt local officials have been removed from power by social protests in some locales but remain entrenched in others, by pointing to factors such as the degree of monopoly control over economic resources enjoyed by elites and the character of local civil societies. Other observers have noted that local political dynasties have risen to dominance in some parts of the country but not others (Buehler 2013; Aspinall and As'ad 2016).[1]

What might explain such variation? In this and the next chapter, we propose an explanation that focuses on the relationship between the worlds of politics and economics, and that probes relations between business and politicians. Taking inspiration from an emerging literature on subnational democratization, we argue that an important determinant of the character of local politics—especially the extent to which clientelistic practices are pervasive—is the degree to which control over economic activities is concentrated in elite hands. Where what we call a "concentrated control economy" arises, the limited dispersion of economic power makes civil society weaker, intensifies collusion between business and politics, and enervates the public sphere. In this context the capacity and willingness of business and societal actors to criticize and constrain the collusive and clientelistic practices of political elites are more limited.

In this chapter, we rely mainly on fieldwork findings to develop this argument, using a comparison between local politics in Central Kalimantan and Surabaya—two locations with strikingly different political economies—as our main illustration. In the next chapter, we use the expert survey to examine whether and to what extent these arguments explain subnational variation across Indonesia.

The Political Economy of Regional Indonesia

As we touched on in chapter 3, during the years of Suharto's rule the state played a prominent role in stimulating and regulating economic activity, creating a wealthy and influential class of regime-allied entrepreneurs who received advantages in the form of state subsidies, concessions, and licenses in exchange for their contributions to Golkar, Suharto's charitable foundations, and other regime leaders and interests. Politics acquired an oligarchic character, as power was concentrated in the hands of a small circle of wealthy business-bureaucratic elites who used control of state institutions to accumulate capital. After the fall of the New Order, authors like Hadiz, Robison, and Winters argued that democratization changed the character of Indonesia's oligarchy but not its dominance. Regional elites have gained ascendance, and a fragmentation of power has made oligarchs less "tamed" (Winters 2011), but, these authors argue, more open politics has not enabled anti-oligarchic forces to significantly challenge oligarchic dominance (Hadiz 2010; Hadiz and Robison 2013). These works have been very influential in the study of Indonesian politics, as they provide a template for interpreting the continuing dominance of economic elites.

Yet in recent times, this oligarchy literature has come under fire for being overly pessimistic and for discounting the influence of other social forces (Ford and Pepinsky 2014). While not denying the prominence of economic elites, critics have proposed that various forms of activism have succeeded in challenging oligarchic influence over aspects of government, pointing to such phenomena as labor laws and expanding health care subsidies (Aspinall 2013b; Mietzner 2014; Pepinsky 2013). One striking feature of this debate, however, is that it has so far been largely waged in general, all-Indonesia terms, as if oligarchic dominance—or challenges to it—are evenly distributed across the archipelago. As Pepinsky (2013, 96) points out, "the theoretical apparatus of oligarchy [does not] provide a framework for building explanations for why or how politics varies." Proponents of the oligarchy thesis have seemed to assume that regional variation is limited and that an all-Indonesia pattern can be established. While this might be expected from those emphasizing political institutions, the lack of attention to regional variation is surprising for political economists.

In contrast, the starting point for our argument in this chapter is a simple observation: Indonesia's economy is highly diverse, encompassing complex and relatively wealthy economic hubs as well as poor backwaters with little private economic activity apart from agriculture and occasional enclaves of natural resource extraction. Per capita income in Jakarta and Surabaya is almost twenty times higher than in many rural districts in eastern Indonesia.[2] A critical political economy approach suggests that such variation will affect the nature of local politics.

Applying the conclusions of earlier chapters about the nature of election campaigns, this chapter discusses how varied economic conditions affect the capacity of economic elites to dominate local politics. For this purpose, we derive inspiration from comparative studies of local politics undertaken elsewhere. A growing body of research compares the character and quality of democracy in different regions *within* a single country (Sidel 2014). While such scholars of subnational democracy formulate their objects of research in different terms—ranging from "subnational authoritarianism" (Gibson 2005) through "hybrid democratic regimes" (McMann 2006) to the "unevenness of democratization" (Behrend 2011)—a striking commonality is that they all relate the character of local politics to economic conditions. Kelly McMann, for example, compares two districts in Russia and two in Kyrgyzstan, attributing differences in local politics to varying levels of "economic autonomy," which she defines as "the ability to earn a living independent of the state" (McMann 2006, 20). She finds that where income opportunities are largely controlled by state authorities, political opposition is much easier to suppress because potential opponents engage in self-censorship or are vulnerable to intimidation. Says an entrepreneur in one such district: "There is a monopoly held by the governor's entourage. One hundred percent. If you want to create a business—a business in a new sphere that is not part of [their] monopoly—officials will simply say, 'No'" (McMann 2006, 154–155).

In a study of local politics in Argentina, Gervasoni focuses on the size of government budgets: "Low levels of democracy are to be expected where states enjoy plentiful central government subsidies and have a weak tax link with local citizens" (Gervasoni 2010, 303; see also Behrend 2011). He finds, like McMann, that democracy does not necessarily function worse in poorer regions, but in regions where government budgets are relatively large and government jobs plentiful. So where McMann focuses on the control of ruling elites over important economic activities, Gervasoni emphasizes the dependence of the economy on the state.

What these studies have in common is that they point to how the concentration of elite control over economic activities can be a key factor in shaping the character of local politics. As Sidel concludes in his overview of this literature on subnational democracy: "The emergence, entrenchment, and endurance of subnational authoritarianism require *not only* constraints on the economic autonomy of citizens in a locality (alas, an all too common condition in developing countries around the world), *but also* concentration of control over the commanding heights of a local economy in the hands of a single individual, family, clan, clique, or organization" (Sidel 2014, 177, emphasis in original).

In this chapter, we use insights drawn from this comparative literature on subnational political variation to interpret the varying character of local politics in Indonesia. We propose that, in the Indonesian context, two interrelated characteristics of local economies are particularly telling indicators of concentrated economic control: dependence on state resources and lack of economic diversification. When local economies rely heavily on state expenditure and government employment, elected officials have a relatively high degree of control over the livelihoods of their constituents. Similarly, economic control is concentrated when the private sector is undiversified and the local economy depends on a small number of capital-intensive activities such as natural resource extraction. Conversely, when local economies are more mixed and especially when industry, finance, and trade make up a larger part of the economy, a wider range of entrepreneurs, enterprises, and other economic actors exercise control over job opportunities and resources. We see high levels of state dependency and low levels of diversification as indicating the presence of a concentrated control economy, and show that different regions of Indonesia vary considerably in their degree of economic concentration.

We argue that the clientelistic embrace between business and politics is most intense in concentrated control economies, because the scope to challenge and constrain patronage-wielding oligarchic politicians is more limited in such contexts. Politicians are more likely to be dependent on a relatively narrow band of often state-dependent elites, while voters, too, are more likely to depend on bureaucrats and a limited number of economic actors for their well-being, and thus are less likely to challenge dominant elites. We identify three main mechanisms that help explain this relationship between economic control and local politics. These mechanisms involve campaign financing, local civil society, and the nature of the public sphere, specifically the media. To illustrate the analysis, we compare local politics in Central Kalimantan and Surabaya, two locations with strikingly different political economies.

Election Campaigns and Oligarchy in Central Kalimantan

On October 2, 2013, Corruption Eradication Commission investigators descended on the house of the chief justice of Indonesia's Constitutional Court, Akil Mochtar, just as two representatives of the district head of Gunung Mas, Hambit Binti, were about to hand over a bribe of 300,000 Singapore dollars. Hambit Binti was paying the bribe in order to get the chief justice to quash a case against him alleging electoral fraud in the disputed election in Gunung Mas, a remote but resource-rich district in Central Kalimantan. In the days following the arrest, SMS texting communication between Akil and Hambit Binti's representatives emerged. When Akil had asked for the bribe to be transferred, some haggling had taken place: "Can it be less? 2.5? For Palangka Raya [the Central Kalimantan capital] it was [only] two tons [i.e., 200,000 Singapore dollars]." Akil had answered: "That was a discounted price. This one [i.e., Hambit Binti] is richer than the Palangkaraya mayor . . . even 3 wouldn't be enough" (B. Hidayat 2014). It turned out that the highest judge of Indonesia's Constitutional Court had been routinely selling his rulings in election disputes to the highest bidder.

The bagman delivering the money was Cornelis Nalau, a major businessman in Gunung Mas. His involvement was not coincidental. Nalau had been instrumental in securing the funding for Binti's lavish election campaign. In 2012, a year before the election, Nalau had allocated land to four newly established oil palm companies with impressive names like Jaya Jadi Utama (Glory Is the Priority) and Berkala Maju Bersama (Step by Step We Progress Together). As district head, Hambit Binti quickly helped these companies to acquire the necessary paperwork so that they could start planting seedlings. These licenses boosted the price of Nalau's new companies: a few months after Nalau arranged the paperwork, he sold the companies to a Malaysian company, CB Industrial Product Holding, while staying on as a commissioner (EIA 2014, 18–19). This windfall helped finance the extensive vote buying that Binti engaged in during the election campaign—informants stated the going rate was the relatively high figure of 200,000 rupiah (eighteen dollars) per person. And when the election results ended up in the Constitutional Court, Nalau and fellow investors were willing to contribute the money to bribe the chief justice (Firdaus 2014). Given the access that Binti could provide to licenses for more plantations, it was a reasonable investment.

The arrest of Akil Mochtar—the highest judicial officer in the country—caused a major stir and dominated headlines for weeks. Even for citizens hardened by a steady stream of corruption scandals over the last decade, the willingness of the country's top judge to sell election victories for bundles of cash was shocking. Yet the case was also revealing of the strategies that Indonesian politicians use to finance their electioneering. It showed how Hambit Binti had used his discretionary power over licensing to help Nalau set up plantations, which in turn helped finance Binti's election campaign. District heads cannot set up palm oil companies in their own names, so they use family members or trusted friends like Nalau to make money out of the discretionary power they possess (see Gecko Project 2018).

During the New Order, the acquisition of such licenses was largely a bureaucratic affair. Business elites needed to spend their energy and money cultivating contacts among bureaucrats, military officers, and political leaders in Jakarta. Binti's dealings illustrate how, in a democratizing Indonesia, popularly elected officials have become an additional focal point for the acquisition of economic privileges. Decentralization has given local elected officials more authority over licensing procedures and spatial planning, much to the dismay of bureaucrats in Jakarta, especially those in the Ministry of Forestry (Gellert and Andiko 2015). As a result, licensing has become a lucrative avenue for local politicians to obtain or recover election campaign funds. In places like Central Kalimantan, palm oil and mining entrepreneurs have quickly learned that making campaign donations can help them get permits and overcome other bureaucratic hurdles. They donate money in the hope and expectation that successful candidates will repay the favor by helping them gain permission for forest conversion and other enterprises. As a recent investigative report on Seruyan (a nearby district in Central Kalimantan) showed, politicians often prefer to bestow such economic privileges on family members in order to make sure that they will derive a considerable part of the profits (Gecko Project 2017).

Such collusion between politicians and entrepreneurs in places like Central Kalimantan undermines the effectiveness of spatial planning and environmental regulation. Local governments are more than willing to creatively interpret Indonesia's already vague and contradictory land regime in ways that benefit big companies (McCarthy 2004). Much money is made by turning a blind eye when oil palm plantations lack the necessary paperwork. According to an assessment made by the Institute for Ecosoc Rights, a Jakarta-based NGO, of the three hundred operational oil palm plantations in Kalimantan, only eighty-two possess all the required licenses (Amirullah 2015). Oil palm plantations located on land designated as forestland are especially likely to lack proper permits. To establish a plantation in these areas, the owner is supposed to acquire a permit from the Ministry of Forestry in Jakarta for release of forestland. This requirement is expensive and troublesome, and most companies ignore it. An investigation by an official body set up in 2009 to investigate Indonesia's "legal mafia" revealed that fewer than 20 percent of plantations on forestland had acquired such a license (Gellert and Andiko 2015, 651). So long as a company has the support of local politicians, it does not need such a license. Local bureaucrats and police are generally happy to heed the wish of the local power holders to overlook such transgressions. Indeed, they often get cut into the bribes.

After a concession is awarded, an additional source of income comes from the land disputes that these concessions generate. Oil palm concession sites are usually inhabited by people who have lived off the land for generations. As these communities generally lack formal land title, oil palm entrepreneurs use the support from politicians and the police to gain the upper hand in the resulting land conflicts. Such collusion makes it difficult for affected communities to demand adequate compensation, let alone resist the incoming tide of oil palm (Afrizal 2013; Colchester and Chao 2013).

The collusion between natural resource businesses and local politicians is thus a major driver of land grabbing in Indonesia and elsewhere. The area devoted to oil palm has expanded dramatically in Central Kalimantan. According to data provided by the provincial government, oil palm went from less than 200,000 hectares in 2001 to 1.7 million in 2015 (Palupi et al. 2015). Using similar data, Walhi, an environmental organization active in Central Kalimantan, has calculated that since 2004, local governments have yearly awarded plantation licenses for between 400,000 and 600,000 hectares. Before 2004 the awarded concessions never exceeded 180,000 hectares per year.[3]

This enthusiastic political support for the palm oil industry can partly be attributed to the nature of election campaigns. Politicians like Hambit Binti do not only make deals with palm oil companies to enrich themselves. They also need to use these deals to recover the expenses they incurred during their last election, and gather funds for the next. Our discussion in previous chapters has illustrated how enormous these debts can be. In a place like Central Kalimantan, even before an election campaign starts, candidates for district head need to spend up to US$500,000 to buy the nominations of political parties. For gubernatorial races, this can cost up to $2 million. Then there are the normal operational expenses of running an election campaign, as well as the costs of building success teams and winning over communities by providing club goods and vote buying. The political observers in our expert survey estimated that, on average, the winning district head in their district spent 28 billion rupiah (about $2.5 million) on his or her election campaign. Estimates ranged from 10 billion rupiah in low-population areas like East Nusa Tenggara to 40 billion rupiah in resource-rich East Kalimantan (i.e., between $880,000 and $3.5 million). The average estimate of our experts of the campaign costs of elected governors was 166 billion rupiah (about $15 million).

These high costs are an important reason why Indonesia's democratization process has not led to curtailment of the dominance of economic elites. As political parties receive only meager state subsidies (Mietzner 2009, 2013b, 2015), candidates need to fund their own campaigns. Most rely on either their own capital, which they later recoup from government, or on donations from business actors. Reliance on campaign donors undermines public policy and weakens state institutions as campaign contributors leverage their donations to gain privileged access to business opportunities and subvert licensing, tendering, land use, and other bureaucratic procedures (Mietzner 2011).

In this sense, it can be argued that democratization is accelerating deforestation and the expansion of oil palm cultivation. Election campaign expenses oblige politicians to form coalitions with palm oil companies, generating various creative and often corrupt ways to circumvent national regulations (EIA 2014). Indeed, a study using satellite images has shown that forest cover loss accelerates in the years leading to local elections: "Deforestation in zones where all logging is illegal increases by as much as 42 percent in the year prior to an election" (Burgess et al. 2012, 2). The struggle to protect Indonesia's remaining forests is therefore not only a struggle to change government policies and reform corporate behavior. It will also need to address the political incentives that sustain collusion between politicians and business.

Mafia Coalitions

These exchanges between politicians and business actors are, for the most part, informal and clientelistic in nature. While politicians sometimes repay their campaign donors by adopting favorable public policies, politicians are more likely to help their business backers by manipulating or circumventing existing regulations on their behalf. For this reason, it is curious that some critics of the oligarchy thesis insist that the dominance of economic elites should be studied by paying "close attention to policy as the fundamental object of contestation" (Pepinsky 2013, 99; Liddle 2013). For local economic elites in particular, the content of public policies is of little consequence so long as bureaucrats and politicians are willing to allow them to ignore these policies. The business of campaign financing is rarely a strategy to influence the drafting of policies; more often it is aimed at undermining them.

Relations between business actors and politicians can take various forms. For the purposes of our analysis, and drawing on Tans (2012), it is useful to highlight a category of "mafia coalitions" that feature strongly personalized and long-lasting informal ties between politicians and business (such as those based on family or long-lasting crony relationships) and that are relatively exclusionary, seeking to maximize resource extraction on behalf of a closed elite faction, clique, or family. The cooperation between Hambit Binti and Nalau in Gunung Mas provides an example. Such coalitions can be distinguished from the more ad hoc and transient deal making and interactions between business and politics that occur across Indonesia, because of the way they direct economic opportunities to a limited network of close allies. As Tans (2012, 11) describes them, in mafia coalitions in North Sumatra, "members divide the spoils among themselves to maintain the coalition and use the remainder to contest elections. The coalition is oriented horizontally because it is limited to members of the local elite." As Tans points out, cooperation within such networks is premised on promises of future control over local state institutions, since this control is necessary to acquire the money needed to keep the coalition afloat. Of course, such distinctions are a matter of degree—all locations in Indonesia feature informal cooperation between political and business actors—but there are some places where local governing coalitions are especially predatory.

In resource-rich areas like Kalimantan, such coalitions coalesce around extractive industries like logging, mining, and palm oil. Elsewhere, especially in remote districts with limited private economic activity and high dependence on government spending, mafia coalitions thrive on the exploitation of government budgets. Not infrequently candidates for district head or governor are supported by a coalition of local contractors who aim to gain control over government contracts for the provision of equipment and infrastructure.

Perhaps the best-known example in Indonesia is the clan of the eventually incarcerated governor Ratu Atut Chosiyah in Banten. This political dynasty used family ties to acquire both political power and business opportunities (see, for example, Ulum 2013). The dominance of the family was built around the construction company set up by Ratu Atut's father, Chasan Sochib. During the New Order period, Chasan used his connections within Golkar and his control of a network of *jawara* (strongmen) to capture lucrative contracts, particularly for building roads.

After the fall of the New Order, Chasan's family used the money thus earned to finance the election campaigns of various family members, which led to Ratu Atut's appointment as governor of Banten in 2005. The family used this position to direct government contracts as well as social assistance funds to companies held by relatives, greatly enlarging their financial clout (Hamid and Facal 2013; Hidayat 2007). According to Indonesia Corruption Watch, this family network managed to obtain 175 government contracts worth US$100 million between 2011 and 2013.[4] Several members of the dynasty, including Ratu Atut herself, were eventually arrested after attempting to bribe Akil Mochtar to secure a favorable ruling in an election dispute, with corruption investigators turning up evidence of extraordinary private wealth. Yet this downturn seemingly did not affect the family's electoral machine. In December 2015, family members once more won impressive electoral victories, so that they now controlled district governments in Serang, South Tangerang, and Pandeglang, with others occupying seats in national and local parliaments.

Two characteristics of such mafia networks stand out. First, these networks develop a monopoly over local state resources, directing government contracts, licenses, and other business opportunities to a relatively small group. For present purposes, and as we explore more fully below, it is important to note that the nature of a local economy shapes the likelihood of the emergence of such mafia coalitions. Such networks face less political competition when they control most of the important economic activities in the region. When, however, a local economy is more diversified and a wider variety of campaign funding is available, excluded business, bureaucratic, and political actors are more likely to launch successful challenges to these mafia coalitions and their hoarding of economic opportunities.

Second, mafia networks require particularly close ties between politicians and business actors in order to ameliorate the risks that both sides face in handling potential opposition, law enforcement, and other threats. Considerable trust and loyalty are needed to ensure that both sides protect each other and that campaign donations are paid back through contracts, licenses, or other benefits. Strained relations not only generate financial losses but can open the door for investigators to obtain proof of corruption. Family networks are for this reason a natural conduit for building such mafia coalitions, as they infuse the exchanges between politics and business with trust and solidarity. As Buehler (2013) puts it, "Establishing a dynasty is often also a protection strategy: incumbents want to be succeeded by their family members in order to shield themselves and their 'nearest and dearest' from being jailed for corruption." The emergence of politico-business families like the Atut dynasty in Banten or the Limpo dynasty in South Sulawesi has sparked considerable public opposition to political dynasties, and there was even an attempt to bar family members of ruling politicians from running as candidates, though it was overturned in court. In the absence of such measures, the protection impulse embodied in such families is likely to ensure that they will remain a feature of local politics.

Corruption and Campaign Finance

Mafia coalitions are a particularly predatory form of political-business cooperation. Not all candidates, however, can build exclusionary ties with business partners, because they lack the capacity to dominate local organs of government. It is the norm for collusion between politicians and business actors to take less exclusionary and more transient forms.

Monopolization can work only if the opposition against such dealings is weak or easily intimidated. As Luky Djani (2013) shows through an analysis of the downfall of a *bupati* in Garut, West Java, if a local government leader centralizes control, disgruntled elites can make common cause with local civil society groups and mobilize to bring down the leader, in this case by exposing evidence of his corruption. Partly for this reason, the ethos of *bagi-bagi*, or sharing (Winters 2011, 143–144), is deeply engrained in local politics, with most local leaders preferring to co-opt potential opponents by providing them with a portion of contracts and other benefits. Taking a large share is feasible only when the leader is confident that he or she can sideline opposition. Such calculations can easily misfire.

By the same token, in many regions relations between politicians and business are flexible, even promiscuous, rather the exclusionary. Indeed, business actors often opt to avoid close ties with one candidate and prefer instead to make campaign contributions to all electable candidates to ensure favorable treatment irrespective of the electoral outcome. Thus, Warburton has shown how large mining companies sometimes employ professional survey organizations to identify strong candidates, with one such company in Sulawesi prior to the 2014 legislative election making "donations to the top 140 candidates, with the expectation that every member of the new parliament would come from that pool" (Warburton 2016b, 349).

Such less personalized and more pragmatic interactions with elected officials do not provide exclusive access to state resources. Yet in such contexts financing an election campaign of a successful district head, governor, or parliament member still yields benefits, including contracts or licenses, help in getting around government regulations, or simply less harassment, obstruction, and bribe seeking from state officials. From the viewpoint of politicians, such deals are a strategic use of their discretionary powers. For businesspeople, campaign contributions are a "prepaid" form of corruption, in the sense that they can reduce the amount of kickbacks necessary to secure government favor. Equally, bribes and kickbacks are a "postpaid" campaign contribution, in the sense that they often help politicians recoup campaign expenses.

The opportunities for such exchanges are vast and depend on the economy of the region. In areas with more industrialized economies, deals between politicians and business actors can focus on, for example, helping factory owners to circumvent environmental regulations, sidestep minimum wage requirements, or solve issues with building permits. During our fieldwork we encountered real estate developers who helped finance an election campaign with the aim of arranging permits to build a new mall, an entrepreneur who helped a candidate with the hope of getting the district government to buy cars from him, and even a supplier of office stationery who reasoned that his campaign support could land him lucrative contracts. In rural, natural-resource-rich areas like Gunung Mas, such campaign donors are thinner on the ground, and politicians have few options beyond construction, palm oil, and mining companies.

The expert survey can illustrate how useful campaign donations are perceived to be for arranging privileged access to economic opportunities. We asked local observers how likely it was that a district head would arrange an *illegal* building permit for a campaign donor. Fully 69 percent of local observers answered that this was likely or very likely (59 percent for governors). Such exchanges were perceived to be more common in eastern Indonesia as well as in Banten (home of the Ratu Atut dynasty) and less common in West and Central Java. These interactions illustrate how clientelistic politics sustain oligarchic dominance: in exchange for campaign support, economic elites can rely on personalized exchanges with power holders to maintain and expand their business activities.

Risma's Struggles in Surabaya

Not every region in Indonesia is dominated by political mafias. Indeed, in some regions even the inclusionary norm of *bagi-bagi* is challenged by reformers. Political leaders sometimes emerge who seem genuinely intent on curbing collusive practices. Surabaya's mayor Tri Rismaharini is one celebrated example. Nominated for the "world mayor award" in 2012 and awarded a host of honors for promoting education, sustainability, and cleanliness, Rismaharini, or Risma, as she is often known, has been lauded as an example of how direct elections can produce new, capable leaders. She was elected in 2010 as a result of factional tensions within PDI-P. A stalemate between two relatively unpopular leaders in the city's party branch stimulated PDI-P's national leaders to support Risma's selection as the party's candidate, despite her being a relative outsider. As a career civil servant in Surabaya's municipal government, including as head of the city's Landscape and Cleanliness Department, she had no previous links to the party. But she had played a critical role in earlier procurement and bureaucratic reform in the city (Mustafa 2017, 165), and her success in both literally and figuratively cleaning up the city had made her popular. She had the support of national party leader Megawati Sukarnoputri, as well as of the minister and local newspaper magnate Dahlan Iskan. In some sense, her selection was the result of the paradoxical challenge that Indonesian political parties face in areas with a more critical media: parties need shady politicians to fund election campaigns, yet they need clean politicians to win them.

Risma sold her small rice field for 70 million rupiah ($6,200) to help fund her campaign. As this was not nearly enough, local PDI-P officials introduced her to potential donors. As *Tempo* reported, "Some wealthy parties approached her. One day there was an emissary from Jakarta who met Risma and offered Rp 60 billion in campaign funds. However, she was asked to agree to a . . . request for assistance [and] the condition was that she had to make a commitment to PDI-P." This was "an effort to bind the 'loyalty' of Risma, who was not raised in PDI-P." Feeling pressured, Risma rejected the offer (Supriyanto et al. 2014). Instead, her campaign managed to attract smaller donations from less demanding actors, and she could still rely on the PDI-P's grassroots network, which is relatively strong in Surabaya. She thus assembled a campaign organization at limited cost, which proved enough—along with the support of Dahlan Iskan's *Jawa Pos* media network—to enable her to scrape by with a narrow election win.

Risma's election victory was thus relatively unencumbered. In contrast to most candidates, she did not have to pay a political party to support her candidacy. The support of national PDI-P leaders made her relatively independent of local party bosses, and she had managed to finance her election campaign without incurring many personal debts. As she did not feel she owed her victory to party bosses or campaign donors, Risma also felt no obligation to defend their personal interests. This independence was difficult to swallow for local PDI-P leaders. As usual, they had backed her in the expectation of future deals. A clash appeared inevitable. In her first week as mayor, the Surabaya PDI-P chairperson, Wisnu Sakti Buana, met with Risma. He gave her a list of the names of eighty civil servants he wanted her to promote. They were civil servants who had supported PDI-P, and some had paid considerable sums of money to be included in the list. Risma refused to consider the promotions. She went ahead with a different selection, in the process demoting several civil servants known to be close to PDI-P (Sugiharto et al. 2014; Setyarso et al. 2014).

Relations soured further when Risma refused to support plans to build a new toll road. This road was going to be built by one of Wisnu's relatives. DPRD members, businesspeople, and even national politicians lobbied her hard to approve the plan. Yet she maintained that she did not want people to pay to travel through the city. Given the massive rents generated by such large-scale infrastructure projects, PDI-P leaders were exasperated. When a third clash ensued over Risma's plans to raise taxes on billboards, PDI-P politicians lobbied five other parties in Surabaya's city council to proceed with a no-confidence vote—just three months after she had been inaugurated as mayor (Taufiq and Abidien 2011; Sugiharto et al. 2014).

At this point, it seemed that Risma's refusal to facilitate the clientelistic deals of fellow politicians would prematurely end her political career. Yet in less than a month, the tables were turned. Local organizations staged protests in her defense, and the media excoriated the DPRD. This wave of support stimulated national PDI-P and Partai Demokrat leaders to pressure members of Surabaya's legislature to compromise. While her relationship with the municipal council remained strained, public support for Risma grew stronger in subsequent years. Her efforts to streamline local bureaucracy and to promote a "Green and Clean" Surabaya landed her both national and international acclaim. In 2015, it took months to find anyone who was even willing to stand against her, and she was eventually reelected with 86 percent of the vote.

Tri Rismaharini is not an isolated example. Over the years since the introduction of direct elections of local government heads in 2005, especially though not exclusively in urban centers in Java, a new type of politician has emerged. Alongside Risma and Jokowi, Ridwan Kamil (Bandung, West Java), Djarot Saiful Hidayat (Blitar, East Java), Bima Arya Sugiarto (Bogor, West Java), I Gede Winasa (Jembrana, Bali), and Ahok (Jakarta) are, to differing degrees, examples of leaders who entered politics after pursuing professional careers, and who relied less than their rivals on conventional clientelistic strategies. Such leaders have excited much positive attention among middle-class liberals and the media (see for example *Jakarta Globe* 2013); in office they have also, again to varying degrees, improved bureaucratic capacity by adopting measures—such as "fit and proper tests" before promoting civil servants, or making impromptu visits to government offices to check on bureaucratic performance—intended to counter bureaucratic sloth and collusion. These politicians have also been more selective in accommodating requests from business actors, with some of them resisting at various points the building of hotels, toll roads, and malls. Some of these local leaders have also appealed to voters by adopting innovative pro-poor policies in areas such as subsidized health care, social housing, and education. Collectively, they have shown that it is possible to win elections by stressing policy platforms and personal commitment to reform, rather than through the usual mix of clientelistic favors and vote buying. Their regions regularly top the various "good governance" benchmarks.[5]

Before we proceed, we should offer an important qualification: we are here discussing differences *in degree*. While the emergence of such reform-oriented leaders is an important development in local politics, we also do not want to naïvely suggest that any of the politicians with reputations as reformers we have mentioned above are paragons of progressive politics. On the contrary, several of them, including Risma, are known for their socially conservative attitudes and, on occasion, for being unsympathetic to marginalized communities (such as with Ahok's program of slum clearance in Jakarta, or Risma's moves against sex workers in Surabaya). Some of them have also made compromises with oligarchic forces: most notably, as Jokowi skyrocketed to the apex of Indonesian politics, he accepted funds from wealthy backers and rewarded oligarchic actors when it came to distributing cabinet and other posts (Fukuoka and Djani 2016; Warburton 2016a; Winters 2013, 23–25). Studies of reformist local leaders in some parts of Java reveal that these leaders often mix programmatic and clientelistic politics (Mas'udi and Kurniawan 2017; Mahsun 2017). Yet another important limitation of these politicians is that they have come to prominence largely outside the party system, relying on personal reputation and initiative to seize voters' imagination, rather than institutionalizing their plans through programmatic parties: this represents a major impediment to their capacity to fundamentally transform Indonesian politics.

Even so, despite these qualifications, the difference between a politician like Risma and one like Hambit Binti is striking, and prompts us to ask: How have such reformist politicians emerged in a political system that is as patronage-saturated as Indonesia's? Both Indonesian media and academic observers (Luebke 2009; Mietzner 2015) have answered this question largely by attributing these success stories to the agency and special character of the elected politicians concerned: their personal styles, leadership attributes, and the like. By focusing, as Luebke (2009, 207) puts it, on the "higher leadership qualities" of these individuals, such arguments pay little attention to how local conditions might facilitate or inhibit the emergence of particular types of politicians.

We argue, however, that the gulf in attitudes to governance between Hambit Binti in Gunung Mas and Risma in Surabaya is due not only to differences in character and personal skills: local context is also key. Risma's reluctance to make deals with business actors to fund her election campaign, as well as her emphasis on government procedure and meritocratic appointment, would have prevented her from being elected in much of Indonesia. Her capacity to win elections and maintain herself in power needs to be understood in light of the particular nature of Surabaya's local economy, which is much more diversified, and much less state dependent than that of Central Kalimantan. Hambit Binti's Gunung Mas district has a concentrated control economy that is centered on government budgets and extraction of natural resources by companies owned by a small elite. In Surabaya, control over economic activities is more dispersed, with the city possessing large industrial, trade, and service sectors. The livelihoods of middle-class residents, and the population as a whole, are much less dependent on government, with employment available in many sectors.

In the remainder of this chapter, we explain why such economic differences have produced politicians—Hambit Bini and Rismaharini—who operate in such contrasting manners. The local economy shapes local politics and political-business interactions. We propose three mechanisms to substantiate this connection, focusing on sources of campaign funding, civil society, and the public sphere.

Patterns of Campaign Funding

A first mechanism linking concentrated control economies to more intimate relations between politics and business concerns the nature of campaign funding. In areas where most wealth is concentrated in a narrow range of sectors and actors, political office is more likely to be captured by dominant elites. A politician like Hambit Binti can ill afford to forgo ties with either the palm oil or the mining industry, since he lacks alternative sources of funds.

In areas with a wider range of economic activity, including much that lies outside the direct control of state officials, campaign funding can originate from a wider range of donors, including those who have no interest in the crassly transactional deals practiced by natural-resource entrepreneurs in Kalimantan. Risma could afford to snub wealthy actors who approached her, because she could count on a relatively wide circle of possible donors (and, as we shall see in a moment, alternative ways to connect her to the voters). She did not need big tycoons because Surabaya also has a broad middle class with means to support a campaign. Joko Widodo showed the potential for such grassroots campaign financing when, during his campaign for Jakarta's governorship, he succeeded in raising campaign funds by selling T-shirts to supporters. Though Jokowi's campaign did receive oligarchic backing (Winters 2013, 23–25), merely raising any funds this way was an impressive feat, seeing that candidates usually hand out T-shirts for free. Likewise, during Jokowi's presidential campaign, he raised funds in small donations from ordinary citizens, rather than providing cash to voters, as is the more usual practice among politicians.

Again, we should not exaggerate this trend: as already noted, as Jokowi moved up through Indonesian politics, he also attracted oligarchic backing. Nor should we expect that politicians like Risma have remained completely free of under-the-table deals with donors. But the availability of a range of funding sources gives such politicians greater room to maneuver. Risma could reject some offers without damaging her electoral chances. Political actors like Hambit Binti do not have this luxury. As most economic activity in Gunung Mas generates little surplus, Binti depended on a limited set of local economic elites to fund his run for office.

Furthermore, in a state-dependent economy with little industry, it is difficult to find donors who do not demand personal favors. In such locations, most economic activity—from construction to plantations to restaurants to mining—is tied either to government budgets or to government approval. As a result, local entrepreneurs have strong incentives to use campaign donations to further their economic interests. Such donors have no interest in promoting the rule of law, transparent tendering procedures, or the like. They are more interested in undermining rather than strengthening government procedures.

In Surabaya's more diversified economy it is more difficult to sustain collusive coalitions such as those found in Gunung Mas, as politicians face a wider range of business actors who are likely to be disadvantaged by, and thus oppose, such coalitions. This was also the conclusion of a comparison of investment climates in Solo (Java) and Manado (North Sulawesi), the authors of which argue that the more open and rule-bound nature of local governance in Solo was due to greater dispersal of economic power there: "The multi-sectoral character of Solo's economy and the balanced influence from Chinese and Javanese firms render the emergence of narrowly defined collusive arrangements less probable. As soon as one group receives illegitimate benefits from the government, another equally influential group is likely to intervene. [This] provides the mayor with an incentive to pursue reforms that will be in the wider interests, rather than policies that benefit one group at the expense of another" (Patunru, McCulloch, and Luebke 2012, 805 and 808).

A similar observation comes from Luky Djani's study of anticorruption campaigns in four districts across Indonesia. Djani partly attributes the successful removal of the corrupt *bupati* of Garut, referred to above, to the composition of the local business community: "The important groups in society that supported the [anticorruption] cause were the business communities who suffered from extortion. Many merchants, especially from an ethnic Chinese background, felt the regular extortions as heavy burdens on their businesses. [Those who opposed] the movement [were] especially those who relied on government projects or contracts" (Djani 2013, 202). Djani relates this more critical attitude of the local business community to the fact that the region had no income from natural resources, which made the local government as well as local politicians more reliant on owners of factories and other small businesses.

Again, we need to be careful to avoid positing an absolute distinction between regions on the basis of the composition of their economies and the types of businesses that operate in those economies; these differences are matters of degree. Moreover, in a political economy founded on particularistic deal making, it can be tempting even for businesses in sectors like finance or retail that are not personally dependent on politicians to take advantage of such personal connections by opportunistically diversifying into a sector where government protection counts. This certainly happens at the local level, where it sometimes seems it is the dream of every small-time chicken wholesaler or cloth merchant to become a construction contractor, if only a friend or relative manages to get into the local parliament. Even so, it is reasonable to conclude that, overall, a more diversified economy makes a less clientelistic form of campaign financing possible. In such a context, political actors can diversify their funding sources and find more donors who are less interested in exchanging their donations for government contracts or permits.

Civil Society against Oligarchy

A second mechanism linking a concentrated control economy to oligarchic politics concerns the capacity of local civil societies to support non-oligarchic candidates or mobilize against clientelistic rulers. Tri Rismaharini's record in Surabaya was partly due to the support she received from a coalition of civil society organizations. Three months after she was first elected, PDI-P politicians would have succeeded in removing her from power were it not for the capacity and willingness of local organizations to rally the media and bring people into the streets to defend her. Moreover, Risma's emergence to prominence came in a city that already had a strong history of civil society mobilization, including street protest against a corrupt mayor about a decade earlier, leading to an earlier round of reforms that had largely broken the back of the "project mafia" in the city (Mustafa 2017).

Risma's experience in Surabaya suggests that alliances between non-clientelistic politicians and civil society organizations can sometimes curtail oligarchic dominance. Surabaya is not the only example. Tans (2012, 15), observing politics in North Sumatra, termed such alliances "mobilizing coalitions" and noted one that had considerable buy-in from local NGOs. He argued that such coalitions can curtail clientelistic politics: "Instead of distributing favors on a personal basis, mobilizing coalitions promise policies that more broadly benefit groups of supporters, such as ethnic or occupational groups." Other observers have also noted the growing willingness of labor unions in industrial areas, mainly in Java, to experiment with electoral politics by supporting candidates who promise to raise the minimum wage or tackle labor outsourcing (Caraway, Ford, and Nugroho 2015; Savirani 2016). Other reform-oriented politicians, such as Jokowi, have been able to mobilize networks of volunteers (*relawan*) to support their election campaigns, partly by drawing on preexisting activist networks, NGOs, and middle-class professionals. Similar in form to the *tim sukses*, such volunteers often campaign without the fees and expectations of personal rewards that typify success teams, even if they carry out many of the same activities—putting up posters and banners, handing out leaflets, designing social media campaigns, and the like (Suaedy 2014).

The importance of such alliances lies, first, in their capacity to reduce election costs and thus financial dependence on donors and, second, as Risma's experience illustrates, in their ability to help politicians deal with the pushback they experience when seeking to curtail informal privileges. Reform-oriented politicians benefit when allies in civil society counter such pressure. A commonality in the experience of Ahok in Jakarta, Rismaharini in Surabaya, and, to a certain extent, Joko Widodo in Solo and Jakarta is that they have used support of civil society groups and the media to counter resistance to their political agendas by civil servants, DPRD members, and politically connected business actors.

A third reason why strong civil society organizations are important is that they can generate demand for more programmatic politics. Organizations like labor unions can engage in interest aggregation (Piattoni 2001), identifying and formulating a set of interests that a particular set of voters—like factory workers—have in common. By doing so, such organizations can stimulate both citizens and politicians to move toward exchanging votes for policy instead of particularistic benefits.

This importance of civil society actors provides another argument against attributing the emergence of non-oligarchic politicians like Rismaharini to individual agency alone. Local economies shape civil society and its mobilizational capacity and hence a society's capacity to support particular politicians. Interest organizations—as opposed to groups whose primary function is to seek patronage—are more likely to thrive when economic activities generate shared experiences that give rise to common concerns among group members. The presence of industrial activity and the role of labor unions are obvious examples of this link: shared concern for improving wages and working conditions stimulates workers to form unions, while regular interaction on the factory floor or in workers' residential areas facilitates organizing. Such tasks are harder for peasants working in rural areas where distances are greater and experiences of shared interests less pronounced.

Furthermore, a concentrated control economy generates dependencies that ruling elites can exploit to weaken civil society and cultivate a command vote at election times. When a wide range of economic activity depends on having good relations with elected politicians, these elites can exploit such ties to sustain their popularity and prevent criticism. For example, during his reelection campaign in Gunung Mas, Hambit Binti relied heavily on the managers of oil palm plantations. As these managers need the district head to obtain permits and solve bureaucratic problems, they are easily persuaded to instruct workers on their plantations to vote for the incumbent. The workers themselves can ill afford to ignore such instructions. Most of them are migrants from Java whose livelihoods are precarious, as they can easily be sent home. Informants commented with some amazement on the speed with which local governments hand out local identity cards to these migrant workers. Formal recognition of residency allows these workers to vote in local elections. Getting these cards can be time-consuming in urban parts of Kalimantan, where migrants arrive under their own steam, compete with others in the labor market, and are often deliberately excluded from local benefits. In areas like Gunung Mas, district heads can develop a secure vote base by relying on plantation companies to mobilize their workers.

In a similar vein, contractors who benefit from government contracts often mobilize all their laborers and dependents during an election campaign. And, as we mentioned in chapter 8, when employment opportunities are scarce and large families depend on a few members holding civil service jobs, such families are readily motivated to campaign for whoever guarantees such employment (or has the power to exile the wage earner to a remote and inaccessible location). More generally, in a place like Gunung Mas, where state expenditure is important to the local economy, many ordinary voters are reliant on the favors they receive from civil servants and officials, who are more able to mobilize a command vote. In all these examples, economic dependencies facilitate political authority.

Such economic dependencies also deter opposition. Being openly critical of power holders is risky in a concentrated control economy. In an area like Gunung Mas, dissent can close the door to jobs and economic opportunities apart from farming. Even if a local dissident finds the courage to risk forgoing a government contract or job, she might well have relatives in government who would feel that a family connection with a critic might threaten their own career. Political opposition in a city like Surabaya is not nearly as risky, because local dissenters can find alternative sources of income outside government employment and networks.

It is also easier for civil society organizations to find independent sources of funding in more diversified economies. In a place like Gunung Mas, local NGOs are regularly mocked with terms like *lembaga suka minta* ("institutes that often beg," or LSM, a play on the Indonesian abbreviation for NGO), or *organisasi plat merah* ("red-plate organizations," a term referring to the red license plates on government cars). Such mockery is not entirely undeserved, as many local organizations serve as vehicles for capturing government projects, not infrequently in return for electoral support. Yet even genuinely committed activists find it difficult to keep aloof from government circles, which are the main local source of funding. Thus, one small local NGO encountered in Gunung Mas was involved in documenting and criticizing the destruction and pollution caused by the BMB plantation set up by Cornelis Nalau. It soon emerged, however, that the NGO's members had decided to join the *tim sukses* of Hambit Binti, Nalau's backer and the very person responsible for the pollution they were campaigning against. Their reasoning was pragmatic: "People have no choice. We need to support someone who will win the elections. We weigh up who can win, and we support that person. In this way we can enter [the circle of the district head] and begin a process of policy making, and making things better." In state-dependent economies, the local state absorbs virtually all social and political networking into itself.

The importance of non-state sources of funding for NGOs is tellingly illustrated in Luky Djani's comparative study of local anticorruption movements (Djani 2013). Alongside the successful anticorruption movement in Garut, mentioned above, Djani also discusses three failed mobilizations in West Sumatra, Central Sulawesi, and East Kalimantan. He attributes these failures largely to the dependence of local civil society on government funding: "As their businesses' and organizations' survival is reliant on government projects or budgets, they could not publicly voice their concerns about the local government's policies. . . . These mayors skillfully distributed government projects and concessions and by doing so were able to maintain the loyalty of their followers and disarm opposition groups" (Djani 2013, 314). In Garut, in contrast, a vibrant civil-society coalition received funding from local businesses wanting to curtail extortion. This coalition succeeded in getting the district head removed from office, and he was convicted on corruption charges.

In sum, a concentrated control economy fosters dependencies that ruling politicians can exploit to stifle opposition. When many livelihoods are dependent on resources and cooperation from the local government, ruling elites can convey a credible threat that opposition and public criticism can lead to dire consequences.

An Open Public Sphere

A third mechanism is found in the public sphere. Particularistic collusion between politicians and businesses thrives on secrecy. Politicians have few incentives to avoid private deals with business backers—as Risma did in Surabaya—when they face little risk of exposure and electoral damage. Without an open public sphere, maintained by an independent media and a critical civil society, politicians have few reasons to keep business actors at arm's length.

A public sphere is largely absent in Central Kalimantan, and this is again largely due to the nature of its economy. The adverse effects of deals made between local politicians and palm oil and mining companies are severe. The forest fires and the resulting haze that afflict Central Kalimantan every year make headlines in international newspapers. Less visible are the numerous land conflicts between local communities and such companies. Friends of the Earth Kalimantan has counted 252 such conflicts in the 2003–2014 period, most of which occur as a result of governments handing out concessions to land that local communities depend on for their livelihoods. Companies with strong contacts among politicians and bureaucrats face little pressure to provide adequate compensation to communities affected by their operations. Protests are regularly quelled by local authorities.

Yet one is hard-pressed to find critical articles in local newspapers about how local politicians contribute to these problems. While newspapers might report on, say, a demonstration against a palm oil company and the changed lifestyles of Dayak communities who have lost their land, local journalists rarely write critical pieces about the support politicians provide to companies involved in these conflicts. This is only partly due to lack of information. Police or local thugs regularly intimidate and harass activists who try to report on the practices of palm oil companies and the land disputes they trigger. The illicit deals that tie companies to politicians are often common knowledge among journalists and other middle-class actors in rural districts like Gunung Mas. Central Kalimantan simply lacks a safe forum where criticism of local governments can be voiced and debated.

This absence of critical reporting is partly due to the ownership and revenues of local newspapers. Three major newspapers in Central Kalimantan—*Palangka Pos*, *Tribun Kalteng*, and *Palangka Express*—are owned by Abdul Rasyid, a notorious and highly successful palm oil entrepreneur and uncle of the man elected governor of Central Kalimantan in 2015, Sugianto Sabran. A fourth paper, *Tabengan*, is owned by the PDI-P. The advertisements in these newspapers illustrate the state dependency of the local economy. In a system known as *kontrak halaman*, or "page contracts," district governments and even local parliaments buy regular half- or full-page spots in these newspapers, expending up to 500 million rupiah (about $44,000) for an annual order. These can add up to about four pages per issue: pages solely reserved for positive reporting on the achievements of local governments and parliaments. The remaining pages are usually no less laudatory: individual politicians not only place advertisements in these newspapers; they also pay journalists to provide favorable reporting. If the journalist is scrupulous, such an article will end with the abbreviation "adv." (for advertorial) in small print. Yet this is often omitted—one journalist said he usually leaves it out because "the politicians do not like it" (interview, May 1, 2013). Another journalist, in the neighboring district of Pulang Pisau, explained that his newspaper did not even pay a salary; he made all his income from selling page contracts and writing puff pieces about politicians, at a price of 35,000 rupiah (about three dollars) per article (interview, April 15, 2013). In the same district, about half of the three hundred daily sales of the province's major newspaper, *Kalteng Pos*, were regular orders in government offices.

With the income of local newspapers heavily dependent on local governments and politicians, editors and journalists exercise self-censorship. Journalist informants regularly commented on how a critical piece had led to an *intervensi*: after a phone call from a politician or a bureaucrat, an editor would instruct the journalist to drop the issue. In at least one instance, Hambit Binti managed to get a journalist fired for writing critical pieces. Not that journalists are necessarily intent on exposing politicians: the payments they receive from politicians and local governments are often enough to discourage efforts in that direction. For the more entrepreneurial journalists, however, it is possible to earn even more by extorting money from a politician in exchange for withholding a critical piece.

Journalists in Surabaya are not necessarily above such practices, and the ownership of newspapers and other media in Java rests, as it does in Central Kalimantan, in the hands of business tycoons, many of whom have their own political connections and ambitions (Tapsell 2015). Even reporters for a renowned national newspaper like *Kompas* can be reluctant to criticize power holders (Wijayanto 2018). But a regional newspaper like *Jawa Pos* does not regularly include pages of government advertisements; instead it carries advertisements for cars, department stores, real estate, and the like. Diversified revenue sources facilitate journalistic independence, as editors do not need to risk financial collapse if they criticize the local government. At the same time, there is also a much larger media-reading public, with strong competition among newspaper and online news sites to increase their readership by reporting on political scandals and covering the doings of popular politicians like Risma.

Reforming politicians like Risma or Jokowi have one weapon at their disposal that their equivalents in Central Kalimantan lack: television. Cities like Jakarta, Surabaya, and Bandung are big enough to sustain their own television markets or at least to contribute stories to national programs. Jokowi most famously, and also politicians like Risma in Surabaya and Ridwan Kamil in Bandung, have been able to use television coverage to promote images of themselves as being uniquely close to ordinary people—inviting television reporters to follow them as they mix with *kampung* dwellers, drop in on traditional markets, pick rubbish off city streets, or berate lazy bureaucrats. As with coverage of populist politicians elsewhere, television exposure has been critical to the success of this new breed of politicians who, lacking control of political parties or other political networks, can use television to appeal to voters directly, over the heads of established clientelistic networks, cutting out the brokers who are so essential to organizing political life in most parts of Indonesia.

Similar comparisons could be made about other constituent elements of a healthy public sphere. For example, Surabaya is home to dozens of universities and other institutions of higher education, and has a relatively lively and critical intellectual culture, in which prominent academics are frequently sought by media outlets for commentary on controversial topics. Campuses host numerous student discussion forums and activist groups. By contrast, in remote and rural districts there are often few or no institutions of higher learning. Even in provincial capitals in Kalimantan and eastern Indonesia, the university sector is generally far weaker than in Java. Many students see education as, above all, a means to get a coveted civil service job, while academics depend on projects and consultancies with local governments to supplement their meager official incomes.

All in all, a city like Surabaya has a much more vibrant and effective public sphere than a place like Central Kalimantan. Unlike in Surabaya, in Central Kalimantan electronic media play little role in linking citizens to their politicians, who must instead rely on clientelistic networks for electoral mobilization. Equally importantly, Central Kalimantan lacks a forum for frank debate about issues of public concern like land conflicts or corruption. Nor do local media play a watchdog role, as their financial circumstances constrain their ability to report critically about local government. A media-facilitated public outcry of the sort that protected Risma against entrenched political elites is hard to imagine in Central Kalimantan, whose rulers can shape media coverage to serve their interests.

This chapter has discussed examples of collusive interactions between the worlds of business and politics. We related the oligarchic character of Indonesian politics to the clientelistic nature of election campaigns. The astronomical cost of campaigns helps explain the failure of Indonesia's democratization to curtail the political dominance of economic elites and to break the personalistic bonds between the worlds of politics and business that were forged during the New Order years. The scramble for campaign funding enables economic elites to dominate politics, either by using their financial clout to enter the political arena themselves, or by backing compliant candidates. As politicians repay their campaign donors with privileges, they ensure that implementation of state policies remains not only informal and personalized, but also skewed in favor of elites.

But this embrace between business and politics is not equally tight throughout the archipelago. Observing that the current debate on oligarchy in Indonesia is often waged in overly general terms, we have discussed in this chapter whether and why the oligarchic character of politics might vary between regions. We proposed that oligarchic dominance will be more intense in areas with concentrated control economies. Reforming politicians who are willing to break with established clientelistic patterns are more likely to emerge in areas with less economic concentration. The comparison of Central Kalimantan and Surabaya yielded explanations for this difference related to the availability of campaign funding, the strength of civil society, and the degree of openness of the public sphere. Such arguments need to be tested. To what extent does the intensity of clientelistic politics indeed vary across Indonesia? And to what extent do the variations correspond to differences in the concentration of control over economic activities? In the next chapter we address these questions.

10

EXPLAINING VARIATION IN INDONESIA'S PATRONAGE DEMOCRACY

As we noted at the start of this book, political scientists know relatively little about conditions that favor or curtail clientelistic politics (Keefer and Khemani 2005, 23; Roniger 2004, 369). In large part, this gap in our knowledge reflects our struggle to identify the extent to which clientelistic practices vary between countries and regions. This lack of knowledge is partly due to methodological challenges. The secretive nature of clientelistic exchanges makes it difficult to gauge and compare the degree to which political systems are clientelistic. Most studies on political clientelism are qualitative and ethnographic in nature. Relying on close-up, detailed observations, they help us to understand the inner logic of clientelism and to identify distinctive forms and local adaptations. We have relied on our own fieldwork to provide such a detailed account of Indonesian-style clientelism through this book. Yet ethnography does not help much when it comes to comparing the *intensity* of clientelistic practices across a large number of locations, a step that is critical if we want to identify what factors might encourage and shape those practices. In order to compare the intensity of clientelism, we need systematic and comparable measures of the phenomenon, something that face-to-face ethnographic research cannot provide.

To overcome this challenge, in this chapter we turn to the expert survey that we introduced at the beginning of the book, and which is detailed in the appendixes. We have already drawn on findings from this expert survey in earlier chapters when explaining how particular aspects of clientelism vary across Indonesia. In this chapter, we bring together the respondents' views on several dimensions of clientelism in order to develop a "Clientelism Perception Index" that measures the extent to which the distribution of different kinds of state resources is perceived to be contingent on electoral support. This measure provides us with an indication of how common clientelistic practices are in different parts of Indonesia. By then comparing this variation with the distribution across Indonesia of underlying conditions that might foster clientelistic practices, we test different explanations for the pervasiveness or absence of clientelistic exchanges.

To summarize our findings in brief: First, as expected, we find that there is indeed considerable variation in the intensity of clientelistic practices, with much lower reported rates in Java and much higher rates in eastern Indonesia and Kalimantan, with Sumatra generally falling in between. Second, in explaining this variation, our findings support the theory we proposed in the preceding chapter: clientelism flourishes best in areas where control over economic activity is highly concentrated. In fact, this explanation matches our data much better than an alternative approach that is much more influential in the comparative literature on the topic, which links clientelism directly to poverty and economic underdevelopment.

What Drives Clientelistic Politics?

Despite the relative paucity of analysis of conditions favoring political clientelism, the literature on the topic contains a rich set of explanations for the pervasiveness of clientelistic electoral strategies. Some of these explanations—such as those focusing on the character of electoral institutions or the relative youthfulness of a democracy (Keefer 2007)—are useful for explaining differences between countries but cannot offer leverage when accounting for subnational variation. Explanations that foreground economic and social factors, however, might do so. Arguably, the most widely shared conclusion in the large and expanding literature on political clientelism is that economic development—defined mostly as growth of per capita income—undermines and curtails clientelistic politics. This proposition is supported by a considerable body of survey-based research that shows that poor countries are more likely to be clientelistic (Bustikova and Corduneanu-Huci 2011; Keefer 2007; Kitschelt and Wilkinson 2007), that poor voters are more likely to receive and respond to money or other clientelistic incentives (Brusco, Nazareno, and Stokes 2004; Stokes 2005; Stokes et al. 2013, 152–171), and that politics in poor regions within one country are more likely to take clientelistic form (Remmer 2007; Wantchekon 2003). Some scholars argue that the relationship is curvilinear, with clientelistic politics first intensifying at low levels of development (Kitschelt and Kselman 2013). What is much less well established, however, is why and how economic development curtails clientelistic practices. As one important review of the literature observed, while "the affinity between poverty (inequality) and clientelism is a settled fact . . . the mechanisms linking the two, and the direction of causality, are not" (Stokes 2007, 623; see also Hicken 2011).

The literature generally analyzes this link between economic development and clientelism by assuming that rising incomes and attendant growth of the middle class reduce the yields and increase the costs of clientelistic strategies. In the words of Magaloni, Diaz-Cayeros, and Estévez (2007, 203): "As a country develops and the pivotal voter becomes wealthier, clientelism should erode as a dominant form of political exchange simply because it becomes too costly." We dub this approach (in shorthand) the *cost perspective*. Starting from marketist assumptions, and conceiving of clientelistic exchanges as being driven by rational calculation and cost-benefit analysis, studies adopting this cost perspective point out, for example, that the marginal utility of material incentives is higher for poor voters than for wealthier voters, and that poor voters are therefore more likely to be won over by clientelistic distribution. Along these lines, one set of scholars has argued that declining poverty rates reduce clientelism because higher incomes lead to higher prices per vote (Calvo and Murillo 2004; Dixit and Londregan 1996). A second group has argued that poor voters are more risk-averse and therefore prefer immediate, concrete benefits over the uncertain benefits held out by politicians who offer only speeches and policies (Keefer 2007; Keefer and Vlaicu 2008). Kitschelt argued, for example, that "poor and uneducated citizens discount the future, rely on short causal chains, and prize instant advantages such that the appeal of direct, clientelist exchanges always trumps that of indirect, programmatic linkages promising uncertain and distant rewards to voters" (Kitschelt 2000, 857).

A third set of arguments has focused on how economic development generates a larger middle class that might dislike clientelistic practices and prefer a strong rule of law. As a result, clientelistic electoral strategies cost votes in middle-class constituencies. As Weitz-Shapiro (2012, 568) put it, "although clientelism is a vote-getting tactic aimed at the poor, non-poor voters are likely to punish politicians who engage in it. The salience of these costs should vary with the share of the population that is non-poor." In a fourth, and slightly different vein, Stokes and her coauthors have argued that when economic development leads to urbanization, it undermines clientelistic practices because densely populated areas complicate the effective monitoring of votes (Stokes et al. 2013, 187).

These arguments have in common a focus on how economic development affects the costs and yields of clientelistic strategies. The cost perspective predicts that clientelistic practices therefore become less effective when incomes rise, the middle class grows, and populations urbanize. A weakness of this literature is that it largely focuses on vote buying, while paying relatively little attention to clientelistic practices that involve provision of other types of resources—public services, welfare benefits, or business opportunities—in exchange for electoral support. Some of these resources may be highly valued by middle-class voters or by wealthy and powerful actors who would thus have interests in continuing clientelistic practices even as incomes rise and populations urbanize.

An alternative explanation for varying levels of clientelism across regions with different economic structures is what we label the *constraint perspective*. We develop this perspective out of the analysis of the relationship between economic development and clientelism we presented in the last chapter. Deriving inspiration from the emerging literature on subnational democracy, we proposed that clientelistic politics are particularly pervasive in regions where control over economic activities is concentrated in the hands of a relatively small elite. We interpreted concentrated control both in terms of the state dependency of the local economy (the degree to which income-generating activities are dependent on state resources) and in terms of its diversification (the relative size of the more advanced sectors of the economy such as industry, trade, and finance). We proposed a number of mechanisms linking concentrated control economies to clientelistic politics: such economies draw politicians and business actors into a collusive embrace, weaken opposition, stifle the public sphere, and inhibit effective scrutiny of politico-business elites. This approach to the relationship between economic development and clientelism can be dubbed the "constraint perspective" because it focuses on the conditions underlying the emergence of a civil society capable of exposing and criticizing clientelistic practices. When economic diversification boosts the independence of citizens from ruling elites, social forces capable of constraining clientelistic practices can emerge.

These cost and constraint perspectives differ not only in terms of the interpretations they offer of the conditions favoring clientelistic politics. Underlying these perspectives are different ideas about what kinds of mechanisms curtail clientelistic practices. Those emphasizing economic costs largely adopt a rational-choice and individualist perspective, focusing on factors that affect how voters and politicians calculate the costs and benefits of clientelistic exchange. In this view, economic growth reduces clientelistic practices because it makes vote buying more expensive while reducing the likelihood that voters will repay patronage with votes. In contrast, the constraint perspective argues that it is not economic growth per se, but rather wider distribution of power and control over economic activities that curtails clientelistic activities. In this view, politicians do not shift away from clientelism because their yields decline, but because political opponents and civil society groups are better able to oppose, expose, and resist such practices.

A similar contrast involves the role of the middle class and industrialization. The cost perspective sees the growth of the middle class as conducive to more programmatic politics, based on the assumption that middle-class voters are more likely to despise clientelistic practices and value the rule of law. The growth of the middle class will thus increase the cost (in terms of lost votes) of clientelism (Weitz-Shapiro 2014) and generate a "constituency for universalism" (Shefter 1994, 28). In contrast, the constraint perspective suggests that it is not the size of the middle class that counts, but rather the extent of its dependence on privileged access to the state for its livelihood. Similarly, in contrast to the cost perspective, industrialization might curtail clientelistic practices not because it generates higher incomes, but rather because it fosters more even distribution of power. As control over sources of livelihoods spreads beyond a narrow oligarchic elite that controls the state, civil society becomes better able (as do rival oligarchs) to criticize clientelistic practices and discipline power holders.

We found evidence to support both sets of arguments during our field research. In chapter 9, we showed how concentrated economic control nurtured clientelistic politics in the district of Gunung Mas, while the more diverse economy of Surabaya created conditions for the rise of a programmatically oriented politician. However, we also encountered many politicians, brokers, and voters who spoke in terms that resonated with the cost perspective. For example, political candidates who practiced vote buying frequently articulated a version of the marginal utility argument, stressing how a payment of 20,000 or 50,000 rupiah would mean little to a middle-class voter, but could make a great difference to a poor voter. Many politicians and brokers explained that they targeted poorer citizens with cash gifts, but to reach more well-to-do voters they used alternative strategies, for example media advertisements, social media campaigns, or publicity campaigns in middle-class neighborhoods. Some candidates, too, complained that it was difficult to reach middle-class voters by way of community-level vote brokers, because such voters often lived in gated communities, apartment buildings, or other types of dwellings that were difficult to access, and interacted little with their neighbors.

An assessment of the validity of these different perspectives is thus needed, not only to identify the conditions fostering clientelism, but also to understand the mechanisms that might promote change: How do socioeconomic changes actually curtail clientelistic practices? These two different perspectives produce different predictions. The cost perspective predicts that clientelistic politics will be more pervasive in regions with higher poverty rates, a more rural population, and a smaller middle class. The constraint perspective, in contrast, predicts that clientelistic politics will be more pervasive in regions with limited economic diversification and greater dependence on state budgets. We use the results of the expert survey to assess the extent to which local politics in Indonesia corresponds to these predictions.

The Clientelism Perception Index

As we explained in chapter 1, given the limitations of measuring clientelism through general surveys and statistical proxies, in this study we used the expert survey conducted by Berenschot in 2014 to develop a picture of how clientelistic practices vary across Indonesia. This expert survey draws inspiration from a similar exercise run by Herbert Kitschelt in 2008 that was designed to measure clientelistic practices across eighty-one countries (Kitschelt et al. 2009). A team interviewed 509 local experts—journalists, academics, NGO activists, and election campaign organizers—in thirty-eight districts in sixteen provinces across Indonesia, with locations chosen to represent a range of socioeconomic and political settings (see appendix A). In recorded interviews the researchers asked these experts about a range of clientelistic practices in their locales, asking them to score how common it was for a range of goods—from government jobs and contracts to public services, welfare support, and cash payments at election time—to be distributed clientelistically (see table 10.1). Taken together, the responses paint a rich picture of variation in perceptions of clientelism across Indonesia.

The expert survey is useful because it helps us to address an important conceptual and methodological challenge: What does "more clientelistic" actually mean? How do we define degrees of clientelism? The literature is remarkably silent about this challenge, with most interpretations remaining implicit. In a recent discussion of "post-clientelist initiatives," for example, Manor (2013) implies that the adoption of government programs that aim to provide impersonal access to welfare support is an indication of a polity becoming "less clientelistic" (see also Nichter 2014). When researchers explicitly define degrees of clientelism, their definitions are often highly pragmatic and attuned to the particular proxy for which statistical material is available, such as a high ratio of civil servants to the general population (Keefer 2007) or greater mayoral intervention in the selection of welfare recipients (Weitz-Shapiro 2014). Herbert Kitschelt's expert survey offers a more comprehensive and explicit conceptualization, defining intensity of clientelistic efforts in terms of how much effort candidates expend on providing preferential access to a range of benefits. Even so, this conceptualization has drawbacks, since it provides no yardstick for interpreting what might constitute a small or large effort. This gap creates an "anchorage problem": respondents might have different interpretations of what a big effort might look like.

To overcome these issues, we have adopted a slightly different conceptualization and define degrees of clientelism in terms of *the share of state benefits and campaign funds that are distributed in a manner perceived to be contingent on electoral support*. A low degree of clientelism thus implies that hardly any state benefits are perceived to be provided as rewards for electoral support, and few voters receive monetary or other material incentives, while a higher degree of clientelism signifies that virtually all state benefits are perceived to be provided in exchange for electoral support.

We avoid the anchorage problem mentioned above because the survey asked respondents to explicitly assess the *proportion* of particular state benefits that are provided as a reward for electoral support. For example, the survey asked, "In your estimation, of all the major contracts that the district government awards, what percentage goes to companies or businesspeople who have supported election campaigns of ruling politicians (district head, governor, DPRD members) during elections?" Similarly, the survey asked, "What percentage of the [higher level] civil servants in the district government (e.g., bureau chiefs, subdistrict heads, regional secretary, etc.) received their current post as a reward for supporting—openly or secretly—a candidate during elections?" To assess vote buying, a slightly different yardstick was used: "What percentage of voters are given money or consumer goods during elections for district head [and governor, DPRD members, and president]?" When such questions were not feasible, the questions were phrased in terms of the *likelihood* of clientelistic distribution: "When implementing welfare programs . . . how likely is it that local government representatives such as village heads and RT/RW heads prioritize people who voted for their preferred candidate?" with respondents then allowed to choose between a range of responses varying from "highly unlikely" to "very likely." Overall, by asking the experts what percentage of particular resources were distributed in a clientelistic manner, or by asking them to estimate the likelihood of clientelistic distribution, we reduced the multi-interpretability of answer categories and are able to develop a comprehensive picture of how the intensity of clientelistic exchanges varies across Indonesia. See appendix B for a brief overview of the survey instrument.

To develop the Clientelism Perception Index (CPI) we combined measures on seven types of personal benefits (see table 10.1) that feature prominently in clientelistic electoral strategies in Indonesia. We selected these seven types on the basis of fieldwork findings and by drawing on Kitschelt's survey tool, as well as on broader comparative literature on clientelism. The survey asked questions

TABLE 10.1   The Clientelism Perception Index

Combines assessments about the degree to which the following resources are distributed in a clientelistic manner:

1. Government contracts (to build a road, supply goods, etc.)
2. Government jobs
3. Public services (preferential access to water, education, sanitation, electricity, etc.)
4. Access to social welfare programs
5. Use of social assistance funds (*hibah/bansos*)
6. Paperwork (licenses, permits, etc.)
7. Money (i.e., vote buying)

---

about the distribution of each of these benefits, with regard to both district and provincial government levels and elections.

Appendix C provides an overview of component scores, as well as an assessment of inter-coder agreement—that is, the degree to which surveyed experts of the same district agreed in their assessments. In general the inter-coder agreement is relatively high in high-scoring regions, while for low-scoring regions, such as Jakarta or Surabaya, disagreement among experts is more common. This might be due to two factors. First, recent reform measures in places like Jakarta and Surabaya might have led to changes in practice. Experts may differ on the extent and rapidity of change, in contrast to regions where political and bureaucratic practices have changed little, where it might be expected that evaluations would be more uniform. A second reason might be that in regions where clientelism is neither absent nor all-pervasive, it is inherently more difficult to assess where exactly the intermediate level lies. Compared to regions where clientelistic practices are all-pervasive or completely absent, it might simply be more difficult to agree in mid-scoring regions on, for example, the proportion of jobs or contracts that are awarded to campaign supporters. In any case, an implication of this varying level of agreement is that the CPI of high-scoring regions like Kupang and Gunung Mas is more reliable, while it is less so in the lower-scoring regions. This poses a challenge for the regression analysis of these results, a point to which we return below.

Table 10.2 illustrates that, in general, scores on different forms of clientelistic exchange are highly intercorrelated. For example, in areas where government contracts are perceived as highly likely to be distributed as rewards to supporters of a successful district-head candidate, government jobs are also likely to be distributed in exchange for electoral support. The exception is vote buying during legislative assembly elections (7b). This exception is an interesting finding, and we return to it below. Because of its lack of correlation with other variables, we excluded vote buying during legislative assembly elections from the Clientelism

TABLE 10.2   Clientelism Perception Index: Correlations

	1	2	3	4	5	6	7A	7B
1. Public services	—							
2. Access to welfare	−.214	—						
3. Social assistance	−.328*	.466**	—					
4. Govt. jobs	−.287	.567**	.811**	—				
5. Govt. contracts	−.361*	.601**	.684**	.710**	—			
6. Business licenses	−.479**	.411*	.693**	.687**	.703**	—		
7a. Vote buying—district-head elections	−.275	.503**	.451**	.416**	.608**	.415**	—	
7b. Vote buying—legislative elections	−.289	.14	.182	.156	.410*	.277	.652**	—

* = p < .05
** = p < .01 (two-tailed)
Note: The question regarding public services (1) was inversely formulated, hence the negative correlations.

Perception Index. The remaining variables allowed for the construction of a relatively strong index variable.[1] To construct this index, we added these scores together to create district-level and provincial-level measures of the extent to which the distribution of state resources is perceived as being contingent on political support in the region concerned. This Clientelism Perception Index was recalculated into a scale from zero to ten. A zero score implies that no state resources are perceived to be distributed in a manner contingent on electoral support. A score of 10 signifies that all state benefits are seen as being distributed clientelistically.

Clientelistic Practices across Indonesia

The expert assessments and the Clientelism Perception Index that was generated from them yield two general conclusions about the nature of clientelistic politics in Indonesia. A first conclusion is that clientelistic practices are perceived to be pervasive—but not all-pervasive. Over 70 percent of all observers, for example, estimated that more than 40 percent of the large contracts that district governments award are given in exchange for electoral support (69 percent thought so about provincial contracts; see chapter 7). Most observers (56 percent) estimated that over 60 percent of higher-level civil servants received their positions as a reward for campaign support (see chapter 8). Asked about the use of social assistance budgets, 66 percent of experts estimated that over 60 percent of these budgets are used to reward campaign supporters.

Yet not all types of clientelistic exchange are perceived to be equally common. Generally speaking, local observers consider exchanges between politicians and their campaign supporters to be more pervasive than exchanges between politicians and voters. When asked about the provision of state resources, such as welfare programs and budgets for village-level infrastructure, directly to voters, significant proportions of our experts (44 and 47 percent, respectively) felt that the provision of these resources is not at all, or is only rarely, contingent on voting behavior. In other words, the general pattern is that elected politicians are seen as being diligent about using state resources to reward their core campaign supporters and donors, but much less successful or willing to use state budgets to reward voters—a pattern that presumably reflects the relatively high level of control still exercised by nonelected bureaucrats (chapter 7). Voters are, it seems, much more likely to be lured through vote buying than through clientelistic distribution of state programs and budgets. Vote buying was considered to be rampant: a large majority of experts (71 percent) estimated that over 60 percent of voters received monetary incentives during parliamentary elections (note, however, that this figure is much higher than figures derived from direct survey questions of voters, and from survey experiments, which point to about 25–33 percent of Indonesian voters receiving payments at election times [Muhtadi 2018]). Vote buying was considered slightly less common in district-head (49 percent), gubernatorial (33 percent), and, particularly, presidential elections (13 percent). In other words, the lower the district magnitude of the electoral contest, the more pervasive the practice of vote buying is perceived to be, a result that is consistent with comparative literature and other fieldwork-based findings from Indonesia (Aspinall et al. 2017).

A second general observation is that the perceived intensity of clientelistic practices varies considerably across Indonesia. With scores on the Clientelism Perception Index ranging from 4.0 (Surabaya) to 8.0 (Kupang) on a scale from 0 to 10, the results suggest that there is considerable variation in the character of local politics. Figure 10.1 provides an overview of the average scores of districts, while figure 10.2 shows how the sixteen provinces scored (appendix D lists the scores for each). These CPI scores reveal a relatively clear pattern, while also throwing up a number of puzzles. The lowest district-level scores are persistently found in Java, particularly its cities like Surabaya (4.0), Jakarta (4.2), and Bandung and Tangerang (both 5.0). The Javanese provinces, excepting Banten, also score lower than other provinces, with the lowest score for Central Java (4.0). The highest CPI scores are in districts in Kalimantan and eastern Indonesia, with particularly high scores for district capitals like Kupang (8.0), Makassar and Palangka Raya (both 7.4), as well as rural areas in Flores (West Manggarai, 7.5), Papua (Jayawijaya, 7.4), and Kalimantan (e.g., Gunung Mas, 7.9, and Kutai Kertanegara, 7.1). On the whole, districts and provinces in Sumatra score between these extremes, with relatively low scores for districts in Aceh and West Sumatra

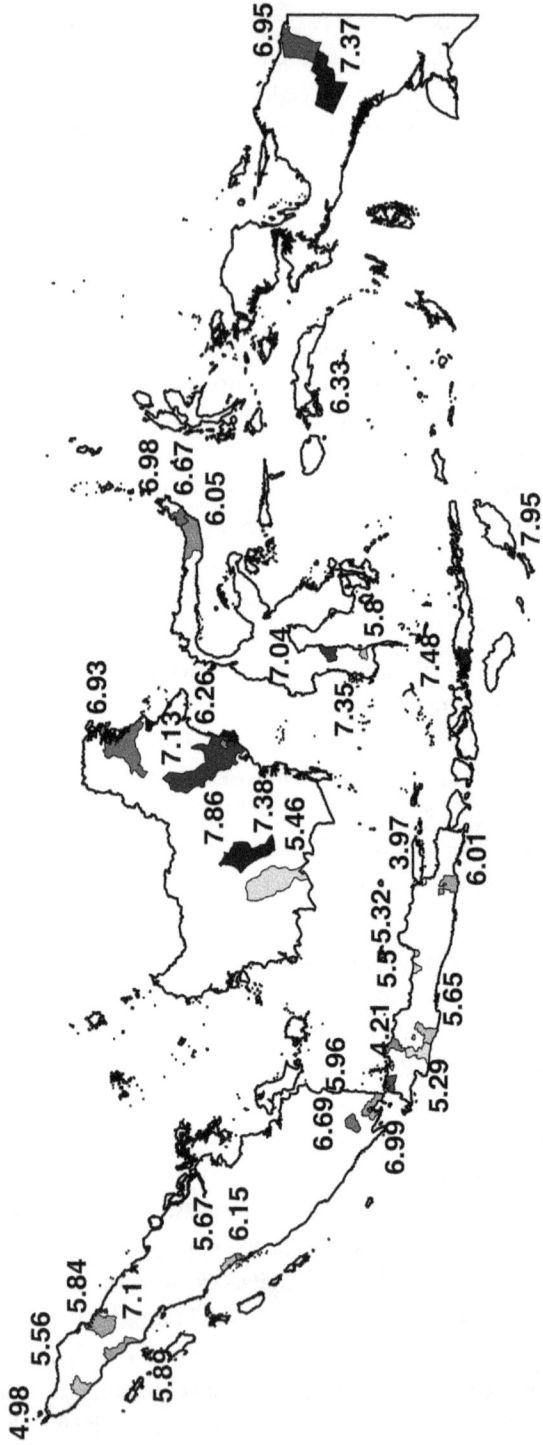

FIGURE 10.1 District CPI scores

FIGURE 10.2 Provincial CPI scores

(e.g., Banda Aceh, 5.0; West Aceh, 5.6; Padang 5.7) and high scores for Medan (7.1) and for both district-level and provincial politics in Lampung (e.g., 6.2 for Lampung Province).

A relatively consistent pattern emerges: low scores throughout Java (except Banten), particularly the cities, and much higher scores in eastern Indonesia, including its provincial capitals. Yet within this general pattern a number of intriguing results are worth highlighting. On Java, the pattern largely follows the expected distribution of low scores in cities and slightly higher scores in rural areas. Outside Java, this pattern is more or less reversed, as provincial capitals like Kupang, Makassar, Medan, and Palangka Raya score higher than the surrounding rural districts. Big and relatively wealthy cities like Medan and Makassar score similarly to Kalimantan's poor countryside, while Java's densely populated and poverty-prone countryside scores lower than natural-resource-rich rural areas like Bulungan, Gunung Mas, and Kutai Kertanegara in Kalimantan. Figure 10.3 plots CPI scores and average household expenditure and illustrates these results, showing little obvious effect of household expenditure on CPI scores. These findings provide an initial hint that the cost perspective does not provide a compelling explanation for variation in clientelism across Indonesia.

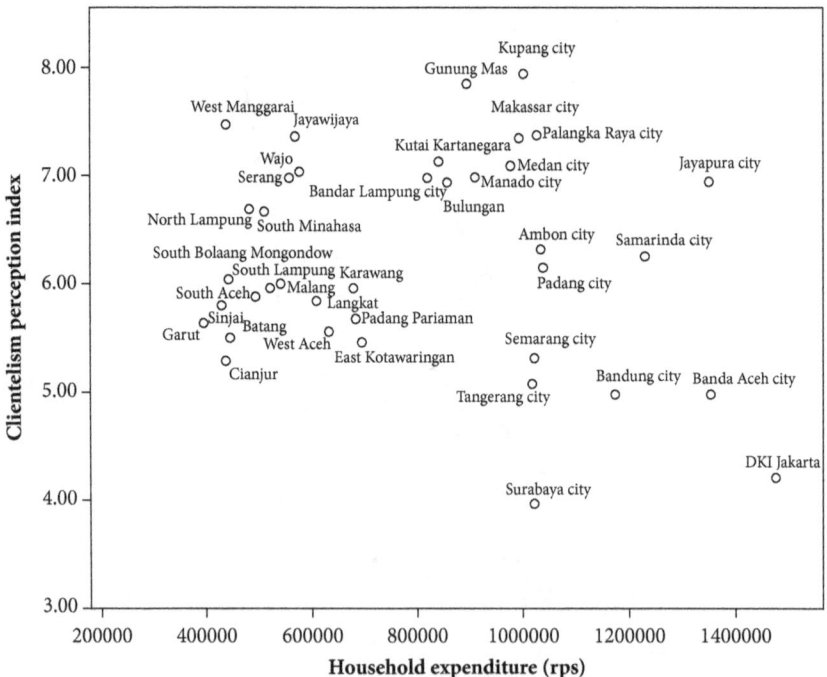

FIGURE 10.3   CPI scores and household expenditure

However, this pattern largely resonates with descriptive assessments of local politics. As we noted in the previous chapter, since not long after the introduction of direct elections, cities in Java have seen the rise of a new breed of local politicians who have gained admiration for adopting a reformist style. Leaders in places like Surabaya, Bandung, and Solo have become known for their emphasis on good governance and meritocratic appointments. These politicians have also been among the first to adopt explicitly programmatic campaign strategies as they start to make policy-based promises about subsidized health care, minimum wages, or free education. In contrast, provinces like Banten, Lampung, Central Kalimantan, and South Sulawesi that received high CPI scores are known for harboring entrenched political dynasties whose dominance largely rests on targeted distribution of state resources (Buehler 2013). Studies that compared the character of politics in different districts (e.g., Djani 2013; Luebke 2009; Patunru 2012; Rosser and Wilson 2012) yielded assessments that also correspond to this pattern.

What Makes Java Less Clientelistic?

How can we explain this pattern? In particular, what is it about these Javanese provinces (excluding Banten) that makes them less prone to clientelistic exchanges? To test to what extent the alternative explanations for clientelism summarized above correspond to our findings, we did our best to operationalize them within the limitations of our data and assess their explanatory power by employing a bivariate and multivariate regression framework. To operationalize the cost perspective we employ poverty rates, years of schooling, urban population percentage, and household expenditure as explanatory variables. To operationalize the constraint perspective we focus on both state dependency and limited economic diversification as indications of concentrated economic control. We use government expenditure (as share of total regional GDP) and the ratio of jobs in trade, industry, and finance to jobs in government as indicators of state dependency. For diversification of local economies we employ both the combined share of the industry, trade, and finance sectors in the district GDP, and the individual share of the industry sector. As control variables we add population size (a factor known to affect clientelistic strategies; see Brusco, Nazareno, and Stokes 2004), the size of the mining sector, and a Java dummy. Finally, in the regression analyses we control for unobserved regional effects by systematically applying robust standard errors that are clustered errors per province. Appendix E contains a correlation table of these main variables. To deal with the above-mentioned lower degree of inter-expert agreement in districts with lower CPI scores, we adopted a weighted least squares (WLS) regression approach instead of the more standard ordinary least squares (OLS) regression approach.[2]

In table 10.3 we present the bivariate regression results, while table 10.4 provides multivariate models.

Given the limited number of cases included in this analysis, these results need to be interpreted with caution. With more districts, the findings would be more robust. Yet a number of conclusions stand out clearly. The variables associated with the constraint perspective—that is, those related to state dependency and economic diversification—generally have more explanatory power. In the bivariate regression framework, all these variables turn up as significant. In contrast, of the variables associated with a cost perspective, only poverty rate and, to a limited extent, urban population are significant in the bivariate models. However, with one partial exception, all the variables associated with the cost perspective turn out to be insignificant in the multivariate models.[3]

The multivariate model associated with the constraint perspective (model 3b) turns out to have much stronger predictive capacity than the model associated

TABLE 10.3　CPI: Bivariate models (WLS regression)

	DEPENDENT VARIABLE: CPI DISTRICT		
	REGR. COEFF. (SE)	CONSTANT	R^2
LN_household expenditure	−0.582 (1.56)	13.927 (2.81)**	0.06
Poverty rate	0.042 (3.03)***	5.566 (18.71)***	0.12
Years of schooling	−0.126 (1.52)	7.194 (10.45)***	0.05
Urban population share	−0.009 (2.03)*	6.585 (29.25)***	0.11
Industry jobs, share of total	−0.063 (3.62)***	6.742 (27.77)***	0.27
Ratio jobs industry / civil servants	−0.096 (2.88)**	6.503 (32.86)***	0.33
Ratio jobs industry, trade, finance / civil servants	−0.035 (4.48)***	6.696 (29.60)***	0.40
Relative size industry/trade/finance sectors	−0.022 (2.77)**	6.961 (20.11)***	0.22
Share govt. expenditure in district GDP	0.029 (2.49)**	5.693 (21.69)***	0.19

* $p < .1$
** $p < .05$
*** $p < .01$
See appendix F for sources of the data used. N = 38.

TABLE 10.4 CPI: Multivariate models with controls (WLS regression)

	DEPENDENT VARIABLE: CPI				
	4A "COST"	4B "CONSTRAINT"	4C MIXED	4D W/ CONTROLS	4E W/ PROV. EFFECTS
LN_household expenditure	0.278 (0.30)		0.043 (0.07)	0.057 (0.08)	−0.957 (0.86)
Poverty rate	0.034 (1.48)		0.006 (0.21)	0.013 (0.56)	0.046 (1.90)*
Years of schooling	0.144 (0.66)		−0.054 (0.23)	0.087 (0.38)	0.730 (2.32)**
Share urban population	−0.013 (1.27)		0.005 (0.54)	0.004 (0.44)	−0.011 (0.91)
Share industry jobs		−0.020 (0.81)	−0.016 (0.41)	0.018 (0.54)	0.066 (1.36)
Ratio jobs ind., trade, fin. / civil servants		−0.035 (4.21)***	−0.037 (2.91)**	−0.064 (4.02)***	−0.070 (3.47)***
Share govt. expenditure in district GDP		0.012 (0.94)	0.010 (0.67)	0.025 (1.35)	0.021 (1.69)
Relative size industry/ trade/finance sectors		0.013 (1.35)	0.009 (0.66)	0.008 (0.51)	0.010 (0.62)
LN_population				0.518 (1.96)*	0.540 (2.33)**
Relative size mining sector				0.025 (0.36)	0.044 (0.42)
Java dummy				−0.807 (1.23)	−1.859 (1.42)
Provincial fixed effects	no	no	no	no	yes
_cons	1.378 (0.12)	6.238 (11.67)***	5.962 (0.72)	−2.174 (0.23)	6.875 (0.44)
R2	0.18	0.44	0.45	0.61	0.78
N	38	38	38	35	35

* $p < .1$
** $p < .05$
*** $p < .01$
See appendix F for data sources.

with the cost perspective (3a). In the combined model (3c), the ratio of jobs in industry, trade, and finance versus government jobs has the strongest impact on the CPI level across districts, a result that appears to be robust when we add control variables (model 3d) and control for provincial fixed effects (3e). In sum, while some variables associated with the cost perspective appear as significant in some model specifications, in general these variables are poor predictors of

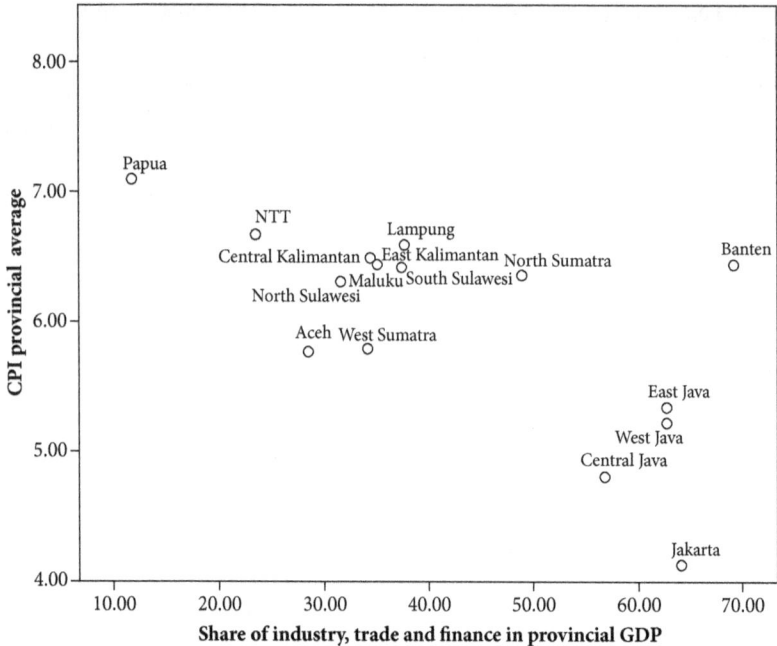

FIGURE 10.4 Average CPI scores per province and share of industry, trade, and finance in provincial GDP

perceived levels of clientelism across Indonesia. In contrast, throughout these different model specifications the variables associated with the constraint perspective consistently have greater explanatory power.

While the small number of provinces does not allow for a meaningful regression analysis of provincial CPI scores, figure 10.4 suggests that a similar pattern might be found if we look at provincial CPI scores. This figure plots the average of provincial and district CPI scores in relation to the relative size of the industry, trade, and finance sectors. Similar to the results of the district-level analysis above, this figure suggests that at the provincial level there is also a relation between economic diversification and the perceived intensity of clientelistic practices.

Clientelism in Indonesia thus turns out to be most strongly related to state dependency and limited economic diversification, while the predictions associated with the cost perspective—such as that clientelism would be most intense in poor regions with a poorly educated, rural population—match the results of the expert survey only weakly. Rural areas in Java, such as Garut, Cianjur, and Batang, have high poverty rates and relatively low household expenditure. Yet their CPI scores are low compared to areas with less poverty and higher incomes and household expenditure in, for example, Kalimantan and Sulawesi. On the whole, the relationship between household expenditure and the CPI scores is not strong. Similarly the CPI scores only show the expected impact of the urban-rural divide in Java, while most provincial capitals outside Java (excepting Banda Aceh and Jayapura) have higher scores than the rural districts selected in those provinces. In short, while the low CPI scores for Javanese cities do match the cost perspective, this perspective cannot account for the comparatively low scores elsewhere in Java and the high scores for urban centers outside Java.

The constraint perspective can better account for these patterns. It offers an explanation for the high CPI scores of provincial capitals like Palangka Raya, Kupang, Manado, Bandar Lampung, and, partly, Samarinda. Many jobs in these cities, where alternative sources of income are lacking, are either directly or indirectly dependent on the state (even sectors like hotels, restaurants, and construction are largely directed toward servicing bureaucrats and government programs). Towns like Kupang grew through a process of "state-sponsored urbanization" (van Klinken 2014, 32), as the city was built around the many offices of district and provincial government it contains. With limited alternative economic activity, and with so many livelihoods dependent on the state, towns like Kupang are characterized by heated, faction-ridden local politics, with intense involvement of civil servants who want to safeguard their privileges and maneuver politically to move up through the bureaucratic hierarchy and gain greater access to resources (Tidey 2012). In that light, it deserves to be pointed out that the weak effect of government expenditure in the regression analysis above is probably an underestimation due to measurement difficulties. As there are no data available of where provincial budgets are spent, we could only assess the size of the public sector by focusing on budgets of *district* governments. This leads to an underestimation of the importance of the public sector in provincial capitals like Kupang, where provincial budgets also contribute significantly to the local economy.

The constraint perspective also provides a better explanation for why the presence of a relatively sizable middle class in these provincial capitals does not produce lower CPI scores. Lacking a broad industrial base, these smaller provincial capitals typically have a middle class engaged in sectors that depend on state budgets, such as contracting, real estate, hospitality, and the civil service (van Klinken and Berenschot 2014). "In the bureaucratic politics that shaped Indonesia's provincial intermediate classes," writes van Klinken about Kupang and other such middle-size towns, the powers "to extract rents from government and to deny them to others are the fundamental driving forces separating the haves from the have-nots" (2014, 17). Their dependency on the state discourages the middle classes of provincial towns like Kupang from punishing politicians for clientelistic practices from which they themselves derive benefit.

The constraint perspective also helps to explain the high CPI scores in districts with large mining, oil, and plantation industries like Kutai Kertanegara, Bulungan, or Gunung Mas. These districts have relatively high incomes, but they also have limited alternative economic activity, and the local economy depends to a significant degree on natural resource extraction. The dominance of big mining and oil palm plantations fosters a concentration of control over economic activities in the hands of a limited number of entrepreneurs. Furthermore, as we discussed in the previous chapter, this sector generates collusion between entrepreneurs and state officials, with licensing and other governance processes offering plenty of opportunities for rent seeking. We discussed in the previous chapter how palm oil entrepreneurs fund election campaigns and promote their own candidates in order to access the government permits or support they need. In other words, the most important economic activities in these regions rely on clientelistic exchanges between business actors and politicians. The Javanese countryside's lower CPI scores fit the constraint perspective in the sense that these areas, while relatively poor, have more diversified and industrialized economies. Some impressive civil society campaigns in, for example, Garut and Batang against sitting district heads (Djani 2013; Mahsun 2017) suggest that the lower degree of state dependence corresponds to more vigorous scrutiny of the behavior of politicians.

However, there is one clear exception to this general pattern. As table 10.2 illustrates, perceptions of vote buying in, particularly, legislative elections do not strongly correlate with other aspects of clientelistic politics. Such vote buying is perceived to be pervasive throughout Indonesia. Levels of vote buying in elections in rural, and indeed, some urban districts in Java are much higher than their scores on other dimensions of the CPI. For example, when asked to score the incidence of vote buying in the most recent DPRD election, several regions in Java scored high: they included Serang (5.43), Karawang (5.46), Surabaya (5.36), and Batang (5.5). Only a few areas outside Java scored higher, and some that scored higher on other aspects of the CPI scored lower on vote buying (e.g., Kupang, with 5.15). There are historical reasons why this may be so (notably, a legacy of vote buying during village-head elections in Java: see Aspinall et al. 2017). It is also possible that the relatively high social influence of community notables in certain regions outside Java makes these areas more susceptible to a command vote or club goods strategy, or both, rather than individualized vote buying, as we argued in chapter 6.

But the finding also suggests that the relatively high levels of poverty among voters in these regions of Java might make them especially likely to be targeted by vote buying.[4] In other words, the widely agreed consensus in the literature—that higher poverty rates and lower levels of economic development explain electoral clientelism—might hold true for vote buying, while being less able to explain the other dimensions of clientelism covered by the CPI. Electoral clientelism—a form of relationship between voters and politicians—might operate according to a logic that is at least in part de-linked from dimensions of clientelism that bind politicians to brokers, civil servants, and other elites.

In this chapter we have compared the intensity of clientelistic politics across Indonesia by using the findings of our expert survey. Our results are highly suggestive, but they require further corroboration. The scope of the survey—executed in only thirty-eight districts—was limited, and expert surveys always contain dangers of bias. Nonetheless, our confidence in our general findings was strengthened by the fact that the assessments of the surveyed local political observers yielded a relatively consistent, yet intriguing, pattern, with low Clientelism Perception Index scores in locations (especially cities) in Java, and high scores in Kalimantan and eastern Indonesia. These findings were relatively consistent in the sense that CPI scores within regions were generally similar across a range of measures, while the contrasts between regions were relatively stark. Furthermore, the findings generally corresponded with our own fieldwork findings, and with other qualitative studies, providing a measure of confidence in the survey results and the general pattern they identified.

We used the survey findings to test the explanatory power of competing explanations for clientelism. Our overall finding is clear: the *character* of economic development is more important than the *level* of economic development for explaining variation in levels of clientelism across Indonesia. While there are outliers (such as Medan and Makassar), generally speaking, clientelistic practices are perceived to be more intense in areas with state-dependent economies and limited economic diversification. This finding supports the constraint perspective that we developed above. In the last chapter we argued that in less state-dependent and more diverse economies, civil society and business actors are better able to expose and criticize clientelistic practices, thus generating stronger societal constraints. In contrast, the cost perspective—focusing on poverty, urbanization, and the size of the middle class—matches the results of the expert survey rather poorly.

These findings draw attention to the nature of politicians' relationships not so much with voters (the focus of most attempts to explain clientelism quantitatively) but instead with what might be called the "political class"—that layer of middle-class civil servants, journalists, businesspeople, and other intermediate groups who, when they possess sufficient sources of economic independence, can threaten or undermine patronage-wielding politicians, or, conversely, when locked into relations of mutual interdependence with those politicians, entrench them in power. In areas of concentrated economic control, much of this political class is dependent on clientelist politicians, and so fails to represent an effective check on them.

Our previous chapters on election campaigns and governance contain observations that support this argument. In chapter 9, for example, we explained that in areas of concentrated economic control, politicians are likely to depend on a relatively small state-linked business elite. Politicians seeking to challenge prevailing clientelist models in such places find it hard to secure election funding, whereas in more economically diverse areas they are better able to raise the finances they need. In the same chapter, we saw how civil society and the media are less likely to challenge incumbent politicians where they are financially dependent on local government or crony businesses. In chapters 7 and 8, we saw how groups such as contractors and civil servants can be crucial to clientelist mobilization around elections. The influence of such state-dependent groups will obviously be greater where they dominate the local political class. Economic dependencies in areas of concentrated economic control also enable ruling politicians to wield a command vote, transforming plantation workers, construction laborers, and civil servants into compliant vote banks.

In this sense, the contrast between the cost and constraint perspectives is partly due to differences in conceptualization and research methods. Authors who propose a relationship between poverty and clientelism often do so largely on the basis of general population surveys on vote buying, rather than on assessments of other dimensions of clientelistic politics. Our findings suggest it is important to use research methods that comparatively assess different aspects of clientelistic politics. The mechanisms driving vote buying might be quite different from those promoting clientelistic distribution of resources to brokers, bureaucrats, and business elites. At the same time, our findings help identify what kind of change processes might curtail clientelism. While much of the literature on clientelism emphasizes economic growth and rising income levels, the analysis presented here suggests that it is not so much the *degree* but rather the *character* of economic development that matters.

CLIENTELISM AND THE SEARCH FOR GOOD GOVERNANCE

A striking feature of Indonesia's democracy is that its winners—the elites who derive power, prestige, and wealth from engaging in politics—harbor considerable misgivings about how it is practiced. During our interviews throughout Indonesia, politicians regularly harped on the expense, uncertainty, moral failings, and destructive effects of the "money politics" they engage in when they run for office. We could cite dozens of examples, but let us return to Tangerang and a candidate for deputy mayor, who expressed these concerns by saying that politicians had "to play two games"—they had to be "idealistic," by which he meant sticking to rules and procedures, but also "tolerant," by which he meant breaking them in order to gain illicit funds:

> If we are not [tolerant], well, the problem is that politics comes with high costs. As politicians we should actually focus on planning and budgets, but sometimes people ask us for favors. That is the time we have to be tolerant and pragmatic. If you are idealistic, the cash flow will be deficient. An income of 3 million rupiah [about $265 per month] is not enough to cover the costs [of election campaigns]. People tell us, you cannot be corrupt, you have to be clean. But on the other hand, they always ask for money, without thinking about how the leader will get the money. And if the leader gets the money from forbidden areas, they will get angry. (Interview, August 16, 2014)

Throughout our research, we frequently encountered candidates who complained about the demands they regularly faced from constituents for cash, club goods, and other benefits, and blamed these demands for forcing them to engage in corruption. We also often heard from candidates who explained that, once they were elected, their main concern was to "*balik modal*"—recoup the capital they had expended on campaign expenses, and so pay back their creditors and accumulate enough money for the next election. Of course, many such comments were doubtlessly self-serving, given that so many politicians accumulate great personal wealth from their profession. But many were heartfelt.

Indonesian politicians feel trapped in patterns of clientelistic exchange: they face pressures from constituents for cash and other benefits, and fear that if they ignore those demands, they will be outbid by rivals. It takes either particular moral courage, or an unusually strong political base, to run for office without distributing patronage, and many candidates who take this path lose. Though we have repeatedly pointed out that monetary transactions do not govern *all* aspects of politics in Indonesia, we have shown also that material exchange can be found at every point of the electoral cycle, while participants in the system themselves often speak as if money is the only thing that counts.

Such complaints illustrate why, contrary to expectations, Indonesia's democratization has so far not worked as an antidote to the corruption inherited from the New Order period. For a long time, the expectation was that democratization would gradually stamp out corruption and generate more dependable, rule-bound state institutions. In normative democratic theory, it is assumed that once politicians are held accountable to voters in the context of a free and open public sphere, they will eventually be forced to change their behavior. Voters will punish corrupt politicians and demand better public services and more efficient delivery, such that clientelistic practices will lose their appeal. Of course, it was obvious to many observers from early in Indonesia's democratic transition that this expectation was going astray; but the assumption that all that is needed to fix corruption is more democracy is still a strongly held view, especially among civil society activists and democracy advocates within Indonesia.

Not just in Indonesia, but across many younger democracies in, mainly, the global South, the realization has begun to sink in that elections are not always an effective tool to curtail corruption or to strengthen state institutions. In this book we described how, because of the pervasiveness of clientelistic practices, election campaigns have become so expensive that elected officials feel they cannot avoid acting corruptly and undermining state institutions. Elections often—though not everywhere or always—resemble a sale of state power, where those individuals with the deepest pockets or the strongest control over state resources stand the biggest chance of winning. As a result, clientelistic politics in Indonesia do not just feed on social inequality; they also contribute to it by enabling—indeed, requiring—a narrow political class to grow rich through privileged access to state resources.[1]

The realization that democracy might not be such an effective antidote to corruption and government failures has in recent years led to a paradigm shift in the thinking about democratization and the promotion of good governance. According to the so-called "principal-agent" approach, which has been dominant until recently, corruption and inadequate public service provision occur when the general public (the "principal") lacks the capacity to hold its "agents"— politicians and bureaucrats—accountable for their failures. In this view, greater democratization and transparency should improve the functioning of governments by making it easier for principal-citizens to check and punish their agent-officials. As a result, until recently, scholars as well as development experts have emphasized empowerment of citizens and accountability relations as pillars of good governance promotion (World Bank 2004).

There is much to be said for this approach. Obviously, without transparency and accountability of officials to mass publics via elections, it can be easy for elites to capture state institutions and use them to further their material interests. However, the problem with this approach is that it adopts an overly idealistic view of citizens. It assumes that citizens, once given enough power and information, will force politicians to pay greater attention to effective policy making, strengthen bureaucratic performance, and promote fair and equitable distribution of state resources. It assumes, in other words, that voters are naturally inclined to favor programmatic delivery and that clientelistic practices originate solely at the initiative of politicians.

As the comments from the candidate in Tangerang above illustrate, such assumptions break down on closer inspection. As we illustrated throughout this book, clientelistic favors—whether delivery of envelopes filled with cash at election time, transfers of loyal bureaucrats to plum posts, or allocation of government grants to *tim sukses* members—are granted not just because politicians supply them, but also because supporters demand them. Politicians are so unhappy about politics, while often hugely benefiting from their positions, because they often feel overwhelmed by expectations of money and favors. The resulting financial risks candidates assume when running for office can cause considerable stress; Indonesia's media regularly carry stories about candidates suffering mental breakdowns or committing suicide after losing and realizing that they face penury (Buehler 2009b).

The fact that both politicians and voters are drivers of clientelistic practices constitutes an important reason why these practices are so difficult to change. Writing about corruption, Mungiu-Pippidi has argued that in conditions where corrupt behavior and other forms of particularistic dealing become deeply entrenched in societal norms, it can become very hard to break out of them. In such conditions, she suggests, framing the issue in terms of victims and perpetrators can become a barrier to clear understanding: "The discussion of whether people are victims or perpetrators seems thus in many ways to miss the main point, which is that there is a comprehensive logic to governance where causes and effects become hard to distinguish, and a vicious circle of rationalizing need and justification is born, which is hard to break" (Mungiu-Pippidi 2015, 9).

The realization that corruption, clientelism, and related forms of particularistic behavior can become deeply entrenched in social orders, and thus seem impervious to good governance interventions, has led to a new approach that views the challenge of tackling clientelistic politics and corruption as a collective-action problem (Booth and Cammack 2013; Mungiu-Pippidi 2015; Persson, Rothstein, and Teorell 2013). A collective-action problem occurs when a group of persons each individually prefers a particular outcome, but they lack the ability to coordinate their actions to bring about change. Addressing collective-action problems thus requires paying attention to the incentive structures that encourage individuals to foreground their immediate interests while inhibiting them from working together to jointly achieve their ultimate preferences. This perspective thus involves moving away from the principal-agent approach that sees eradicating corruption and clientelism primarily as a problem of devising ways to ensure that governmental agents act in ways that accord with the preference of the populace-principals: "Governance challenges are not fundamentally about one set of people getting another set of people to behave better in the interest of development. They are about both sets of people finding ways of being able to act collectively in their own and others' best interests" (Booth and Cammack 2013, 5).

With regard to clientelism specifically, this approach needs to start with the proposition that voters cannot always be relied on to discipline wayward power holders. On the contrary, the main challenge when curbing clientelistic practices is that everybody involved—not just politicians and bureaucrats but also voters—individually stands to lose by forgoing clientelistic practices, at least in circumstances in which they expect others to continue to act clientelistically. Politicians, like the deputy mayoral candidate we quoted above, might individually wish the character of politics to be different, but they fear that if they depart from the conventional approach they will be defeated by rivals who mobilize money and resources. Voters, for their part, do not demand money and favors from politicians because they are ignorant, greedy, or lack education. Rather, they demand these things because it makes sense to do so in a context where they believe policies have little impact, politicians enrich themselves while in office, and other voters are going to take whatever the politicians give them. As we saw in chapter 5, voters often speak explicitly in just such terms: they express cynicism about political life, and recognize that money politics is destructive, but take heart that they at least have the opportunity to take some private profit from the system at election times. Similarly, many bureaucrats would personally prefer universalistic implementation of government policies and rule-based provision of public services. But they would risk their careers by refusing to entertain particularistic requests from politicians or their superiors. Such dynamics explain why curbing clientelistic practices is a collective-action problem: while all the actors might wish the system to be different, they each require other actors in the system to change before they do so themselves, and lack incentives to be the one to go out ahead of the crowd. As a result, a clientelistic political arena—sometimes referred to as a "limited access order" (North, Wallis, and Weingast 2009)—constitutes a stable social equilibrium that is not easy to change.

This paradigm shift has led to growing awareness that in order to change a corruption-ridden and clientelistic political system, it is necessary to first develop deep knowledge about its actual workings and the incentive structures that operate within it. There is growing awareness among policy makers and development specialists that the quest for good governance (Mungiu-Pippidi 2015) requires engagement with politics as it actually is, rather than as formal rules suppose it to be. This view, for example, infuses the 2017 *World Development Report* (World Bank 2017), as well as a host of publications on corruption, good governance, and natural resource management produced since around 2010 (e.g., Mungiu-Pippidi 2015; Persson, Rothstein, and Teorell 2013; Hickey 2012). For example, an advisory institution for development organizations in the UK argues that "instead of prioritizing reform of formal institutions, they [i.e., development practitioners] should look at the structures, relationships, interests and incentives that underpin them. This does not mean rejecting the longer-term goal of helping poor countries to build inclusive, rules-based public authority. But in the short-to-medium term it may be more useful to explore whether relationship-based arrangements could offer a way to make progress" (Centre for the Future State 2010).

Indonesia's Patronage Democracy in Comparative Perspective

These studies all have in common that they argue that knowledge about the informal, inner workings of politics is essential to developing more effective policies, promoting a programmatic orientation, and improving governance.

Such knowledge is what this book has aimed to provide. In particular, we have argued that the *specific* forms of informal politics practiced in a particular country—ranging from the character of election campaigns to the pattern of control exercised by politicians, bureaucrats, and other actors over state resources—matter greatly for the nature of governance and democracy and, by implication, for pathways toward reform. We have argued that the comparative study of clientelistic politics is much neglected, but greatly needed if we are to understand the challenges that beset many of the world's democracies and which can frequently prompt authoritarian regression—as when populist or authoritarian leaders offer strong leadership to stem corruption, favoritism, and money politics (Kenny 2017). In response to this need, we have developed a comparative framework to identify and analyze the nature of Indonesia's patronage democracy. We proposed four comparative dimensions—networks, resources, discretionary control, and degree of clientelism—which we employed to show that Indonesia's patronage democracy differs considerably from our two main comparators, India and Argentina, and in the modest hope that this effort might stimulate more systematic comparison of patronage democracies in the future.

Using these comparative dimensions, we highlighted in this book three specific features of Indonesia's patronage democracy. First, we emphasized the importance of personal networks. In contrast to their counterparts in India and, particularly, Argentina, where politicians depend much more on political parties to organize their election campaigns, politicians in Indonesia instead rely on ad hoc, candidate-centered structures, or *tim sukses*—success teams. We discussed in chapter 5 how candidates build their campaign organizations by drawing on personal connections while promising *tim sukses* members favors—such as government contracts, projects, or subsidies—should they succeed. In chapters 3 and 4 we traced the origins of this system of freewheeling clientelism to Indonesia's authoritarian past and the candidate-centered nature of its electoral system.

Second, we argued that the mobilizational weaknesses of political parties spur intense politicization of social life during election campaigns. As candidates need strong social networks to build their campaign organizations and connect with voters, they enlist support from virtually every kind of formal and informal social network and association. We explained in chapter 6 that this instrumentalization of social networks fosters a particular type of clientelistic exchange. Politicians provide targeted communities with club goods that offer collective benefits—ranging from street paving to mosque renovation, from excursions to new water taps—in order to obtain the support of community members. Furthermore, Indonesian politicians expend considerable effort identifying local leaders with influence at the community level. Doing so is important, because the effectiveness of their clientelistic strategies largely depends on their using local brokers who enjoy strong personal connections with targeted voters.

Third, we argued that—again in contrast with India and Argentina—state actors (civil servants as well as community-level state representatives like village and neighborhood heads) play an important role in election campaigns. In chapter 8, we attributed the capacity of such actors to deliver votes to the discretionary control over state resources they continue to exert. While in India and Argentina political parties have managed to wrest much control over the allocation of state benefits away from bureaucrats, an important heritage of Indonesia's New Order is that state functionaries retain considerable authority in determining what persons and areas get programs and benefits. We argued in chapter 9 that this heritage means that control over the bureaucracy constitutes highly valuable political capital in contemporary Indonesia, with effects for the outcomes of local elections. In comparative terms, elected district heads and governors frequently come from the civil service, and incumbents enjoy strong advantages when trying to win reelection. Lacking control over the allocation of state resources, and unable to direct the bureaucracy, outsider candidates face obstacles when trying to cultivate electoral support. The most significant political competition often occurs *within* local bureaucracies as contending bureaucratic actors vie for control over government budgets and projects. For this reason, we called Indonesia a democratized bureaucratic polity.

These three elements have led us to argue that, in comparison to India and Argentina's party-centered patronage democracies, Indonesia represents an example of a more state-centered patronage democracy. A significant proportion of clientelistic vote mobilization is facilitated not by parties, but by bureaucratic networks. Vote buying and other forms of private patronage distribution are prevalent because most candidates—excluding incumbent executive government heads—lack the access to state resources needed to build the kind of sustained relationships with voters that scholars have observed being organized by parties in India and Argentina, as well as in other countries. Similarly, we argued that the limited control of Indonesia's political parties over the bureaucracy has fostered the notably freewheeling, ad hoc, and flexible form of campaign organization associated with elections in the country. Political parties lack the access to state resources to build more institutionalized political networks and to consolidate ongoing relationships of dependency with large groups of constituents.

In the final two chapters of the book, we highlighted the relationship between economic conditions and clientelistic practices. Personal exchange relationships between politicians, bureaucrats, and business actors play an important role in sustaining clientelism, but there is considerable variation in how sustained and deep-going such relationships are across Indonesia. Employing our expert survey, we showed that clientelistic practices are perceived to be particularly pervasive in Kalimantan and eastern Indonesia, and much less so in Java. We attributed this variation to the character of local economies. The greater diversification of Java's economy, coupled with its more limited dependence on state resources, has led to a somewhat more equitable distribution of political resources there, generating greater constraints on clientelistic practices and weaker incentives to behave clientelistically. In the concentrated-control economies of Kalimantan and eastern Indonesia, interactions between the world of politics and business are deeply clientelistic, while the public sphere is weak, with local media outlets possessing little ability to act independently of the local state, and civil society groups being feeble.

As well as hoping to contribute to more systematic comparative analysis of patronage democracies, we of course hope that the arguments presented in this book will encourage further analysis of informal dimensions of politics within Indonesia itself. As we have pointed out, though the existing scholarly literature frequently recognizes that informal interactions, personal relationships, and hidden exchanges of material resources and political favors are important in, even central to, Indonesian politics, such phenomena are frequently merely noted as signs of dysfunction or of what is lacking in Indonesian politics, without attempts at systematic or detailed analysis.[2]

We are especially keen to promote serious attention to informal politics by Indonesian scholars, who are often the best placed to study them. Both authors have had the experience of attending seminars and conferences in Indonesia during which the latest political gossip about under-the-table deal making and influence peddling at the highest echelons of government dominates discussion during the breaks, but when the formal sessions reconvene participants go back to discussing formal rules and institutions, often using theories devised in the context of very different political systems, as if the informal dimensions of politics that have just animated conversation are no longer important. This gap between how politics is discussed in everyday conversations and in formal academic analysis must be bridged, even if doing so will be challenging.

We think the way forward will likely require combinations similar to what we have used in this book: ethnography, crucial because it provides insights into interactions that are invisible to those surveying formal politics, and attempts to systematically compare patterns of informal politics in varying social and political settings across the archipelago. We note that important studies have already appeared (for ethnographic studies that look into aspects of informal politics, for example, see Hanani 2016; Sambodho 2016; Tidey 2012; for comparative studies see Clark 2013; Djani 2013; Muhtadi 2018; Mustafa 2017; Tans 2012), though attention will need to be paid to developing better quantitative tools for assessing informal politics systematically. Developing such a dual-pronged line of scholarship will be important for Indonesian scholars, many of whom are strongly committed to improving the functioning of their political system and ensuring it provides greater welfare for ordinary people.

Indonesia's Quest for Good Governance

Knowledge about the inner workings of Indonesia's politics and bureaucracy is an essential prerequisite for addressing many of the key challenges that Indonesia faces. Corruption, environmental degradation, the quality of public services, social inequality, improving infrastructure: the nature of politics in Indonesia constitutes a large, if not the largest, obstacle to addressing these issues. Awareness of that reality was the driving motivation for us to write this book. Throughout, we have provided illustrations of the relationship between politics and governance. We noted in chapter 10, for example, how the rate of deforestation is related to the financing of election campaigns by politicians in Kalimantan. We discussed in chapter 8 how the cost of elections stimulates political actors to demand hefty kickbacks when awarding government tenders, reducing the quality of Indonesia's public infrastructure. In chapter 9, we showed how the quality and the capacity of Indonesian bureaucracy suffer because politicians need to cultivate personal support among bureaucrats. In short, informal politics and personal exchange relationships shape virtually every aspect of the state's operations in Indonesia.

Policies and development interventions are destined to fail if they operate on the assumption that Indonesia's state is a rule-bound, Weberian institution only occasionally waylaid by deviant behavior. Clientelistic exchange relations pervade state institutions and affect their basic functioning. Any policy intervention or development initiative should start by recognizing this reality, rather than wishing it away. As we mentioned above, a similar realization has led to calls to "work with the grain" (Booth 2011) of existing local political orders and their incentive structures, and to numerous initiatives by the international development community to pay more attention to political economy. This certainly does not mean acceding to perverse incentive structures when they are present, but it does require a careful reading of the mixture of constraints on, and opportunities for, reform in any given setting, and the design of focused strategies that might nudge the existing societal equilibrium in the direction of "ethical universalism" (Mungiu-Pippidi 2015).

In our experience, policy makers as well as development organizations struggle to incorporate this political dimension into their work. This is understandable:

it is much easier and less risky for them to work on training in technical skills or the preparation of guidelines and operating procedures than to deal with politics head-on. Compared to technical fixes, political approaches are messy and controversial since they involve, in one way or another, addressing power inequalities. Consequently, much policy making and development cooperation still proceeds on the assumption (or hope) that the provision of knowledge and skills, the training of a few bureaucrats or judges, or the adoption of a particular policy will fix a problem. This logic gives rise to a never-ending seminar circuit in Jakarta's upmarket hotels, where new skills and policies are eagerly discussed, whether the topic at hand is legal development, the environment, urban planning, or bureaucratic reform. We have often participated in such seminars; it is very common that someone in the course of the discussions will observe that even if the policy or law being suggested is adopted, it will have little effect, because Indonesia's major problems relate to implementation rather than policy design. Often everyone agrees—but the conversation typically then resumes its course. The elephant in these hotel rooms, in other words, is informal politics.

This book does not suggest that the pervasiveness of clientelistic practices within Indonesian politics can be changed easily. We have described how clientelistic practices are deeply rooted in history and embedded in widely shared norms and in particular distributions of power within Indonesia's society. Even so, this book does provide hints about how to more actively engage with Indonesia's political structures in ways that might help to nudge incentive structures in the direction of more programmatic politics. Our finding of considerable variation in the intensity of clientelistic politics across the country suggests that different strategies will be needed in different areas. In relatively low-intensity zones of clientelism, notably in Java, especially in urban areas, a new breed of programmatic local politicians has already begun to emerge, though they have faced considerable resistance, suggesting that even in such relatively conducive settings the emergence of more programmatic politics will be highly contentious. Even so, both the emergence of such politicians, and the findings of our expert survey indicating that the social-political contexts in which they operate are less clientelistic, suggest that traditional interventions aimed at improving bureaucratic functioning, oversight mechanisms, and strengthening civil society will stand greater chances of success in these areas.

There are much greater barriers to programmatic politics in areas such as those in eastern Indonesia and Kalimantan, where we showed that concentrated control economies nurture more intense clientelistic politics, with few possibilities for checking by social actors independent of clientelist networks and imperatives. In such areas, attempts to implement bureaucratic reform or improve enforcement are likely to be swallowed up by locally dominant political orders and to produce little meaningful change. In these areas, our analysis identifies the key problems as lack of economic diversification and crippled public spheres and civil societies, suggesting that attempts at reform in such places might do best to start by directly addressing these problems. For example, programs that help to diversify local economies, or strengthen the capacity of citizens to articulate their interests and operate independently of the local state, as through legal aid programs, are likely to be helpful.

Overall, in fact, we suggest that for Indonesia as a whole, the civil society dimension remains a critical one (Mietzner 2013a). The issue is not simply whether Indonesia has dense associational life, a feature of Indonesian society that has been widely recognized (Lussier and Fish 2012). We have seen that many of Indonesia's societal organizations, especially those at the grass roots, are readily hijacked for purposes of patronage distribution, and thus may be seen as nurturing hierarchical social relationships and facilitating rather than inhibiting clientelistic politics. Instead, Indonesia needs more and stronger associations able to aggregate the interests of distinctive social groups and advocate for long-term goals rather than simply trading for short-term clientelistic gain. The development of such a civil society would strengthen demands for programmatic rather than clientelistic delivery. Agencies interested in improving governance in Indonesia therefore need to keep doing what they can to strengthen the diversity of Indonesia's associational life, rather than simply focusing on internal mechanisms and procedures within government.

Another critical conclusion that arises from our book concerns the centrality of electoral system design. Though our focus has been informal politics, we have from the start shown that informal patterns of politics, including clientelism, interact strongly with formal institutional structures and respond to the incentives they provide, with the electoral system featuring strongly in our account. Electoral reform is a recurring topic on the policy agenda in Jakarta. Unease with the flourishing of money politics during elections, and with how this dynamic feeds corruption, has fostered persistent debate about whether and in what way Indonesia's electoral laws need to be changed. In late 2014, a coalition of parties opposed to the newly elected president Joko Widodo even agreed to abolish direct elections of local government leaders, citing their high cost, though this change was soon overturned following a public outcry. Short-term political calculus on the part of President Widodo's opponents motivated this attempted change (opposition parties dominated most local legislatures and therefore believed they would benefit from a return to indirect elections). The then leader of the coalition of opposition parties promoting the change, Prabowo Subianto, was also motivated by authoritarian impulses. But the fact that this debate was deeply politicized should not surprise us. Authoritarian backlashes and populist leaders frequently feed off public and elite perceptions that electoral competition is corrupt and a barrier to clean government and better development. Indonesia's money-infused electoral system increases the chances of authoritarian regression.

While party politicians have often expressed support for abolition of direct elections, hoping that this change might strengthen the parties and reduce the costs that individual candidates bear in election campaigns, civil society organizations have typically defended direct elections and called for more democracy, as during the episode in late 2014. What is needed, however, is to find ways to reconcile democratic accountability with reducing the costs of election campaigns for individual candidates and encouraging programmatic rather than personalistic competition. If we conceive of Indonesia's governance challenges as a collective-action problem, then it becomes clear that all of these goals are important. So far, electoral reforms have focused on democratic accountability by increasing the role of the personal vote, and so have had the unintended effect of greatly increasing the financial burden on individual candidates and encouraging clientelistic mobilization. We highlighted in chapter 4, for example, how the decision of Indonesia's Constitutional Court to switch to an open-list PR system in legislative elections led to an increase in vote buying. The court's support for this open-list system was based on an everyday version of the principal-agent approach outlined above: the court and its supporters assumed that the more direct influence voters exercised over the selection of their representatives, the better those representatives would operate. However, by turning candidates from the same parties into rivals, this decision significantly increased barriers to collective action among politicians. It provided candidates with incentives to differentiate themselves from their intra-party rivals by engaging in vote buying and other forms of individualized patronage politics.

This is but one example of the ways in which Indonesia's current candidate-centered electoral system contributes to the cost of election campaigns and, consequently, to the pervasiveness of corruption. A fruitful avenue for pursuing electoral reform lies in reconsidering the role that political parties should play in Indonesia's democracy. We highlighted throughout this book their peripheral role in election campaigns, which we attributed partly to Indonesia's electoral system. High distrust in parties has led to the adoption of various measures that have weakened their role. The thrust of this book supports those who believe there is a need to overcome the antiparty sentiment that has infused Indonesian politics. Stronger parties may not be a sufficient condition for overcoming clientelistic politics, but they are certainly a necessary prerequisite for doing so: when candidates run for office on the basis of personal appeal and by providing whatever they can to voters as individuals, they have strong incentives to act clientelistically; parties provide them with a means to coordinate their campaign promises around programmatic offerings and thus—potentially at least—overcome at least one of the collective-action problems we discussed above. Stronger party-candidate links might also reduce the amount of money that candidates spend on buying party support, and stronger parties might be able to coordinate fund-raising and so reduce the predominance of economic elites in Indonesia's political life. Stronger parties could also give voters more insight into the different opinions and policy preferences of candidates, thus fostering programmatic voting behavior. Of course, strong parties, too, can be deeply clientelistic—as our repeated references to India and Argentina make clear—but it is very hard to imagine programmatic politics without them.

Especially if combined with other party-strengthening reforms, such as increased government subsidies for parties and their election campaigns, a return to a more party-centered electoral system, such as closed-list PR in legislative elections, might help foster stronger parties, reducing pressures on individual candidates to raise their own funds and design their own clientelistic election campaigns. While we would not advocate abolition of direct elections for heads of local governments (as we noted in chapter 4, indirect elections of local government heads can also undermine parties by allowing wealthy contenders to bribe individual parliamentarians to support them), we do believe it is important to think about how to better align party and candidate incentives in these races. Various methods might be devised to further this aim: for example, ensuring that leaders of the first-placed parties in a legislative election are automatically nominated as district-head candidates in the region concerned (Berenschot 2015b).

Of course, each institutional change carries risks of unintended consequences, and thus electoral system redesign should proceed cautiously: stronger party-based competition, reduction of patronage politics, and an increase in programmatic mobilization can produce political polarization and so give rise to harmful effects of a different kind. For example, party-strengthening reforms in Thailand in the late 1990s, after a decade of very similar complaints about the weakness and corruption of that country's parties and the pervasiveness of vote buying, had the desired effect of building up parties and increasing programmatic competition, but also helped fuel political conflict, authoritarian regression, and two coups. The extreme flexibility and pragmatism fostered by Indonesia's candidate-focused system have helped defuse conflict in Indonesian elections, for example by facilitating cross-ethnic alliance building during elections (Aspinall 2011), and care would need to be taken to ensure that such benefits are not lost.

Overall, change processes are slow and difficult to achieve, and we do not suggest there is any easy panacea, including electoral reform. The lesson of countries that successfully made the transition away from clientelism toward ethical universalism is that these transitions typically take decades and are often marked by sharp moments of disequilibrium followed by a slow process of institution building and normative change (Mungiu-Pippidi 2015). This is an important caveat, but it should also remind us that the character of politics in Indonesia, as elsewhere, is not beyond human control. The political patterns we have discussed in this book, including their drawbacks, partly result from complex and slow-moving historical and economic forces, which have fostered an unequal distribution of power in society upon which clientelistic politics thrive. But they also arise from policies and laws that are much easier to control. In this regard, we view our book as standing in a tradition that sees social inquiry as a means to achieve some degree of liberation from the social and economic forces that guide human lives. We wrote this book with the modest hope that knowledge of the inner workings of politics can serve to facilitate debate and conscious choices about how politics might be reimagined and redesigned.

THE EXPERT SURVEY

For the analysis in this book we relied in part on an expert survey, executed among over five hundred academics, journalists, NGO activists, and campaign organizers from thirty-eight districts in sixteen provinces across Indonesia. This appendix discusses the design and execution of this expert survey. The data and the questionnaire can be found online at http://www.kitlv.nl/democracy-for-sale/ as well as at the DANS data archive: https://doi.org/10.17026/dans-xm4-exy3.

Design of the Survey Questionnaire

The expert survey used an elaborate survey instrument divided into three sections: voter-politician exchanges, campaign organization, and voting behavior. The questions in this survey concerned elections for district heads, governors, and district parliaments, as well as (to a more limited extent) for the president.

The questionnaire was designed based on initial fieldwork on election campaigns. The fieldwork was also used to test and adapt the exact phrasing of questions, in order to avoid misunderstandings. The questions on clientelistic electoral strategies focused on seven types of patronage resources—jobs, access to public services, money, licenses, social assistance, government contracts, and access to welfare programs—that are commonly used for clientelistic politics in Indonesia and beyond (Kitschelt et al. 2009).

The exact phrasing of questions about these resources was attuned to local context, to correspond with how such clientelistic exchanges are usually organized in Indonesia. For example, as the access to public services often depends on government projects and grants awarded to whole villages and neighborhoods, the survey question was phrased in terms of whether the voting behavior of a village or neighborhood might affect its chances of securing such government funds. Similarly, as village, RW, and RT heads are important brokers mediating access to welfare programs and subsidized health care, the survey question on access to welfare focused on whether it was likely that such local leaders prioritized people on the basis of their voting behavior. In all survey questions, technical terms that could easily be misunderstood—like "clientelism"—were avoided. Instead, the experts were asked to assess the *proportion* of particular state benefits provided as rewards for electoral support. This phrasing also minimized possible confusion about answer categories, since experts were generally asked to answer in terms of percentages of a total of jobs, contracts, or social assistance provided by the district government. For example, the survey asked, "In your estimation, of all the major contracts that the district government awards, what percentage goes to companies or businesspeople who have supported election campaigns of ruling politicians (district head, governor, DPRD members) during elections?" The answer categories to this question ranged from "no one" to "80–100 percent."

The survey not only included questions about clientelist exchange. We also asked experts about campaign organization, voting behavior, and the influence of various types of local leaders. While we do not include discussions of the survey results on all these matters in this book, this material does support our analysis.

Execution of the Survey

The survey was executed by one of us (Berenschot), together with a group of thirty-eight Indonesian researchers. These were mostly researchers and lecturers at local universities, as well as a number of independent researchers. They all lived in or nearby the district in which they executed the survey. They were chosen for their knowledge of the region and, hence, their capacity to select reliable experts. All had experience executing expert surveys, mostly with Indonesia's Academy of Sciences and/or the political science department of the Universitas Gadjah Mada (see Prasetyo et al. 2004; Törnquist 2006). Before executing the survey, all researchers also participated in a two-day training workshop to familiarize them with the survey instrument.

The survey was executed between the end of April and late June 2014 (with the exceptions of the districts of Bulungan, Gunung Mas, and Garut, where the survey was executed in late July 2014). To ensure reliability, all researchers were instructed to read out the questions as formulated on the questionnaire, and they recorded all their interviews. Unfortunately, despite these precautions, the survey was not always reliably executed. The material from six of the original forty-four surveyed districts had to be discarded. In three cases, this was because the interviews were not recorded, in two it was because the survey questions were not read out during the interviews, and in one district the researcher skipped questions. In another district, the survey was executed within six months of the inauguration of the new district head, with the result that experts could not assess how the new district head awarded jobs, contracts, and other benefits. These six districts were excluded from the analysis presented in this book, which focuses on the remaining thirty-eight districts.

Selection of Districts

To select the districts, Berenschot tried to balance the wish to have a representative sample with the need to work with experienced researchers with local knowledge. The general goal was to select three districts—the provincial capital and two rural districts—in sixteen of the then thirty-three provinces across Indonesia. The provincial capital was selected because these towns are the focal point of regional politics. The selected rural districts were, ideally, representative of the character of the economy of the region, yet the choice had to be adapted to the availability of researchers. Furthermore, in some regions we lacked sufficient researchers. In Maluku we surveyed only one district (Ambon). In other provinces—North Sumatra, West Sumatra, East Nusa Tenggara, Papua, East Java, Banten—we ended up with only two districts, either because of a lack of researchers or because of problems with the implementation in the third district.

Selection of Experts

As explained in chapter 1, an expert survey has certain advantages compared to the (few) other available methods to study clientelistic politics comparatively. While both general surveys and studies based on statistical proxies focus only on one dimension of clientelistic politics (e.g., vote buying), the expert survey contained questions about a range of clientelistic exchanges. Furthermore, perceptions of informed experts about the pervasiveness of such exchanges constitute a closer and more reliable proxy for degrees of clientelism than proxies used previously (e.g., rule-of-law measures, corruption indicators, or government spending on personnel).

Execution of an expert survey, however, also poses challenges. One is the possibility that the partisanship of the interviewed experts affects their assessments. An expert supportive of a district head or governor might underestimate the pervasiveness of clientelistic practices, while a critic might overstate them. Indeed, we found a limited but statistically significant correlation between experts' evaluations of ruling politicians and their assessments in the Clientelism Perception Index. This means that a balanced selection of experts is important to ensure reliability and comparability of the results.

Another important challenge concerns the selection of knowledgeable observers. Four different groups of experts were included in the survey: journalists, NGO activists, academics, and election campaign organizers. Members of these groups were chosen because their backgrounds allowed them to follow politics on a regular basis, enabling accumulation of insider knowledge on local politics. Assessments of the first three groups were broadly similar, while campaign organizers generally considered clientelistic practices to be slightly less pervasive. In each district, fourteen experts were selected. This number was chosen to ensure that, on the one hand, the average scores for each district were based on a wide range of views. On the other hand, the total number of interviewed experts could not be too high because, particularly in remote rural districts, the number of informed and reliable observers was limited. Increasing the number of experts might have led to the inclusion of observers with poor knowledge of local politics.

To select the experts, we relied on the local knowledge of the researchers. They were asked to propose a list of experts on the basis of two criteria: the experts needed to be knowledgeable about local politics and, as much as possible, nonpartisan. However, particularly in small districts with state-dependent economies, the supply of neutral observers was limited. To address this, researchers made assessments of the partisanship of the experts they proposed. In consultation with Berenschot, they tried to ensure that, if they had selected an expert known to be supportive of ruling politicians, they also included an expert known to be critical.

To further boost the reliability of the results, we asked the researchers to rate the trustworthiness of the experts. They were also given the option of recommending exclusion of particular experts from the analysis if they considered them to be particularly untrustworthy on the basis of their assessments during the interview. Out of the 533 experts interviewed in the thirty-eight districts, 24 were excluded in this way. As a result, the analysis in this book is based on assessments of 509 experts. The table below gives an overview of the background of these experts. The selection process described above led to a large overrepresentation of male experts. Partly reflecting the male-dominated nature of (much of) Indonesia's public sphere, the selected experts were 87 percent men.

For an assessment of the reliability of the expert assessments and the degree to which experts of the same district agreed in their evaluations, see appendix C.

TABLE A.1 Profession and age of surveyed experts

		AGE						
		UNDER 30	30–40	40–50	50–60	ABOVE 60	UNKNOWN	TOTAL
Profession	Journalist	15	52	25	6	2	17	117
	Academic	7	24	30	24	2	19	106
	NGO	11	36	35	10	1	20	113
	Campaign organizer	6	22	32	10	4	12	86
	Other / not recorded	5	38	23	13	1	7	87
Total		44	172	145	63	10	75	509

Appendix B

TABLE B.1 Survey tool Clientelism Perception Index (CPI)—district

RESOURCE EXCHANGED:	Q:	SCALE:
1. Public services	A1a. In your opinion, can a village or neighborhood where very few people voted for the current district head succeed in getting funding from the district government to improve their basic amenities (roads, electricity, sanitation, schools)?	1. Very unlikely (voting behavior plays a big role in allocating government budgets) to 5. Very likely (voting behavior plays no role in allocating budgets)
2. Access to welfare programs	A3a. In your estimation, when implementing welfare programs (such as handouts of cash and rice, or subsidized health care), after elections how often do these local government representatives [village heads, RT heads or *lurah*] prioritize people who voted for their preferred candidate for *bupati*?	1. Never (local government officials will never prioritize people because of their vote) to 5. Very common (most officials will prioritize people who voted for their candidate)
3. Use of social assistance budgets	A10a. In your estimation, what percentage of social assistance budgets of the district government is used by the sitting district head to reward his/her supporters for their campaign efforts?	1. None is used to reward supporters, 2. 0–20% of these budgets, to 6. 80%–100%

RESOURCE EXCHANGED:	Q:	SCALE:
4. Jobs	A5a. In your estimation, what percentage of the civil servants in echelon two and three of the district government [e.g., bureau chiefs, subdistrict heads, regional secretary, etc.] have been promoted to this position as a reward for supporting—openly or secretly—a candidate during an election?	1. None, 2. Up to 20 percent of these civil servants, to 6. 80%–100%
5. Government contracts	A8a. In your estimation, of all the major contracts that the *district government* awards, how many go to companies or businesspersons who supported election campaigns of ruling politicians (district head, governor, members of DPRD) during elections?	1. No contract goes to companies that support politicians, 2. 0–20% of all major contracts, to 6. 80%–100%
6. Influencing regulatory proceedings	A11a. When a campaign donor asks for help to get a permit to build a commercial building in an area officially designated for farming, how likely is it that the district head / mayor will arrange the building permit?	1. Very unlikely (will never help to arrange a permit that does not accord with spatial planning) to 5. Very likely (will arrange the permit for any campaign donor)
7a. Money—district head elections	A6a. What percentage of voters is given money or consumer goods during elections for district head?	1. None, 2. Between 0–20% of *all voters* get money or consumer goods from candidates, to 6. 80%–100%
7b. Money—Legislative Assembly	A6a. What percentage of voters is given money or consumer goods during elections for the district-level legislative assembly?	1. None, 2. Between 0–20% of *all voters* get money or consumer goods from candidates, to 6. 80%–100%

Appendix C

CPI AND COMPONENT VARIABLES: SCORES AND DEGREE OF INTER-EXPERT AGREEMENT

To assess the reliability of the results of the expert survey, we looked at inter-expert agreement. This degree to which experts (within the same districts) offer similar judgments can be used as an indicator of the reliability of their assessments. A commonly used measure of such intercoder agreement is Rwg, which is an assessment of the variance among expert answers in proportion of the variance expected if there was a complete lack of agreement.[1] This measure ranges from 0 to 1, where 1 indicates full agreement among experts. For an index variable like CPI, this measure is called Rwg(j), as it is calculated slightly differently using the average variance of all component variables in relation to not only the null distribution but also the number of items. As the inclusion of additional items in an index variable reduces measurement error, the Rwg(j) scores are generally higher than assessments of intercoder agreement of component variables (see Bieman, Cole, and Voelpel 2012, 68; LeBreton and Senter 2008; Lindstadt, Proksch, and Slapin 2015). The table below provides an overview of the Clientelism Perception Index scores per district and district averages of component variables, as well as the Rwg and Rwg(j) scores for all these variables. (The CPI was constructed by, first, standardizing the scores of variables with a deviant scale [A1, A3, and A11, which had answer categories that ranged from 1 to 5, while A1 also had a reverse scale]. The index variable CPI district was subsequently constructed by adding up the district averages of all component variables and recalculating these scores to a scale of 0 to 10.)

Three aspects of the data in this table deserve highlighting. First, the degree of intercoder agreement for the CPI is for almost all districts above 0.70, which is generally taken as an acceptable level of agreement for such index variables. On this measure, higher-scoring districts like Kupang or Gunung Mas score a 0.92 and 0.93 for the CPI index variable, while lower districts like Jakarta or Semarang score much lower (respectively, 0.78 and 0.68). Second, the table also shows that for some component variables and in some districts, the experts sometimes differed considerably in their answers, suggesting that the results for the individual component variables have a considerable margin of error. Experts found it particularly difficult to assess the degree to which welfare programs are distributed in a clientelistic manner (question A3). This suggests that either the wording of this question was less clear than others, or that experts lacked knowledge to address it. A third observation is that there is considerable variation between districts in terms of intercoder agreement. In general, in the districts where clientelism is considered to be pervasive, such as Kupang, Palangka Raya, or Medan, such agreement is rather high. Yet in districts with the lowest CPI scores, such as Surabaya, Semarang, or Batang, expert assessments show much lower levels of agreement.

This strong correlation between CPI scores and Rwg(j) (R = 0.621) deserves further reflection. It might be due to two reasons. Firstly, it suggests that at moderate levels of clientelism these assessments are more difficult to make, compared to areas where clientelism is intense (or absent, but such districts are not found in Indonesia). When asked to estimate the proportion of, for example, contracts, jobs, or social assistance to be awarded clientelistically, it is likely more difficult for experts to indicate a percentage range when they consider clientelism to be neither absent nor pervasive. In contrast, in areas where clientelism is pervasive, the experts are all likely to converge on the highest answer category. A second reason might be that a changing situation in terms of clientelism in, particularly, Java, led to lower levels of agreement. As reform measures such as bureaucratic reforms and stricter budgeting have been enacted most extensively in these areas, it might be that experts differ in the degree to which these reforms have been effective. Such a more fluid situation makes it difficult to make assessments, thus generating higher levels of expert disagreement.

Whatever the reason, the CPI scores for low-scoring districts are less reliable. These differing levels of expert agreement in relation to CPI scores pose a challenge for statistical interference, since higher degrees of measurement error of the lower-scoring districts make the results of a regression analysis less reliable. To address the impact of these varying levels of measurement error, we adopted in chapter 10 a WLS (weighted least squares) regression approach. In this approach, differing weights are assigned to the dependent variable (i.e., CPI district) on the basis of the degree of variation in expert ratings. For this weightage we employed the average within-district variance of expert responses for the seven component variables. The advantage of using this approach is that it takes differential levels of measurement error into account, thus providing a means to correct for the bias resulting from the differing levels of expert agreement. The results are not very different from the results of the more standard OLS regression approach.

TABLE C.1 CPI and component variables: Scores and degree of inter-expert agreement

DISTRICT	CPI DISTRICT		PUBLIC SERVICES (INVERSE SCALE, A1)		WELFARE (A3)		JOBS (A5)		VOTE BUYING (A6)		CONTRACTS (A8)		SOCIAL ASSISTANCE (A10)		BUSINESS LICENSE (A11)	
	CPI	RWG(J)	MEAN	RWG	MEAN	RWG	MEAN	RWG	MEAN	RWG	MEAN	RWG	MEAN	RWG	MEAN	RWG
Scale	0 to 10	0 to 1	1–5	0–1	1–5	0–1	1–6	0–1	1–6	0–1	1–6	0–1	1–6	0–1	1–5	0–1
Kota Banda Aceh	4.98	0.82	4.07	0.71	2.64	0.04	4.00	0.38	3.69	0.35	4.00	0.38	3.85	0.44	3.69	0.30
Aceh Barat	5.56	0.84	3.77	0.45	3.08	0.00	4.54	0.68	4.00	0.59	4.08	0.68	3.45	0.63	4.25	0.38
Aceh Selatan	5.89	0.83	2.57	0.45	2.57	0.03	4.31	0.58	4.00	0.42	4.14	0.58	3.33	0.42	4.85	0.60
Langkat	5.84	0.83	3.57	0.53	3.00	0.00	4.14	0.32	4.50	0.48	3.85	0.32	3.64	0.49	5.02	0.65
Kota Medan	7.10	0.91	2.79	0.16	4.07	0.47	4.64	0.60	4.86	0.64	4.15	0.60	4.31	0.81	5.29	0.86
Padang Pariaman	5.67	0.75	3.23	0.27	2.85	0.30	4.31	0.58	4.15	0.21	4.42	0.58	3.55	0.22	3.88	0.07
Kota Padang	6.15	0.77	3.92	0.42	3.08	0.00	4.85	0.78	4.20	0.48	4.42	0.78	4.18	0.46	4.94	0.30
Lampung Utara	6.69	0.88	3.67	0.58	3.45	0.10	5.08	0.66	4.25	0.43	5.08	0.66	4.42	0.66	4.85	0.47
Lampung Selatan	5.96	0.86	3.43	0.36	3.07	0.00	4.50	0.70	4.14	0.74	4.14	0.66	3.50	0.70	5.02	0.49
Kota Bandar Lampung	6.99	0.84	2.79	0.00	3.36	0.04	4.64	0.55	4.86	0.74	4.50	0.55	4.23	0.53	5.52	0.68
Kota Tangerang	5.08	0.70	3.64	0.00	3.33	0.00	4.08	0.41	3.92	0.47	3.42	0.41	2.83	0.39	3.92	0.28
Serang	6.99	0.86	3.29	0.55	4.00	0.26	4.14	0.37	5.14	0.74	4.79	0.37	4.29	0.50	5.20	0.45
DKI Jakarta	4.21	0.76	3.62	0.09	2.86	0.27	2.62	0.57	3.57	0.54	2.92	0.57	3.00	0.42	3.59	0.00
Karawang	5.96	0.85	3.23	0.09	3.38	0.24	3.77	0.36	4.77	0.65	3.77	0.36	4.08	0.80	4.27	0.41
Cianjur	5.29	0.91	3.62	0.59	2.15	0.39	4.85	0.72	3.67	0.73	3.73	0.72	3.25	0.49	4.85	0.69
Kota Bandung	4.99	0.62	3.80	0.37	3.29	0.14	3.64	0.33	3.31	0.29	3.46	0.33	3.53	0.07	4.17	0.00
Batang	5.50	0.66	3.79	0.65	3.57	0.28	4.07	0.13	5.00	0.52	3.46	0.13	3.86	0.21	3.14	0.00
Kota Surabaya	3.97	0.58	3.71	0.00	1.92	0.15	3.08	0.34	3.92	0.34	3.09	0.34	3.08	0.22	2.96	0.00
Malang	6.01	0.82	3.67	0.41	3.60	0.48	4.07	0.49	4.54	0.45	4.00	0.49	3.93	0.24	4.58	0.32
Kutai Kartanegara	7.13	0.90	3.77	0.72	3.46	0.00	5.38	0.80	5.00	0.66	5.15	0.80	4.38	0.57	5.42	0.68
Kota Palangka Raya	7.38	0.94	2.60	0.74	4.00	0.52	5.00	0.93	4.60	0.83	4.45	0.93	4.60	0.53	5.43	0.85
Kotawaringin Timur	5.46	0.81	4.46	0.86	4.31	0.52	4.08	0.22	4.33	0.35	4.17	0.22	3.33	0.48	3.40	0.00
Gunung Mas	7.86	0.92	2.64	0.45	4.14	0.10	5.43	0.86	4.71	0.61	5.36	0.86	4.92	0.74	5.20	0.78

(Continued)

TABLE C.1 (Continued)

DISTRICT	CPI DISTRICT		PUBLIC SERVICES (INVERSE SCALE, A1)		WELFARE (A3)		JOBS (A5)		VOTE BUYING (A6)		CONTRACTS (A8)		SOCIAL ASSISTANCE (A10)		BUSINESS LICENSE (A11)	
	CPI	RWG(J)	MEAN	RWG	MEAN	RWG	MEAN	RWG	MEAN	RWG	MEAN	RWG	MEAN	RWG	MEAN	RWG
Kota Makassar	7.35	0.93	3.14	0.52	4.07	0.38	5.07	0.76	4.50	0.59	4.71	0.76	5.07	0.87	5.20	0.70
Sinjai	5.80	0.90	3.42	0.86	4.00	0.32	3.92	0.47	4.25	0.68	4.00	0.47	3.44	0.22	3.95	0.65
Wajo	7.04	0.91	3.33	0.38	4.17	0.43	4.92	0.66	4.50	0.72	4.18	0.66	4.83	0.70	5.17	0.48
Kota Manado	6.98	0.91	4.21	0.49	4.00	0.34	4.93	0.66	5.08	0.69	4.86	0.66	4.71	0.61	5.11	0.72
Minahasa Selatan	6.67	0.65	3.14	0.00	3.64	0.04	4.86	0.53	4.85	0.49	4.15	0.53	4.50	0.47	4.37	0.07
Bolaang Mongondow Selatan	6.05	0.77	4.07	0.38	3.79	0.24	4.71	0.50	4.50	0.33	4.46	0.50	3.77	0.19	4.08	0.14
Kota Ambon	6.33	0.88	3.38	0.68	3.92	0.60	4.31	0.35	3.50	0.41	4.54	0.35	4.27	0.58	4.85	0.47
Kota Kupang	7.95	0.95	3.00	0.46	4.69	0.79	5.38	0.80	4.62	0.68	5.45	0.80	4.54	0.79	5.71	0.90
Mangarai Barat	7.48	0.82	2.79	0.24	3.93	0.00	5.07	0.50	4.36	0.39	5.57	0.50	4.64	0.60	5.11	0.30
Kota Jayapura	6.95	0.91	3.46	0.14	3.33	0.28	5.31	0.81	4.69	0.69	4.69	0.81	4.67	0.85	5.13	0.88
Jayawijaya	7.37	0.73	2.85	0.12	4.23	0.36	5.38	0.51	4.38	0.17	5.46	0.51	4.00	0.00	4.85	0.15
Semarang	5.32	0.75	3.15	0.57	3.38	0.15	4.33	0.29	4.23	0.53	3.08	0.29	3.08	0.00	3.60	0.24
Garut	5.65	0.84	4.00	0.11	3.62	0.33	3.92	0.23	4.00	0.75	3.85	0.23	3.83	0.64	4.65	0.42
Bulungan	6.93	0.85	2.58	0.47	3.67	0.00	4.33	0.42	5.00	0.44	3.91	0.42	4.58	0.78	5.06	0.89
Samarinda	6.26	0.83	3.14	0.43	3.43	0.00	4.79	0.78	4.29	0.66	4.18	0.78	4.08	0.60	4.21	0.36
Average	**6.23**	**0.78**	**3.41**	**0.40**	**3.50**	**0.23**	**4.49**	**0.44**	**4.37**	**0.50**	**4.27**	**0.44**	**3.99**	**0.42**	**4.59**	**0.44**

Appendix D

TABLE D.1 Clientelism Perception Index scores of surveyed districts and provinces

DISTRICT/*PROVINCE*	IN PROVINCE:	CPI
Surabaya City	East Java	3.97
Central Java		*4.02*
DKI Jakarta		*4.21*
West Java		*4.64*
Banda Aceh City	Aceh	4.98
Bandung City	West Java	4.99
Tangerang City	Banten	5.08
West Sumatra		*5.26*
Cianjur	West Java	5.29
Semarang	Central Java	5.32
East Java		*5.33*
East Kotawaringin	Central Kalimantan	5.46
Batang	Central Java	5.50
West Aceh	Aceh	5.56
Aceh		*5.63*
Garut	West Java	5.65
Padang Pariaman	West Sumatra	5.67
East Kalimantan		*5.69*
North Sulawesi		*5.70*

(Continued)

TABLE D.1 (Continued)

DISTRICT/*PROVINCE*	IN PROVINCE:	CPI
Central Kalimantan		5.78
Sinjai	South Sulawesi	5.80
Langkat	North Sumatra	5.84
South Aceh	Aceh	5.89
South Sulawesi		5.89
North Sumatra		5.91
South Lampung	Lampung	5.96
Karawang	West Java	5.96
Malang	East Java	6.01
South Bolaang Mongondow	North Sulawesi	6.05
Maluku		6.06
Padang City	West Sumatra	6.15
NTT		6.21
Lampung		6.23
Samarinda City	East Kalimantan	6.26
Ambon City	Maluku	6.33
Banten		6.52
South Minahasa	North Sulawesi	6.67
Papua		6.67
North Lampung	Lampung	6.69
Bulungan	East Kalimantan	6.93
Jayapura City	Papua	6.95
Manado City	North Sulawesi	6.98
Bandar Lampung City	Lampung	6.99
Serang City	Banten	6.99
Wajo	South Sulawesi	7.04
Medan City	North Sumatra	7.10
Kutai Kartanegara	East Kalimantan	7.13
Makassar City	South Sulawesi	7.35
Jayawijaya	Papua	7.37
Palangka Raya City	Central Kalimantan	7.38
West Manggarai	NTT	7.48
Gunung Mas	Central Kalimantan	7.86
Kupang City	NTT	7.95

Appendix E

TABLE E.1 Clientelism Perception Index and selected economic variables: Correlations

	1. CPI DISTRICT	2	3	4	5	6	7	8	9	10	11
2. Income per capita (no oil) 2010[b]	-0.428**	—									
3. Household expenditure 2013[a]	-0.133	.681**	—								
4. City[e]	-0.096	.528**	.852**	—							
5. Poverty rate 2010[a]	0.218	-.433**	-.488**	-.474**	—						
6. Av. years of schooling 2010[d]	-0.058	.540**	.846**	.892**	-.567**	—					
7. HDI 2013[a]	-0.135	.513**	.719**	.751**	-.771**	.883**	—				
8. Population 2010[a]	-0.536**	.652**	.351*	0.262	-0.32	0.184	0.2	—			
9. Industry, trade, finance sectors, share of GDPR 2010[b]	-0.405*	.422*	.405*	.528**	-.452**	.351*	.358*	.533**	—		
10. Govt. expenditure, share of GDPR 2010[c]	0.375*	-.424**	-0.301	-.410*	.551**	-.436**	-.528**	-.378*	-.587**	—	
11. Ratio jobs in industry, trade, finance / civil servants 2010[a,d]	-0.606**	.653**	.411*	.454**	-.360*	0.301	0.323	.797**	.779**	-.524**	—
12. Industry jobs, share of total 2010[a]	-0.517**	0.246	0.094	0.162	-.402*	0.071	0.131	.463**	.765**	-.508**	.729**

* = p < .05
** = p < .01
N = 38

Sources: See appendix F.

Appendix F

TABLE F.1 Variables and sources used in chapter 10

		(1)	(2)	(3)	(4)	(5)
VARIABLES	**SOURCE (YEAR)**	**N**	**MEAN**	**SD**	**MIN.**	**MAX.**
CPI	Expert survey (2014)	38	6.231	0.968	3.970	7.950
HH_Exp	Indo Dapoer (2013)	38	794,675	300,986	394,653	1.479e+06
GDPRcapnoil	BPS 2012 (2010)	38	22.72	17.34	4.560	81.81
LN_GDPRcapnoil	BPS 2012 (2010)	38	2.897	0.668	1.517	4.404
YearsSchooling	BPS 2011 (2010)	38	8.954	1.749	5.320	12.27
Poverty_Rate	Indo Dapoer (2010)	38	12.02	7.595	3.480	41.84
RelSize_ITF	BPS 2012 (2012)	38	39.46	19.91	4.440	82.35
Share_GovExp	Kememkeu (2010)	38	13.04	14.08	2.040	54.99
Population	Indo Dapoer	38	1.174e+06	1.691e+06	60,220	9.970e+06
RatioJobs_Priv Sect_CivServ	Indo Dapoer & BPS 2011 (2010)	38	16.42	16.06	0.398	68.92
ShareJobs_Ind	Indo Dapoer	38	9.851	7.497	0	32.72
RatioJobs_Ind_ CivServ	Indo Dapoer & BPS 2011 (2010)	38	3.920	5.305	0	26.35
GDP_Mining	Indo Dapoer	38	719,395	3.649e+06	0	2.258e+07
Distance to JKT	Author calculation	38	1,110	874.0	0	3,404
GDP_Mining_cap	Indo Dapoer	38	1.097	5.354	0	33.05
d_Java	Author coding	38	0.289	0.460	0	1
d_Aceh	Author coding	38	0.0789	0.273	0	1
d_Sumatra	Author coding	38	0.263	0.446	0	1
d_Kalimantan	Author coding	38	0.158	0.370	0	1
d_Papua	Author coding	38	0.0526	0.226	0	1
d_Maluku	Author coding	38	0.0263	0.162	0	1

VARIABLES	SOURCE (YEAR)	(1) N	(2) MEAN	(3) SD	(4) MIN.	(5) MAX.
d_NTT	Author coding	38	0.132	0.343	0	1
d_Sulawesi	Author coding	38	0.0789	0.273	0	1

Sources: INDO-DAPOER (Indonesia Database for Policy and Economic Research),

http://databank.worldbank.org/data/reports.aspx?source=indo~dapoer-(indonesia-database-for-policy-and-economic-research).

BPS 2011. Kabupaten / Kota Dalam Angka, several volumes (Jakarta: Badan Pusat Statistik).

BPS 2012. Tinjauan Regional Berdasarkan PDRB Kabupaten/Kota 2009–2012 (Jakarta: BPS).

Kemenkeu 2010. Data APBD (district government budget data), http://www.djpk.depkeu.go.id/?page_id=316.

Notes

1. INDONESIA'S PATRONAGE DEMOCRACY

1. Throughout this volume we use the exchange rate of April 2014, when Indonesia held its most recent election, and when one US dollar was equivalent to 11,300 rupiah.

2. See for example Held's famous *Models of Democracy* (1994). His various models all involve more or less programmatic forms of accountability between politicians and groups of voters. Clientelistic modes of accountability are not discussed.

3. The Gini coefficient of Argentina is 42.3, while India's is 33.6, and Indonesia's 35.6. See http://data.worldbank.org/data-catalog/all-the-ginis.

2. CAPTURING VARIETIES OF CLIENTELISM

1. We draw particular inspiration from Hutchcroft 2014 and would like to acknowledge our intellectual debt to him as well as to Allen Hicken and Meredith Weiss, who are involved with Aspinall in a project on clientelism in Southeast Asia.

2. Examples of such handbooks are Goodin and Klingemann 1998, Goodin and Tilly 2006, and Ishiyama and Breuning 2011. In contrast, the *Oxford Handbook of Comparative Politics* (Boix and Stokes 2007) contains an excellent contribution by Stokes (2007) on political clientelism. The focus of this piece, however, is on defining the phenomenon and providing a general account of the causes and the strategic choices driving it. The article does not provide a framework for comparing different forms of clientelism across countries.

3. We adopt a slightly different definition from that of Kitschelt and Wilkinson, whose definition focuses on a citizen's vote. Other forms of electoral support are also objects of clientelistic exchange.

4. The term "patronage" has widely differing uses. As noted, some scholars treat the term as synonymous with clientelism: e.g., Kitschelt and Wilkinson 2007, 7; Piattoni 2001. Fukuyama (2014) reserves the word for personal patron-client exchange relationships and sees clientelism as a practice of "massified patronage" that politicians adopt in the context of mass democracies. Stokes et al. (2013, 14) use patronage to refer to "intra-party flows of benefits," while others use it yet more narrowly to describe the awarding of public service jobs to supporters (e.g., Grindle 2013).

5. Our definition of patronage democracy differs from that used by Kanchan Chandra, who is credited with coining the term. She defines a patronage democracy as "a democracy in which the state monopolizes access to jobs and services, *and* in which elected officials have discretion in the implementation of laws allocating the jobs and services at the disposal of the state" (Chandra 2004, 6). We feel that this definition refers to *causes* of the phenomenon (state dominance in the economy and discretionary control over the distribution of state benefits) rather than the phenomenon itself, which is the predominance of clientelistic strategies as a means to mobilize electoral support.

6. Stokes (2005) uses the term "perverse accountability" to describe the capacity of politicians to punish voters for their voting behavior by withholding access to state resources. We would suggest that the capacity of politicians to do this will depend on the degree to which control over distribution of state resources is dispersed or centralized.

5. SUCCESS TEAMS AND VOTE BUYING

1. Indeed, one of the common problems with vote buying in Indonesia is that informed persons, including practitioners, often exaggerate its effectiveness. For example, in the expert survey, 66 percent of respondents said that they believed vote buying was either very or extremely effective in DPRD elections, meaning either that a majority of voters would sell their votes to the highest bidder or that it was "possible to buy an election." Figures such as those from Central Java cited above, showing that a large proportion of payments are wasted, do not support such estimates.

2. We thank David Henley for this point.

6. SOCIAL NETWORKS AND CLUB GOODS

1. We should note that our usage differs somewhat from the standard interpretation in wider political-economy literature, which sees club goods as those goods that are "excludable" but "non-rivalrous" in consumption (e.g., Cornes and Sandler 1996). We include in our definition goods such as carpets, tents, and fertilizer, which might normally be considered standard private goods, precisely because they are often distributed through, and intended for consumption by, clubs.

2. And vice versa: in fact, a more common argument in the literature on political clientelism is that ethnic heterogeneity boosts clientelism by undermining trust in unbiased implementation of government policies, such that "politicians simply cannot make credible commitments to universalism in an ethnically complex polity" (Kitschelt and Wilkinson 2007, 33).

3. Studies of Indonesian provinces provide examples of the instrumental use of ethnicity and its connection to patronage politics, especially at times of violent conflict: see van Klinken 2007; Davidson 2008; C. Wilson 2013.

7. GOVERNANCE AND PUBLIC SPENDING

1. Using econometric methods, Auerbach showed not only that party networks pervade India's slums, but also that the presence of party representatives is positively related to the quality of public services: "Party networks significantly influence the ability of poor urban communities to secure development from the state. In slums with dense party networks, competition among party workers generates a degree of accountability in local patron-client hierarchies that encourages development" (Auerbach 2016, 112).

2. For an illustration of the importance of nurturing clientelistic ties in order to deal with insecurity and risk see Roanne van Voorst's study of Jakarta's urban poor faced with recurrent flooding (van Voorst 2016).

3. The survey question was: "Are there people in your surrounding whose opinions or advice you follow on political matters?" (Muhtadi 2015).

4. See http://www.lokniti.org/nes2009-finding_of_the_survey.pdf (accessed June 4, 2015).

5. In fact, even the regular development planning process is supposed to involve popular participation. Through a process known as Development Planning Consultations, or Musrenbang, district governments are supposed to involve local communities in order to ascertain their needs and decide on development priorities. However, close studies of these processes suggest that community involvement in often token and that the budgeting process is subject to capture for patronage purposes, with politicians seeking to use it to reward political supporters with projects. See Djani, Wilson, and Masduki 2009.

6. Such observations led to debate in policy circles about how to curtail the misuse of *bansos* funds. See for example *Kompas* 2013.

7. These figures are author calculations based on budget reports of local governments compiled by the Ministry of Finance, available at http://www.kemenkeu.go.id/Page/data-keuangan-daerah.

8. Often legislators direct grants to fictitious organizations, or beneficiary groups receive a fraction of the payment that is their due. See for example a special edition of the tabloid *Modus Aceh* (vol. 10, no. 47, March 25–31, 2013), titled "Konspirasi Bertopeng Dana Aspirasi" (A conspiracy wearing the Aspiration Fund mask).

8. BUREAUCRATS AND THE POWER OF OFFICE

1. We need to treat these perceptions of experts with some caution—some distortion, for example, might be due to the fact that non-jobbed civil servants prefer to explain their own downfall as being the result of politicking rather than their own misconduct or incompetence. Their stories might in turn influence wider perceptions regarding the incidence of political appointments.

2. In contrast, Mietzner (2010, 179) had found that 22 percent of nominees in his sample were party leaders and members of parliament.

3. Our dataset of the results of the 2015 *pilkada* is available at http://www.kitlv.nl/democracy-for-sale/.

4. We could not find studies detailing the professional background of Indian chief ministers; available studies focus on members of legislative assemblies (which includes chief ministers).

5. These figures were compiled from Litbang Kompas (2015) and online sources. See online data file at http://www.kitlv.nl/democracy-for-sale/.

6. Our database of election results is available at http://www.kitlv.nl/democracy-for-sale/. These data were collected from https://pilkada2015.kpu.go.id. On December 9, 2015, elections were held in 269 districts and provinces; we were able to obtain election results for only 223 cases.

7. See data file at http://www.kitlv.nl/democracy-for-sale/.

9. CAMPAIGN FINANCING, BUSINESS, AND THE PUBLIC SPHERE

1. For other accounts pointing to subnational political variation see Djani 2013; Mustafa 2017; Patunru, McCulloch, and Luebke 2012; Rosser and Wilson 2012; Tomsa 2015.

2. For example, in 2010 per capita income in Jakarta was 82.15 million rupiah (73.94 million in Surabaya), while residents of West Manggarai (East Nusa Tenggara) earned on average 4.56 million rupiah, and residents of Jayawijaya (Papua) made 5.66 million. See BPS 2012.

3. Powerpoint presentation by Arie Rompas, director of Walhi Central Kalimantan, July 12, 2015.

4. "Ratu Atut's Banten Projects Worth $100m since 2011: ICW," *Jakarta Globe*, October 16, 2013, http://jakartaglobe.beritasatu.com/news/ratu-atuts-banten-projects-worth-100m-since-2011-icw/.

5. See Kemitraan's "Indonesia Governance Index," where Jakarta, East Java, and Bali top the chart (after Yogyakarta), at http://www.kemitraan.or.id/igi/ (accessed January 25, 2016).

10. EXPLAINING VARIATION IN INDONESIA'S PATRONAGE DEMOCRACY

1. A common measure of the strength of an index variable is Cronbach's Alpha. For the district-level index, Cronbach's Alpha is .878; for the provincial index it is .886.

2. As already mentioned, the responses of the surveyed experts varied more in districts with lower CPI scores. This unequal variance in inter-expert agreement prevented

us from adopting the standard ordinary least squares (OLS) regression approach, because this approach assumes the variance to be constant. To correct for the potential bias in the results, we adopted a weighted least squares (WLS) approach in which the dependent variable (CPI) is given differential weights across districts. More specifically, the regression analysis was computed by giving different analytical weights to the CPI scores, proportional to the degree of inter-expert agreement (which we measure by taking the inverse of the squared standard deviations of the average district-level variance of expert assessments for all seven component variables). In this way the observations with smaller variance carry larger weight in the regression. The results of the more standard OLS regression are largely similar, with the main difference being that poverty does not turn out to be significant in the bivariate analysis. See Berenschot 2018.

3. The exception is in the model that controls for provincial fixed effects, where, contrary to what one would expect, years of schooling suddenly turns out to be positively related to CPI.

4. On the other hand, it should be noted that Muhtadi's (2018, 87) analysis of Indonesian survey data suggests that poverty and lower education do not make voters significantly more likely to be targeted by vote buying, while Javanese ethnicity does. Higher poverty and lower education levels, however, make voters more likely to view vote buying as acceptable. He notes that candidates explain the effect of Javanese ethnicity by reaching for culturally essentialist arguments: "The dominant discourse among politicians is that Javanese voters, especially those who live in rural settings where public goods are still limited, are more likely to reward providers of material benefits than are other voters" (Muhtadi 2018, 94).

CONCLUSION

1. The connection between inequality and clientelism has been convincingly documented by Jong-Sung You (2016) for the cases of Korea, Taiwan, and the Philippines.

2. Though we acknowledge that other works before this one have analyzed such interactions as central: see, for example, Aspinall and van Klinken 2011; Aspinall and Sukmajati 2016; Buehler and Tan 2007; van Klinken 2014; van Klinken and Barker 2009; Simandjuntak 2012.

APPENDIX C

1. Rwg is calculated as follows: Rwg = 1 – (variance / null distribution). The null distribution is a function of the number of answer categories. For a variable with six answer categories, the null distribution is 2.91. See LeBreton and Senter 2008.

References

Afrizal. 2013. "Oil Palm Plantations, Customary Rights, and Local Protests: A West Sumatran Case Study." In *Land for the People: The State and Agrarian Conflict in Indonesia*, edited by Anton Lucas and Carol Warren, 149–183. Athens: Ohio University Press.

Alamsyah. 2016. "Musi Banyuasin, South Sumatra: Nine Steps to Victory." In Aspinall and Sukmajati, *Electoral Dynamics in Indonesia*, 102–119.

Allen, Nathan Wallace. 2012. "Diversity, Patronage and Parties: Parties and Party System Change in Indonesia." PhD diss., University of British Columbia.

Amirullah. 2015. "Ekspansi Industri Sawit di Kalteng Tak Terkendali." *Tempo*, January 28, 2015. https://nasional.tempo.co/read/638155/ekspansi-industri-sawit-di-kalteng-tak-terkendali.

Anderson, Benedict R. O'G. 1983. "Old State, New Society: Indonesia's New Order in Comparative Historical Perspective." *Journal of Asian Studies* 42 (3): 477–496.

Antlöv, Hans. 1994. *Village Leaders and the New Order*: Richmond, UK: Curzon.

——. 1995. *Exemplary Centre, Administrative Periphery: Rural Leadership and the New Order in Java*. Richmond, UK: Curzon.

Arghiros, Daniel. 2001. *Democracy, Development and Decentralization in Provincial Thailand*. Richmond, UK: Curzon.

Aspinall, Edward. 2005. *Opposing Suharto: Compromise, Resistance, and Regime Change in Indonesia*. Palo Alto, CA: Stanford University Press.

——. 2011. "Democratization and Ethnic Politics in Indonesia: Nine Theses." *Journal of East Asian Studies* 11 (2): 289–301.

——. 2013a. "A Nation in Fragments: Patronage and Neoliberalism in Contemporary Indonesia." *Critical Asian Studies* 45 (1): 27–54.

——. 2013b. "Popular Agency and Interests in Indonesia's Democratic Transition and Consolidation." *Indonesia* 96:101–121.

——. 2014a. "Health Care and Democratization in Indonesia." *Democratization* 21 (5): 803–823.

——. 2014b. "Indonesia's 2014 Elections: Parliament and Patronage." *Journal of Democracy* 25 (4): 96–110.

——. 2014c. "When Brokers Betray: Clientelism, Social Networks, and Electoral Politics in Indonesia." *Critical Asian Studies* 46 (4): 545–570.

——. 2015. "Oligarchic Populism: Prabowo Subianto's Challenge to Indonesian Democracy." *Indonesia* 99:1–28.

Aspinall, Edward, and Muhammad Uhaib As'ad. 2015. "The Patronage Patchwork." *Bijdragen tot de Taal-, Land-en Volkenkunde* 171 (2–3): 165–195.

——. 2016. "Understanding Family Politics: Successes and Failures of Political Dynasties in Regional Indonesia." *South East Asia Research* 24 (3): 420–435.

Aspinall, Edward, Michael Davidson, Allen Hicken, and Meredith Weiss. 2015. "Inducement or Entry Ticket? Broker Networks and Vote Buying in Indonesia." Paper presented at the annual meeting of the American Political Science Association, September 3–6, San Francisco.

Aspinall, Edward, and Greg Fealy, eds. 2003. *Local Power and Politics in Indonesia*. Singapore: Institute of Southeast Asian Studies.

Aspinall, Edward, and Noor Rohman. 2017. "Village Head Elections in Java: Money Politics and Brokerage in the Remaking of Indonesia's Rural Elite." *Journal of Southeast Asian Studies* 48 (1): 31–52.

Aspinall, Edward, Noor Rohman, Ahmad Zainul Hamdi, Rubaidi, and Zusiana Elly Triantini. 2017. "Vote Buying in Indonesia: Candidate Strategies, Market Logic and Effectiveness." *Journal of East Asian Studies* 17 (1): 1–27

Aspinall, Edward, and Mada Sukmajati, eds. 2016. *Electoral Dynamics in Indonesia: Money Politics, Patronage and Clientelism at the Grassroots*. Singapore: NUS Press.

Aspinall, Edward, and Gerry van Klinken, eds. 2011. *The State and Illegality in Indonesia*. Leiden: KITLV Press.

Auerbach, Adam Michael. 2016. "Clients and Communities." *World Politics* 68 (1): 111–148.

Auyero, Javier. 2001. *Poor People's Politics: Peronist Survival Networks and the Legacy of Evita*. Durham, NC: Duke University Press.

Auyero, Javier, and Claudio Benzecry. 2017. "The Practical Logic of Political Domination: Conceptualizing the Clientelist Habitus." *Sociological Theory* 35 (3): 179–199.

Aziza, Kurnia Sari. 2015. "Ahok: Anggaran Dinas Olahraga dan Dinas Pendidikan Paling Banyak yang Aneh-aneh." *Kompas*, May 12. http://properti.kompas.com/read/2015/05/12/21290751/Ahok.Anggaran.Dinas.Olahraga.dan.Dinas.Pendidikan.Paling.Banyak.yang.Aneh-aneh.

Baker, Jacqui. 2013. "The 'Parman' Economy: Post-Authoritarian Shifts in Indonesia's Illicit Security Economy." *Indonesia* 96:123–150.

Banfield, Edward C., and James Quinn Wilson. 1963. *City Politics*. Cambridge, MA: Harvard University Press and MIT Press.

Bayart, Jean-François. 1993. *The State in Africa: The Politics of the Belly*. New York: Longman.

Beck, Linda J. 2008. *Brokering Democracy in Africa: The Rise of Clientelist Democracy in Senegal*. New York: Palgrave Macmillan.

Behrend, Jacqueline. 2011. "The Unevenness of Democracy at the Subnational Level: Provincial Closed Games in Argentina." *Latin American Research Review* 46 (1): 150–176.

Berenschot, Ward. 2010. "Everyday Mediation: The Politics of Public Service Delivery in Gujarat, India." *Development and Change* 41 (5): 883–905.

——. 2011a. "Political Fixers and the Rise of Hindu Nationalism in Gujarat, India: Lubricating a Patronage Democracy." *Journal of South Asian Studies* 34 (3): 382–401.

——. 2011b. *Riot Politics: India's Hindu-Muslim Violence and the Indian State*. London: Hurst.

——. 2014. "Political Fixers and India's Patronage Democracy." In *Patronage as Politics in South Asia*, edited by Anastasia Piliavsky, 196–217. Cambridge: Cambridge University Press.

——. 2015a. "Clientelism, Trust Networks, and India's Identity Politics: Conveying Closeness in Gujarat." *Critical Asian Studies* 47 (1): 24–43.

——. 2015b. "Misdirecting Elections." *Jakarta Post*, October 1. http://www.thejakartapost.com/news/2014/10/01/misdirecting-elections.html.

——. 2018. "The Political Economy of Clientelism: A Comparative Study of Indonesia's Patronage Democracy." *Comparative Political Studies* 51: 1163–1193. doi: https://doi.org/10.1177/0010414018758756.

Berenschot, Ward, Retna Hanani, and Prio Sambodho. 2018. "Brokers and Citizenship: Access to Healthcare in Indonesia." *Journal of Citizenship Studies* 22 (2): 129–144.

Berenschot, Ward, Henk Schulte Nordholt, and Laurens Bakker, eds. 2016. *Citizenship and Democratization in Southeast Asia.* Leiden: Brill.

Berenschot, Ward, and Gerry van Klinken. 2018. "Informality and Citizenship: The Everyday State in Indonesia." *Journal of Citizenship Studies* 22 (2): 95–111.

Bertrand, Jacques. 2004. *Nationalism and Ethnic Conflict in Indonesia.* Cambridge: Cambridge University Press.

Bickers, Kenneth N., and Robert M. Stein. 1996. "The Electoral Dynamics of the Federal Pork Barrel." *American Journal of Political Science* 40 (4): 1300–1326.

Biemann, Torsten, Michael S. Cole, and Sven Voelpel. 2012. "Within-Group Agreement: On the Use (and Misuse) of Rwg and Rwg(j) in Leadership Research and Some Best Practice Guidelines." *Leadership Quarterly* 23 (1): 66–80.

Björkman, Lisa. 2014. "'You Can't Buy a Vote': Meanings of Money in a Mumbai Election." *American Ethnologist* 41 (4): 617–634.

Blunt, Peter, Mark Turner, and Henrik Lindroth. 2012a. "Patronage, Service Delivery, and Social Justice in Indonesia." *International Journal of Public Administration* 35 (3): 214–220.

Blunt, Peter, Mark Turner, and Henrik Lindroth. 2012b. "Patronage's Progress in Post-Soeharto Indonesia." *Public Administration and Development* 32 (1): 64–81.

Boix, Carles, and Susan Carol Stokes, eds. 2007. *The Oxford Handbook of Comparative Politics.* Oxford: Oxford University Press.

Booth, David. 2011. "Introduction: Working with the Grain? The Africa Power and Politics Programme." *IDS Bulletin* 42 (2): 1–10.

Booth, David, and Diana Cammack. 2013. *Governance for Development in Africa: Solving Collective Action Problems.* London: Zed Books.

BPS (Badan Pusat Statistik). 2011. Kabupaten/Kota Dalam Angka, several volumes. Jakarta: Badan Pusat Statistik.

——. 2012. Tinjauan Regional Berdasarkan PDRB Kabupaten/Kota 2009–2012. Jakarta: Badan Pusat Statistik.

Brusco, Valeria, Marcelo Nazareno, and Susan C. Stokes. 2004. "Vote Buying in Argentina." *Latin American Research Review* 39 (2): 66–88.

Buehler, Michael. 2009a. "The Rising Importance of Personal Networks in Indonesian Local Politics: An Analysis of the District Government Head Elections in South Sulawesi in 2005." In *Deepening Democracy in Indonesia*, edited by Maribeth Erb and Priyambudi Sulistiyanto, 101–124. Singapore: Institute of Southeast Asian Studies.

——. 2009b. "Suicide and Progress in Modern Nusantara." *Inside Indonesia* 97. http://www.insideindonesia.org/suicide-and-progress-in-modern-nusantara.

——. 2010. "Decentralization and Local Democracy in Indonesia: The Marginalisation of the Public Sphere." In *Problems of Democratisation in Indonesia: Elections, Institutions and Society*, edited by Edward Aspinall and Marcus Mietzner, 267–286. Singapore: Institute of Southeast Asian Studies.

——. 2011. "Indonesia's Law on Public Services: Changing State-Society Relations or Continuing Politics as Usual?" *Bulletin of Indonesian Economic Studies* 47 (1): 65–86.

——. 2013. "Married with Children." *Inside Indonesia* 112. http://www.insideindonesia.org/married-with-children.

Buehler, Michael, and Paige Tan. 2007. "Party-Candidate Relationships in Indonesian Local Politics: A Case Study of the 2005 Regional Elections in Gowa, South Sulawesi Province." *Indonesia* 84: 41–69.

Burgess, Robin, Matthew Hansen, Benjamin A. Olken, Peter Potapov, and Stefanie Sieber. 2012. "The Political Economy of Deforestation in the Tropics." *Quarterly Journal of Economics* 127 (4): 1707–1754.

Bustikova, Lenka, and Cristina Corduneanu-Huci. 2011. "Clientelism, State Capacity and Economic Development: A Cross-National Study." Paper presented at the annual meeting of the American Political Science Association, 2009, Toronto (revised and presented at MPSA 2011).

Butt, Simon, and Tim Lindsey. 2011. "Judicial Mafia: The Courts and State Illegality in Indonesia." In Aspinall and van Klinken, *State and Illegality in Indonesia*, 189–213.

Callahan, William A., and Duncan McCargo. 1996. "Vote-Buying in Thailand's Northeast: The July 1995 General Elections." *Asian Survey* 36 (4): 376–392.

Calvo, Ernesto, and Maria Victoria Murillo. 2004. "Who Delivers? Partisan Clients in the Argentine Electoral Market." *American Journal of Political Science* 48 (4): 742–757.

Caraway, Teri L., Michele Ford, and Hari Nugroho. 2015. "Translating Membership into Power at the Ballot Box? Trade Union Candidates and Worker Voting Patterns in Indonesia's National Elections." *Democratization* 22 (7): 1296–1316.

Cederroth, Sven. 2004. "Traditional Power and Party Politics in North Lombok, 1965–1999." In *Elections in Indonesia: The New Order and Beyond*, edited by Hans Antlöv and Sven Cederroth, 77–110. London: RoutledgeCurzon.

Centre for the Future State. 2010. *An Upside View of Governance*. Brighton, UK: Institute for Development Studies.

Chabal, Patrick, and Jean Pascal Daloz. 1999. *Africa Works: Disorder as Political Instrument*. Bloomington: Indiana University Press.

Chandra, Kanchan. 2004. *Why Ethnic Parties Succeed: Patronage and Ethnic Head Counts in India*. Cambridge: Cambridge University Press.

Chattharakul, Anyarat. 2010. "Thai Electoral Campaigning: Vote-Canvassing Networks and Hybrid Voting." *Journal of Current Southeast Asian Affairs* 29 (4): 67–95.

Choi, Ina, and Yuki Fukuoka. 2015. "Co-opting Good Governance Reform: The Rise of a Not-so-Reformist Leader in Kebumen, Central Java." *Asian Journal of Political Science* 23 (1): 83–101.

Chubb, Judith. 1981. "The Social Bases of an Urban Political Machine: The Christian Democratic Party in Palermo." In *Political Clientelism, Patronage and Development*, edited by S. N. Eisenstadt and René Lemarchand, 57–90. London: Sage.

Clark, Samuel. 2013. "Enforcing Corruption Laws: The Political Economy of Subnational Prosecutions in Indonesia." PhD diss., University of Oxford.

Colchester, Marcus, and Sophie Chao. 2013. *Conflict or Consent? The Oil Palm Sector at a Crossroads*. London: Forest Peoples Programme.

Collins, Kathleen. 2006. *Clan Politics and Regime Transition in Central Asia*. Cambridge: Cambridge University Press.

Cornes, Richard, and Todd Sandler. 1996. *The Theory of Externalities, Public Goods, and Club Goods*. Cambridge: Cambridge University Press.

Cox, Gary W. 2009. "Swing Voters, Core Voters, and Distributive Politics." In *Political Representation*, edited by Ian Shapiro, Susan Stokes, Elisabeth Wood, and Alexander Kirshner, 342–357. Cambridge: Cambridge University Press.

Crouch, Harold. 1979. "Patrimonialism and Military Rule in Indonesia." *World Politics* 31 (4): 571–587.

Davidson, Jamie. 2008. *From Rebellion to Riots: Collective Violence on Indonesian Borneo*. Madison: University of Wisconsin Press.

Davidson, Jamie, and David Henley, eds. 2007. *The Revival of Tradition in Indonesian Politics: The Deployment of Adat from Colonialism to Indigenism*. London: Routledge.

Day, Tony. 2002. *Fluid Iron: State Formation in Southeast Asia*. Honolulu: University of Hawai'i Press.

De Luca, Miguel. 2008. "Political Recruitment and Candidate Selection in Argentina: Presidents and Governors, 1983 to 2006." In *Pathways to Power: Political Recruitment and Candidate Selection in Latin America*, edited by Peter M. Siavelis and Scott Morgenstern, 189–217. University Park: Pennsylvania State University Press.

Dewi, Sita W., S. L. Hajanto, and Olivia D. Purba. 2016. "Central and South Jakarta: Social Welfare and Constituency Service in the Metropolis." In Aspinall and Sukmajati, *Electoral Dynamics in Indonesia*, 167–183.

De Wit, Joop. 2016. *Urban Poverty, Local Governance and Everyday Politics in Mumbai*. London: Routledge.

Dixit, Avinash, and John Londregan. 1996. "The Determinants of Success of Special Interests in Redistributive Politics." *Journal of Politics* 58 (4): 1132–1155.

Djani, Luky. 2013. "Reform Movements and Local Politics in Indonesia." PhD diss., Murdoch University.

Djani, Luky, Ian Douglas Wilson, and Teten Masduki. 2009. "Governing Favors: An Investigation of Accountability Mechanisms in Local Government Budget Allocation in Indonesia." *AIGRP Policy Brief* 8. Canberra.

Dwicaksono, Adenantera, Ari Nurman, and Panji Yudha Prasetya. 2012. *JAMKESMAS and District Health Care Insurance Schemes: Assessment Reports from 8 Districts/ Municipalities and 2 Provinces*. Jakarta: Perkumpulan Initiatif.

EIA (Environmental Investigation Agency). 2014. *Permitting Crime: How Palm Oil Expansion Drives Illegal Logging in Indonesia*. London: EIA.

Eisenstadt, Shmuel N., and Louis Roniger. 1980. "Patron-Client Relations as a Model of Structuring Social Exchange." *Comparative Studies in Society and History* 22 (1): 42–77.

Fealy, Greg. 1998. "Ulama and Politics in Indonesia: A History of Nahdlatul Ulama, 1952–1967." PhD diss., Monash University.

——. 2015. "Politics and Principle at the NU Congress." *Jakarta Post*, August 8.

Fealy, Greg, and Greg Barton, eds. 1996. *Nahdlatul Ulama, Traditional Islam and Modernity in Indonesia*. Clayton, Australia: Monash Asia Institute.

Feith, Herbert. 1962. *The Decline of Constitutional Democracy in Indonesia*. Ithaca, NY: Cornell University Press.

Finan, Frederico, and Laura Schechter. 2012. "Vote-Buying and Reciprocity." *Econometrica* 80 (2): 863–881.

Firdaus, Edwin. 2014. "2 Pengusaha Kalimantan Akui Pinjamkan 'Uang Suap' untuk Akil." *Tribunnews*, February 6. http://www.tribunnews.com/nasional/ 2014/02/06/2-pengusaha-kalimantan-akui-pinjamkan-uang-suap-untuk-akil.

Ford, Michele, and Thomas B. Pepinsky, eds. 2014. *Beyond Oligarchy: Wealth, Power, and Contemporary Indonesian Politics*. Ithaca, NY: Southeast Asia Program Publications.

Fossati, Diego. 2017. "A Tale of Three Cities: Electoral Accountability in Indonesian Local Politics." *Journal of Contemporary Asia* 48 (1): 23–49. https://doi.org/10.10 80/00472336.2017.1376345.

Fox, Colm. 2014. "Appealing to the Masses: Understanding Ethnic Politics and Elections in Indonesia." PhD diss., George Washington University.

Fukuoka, Yuki, and Luky Djani. 2016. "Revisiting the Rise of Jokowi: The Triumph of Reformasi or an Oligarchic Adaptation of Post-clientelist Initiatives?" *South East Asia Research* 24 (2): 204–221.

Fukuyama, Francis. 1995. *Trust: The Social Virtues and the Creation of Prosperity.* New York: Free Press.

——. 2011. *The Origins of Political Order: From Prehuman Times to the French Revolution.* New York: Farrar, Straus and Giroux.

——. 2014. *Political Order and Political Decay: From the Industrial Revolution to the Globalization of Democracy.* New York: Farrar, Straus and Giroux.

Fuller, Chris J., and John Harriss. 2001. "For an Anthropology of the Modern Indian State." In *The Everyday State and Society in Modern India*, edited by Chris J. Fuller and Véronique Bénéï, 1–30. London: Hurst.

Gans-Morse, Jordan, Sebastián Mazzuca, and Simeon Nichter. 2014. "Varieties of Clientelism: Machine Politics during Elections." *American Journal of Political Science* 58 (2): 415–432.

Gay, Robert. 1998. "Rethinking Clientelism: Demands, Discourses and Practices in Contemporary Brazil." *European Review of Latin American and Caribbean Studies* (65): 7–24.

Gecko Project. 2017. "The Making of a Palm Fiefdom." https://thegeckoproject.org/the-making-of-a-palm-oil-fiefdom-7e1014e8c342.

——. 2018. "Ghosts Is the Machine." https://thegeckoproject.org/ghosts-in-the-machine-4acb5c5236cc.

Geertz, Clifford. 1959. "The Javanese Village." In *Local, Ethnic, and National Loyalties in Village Indonesia*, edited by G. William Skinner, 34–51. New Haven, CT: Yale University Press.

Gellert, Paul K., and Andiko. 2015. "The Quest for Legal Certainty and the Reorganization of Power: Struggles over Forest Law, Permits, and Rights in Indonesia." *Journal of Asian Studies* 74 (3): 639–666.

Gervasoni, Carlos. 2010. "A Rentier Theory of Subnational Regimes: Fiscal Federalism, Democracy, and Authoritarianism in the Argentine Provinces." *World Politics* 62 (2): 302–340.

Gibson, Christopher, and Michael Woolcock. 2008. "Empowerment, Deliberative Development, and Local-Level Politics in Indonesia: Participatory Projects as a Source of Countervailing Power." *Studies in Comparative International Development* 43 (2): 151–180.

Gibson, Edward L. 2005. "Boundary Control: Subnational Authoritarianism in Democratic Countries." *World Politics* 58 (1): 101–132.

Golden, Miriam A. 2003. "Electoral Connections: The Effects of the Personal Vote on Political Patronage, Bureaucracy and Legislation in Postwar Italy." *British Journal of Political Science* 33 (2): 189–212.

Goodin, Robert E., and Hans-Dieter Klingemann, eds. 1998. *A New Handbook of Political Science.* Oxford: Oxford University Press.

Goodin, Robert E., and Charles Tilly, eds. 2006. *The Oxford Handbook of Contextual Political Analysis.* Oxford: Oxford University Press.

Grindle, Merilee S. 2013. *Jobs for the Boys: Patronage and the State in Comparative Perspective.* Cambridge, MA: Harvard University Press.

Guggenheim, Scott. 2006. "Crises and Contradictions: Understanding the Origins of a Community Development Project in Indonesia." In *The Search for Empowerment: Social Capital as Idea and Practice at the World Bank*, edited by Anthony Bebbington, Michael Woolcock, Scott Guggenheim, and Elizabeth A. Olson, 111–144. Bloomfield, CT: Kumarian.

Guinness, Patrick. 2009. *Kampung, Islam and State in Urban Java*. Singapore: NUS Press.

Hadiz, Vedi R. 2004. "Indonesian Local Party Politics: A Site of Resistance to Neoliberal Reform." *Critical Asian Studies* 36 (4): 615–636.

——. 2010. *Localising Power in Post-authoritarian Indonesia: A Southeast Asia Perspective*. Palo Alto, CA: Stanford University Press.

Hadiz, Vedi R., and Richard Robison. 2013. "The Political Economy of Oligarchy and the Reorganization of Power in Indonesia." *Indonesia* 96:35–57.

Hale, Henry E. 2011. "Formal Constitutions in Informal Politics: Institutions and Democratization in Post-Soviet Eurasia." *World Politics* 63 (4): 581–617.

Hamdi, Ahmad Zainul. 2016. "Madiun, East Java: Brokers in Territorial, Social Network and Vote Buying Strategies." In Aspinall and Sukmajati, *Electoral Dynamics in Indonesia*, 279–299.

Hamid, Abdul, and Gabriel Facal. 2013. "Nationalism, Islam, and Political Influence: The Ethics of the Enterprises in Banten (Indonesia)." *Moussons* 21:51–64.

Hanani, Retna. 2016. "Performing Care: Rights Claiming and Urban Poor Access to Health Care in Jakarta." Paper presented at the KITLV-UGM conference "From Clients to Citizens? Citizenship in Democratising Indonesia," at Universitas Gadjah Mada, December 8–10.

Hansen, Thomas Blom. 2005. "Sovereigns beyond the State: On Legality and Public Authority in India." In *Religion, Violence and Political Mobilisation in South Asia*, edited by Ravinder Kaur, 109–144. New Delhi: Sage.

Hanusch, Marek, and Philip Keefer. 2013. "Promises, Promises: Vote-Buying and the Electoral Mobilization Strategies of Non-credible Politicians." World Bank Policy Research Working Paper 6653.

Harimurti, Pandu, Eko Pambudi, Anna Pigazzini, and Ajay Tandon. 2013. *The Nuts and Bolts of Jamkesmas, Indonesia's Government-Financed Health Coverage Program*. Washington, DC: World Bank.

Hart, Gillian Patricia. 1986. *Power, Labor, and Livelihood: Processes of Change in Rural Java*. Berkeley: University of California Press.

Haryanto. 2017. "Adaptation and Continuities in Clientelism in a Fishing Community in Takalar, South Sulawesi." *Contemporary Southeast Asia* 39 (3): 511–531.

Hastuti, Sudarno Sumarto, and Asep Suryahadi. 2007. *The Effectiveness of the Raskin Program*. Jakarta: SMERU Institute.

Held, David. 1994. *Models of Democracy*. London: Polity.

Helmke, Gretchen, and Steven Levitsky. 2004. "Informal Institutions and Comparative Politics: A Research Agenda." *Perspectives on Politics* 2 (4): 725–740.

Hicken, Allen. 2007. "How Do Rules and Institutions Encourage Vote Buying?" In *Elections for Sale: The Causes and Consequences of Vote Buying*, edited by Frederic C. Schaffer, 47–60. Boulder, CO: Lynne Reinner.

——. 2009. *Building Party Systems in Developing Democracies*. Cambridge: Cambridge University Press.

——. 2011. "Clientelism." *Annual Review of Political Science* 14 (1): 289–310.

Hicken, Allen, Edward Aspinall, and Meredith Weiss, eds. Forthcoming. *Electoral Dynamics in the Philippines. Machines and Money Politics at the Grassroots*. Singapore: NUS Press.

Hickey, Sam. 2012. "Turning Governance Thinking Upside-Down? Insights from 'The Politics of What Works.'" *Third World Quarterly* 33 (7): 1231–1247.

Hidayat, Bagja. 2014. "Fixing Court Verdicts." *Tempo*, January 28. https://magz.tempo.co/konten/2014/01/28/LU/27747/Fixing-Court-Verdicts/23/14.

Hidayat, Syarif. 2007. "Shadow State? Business and Politics in the Province of Banten." In *Renegotiating Boundaries: Local Politics in Post-Suharto Indonesia*, edited by Henk Schulte Nordholt and Gerry van Klinken, 203–224. Leiden: KITLV Press.

Hilgers, Tina. 2012. "Clientelism and Conceptual Stretching: Differentiating among Concepts and among Analytical Levels." *Theory and Society* 40 (5): 567–588.

Holland, Alisha C., and Brian Palmer-Rubin. 2015. "Beyond the Machine: Clientelist Brokers and Interest Organizations in Latin America." *Comparative Political Studies* 48 (9): 1186–1223.

Honna, Jun. 2012. "Inside the Democrat Party: Power, Politics and Conflict in Indonesia's Presidential Party." *South East Asia Research* 20 (4): 473–489.

Horowitz, Donald L. 2013. *Constitutional Change and Democracy in Indonesia.* Cambridge: Cambridge University Press.

Hutchcroft, Paul D. 2014. "Linking Capital and Countryside: Patronage and Clientelism in Japan, Thailand, and the Philippines." In *Clientelism, Social Policy, and the Quality of Democracy*, edited by Diego Abente Brun and Larry Diamond, 174–203. Baltimore: Johns Hopkins University Press.

Indikator Politik Indonesia. 2014. *Sikap dan Perilaku Pemilih terhadap Vote Buying dalam Pemilu Legislatif 2014. Temuan Survei Nasional 20–26 April 2014.* Jakarta: Indikator Politik Indonesia.

Ishiyama, John T., and Marijke Breuning, eds. 2011. *21st Century Political Science: A Reference Handbook.* London: Sage.

Ismanto, Gandung, and Idris Thaha. 2016. "Banten: Islamic Parties, Networks and Patronage." In Aspinall and Sukmajati, *Electoral Dynamics in Indonesia*, 137–154.

Jackson, Karl D. 1978. "Bureaucratic Polity: A Theoretical Framework for the Analysis of Power and Communications in Indonesia." In *Political Power and Communications in Indonesia*, edited by Karl D. Jackson and Lucien Pye, 3–22. Berkeley: University of California Press.

Jaffrelot, Christophe. 1996. *The Hindu Nationalist Movement and Indian Politics.* London: Hurst and Company.

Jaffrelot, Christophe, and Sanjay Kumar, eds. 2009. *Rise of the Plebeians? The Changing Face of Indian Legislative Assemblies.* New Delhi: Routledge.

Jakarta Globe. 2013. "New Generation of Local Leaders Cleaning House." September 23. http://jakartaglobe.beritasatu.com/news/new-generation-of-local-leaders-cleaning-house/.

Jalal, Ayesha. 1995. *Democracy and Authoritarianism in South Asia: A Comparative and Historical Perspective.* Cambridge: Cambridge University Press.

Jones, Mark P. 2002. "Explaining the High Level of Party Discipline in the Argentine Congress." In *Legislative Politics in Latin America*, edited by Scott Morgenstern and Benito Nacif, 147–184. Cambridge: Cambridge University Press.

Jones, Mark P., Sebastian Saiegh, Pablo T. Spiller, and Mariano Tommasi. 2002. "Amateur Legislators–Professional Politicians: The Consequences of Party-Centered Electoral Rules in a Federal System." *American Journal of Political Science* 46 (3): 656–669.

JPNN.com. 2011. "Jelang Pilkada Dana Bansos dan Hibah Membengkak." August 28. http://www.jpnn.com/read/2011/08/28/101805/Jelang-Pilkada-Dana-Bansos-dan-Hibah-Membengkak-.

Keefer, Philip. 2007. "Clientelism, Credibility, and the Policy Choices of Young Democracies." *American Journal of Political Science* 51 (4): 804–821.

Keefer, Philip, and Stuti Khemani. 2005. "Democracy, Public Expenditures, and the Poor: Understanding Political Incentives for Providing Public Services." *World Bank Research Observer* 20 (1): 1–27.

Keefer, Philip, and Razvan Vlaicu. 2008. "Democracy, Credibility, and Clientelism." *Journal of Law, Economics, and Organization* 24 (2): 371–406.

Kemenkeu (Indonesian Ministry of Finance). 2010. APBD [Regional Budgets] http://www.djpk.depkeu.go.id/?page_id=316.

Kenny, Paul D. 2015. "The Origins of Patronage Politics: State Building, Centrifugalism, and Decolonization." *British Journal of Political Science* 45 (1): 141–171.

——. 2017. *Patronage and Populism: Explaining Populist Success in Asia and Latin America*. Oxford: Oxford University Press.

Kitschelt, Herbert. 2000. "Linkages between Citizens and Politicians in Democratic Polities." *Comparative Political Studies* 33 (6–7): 845–879.

Kitschelt, Herbert, Kent Freeze, Kiril Kolev, and Yi-Ting Wang. 2009. "Measuring Democratic Accountability: An Initial Report on an Emerging Data Set." *Revista de Ciencia Política* 29 (3): 741–773.

Kitschelt, Herbert, and Daniel M. Kselman. 2013. "Economic Development, Democratic Experience, and Political Parties' Linkage Strategies." *Comparative Political Studies* 46 (11): 1453–1484.

Kitschelt, Herbert, and Steven Wilkinson. 2007. "Citizen-Politician Linkages: An Introduction." In *Patrons, Clients and Policies: Patterns of Democratic Accountability and Political Competition*, edited by Herbert Kitschelt and Steven I. Wilkinson, 1–50. Cambridge: Cambridge University Press.

Kompas. 2013. "Hentikan Dana Bansos." January 20. http://nasional.kompas.com/read/2013/02/20/02070085/hentikan.dana.bansos.

Kopecký, Petr, Peter Mair, and Maria Spirova. 2012. *Party Patronage and Party Government in European Democracies*. Oxford: Oxford University Press.

Kothari, Rajni. 1964. "The Congress 'System' in India." *Asian Survey* 4 (12): 1161–1173.

Kramon, Eric. 2016. "Electoral Handouts as Information: Explaining Unmonitored Vote Buying." *World Politics* 68 (3): 454–498.

Krishna, Anirudh. 2007. "Politics in the Middle: Mediating Relationships between the Citizens and the State in Rural North India." In *Patrons, Clients and Policies: Patterns of Democratic Accountability and Political Competition*, edited by Herbert Kitschelt and Steven Wilkinson, 141–159. Cambridge: Cambridge University Press.

Kristiansen, Stein, and Muhid Ramli. 2006. "Buying an Income: The Market for Civil Service Positions in Indonesia." *Contemporary Southeast Asia* 28 (2): 207–233.

Kurasawa, Aiko. 2009. "Swaying between State and Community. The Role of RT/RW in Post-Suharto Indonesia." In *Local Organizations and Urban Governance in East and Southeast Asia: Straddling State and Society*, edited by Benjamin L. Read and Robert Pekkanen, 58–83. London: Routledge.

Lange, Matthew. 2009. *Lineages of Despotism and Development: British Colonialism and State Power*. Chicago: University of Chicago Press.

Larreguy, Horacio, John Marshall, and Pablo Queribín. 2016. "Parties, Brokers and Voter Mobilization: How Turnout Buying Depends upon the Party's Capacity to Monitor Brokers." *American Political Science Review* 110 (1): 160–179.

Lauth, Hans-Joachim. 2000. "Informal Institutions and Democracy." *Democratization* 7 (4): 21–50.

Lawson, Chappell, and Kenneth F. Greene. 2014. "Making Clientelism Work: How Norms of Reciprocity Increase Voter Compliance." *Comparative Politics* 47 (1): 61–85.

Lay, Cornelis, Hasrul Hanif, Ridwan, and Noor Rohman. 2017. "The Rise of Uncontested Elections in Indonesia: Case Studies of Pati and Jayapura." *Contemporary Southeast Asia* 39 (3): 427–448.

LeBreton, James M., and Jenell L. Senter. 2008. "Answers to 20 Questions about Interrater Reliability and Interrater Agreement." *Organizational Research Methods* 11 (4): 815–852.

Lemarchand, René. 1972. "Political Clientelism and Ethnicity in Tropical Africa: Competing Solidarities in Nation-Building." *American Political Science Review* 66 (1): 68–90.

Lemarchand, René, and Keith Legg. 1972. "Political Clientelism and Development: A Preliminary Analysis." *Comparative Politics* 4 (2): 149–178.

Levitsky, Steven. 2003. *Transforming Labor-Based Parties in Latin America: Argentine Peronism in Comparative Perspective.* Cambridge: Cambridge University Press.

Li, Tania Murray. 2007. *The Will to Improve: Governmentality, Development, and the Practice of Politics.* Durham, NC: Duke University Press.

——. 2016. "Governing Rural Indonesia: Convergence on the Project System." *Critical Policy Studies* 10 (1): 79–94.

Liddle, R. William. 1985. "Soeharto's Indonesia: Personal Rule and Political Institutions." *Pacific Affairs* 58 (1): 68–90.

——. 1988. "Indonesia in 1987: The New Order at the Height of Its Powers." *Asian Survey* 28 (2): 180–191.

——. 1996. "A Useful Fiction: Democratic Legitimation in New Order Indonesia." In *The Politics of Elections in Southeast Asia*, edited by R. H. Taylor, 34–60. Cambridge: Cambridge University Press.

——. 2013. "Improving the Quality of Democracy in Indonesia: Toward a Theory of Action." *Indonesia* 96:59–80.

Lijphart, Arend. 2012. *Patterns of Democracy: Government Forms and Performance in Thirty-Six Countries.* New Haven, CT: Yale University Press.

Litbang Kompas. 2015. *Profil Anggota DPR DAN DPD 2014–2019.* Jakarta: Kompas.

Lindstadt, Rene, Sven-Oliver Proksch, and Jonathan B Slapin. 2015. "Assessing the Measurement of Policy Positions in Expert Surveys." Paper presented at the Annual Meeting of the American Political Science Association, September 6–9, San Francisco.

Lucas, Anton, and Carol Warren, eds. 2013. *Land for the People: The State and Agrarian Conflict in Indonesia.* Athens: Ohio University Press.

Luebke, Christian von. 2009. "The Political Economy of Local Governance: Findings from an Indonesian Field Study." *Bulletin of Indonesian Economic Studies* 45 (2): 201–230.

Lussier, Danielle N., and M. Steven Fish. 2012. "Indonesia: The Benefits of Civic Engagement." *Journal of Democracy* 23 (1): 70–84.

Magaloni, Beatriz, Alberto Diaz-Cayeros, and Federico Estévez. 2007. "Clientelism and Portfolio Diversification: A Model of Electoral Investment with Applications to Mexico." In *Patrons, Clients, and Policies: Patterns of Democratic Accountability and Political Competition*, edited by Herbert Kitschelt and Steven I. Wilkinson, 182–205. Cambridge: Cambridge University Press.

Mahsun, Muhammad. 2016. "Palembang, South Sumatra: Aspiration Funds and Pork Barrel Politics." In Aspinall and Sukmajati, *Electoral Dynamics in Indonesia*, 120–137.

——. 2017. "Peasants and Politics: Achievements and Limits of Popular Agency in Batang, Central Java." *Contemporary Southeast Asia* 39 (3): 470–490.

Malley, Michael S. 2002. "New Rules, Old Structures and the Limits of Democratic Decentralisation." In *Local Power and Politics in Indonesia: Decentralisation and Democratisation*, edited by Edward Aspinall and Greg Fealy, 102–117. Singapore: Institute of Southeast Asian Studies.

Mamdani, Mahmood. 1996. *Citizen and Subject: Contemporary Africa and the Legacy of Late Colonialism.* Princeton, NJ: Princeton University Press.

Manor, James. 2010. "Prologue: Caste and Politics in Recent Times." In *Caste in Indian Politics*, edited by Rajni Kothari, i–xvii. Hyderabad: Orient Blackswan.

———. 2013. "Post-clientelist Initiatives." In *Democratization in the Global South: International Political Economy*, edited by Kristian Stokke and Olle Törnquist, 243–253. London: Palgrave Macmillan.

Mas'udi, Wawan. 2016. "Creating Legitimacy in Decentralized Indonesia: Joko 'Jokowi' Widodo's Path to Legitimacy in Solo, 2005–2012." PhD diss., University of Melbourne.

Mas'udi, Wawan, and Nanang Indra Kurniawan. 2017. "Programmatic Politics and Voter Preferences: The 2017 Election in Kulon Progo, Yogyakarta." *Contemporary Southeast Asia* 39 (3): 449–69.

McCarthy, John F. 2004. "Changing to Gray: Decentralization and the Emergence of Volatile Socio-legal Configurations in Central Kalimantan, Indonesia." *World Development* 32 (7): 1199–1223.

McLeod, Ross. 2000. "Soeharto's Indonesia: A Better Class of Corruption." *Agenda: A Journal of Policy Analysis and Reform* 7 (2): 99–112.

———. 2011. "Institutionalized Public Sector Corruption: A Legacy of the Soeharto Franchise." In Aspinall and van Klinken, *State and Illegality in Indonesia*, 45–64.

McMann, Kelly M. 2006. *Economic Autonomy and Democracy: Hybrid Regimes in Russia and Kyrgyzstan*. Cambridge: Cambridge University Press.

McVey, Ruth. 1982. "The Beamtenstaat in Indonesia." In *Interpreting Indonesian Politics: Thirteen Contributions to the Debate*, edited by Benedict R. Anderson and A. Kahin, 84–91. Ithaca, NY: Cornell University Press.

Mietzner, Marcus. 2006. "Local Democracy." *Inside Indonesia* 85:17–18.

———. 2007. "Party Financing in Post-Soeharto Indonesia: Between State Subsidies and Political Corruption." *Contemporary Southeast Asia* 29 (2): 238–263.

———. 2008. "Comparing Indonesia's Party Systems of the 1950s and the Post-Suharto Era: From Centrifugal to Centripetal Inter-party Competition." *Journal of Southeast Asian Studies* 39 (3): 431–453.

———. 2009. "Political Opinion Polling in Post-authoritarian Indonesia: Catalyst or Obstacle to Democratic Consolidation?" *Bijdragen tot de Taal-, Land-en Volkenkunde* 165 (1): 95–126.

———. 2010. "Indonesia's Direct Elections: Empowering the Electorate or Entrenching the New Order Oligarchy?" In *Soeharto's New Order and Its Legacy*, edited by Edward Aspinall and Greg Fealy, 173–192. Canberra: ANU E Press.

———. 2011. "Funding *Pilkada*: Illegal Campaign Financing in Indonesia's Local Elections." In Aspinall and van Klinken, *State and Illegality in Indonesia*, 173–190.

———. 2013a. "Fighting the Hellhounds: Pro-democracy Activists and Party Politics in Post-Suharto Indonesia." *Journal of Contemporary Asia* 43 (1): 28–50.

———. 2013b. *Money, Power, and Ideology: Political Parties in Post-authoritarian Indonesia*. Singapore: NUS Press.

———. 2014. "Oligarchs, Politicians and Activists: Contesting Party Politics in Post-Suharto Indonesia." In *Beyond Oligarchy: Wealth, Power, and Contemporary Indonesian Politics*, edited by Michele Ford and Thomas B. Pepinsky, 51–86. Ithaca, NY: Southeast Asia Program Publications.

———. 2015. *Reinventing Asian Populism: Jokowi's Rise, Democracy, and Political Contestation in Indonesia*. Honolulu: East West Center.

Mortimer, Rex. 1974. *Indonesian Communism under Sukarno: Ideology and Politics, 1959–1965*. Ithaca, NY: Cornell University Press.

Muhtadi, Burhanuddin. 2015. "The Interplay between Partisanship and Money Politics: The 2014 Legislative Election in Indonesia." Paper presented to Euroseas Conference, Vienna, August 11–14.

———. 2018. "Buying Votes in Indonesia: Partisans, Personal Networks, and Winning Margins." PhD diss., Australian National University.

Mujani, Saiful, R. William Liddle, and Kuskridho Ambardi. 2012. *Kuasa Rakyat: Analisis tentang Perilaku Memilih dalam Pemilihan Legislatif dan Presiden Indonesia pasca-Orde Baru*. Jakarta: Mizan.

Mulyadi. 2013. "Welfare Regime, Social Conflict, and Clientelism in Indonesia." PhD diss., Australian National University.

Mungiu-Pippidi, Alina. 2015. *The Quest for Good Governance: How Societies Develop Control of Corruption*. Cambridge: Cambridge University Press.

Muno, Wolfgang. 2010. "Conceptualizing and Measuring Clientelism." Paper presented at "Neopatrimonialism in Various World Regions" workshop, German Institute of Global and Area Studies, Hamburg, August 23.

Mustafa, Mochamad. 2017. "Democratic Decentralisation and Good Governance: The Political Economy of Procurement Reform in Decentralised Indonesia." PhD diss., University of Adelaide.

Myrdal, Gunnar. 1968. *Asian Drama: An Inquiry into the Poverty of Nations*. New York: Pantheon.

Newberry, Janice C. 2006. *Back Door Java: State Formation and the Domestic in Working Class Java*. Toronto: University of Toronto Press.

Nichter, Simeon. 2008. "Vote Buying or Turnout Buying? Machine Politics and the Secret Ballot." *American Political Science Review* 102 (1): 19–31.

———. 2011. "Electoral Clientelism or Relational Clientelism? Healthcare and Sterilization in Brazil." Paper presented at the annual meeting of the American Political Science Association in Seattle, WA, September 1–4.

———. 2014. "Political Clientelism and Social Policy in Brazil." In *Clientelism, Social Policy, and the Quality of Democracy*, edited by Diego Abente Brun and Larry Diamond, 130–151. Baltimore: Johns Hopkins University Press.

Nichter, Simeon, and Michael Peress. 2016. "Request Fulfilling: When Citizens Demand Clientelist Benefits." *Comparative Political Studies* 50 (8): 1086–1117.

Nilawati, Sri, Robert Endi Jaweng, and Darwanto. 2013. *APBD yang Tergerus: Politisasi Anggaran Pemilukada DKI Jakarta 2012*. Jakarta: Tifa Foundation.

Nooruddin, Irfan, and Pradeep Chibber. 2008. "Unstable Politics: Fiscal Space and Electoral Volatility in the Indian States." *Comparative Political Studies* 41 (8): 1069–1091.

Nordholt, Henk Schulte, and Gerry van Klinken, eds. 2007. *Renegotiating Boundaries: Local Politics in Post-Suharto Indonesia*. Leiden: KITLV Press.

North, Douglass C., John Joseph Wallis, and Barry R. Weingast. 2009. *Violence and Social Orders: A Conceptual Framework for Interpreting Recorded Human History*. Cambridge: Cambridge University Press.

O'Donnell, Guillermo. 1973. *Modernization and Bureaucratic-Authoritarianism: Studies in South American Politics*. Berkeley, CA: Institute of International Studies.

———. 1978. "State and Alliances in Argentina, 1956–1976." *Iberoamericana–Nordic Journal of Latin American and Caribbean Studies* 7 (2): 20–54.

O'Dwyer, Conor. 2006. *Runaway State-Building: Patronage Politics and Democratic Development*. Baltimore: Johns Hopkins University Press.

Palupi, Sri, P. Prasetyohadi, Chelluz Pahun, Andriani S. Kusni, Kusni Sulang, Johanes Jenito, and Dudik Warnadi. 2015. *Industri Perkebunan Sawit dan Hak Asasi Manusia: Potret Pelaksanaan Tanggung Jawab Pemerintah dan Korporasi terhadap Hak Asasi Manusia di Kalimantan Tengah*. Jakarta: Institute for Ecosoc Rights.

Paskarina, Caroline. 2016. "Bandung, West Java: *Silaturahmi*, Personalist Networks and Patronage Politics." In Aspinall and Sukmajati, *Electoral Dynamics in Indonesia*, 203–216.

Patunru, Arianto A., Neil McCulloch, and Christian von Luebke. 2012. "A Tale of Two Cities: The Political Economy of Local Investment Climates in Indonesia." *Journal of Development Studies* 48 (7): 799–816.

Pelras, Christian. 2000. "Patron-Client Ties among the Bugis and Makassarese of South Sulawesi." *Bijdragen tot de Taal-, Land-en Volkenkunde* 156 (3): 393–432.

Pepinsky, Thomas B. 2013. "Pluralism and Political Conflict in Indonesia." *Indonesia* 96 (1): 81–100.

Persada, Syailendra, Yolanda Ryan Armindya, Erwan Hernawan, and Dimas Siregar. 2015. "Perusahaan Tunggangan Kantor Sebelah." *Tempo*, March 9. https://majalah. tempo.co/konten/2015/03/09/NAS/147660/Perusahaan-Tunggangan-Kantor-Sebelah/02/44.

Persson, Anna, Bo Rothstein, and Jan Teorell. 2013. "Why Anticorruption Reforms Fail—Systemic Corruption as a Collective Action Problem." *Governance* 26 (3): 449–471.

Piattoni, Simona. 2001. *Clientelism, Interests, and Democratic Representation: The European Experience in Historical and Comparative Perspective*. Cambridge: Cambridge University Press.

Pierskalla, Jan, and Audrey Sacks. 2015. "Personnel Politics: Elections, Clientelistic Competition, and Teacher Hiring in Indonesia." Working paper. Jakarta: World Bank.

Piliavsky, Anastasia. 2014. Introduction to *Patronage as Politics in South Asia*, edited by Anastasia Piliavsky, 1–35. Cambridge: Cambridge University Press.

Pompe, Sebastiaan. 2005. *The Indonesian Supreme Court: A Study of Institutional Collapse*. Ithaca, NY: Southeast Asia Program Publications.

Power, Tom. 2014. "Creative Campaigners." *Inside Indonesia* 116. http://www.insideindonesia. org/creative-campaigners.

Prasetyo, Stanley Adi, A. E. Priyono, and Olle Törnquist, eds. 2004. *Indonesia's Post-Soeharto Democracy Movement*. Jakarta: Demos.

Puspitasari, Maya Ayu. 2017. "Suap Bupati, Ini Daftar Harga Jabatan di Pemkab Klaten." *Tempo*, January 6. https://m.tempo.co/read/news/2017/01/06/078833341/ suap-bupati-ini-daftar-harga-jabatan-di-pemkab-klaten.

Putnam, Robert D., Robert Leonardi, and Raffaella Y. Nanetti. 1993. *Making Democracy Work: Civic Traditions in Modern Italy*. Princeton, NJ: Princeton University Press.

Qodari, Muhammad. 2010. "The Professionalisation of Politics: The Growing Role of Polling Organisations and Political Consultants." In *Problems of Democratisation in Indonesia: Elections, Institutions and Society*, edited by Edward Aspinall and Marcus Mietzner, 122–140. Singapore: Institute of Southeast Asian Studies.

Reeve, David. 1990. "The Corporatist State: The Case of Golkar." In *State and Civil Society in Indonesia*, edited by Arief Budiman, 151–176. Clayton, Australia: Monash Asia Institute.

Remmer, Karen L. 2007. "The Political Economy of Patronage: Expenditure Patterns in the Argentine Provinces, 1983–2003." *Journal of Politics* 69 (2): 363–377.

Republika. 2014. "Ini Dia Profil Anggota Legislatif 2014–2019." October 9. http:// www.republika.co.id/berita/koran/teraju/14/10/09/nd6caa-ini-dia-profil-anggota-legislatif-20142019.

Robinson, James A., and Thierry Verdier. 2013. "The Political Economy of Clientelism." *Scandinavian Journal of Economics* 115 (2): 260–291.

Robison, Richard. 1986. *Indonesia: The Rise of Capital*. St. Leonards, UK: Allen and Unwin.

Robison, Richard, and Vedi R. Hadiz. 2004. *Reorganising Power in Indonesia: The Politics of Oligarchy in an Age of Markets*. London: Routledge.

Rohi, Rudi. 2016. "East Nusa Tenggara: Patronage Politics, Clientelism and the Hijacking of Social Trust." In Aspinall and Sukmajati, *Electoral Dynamics in Indonesia*, 363–382.

Rohman, Noor. 2016. "Pati, Central Java: Targets, Techniques and Meanings of Vote Buying." In Aspinall and Sukmajati, *Electoral Dynamics in Indonesia*, 233–248.

Roniger, Luis. 2004. "Political Clientelism, Democracy, and Market Economy." *Comparative Politics* 36 (3): 353–375.

Rosser, Andrew, and Mohamad Fahmi. 2016. "The Political Economy of Teacher Management in Decentralized Indonesia." Policy Research Working Paper WPS7913. Washington, DC: World Bank.

Rosser, Andrew, and Ian Wilson. 2012. "Democratic Decentralisation and Pro–Poor Policy Reform in Indonesia: The Politics of Health Insurance for the Poor in Jembrana and Tabanan 1." *Asian Journal of Social Science* 40 (5–6): 608–634.

Rubaidi. 2016. "East Java: New Clientelism and the Fading of *Aliran* Politics." In Aspinall and Sukmajati, *Electoral Dynamics in Indonesia*, 264–278.

Rudolph, Lloyd I., and Suzanne H. Rudolph. 1987. *In Pursuit of Lakshmi: The Political Economy of the Indian State*. Chicago: University of Chicago Press.

Sambodho, Prio. 2016. "Menyindir the State: Everyday Citizenship Claims in West Java Village." Paper presented at the KITLV-UGM conference "From Clients to Citizens? Citizenship in Democratising Indonesia," at Universitas Gadjah Mada, December 8–10.

Samuels, David J. 2002. "Pork Barreling Is Not Credit Claiming or Advertising: Campaign Finance and the Sources of the Personal Vote in Brazil." *Journal of Politics* 64 (3): 845–863.

Savirani, Amalinda. 2014. "Resisting Reforms: The Persistence of Patrimonialism in Pekalongan's Construction Sector." In *In Search of Middle Indonesia*, edited by Gerry van Klinken and Ward Berenschot, 133–147.

——. 2016. "Bekasi, West Java: From Patronage to Interest Groups Politics?" In Aspinall and Sukmajati, *Electoral Dynamics in Indonesia*, 184–202.

Schaffer, Frederic C. 2007. *Elections for Sale: The Causes and Consequences of Vote Buying*. Boulder, CO: Lynne Rienner.

Schiller, Jim. 1996. *Developing Jepara: State and Society in New Order Indonesia*. Clayton, Australia: Monash Asia Institute.

Schmidt, Steffen W., Laura Guasti, Carl H. Landé, and James C. Scott, eds. 1977. *Friends, Followers, and Factions: A Reader in Political Clientelism*. Berkeley: University of California Press.

Schneider, Mark. 2014. "Does Clientelism Work? A Test of Guessability in India." Paper presented at Annual Meeting of the Midwest Political Science Association, April 3–6, Chicago.

Schulte Nordholt, Henk. 2015. "From Contest State to Patronage Democracy: The *Longue Durée* of Clientelism in Indonesia." In *Environment, Trade and Society in Southeast Asia: A* Longue Durée *Perspective*, edited by David Henley and Henk Schulte Nordholt, 166–180. Leiden: Brill.

Schulte Nordholt, Henk, and Gerry van Klinken, eds. 2007. *Renegotiating Boundaries: Local Politics in Post-Suharto Indonesia*. Leiden: KITLV Press.

Schulze, Günther G., and Bambang Suharnoko Sjahrir. 2014. "Decentralisation, Governance, and Public Service Delivery." In *Regional Dynamics in a*

Decentralised Indonesia, edited by Hal Hill, 186–207. Singapore: Institute of Southeast Asian Studies.

Scott, James C. 1969. "Corruption, Machine Politics, and Political Change." *American Political Science Review* 63 (4): 1142–1558.

———. 1972a. "The Erosion of Patron-Client Bonds and Social Change in Rural Southeast Asia." *Journal of Asian Studies* 32 (1): 5–37.

———. 1972b. "Patron-Client Politics and Political Change in Southeast Asia." *American Political Science Review* 66 (1): 91–113.

Setyarso, Budi, Khairul Anam, Agus Supriyanto, Dewi Suci Rahayu, Agita Sukma Listyanti, Edwin Fajerial, and Kukuh S. W. 2014. "Surabaya Showdown." *Tempo*, February 18. https://magz.tempo.co/konten/2014/02/18/LU/27871/Surabaya-Showdown/26/14.

Shefter, Martin. 1977. "Party and Patronage: Germany, England, and Italy." *Politics and Society* 7 (4): 403–451.

———. 1994. *Political Parties and the State: The American Historical Experience*. Princeton, NJ: Princeton University Press.

Sherlock, Stephen. 2010. "The Parliament in Indonesia's Decade of Democracy: People's Forum or Chamber of Cronies?" In *Problems of Democratisation in Indonesia: Elections, Institutions and Society*, edited by Edward Aspinall and Marcus Mietzner, 160–178. Singapore: Institute of Southeast Asian Studies.

Sidel, John. 2006. *Riots, Pogroms, Jihad: Religious Violence in Indonesia*. Ithaca, NY: Cornell University Press.

———. 2014. "Economic Foundations of Subnational Authoritarianism: Insights and Evidence from Qualitative and Quantitative Research." *Democratization* 21 (1): 161–184.

Simanjuntak, Deasy. 2010. "Who Shall Be Raja? Patronage Democracy in North Sumatra, Indonesia." PhD diss., University of Amsterdam.

———. 2012. "Gifts and Promises: Patronage Democracy in a Decentralised Indonesia." *European Journal of East Asian Studies* 11 (1): 99–126.

Sjahrir, Bambang Suharnoko, Krisztina Kis-Katos, and Günther G. Schulze. 2014. "Administrative Overspending in Indonesian Districts: The Role of Local Politics." *World Development*, no. 59: 166–183.

Skoufias, Emmanuel, Ambar Narayan, Basab Dasgupta, and Kai Kaiser. 2014. "Electoral Accountability and Local Government Spending in Indonesia." Policy Research Working Paper 6782. Washington, DC: World Bank.

Slater, Dan. 2004. "Indonesia's Accountability Trap: Party Cartels and Presidential Power after Democratic Transition." *Indonesia* 78:61–92.

Slater, Dan, and Erica Simmons. 2013. "Coping by Colluding: Political Uncertainty and Promiscuous Powersharing in Indonesia and Bolivia." *Comparative Political Studies* 46 (11): 1366–1393.

Stokes, Susan C. 2005. "Perverse Accountability: A Formal Model of Machine Politics with Evidence from Argentina." *American Political Science Review* 99 (3): 315–325.

———. 2007. "Political Clientelism." In *The Oxford Handbook of Comparative Politics*, edited by Carles Boix and Susan Stokes, 604–627. Oxford: Oxford University Press.

Stokes, Susan C., Thad Dunning, Marcelo Nazareno, and Valeria Brusco. 2013. *Brokers, Voters, and Clientelism: The Puzzle of Distributive Politics*. Cambridge: Cambridge University Press.

Suaedy, Ahmad. 2014. "The Role of Volunteers and Political Participation in the 2012 Jakarta Gubernatorial Election." *Journal of Current Southeast Asian Affairs* 33 (1): 111–138.

Sugiharto, Jobpie, Khairul Anam, Agus Supriyanto, Agita Sukma Listyanti, Edwin Fajerial, Dewi Suci Rahayu, and Endri Kurniawati. 2014. "Conflict at City Hall." *Tempo*, February 18. https://magz.tempo.co/konten/2014/02/18/LU/27872/ Conflict-at-City-Hall/26/14.

Sulaiman, Teuku Muhammad Jafar. 2016. "Bener Meriah, Aceh: The Aftermath of Post-conflict Politics and the Decline of Partai Aceh." In Aspinall and Sukmajati, *Electoral Dynamics in Indonesia*, 54–70.

Sumampouw, Nono S. A. 2016. "North Sulawesi: Clan, Church and State." In Aspinall and Sukmajati, *Electoral Dynamics in Indonesia*, 321–340.

Supriyanto, Agus, Dewi Suci Rahayu, Agita Sukma Listyanti, Edwin Fajerial, Endri Kurniawati, Budi Setyarso, and Khairul Anam. 2014. "The Party 'Boarder.'" *Tempo*, February 18. https://magz.tempo.co/konten/2014/02/18/LU/27873/ The-Party-Boarder/26/14.

Sutherland, Heather. 1979. *The Making of a Bureaucratic Elite: The Colonial Transformation of the Javanese Priyayi*. Singapore: Heinemann.

Szwarcberg, Mariela. 2012. "Uncertainty, Political Clientelism, and Voter Turnout in Latin America: Why Parties Conduct Rallies in Argentina." *Comparative Politics* 45 (1): 88–106.

——. 2015. *Mobilizing Poor Voters: Machine Politics, Clientelism, and Social Networks in Argentina*. Cambridge: Cambridge University Press.

Talib, Herdiansyah. 2016. "Gila! Gubernur Gatot Sebut DPRD Sumut Minta Uang Ketok APBD 2014 Rp1,3 Triliun." Medansatu.com, March 2. http://medansatu. com/berita/15757/gila-gubernur-gatot-sebut-dprd-sumut-minta-uang-ketok-apbd-2014-rp13-triliun.

Tan, Paige Johnson. 2006. "Indonesia Seven Years after Soeharto: Party System Institutionalization in a New Democracy." *Contemporary Southeast Asia* 28 (1): 88–114.

Tans, Ryan. 2012. *Mobilizing Resources, Building Coalitions: Local Power in Indonesia*. Honolulu: East–West Center.

Tapsell, Ross. 2015. "Indonesia's Media Oligarchy and the 'Jokowi Phenomenon.'" *Indonesia* 99 (1): 29–50.

Taufiq, Fatkhurrohman, and Zed Abidien. 2011. "Walikota Surabaya Diberhentikan DPRD." *Tempo*, January 31. https://nasional.tempo.co/read/310080/ walikota-surabaya-diberhentikan-dprd.

Tawakkal, George Towar Ikbal, and Andrew Gardner. 2017. "Unopposed but Not Uncontested: Brokers and 'Vote Buying' in the 2017 Pati District Election." *Contemporary Southeast Asia* 39 (3): 491–510.

Tempo. 2015. "Budget Buster." March 10. https://magz.tempo.co/konten/2015/03/10/ OPI/29689/Budget-Buster/29/login.

Tidey, Sylvia. 2012. "A Divided Provincial Town: The Development from Ethnic to Class Segmentation in Kupang, West Timor." *City and Society* 24 (3): 302–320.

——. 2013. "Corruption and Adherence to Rules in the Construction Sector: Reading the 'Bidding Books.'" *American Anthropologist* 115 (2): 188–202.

Tilly, Charles. 2005. *Trust and Rule*. Cambridge: Cambridge University Press.

Tomsa, Dirk. 2008. *Party Politics and Democratization in Indonesia: Golkar in the Post-Suharto Era*. London: Routledge.

——. 2009. "Electoral Democracy in a Divided Society: The 2008 Gubernatorial Election in Maluku, Indonesia." *South East Asia Research* 17 (2): 229–259.

——. 2014. "Party System Fragmentation in Indonesia: The Subnational Dimension." *Journal of East Asian Studies* 14 (2): 249–278.

——. 2015. "Local Politics and Corruption in Indonesia's Outer Islands." *Bijdragen tot de Taal-, Land-en Volkenkunde* 171 (2–3): 196–219.

Törnquist, Olle. 2006. "Assessing Democracy from Below: A Framework and Indonesian Pilot Study." *Democratization* 13 (2): 227–255.

Triantini, Zusiana Elly. 2016. "Blora, Central Java: Local Brokers and Vote Buying." In Aspinall and Sukmajati, *Electoral Dynamics in Indonesia*, 249–263.

Tudor, Maya, and Dan Slater. 2016. "The Content of Democracy: Nationalist Parties and Inclusive Ideologies in India and Indonesia." In *Parties, Movements, and Democracy in the Developing World*, edited by Nancy Bermeo and Deborah J. Yashar, 28–60. New York: Cambridge University Press.

Ufen, Andreas. 2006. "Parties in Post-Suharto Indonesia: Between *Politik Aliran* and 'Philippinisation.'" GIGA Working Papers 37, Hamburg: German Institute of Global and Area Studies.

——. 2012. "Lipset and Rokkan in Southeast Asia: Indonesia in Comparative Perspective." In *Party Politics in Southeast Asia: Clientelism and Electoral Competition in Indonesia, Thailand and the Philippines*, edited by Dirk Tomsa and Andreas Ufen, 40–61. London: Routledge.

Ulum, Wasi'ul. 2013. "Atut Dynasty Gains Power Using Regional Budget." *Tempo*, October 22. https://en.tempo.co/read/news/2013/10/22/055523809/Atut-Dynasty-Gains-Power-Using-Regional-Budget.

Uppal, Yogesh. 2009. "The Disadvantaged Incumbents: Estimating Incumbency Effects in Indian State Legislatures." *Public Choice* 138 (1–2): 9–27.

van Bruinessen, Martin. 2010. "New Leadership, New Policies? The Nahdlatul Ulama Congress in Makassar." *Inside Indonesia* 101. http://www.insideindonesia.org/new-leadership-new-policies.

van de Walle, Nicolas. 2007. "Meet the New Boss, Same as the Old Boss? The Evolution of Political Clientelism in Africa." In *Patrons, Clients, and Policies: Patterns of Democratic Accountability and Political Competition*, edited by Herbert Kitschelt and Steven I. Wilkinson, 50–67. Cambridge: Cambridge University Press.

van Klinken, Gerry. 2007. *Communal Violence and Democratization in Indonesia: Small Town Wars*. New York: Routledge.

——. 2009. "Patronage Democracy in Provincial Indonesia." In *Rethinking Popular Representation*, edited by Olle Törnquist, Neil Webster, and Kristian Stokke, 141–159. New York: Palgrave Macmillan.

——. 2014. *The Making of Middle Indonesia: Middle Classes in Kupang Town, 1930s–1980s*. Leiden: Brill.

van Klinken, Gerry, and Joshua Barker, eds. 2009. *State of Authority: State in Society in Indonesia*. Ithaca, NY: Southeast Asia Program Publications.

van Klinken, Gerry, and Ward Berenschot, eds. 2014. *In Search of Middle Indonesia*. Leiden: Brill.

van Voorst, Roanne. 2016. *Natural Hazards, Risk and Vulnerability: Floods and Slum Life in Indonesia*. London: Routledge.

Vel, Jacqueline A. C. 2008. *Uma Politics: An Ethnography of Democratization in West Sumba, Indonesia, 1986–2006*. Leiden: KITLV Press.

Wantchekon, Leonard. 2003. "Clientelism and Voting Behaviour: Evidence from a Field Experiment." *World Politics* 55 (3): 399–422.

Warburton, Eve. 2016a. "Indonesian Politics in 2016: Jokowi and the New Developmentalism." *Bulletin of Indonesian Economic Studies* 52 (3): 297–320.

——. 2016b. "Southeast Sulawesi: Money Politics in Indonesia's Nickel Belt." In Aspinall and Sukmajati, *Electoral Dynamics in Indonesia*, 341–363.

Wardhani, Dewanti A., and Haeril Halim. 2015. "Ahok Reveals History of Suspicious Budget Allocations." *Jakarta Post*, March 27. http://www.thejakartapost.com/news/2015/03/27/ahok-reveals-history-suspicious-budget-allocations.html.

Warren, Carol, and Leontine Visser. 2016. "The Local Turn: An Introductory Essay Revisiting Leadership, Elite Capture and Good Governance in Indonesian Conservation and Development Programs." *Human Ecology* 44 (3): 277–286.

Weiner, Myron. 1967. *Party Building in a New Nation: The Indian National Congress.* Chicago: University of Chicago Press.

Weingrod, Alex. 1968. "Patrons, Patronage, and Political Parties." *Comparative Studies in Society and History* 10 (4): 377–400.

Weitz-Shapiro, Rebecca. 2012. "What Wins Votes: Why Some Politicians Opt Out of Clientelism." *American Journal of Political Science* 56 (3): 568–583.

——. 2014. *Curbing Clientelism in Argentina.* Cambridge: Cambridge University Press.

Wijayanto, Wija. 2018. "Between Fear and Power: Kompas, Indonesia's Most Influential Newspaper, 196–-2015." PhD diss., Leiden University.

Wilson, Chris. 2013. "'Ethnic Outbidding' for Patronage: The 2010 Riots in Tarakan, Indonesia." *South East Asia Research* 21 (1): 105–129.

Wilson, Ian. 2015. *The Politics of Protection Rackets in Post–New Order Indonesia: Coercive Capital, Authority and Street Politics.* London: Routledge.

Winters, Jeffrey A. 2011. *Oligarchy.* Cambridge: Cambridge University Press.

——. 2013. "Oligarchy and Democracy in Indonesia." *Indonesia* 96 (1): 11–33.

Witsoe, Jeffrey. 2012. "Everyday Corruption and the Political Mediation of the Indian State." *Economic & Political Weekly* 47 (6): 47–54.

——. 2013. *Democracy against Development: Lower-Caste Politics and Political Modernity in Postcolonial India.* Chicago: University of Chicago Press.

Wood, Terence. 2014. "Ties That Unbind? Ethnic Identity, Social Rules and Electoral Politics in Solomon Islands." PhD diss., Australian National University.

World Bank. 2003. *Combating Corruption in Indonesia: Enhancing Accountability for Development.* Jakarta: World Bank.

——. 2004. *World Development Report 2004: Making Services Work for Poor People.* Washington, DC: World Bank.

——. 2017. *World Development Report: Governance and the Law.* Washington, DC: World Bank.

You, Jong-Sung. 2016. *Democracy, Inequality, and Corruption: Korea, Taiwan, and the Philippines Compared.* Cambridge: Cambridge University Press.

Young, Daniel J. 2009. "Is Clientelism at Work in African Elections? A Study of Voting Behaviour in Kenya and Zambia." Afrobarometer Working Paper 106.

Zerinini, Jasmine. 2009. "The Marginalisation of the Savarnas in Uttar Pradesh?" In *Rise of the Plebeians? The Changing Face of Indian Legislative Assemblies*, edited by Christophe Jaffrelot and Sanjay Kumar, 27–64. New Delhi: Routledge.

Index

Page locators followed by *t* and *fig* indicate tables and figures, respectively.